FINDING THE
Hidden Horse

Profiles of Long Shots

CONRAD CREASE

BLUE MAX PRESS LLC

1607 Berkshire Avenue

Myrtle Beach, SC 29577

SOFTWARE AVAILABLE!

vkress15@hotmail.com

ISBN: 1451540167

ISBN-13: 9781451540161

Library of Congress Control Number: 2010903545

...Once again to the lovely Lillian Louise, my partner for 48 years in the *race of life*...

CONTENTS

ACKNOWLEDGEMENTS

Special thanks to former racing partner Marvin Small and to the knowledgeable Rich Meyer for their reviews of the raw manuscript and their invaluable suggestions and insights.

Additional recognition is due the Bloodstock Research Information Services (Brisnet).

Their past performance and results charts were invaluable contributions to the goal of clarity of the work. Their *late pace ratings* are a particularly useful tool in handicapping distance races.

The examples reprinted are the property of Brisnet and are included with their permission.

FORWARD

Theories are a sometime thing: easily promulgated until - in the crucible of incontrovertible facts and clinically demonstrable experience - most fail. This is especially true of pari-mutual thoroughbred horse race wagering systems.

The methodology set out here has been validated with over sixty examples recorded over a two year period, culminating in the *Hidden Horse* system predicting the first four finishers in the 2010 *Run for the Roses;* the place and show finishers in the Preakness, and the winner of the Belmont at odds of 13/1.

A one dollar superfecta box in the Derby, costing all of twenty-four dollars, returned $101,284.60; a "life-changing" win by any measure.

CKC

INTRODUCTION

Daughter Elaine was the first person to review the raw manuscript as I asked her to assist in editing the book for grammar and punctuation. With ten years of professional experience as an editor, she was of immense value in keeping the author on the road of clarity. For filial reasons, she may have been somewhat prejudiced in her review; nevertheless, it appears below – unedited.

Hi, Dad:

Sorry I'm about 24 hours late with this; Life just got in my way this weekend…

I found very few mistakes or unclear use of language. The writing style of this book is more Hemingway, while *The Desert Baron* **was more Fitzgerald, or maybe Dickens…which makes sense because that was a biography of a family member, and it had intimately personal meaning for you. It's natural that the language was more effusive…**

I have to say I was surprised at how much I enjoyed *Finding the Hidden Horse* **– guess I thought the subject matter (being so technical, in a way) would not have lent itself to being as exciting as it was. Your writing was entertaining, warm, funny, and down-to-earth. It was like being led on a fascinating adventure to understand the tools that could lead to, as you put it, "a life-changing win."**

Finding The Hidden Horse: Profiles of Long Shots

I also think this book was different because it's educational – you were teaching the reader something, and in that endeavor you have hit it out of the park, Dad. Even I, as a complete novice regarding the handicapping of horse races, have come away with some clear ideas:

- ignore the setting of the morning line; past performance and works are everything;
- a horse that has been away from racing for more than 30 days is refreshed, and strong;
- it's really suspect when a horse drops a class after a win;
- betting on two year olds is risky and, if it's their first start ("maiden" race?) betting on one is insane;
- a recent poor performance doesn't automatically mean a problem, especially if that performance was bad because of a reason singular to that race, i.e., traffic problems, bumped, steadied, caught extremely wide and so forth;
- not bad, huh? That's a tribute to your clear writing style here, definitely a function of years of expertise – in other words, when you know a subject inside and out, you can explain it really clearly and well...
- I also love the forest motif you use throughout the book, makes it fun...

I've attached a document with the few suggestions that I have – believe me, they are absolutely miniscule...

there's almost no suggested rewording of language this time, Dad, you've done an incredible job of writing very clearly, with very few run-on sentences. The rhythm of the language…is crisp and clear…the suggestions are mostly when you've used a semicolon when a comma would be correct, or a colon when a semicolon is correct…no biggie.

Elaine Crease

INTRODUCTION ADDENDUM

The author – a friend and fellow punter for over twenty years – has an incredible knack for combing through the nearly infinite variables contained in the racing form in order to find the hidden horse. As an accountant he has a very analytical mind, while at the same time possessing tremendous intuitive reasoning ability; both of which are invaluable tools in pursuing – and finding – *hidden horses* that pay huge prices.

Rich Meyer

Chapter 1

When Shakespeare's King Richard III cried out his famous plea: "A horse! A horse! My kingdom for a horse!" no doubt the last thing on his mind was pari-mutual thoroughbred horse racing. Yet today that famous cry has descended the ages to resound in its purest form in the hopes and dreams of thoroughbred owners, trainers, breeders and their connections. Not for just any steed do they covet; no, the longing is for one of Eclipse's progeny in his purest inbred form; a horse - if not with wings - with winged hoofs that touch the ground for fleeting milliseconds, propelling their torso forward for a full five lengths a second, and with those giant strides push their half-ton bodies to the finish line, and sometimes glory for themselves and often riches for their masters.

The New Orleans Fairground racetrack is something right out of *The Streetcar Named Desire,* situated among a neighborhood of dwellings, some of which are over 300 years old. In the fall of

1965 most of those homes and their slate tile roofs were damaged by Hurricane Carla. As the storm manager for a mid-west independent claims adjusting firm, I had the responsibility of supervising the some 15 independent insurance catastrophe specialist adjusters who came from as far away as California and New York to work with our firm on a split-fee basis. Supervising this independent crew was like trying to herd cats. The pressure from insurance company claims managers was considerable; they wanted the claims closed quickly, and not necessarily at the lowest cost. It did not take long to discover that the New Orleans citizens would not be pressured nor hurried; the temperament that prevailed among a majority of policyholders in the Emerald City soon led to a back up of unclosed claims followed by a considerable amount of pressure from the home office.

The general feedback from the adjusters was: "All these people want to fight, especially the French and the Italians!" It was left to our man from Brooklyn to solve the problem of the differences in sensibilities between the Louisiana policyholders and the adjusters from the west, the mid-west, and the northeast.

On a day when several of the adjusters were in the office checking their phone messages and making call backs, I couldn't help overhearing our Brooklyn adjuster shouting into the phone at a policyholder. It was plain from his periodic pauses that the policyholder was shouting back. I was tempted to interrupt, but before I could our Brooklyn man concluded with: "Ok then, it's settled. You drive a hard bargain Mrs. De Ardenville, but I'll send you the proof claim form today."

Upon being asked, he explained: "You have to let these people vent, and sometimes you have to shout back, but most of all you have to leave them thinking they got the better part of the deal." I called a meeting of all of the adjusters for the next morning. Our man from Brooklyn explained his method of negotiating with the high blooded New Orleans policyholders. Shortly the log jam was broken; closed claims then flowed into the office at a rapid pace.

A few days later Phil from Phoenix was in the office and asked what I was doing for lunch. "Thought we might run out to the race track and have lunch and play a few races." It was an offer I couldn't refuse for I had never witnessed a live horse race, Kansas at that time being a non pari-mutuel state.

Four decades ago the New Orleans Fairgrounds race track was a sight of nostalgia to behold; with its wood framed cupola topped grandstand it was a classic picture of late nineteenth century southern gentility. Some years later it burned to the ground. On that afternoon; however, it gleamed in the southern sun with a promise of excitement, and pulsed with the gambling fever; one of mankind's most primordial of instincts.

As Phoenix Phil and I sat down at a table near the window of the lush clubhouse, he handed me the Daily Racing Form, a periodical I had never before perused. It is - forgive the blasphemy - the "Bible" of the horse racing community. As I wolfed down a tuna salad sandwich and fries, our man from Phoenix gave me some elemental handicapping pointers; to this day I remember the details of that day.

"Why don't you pick three horses in the first race and I'll pick three in the second. We can play the daily double for just $18 for that bet." I countered that we should play a $5 bet that would cost us $45 each. (I later learned that the nomenclature of that kind of wager was a "partial wheel.")

It was ten minutes to post time for the first race when we finished our beers and headed for trackside after Phil made our bets. Handing me the tickets, he gave me a thumbs-up, saying: "Beginner's luck!" We moved to the fence near the finish line and awaited the opening of the gates. The bell rang: the gates opened; a steady roar came up from the crowd behind us - the magnificent thoroughbreds pounded forward. As they turned into the stretch, one of our horses was third and moving up. I began a steady drumbeat on Phil's shoulder with my rolled up racing form. The thunder of the horse's hooves shook the ground beneath us. When our horse surged to win by a nose at the wire, I'm sure I made a perfect fool of myself, transported as I was by the adrenaline rush of having picked a winner on my first try. Our man from Phoenix was laughing and rubbing his shoulder, then admonishing: "Ok, that's the first half. Now we have to get the winner of the second in order to collect our daily double." (Years later I learned that most professional handicappers call that bet "the daily do-do.")

Yes - one of Phil's picks won the second race; some ten minutes later my feet touched the ground. The double paid $178 for each $2 bet; we collected our $445 and after deducting our bet split the profit of $355. My remaining time in New Orleans found me at the Fairgrounds on each weekend. I was hooked for life; not necessarily on the gambling, though that was part of it - the reward for being right, but on the never diminishing thrill of seeing the flight of those magnificent animals, their hooves pounding to a drum beat crescendo as they thunder down the stretch, nostrils flaring, broad chests heaving, hind legs thrusting, hips powering to be first to the finish line and the roaring acclaim of the crowd. The beauty of it is that thoroughbred racing is elemental; the thoroughbreds' instinct to run as fast as they can for as long as they can is equal to our will to live.

Many a race has been run and many a year has rolled by since that first day of luck at the Fairgrounds. Little did I dream that one day many years later a thoroughbred handicapper would be able to watch and wager on nearly any racetrack in the United States and, for that matter, wherever in the world simulcast signals could be beamed; all from their home or office by way of an online wagering account on their computer.

Before the internet, you had to be at the track to place a bet - or gamble with a bookie - akin to playing financial Russian roulette. So it was that for many years the lovely Lillian Louise and I would on selected weekends travel to the nearest racetrack some 300 miles away for a get-away weekend holiday. Ak-Sar-Ben (Nebraska spelled backward) was located in Omaha and had been since 1938. Some 60 years later the city fathers tore it down in a fit of religious temper. Live thoroughbred racing in Nebraska has headed downhill since that debacle, today being limited to the smaller tracks at Grand Island, Lincoln, and Columbus. Live racing; however, continues in Omaha at Horsemen's Park, a combination five-eighths of a mile dirt track with limited barns situated next to a luxurious simulcast facility. For four days a year about four races a day are run; a requirement for keeping the simulcast facility license in force. The purses are substantial and the crowds are large and there is a festival ambience to the annual event; so many players so badly miss Ak-Sar-Ben and the "good old days," when on any given Saturday upwards of 40,000 bettors screamed at the top of their lungs for their selected steed with winged hooves to cross the finish line first, then most moaned in defeat as their horses finished back in the pack.

It did not occur to me on that Fairgrounds day when first I sipped the wine of picking a thoroughbred race winner that one day I would be an owner and breeder of these magnificent animals. In the next ten years thoroughbred racing would become a major source of entertainment for Lillian Louise and me, the sport never losing its edge for us. Over time she became an excellent handicapper in her own right; with her one, two, and three star system of selecting the contenders in any given race. Rarely did her "three star horses" finish up the track.

A half dozen times a year we were able to take weekend trips to Omaha, Oaklawn Park in Hot Springs, Arkansas, and Remington Park in Oklahoma City. We considered our handicapping a success if we met our trip expenses with our winnings. Over this time we "paid our dues" in learning the difficult lessons that the course of *Handicapping 101* teaches novice punters.

After spending some ten years in property insurance claims administration, I found myself burned out. The field just didn't hold for me the challenge on which I had thrived in my early thirties. In as much as I aced my tax accounting class when I returned to college to complete my accounting courses which would allow me to hang out my shingle as a tax accountant, I decided to set up my own practice. It is surprising the degree to which both handicapping thoroughbred horse races and the accounting profession are alike; both requiring a high degree of objective, critical, analytical, and cognitive ability. My four children might attest that their father is: "analytical to a fault." Perhaps, as the years come on, they will see my penchant for critical analysis as more of an asset.

Two years into the development of my practice, a life changing coincidence occurred with the appearance at my office door of a newly referred client whose avocation was the breaking and training of two year old unraced thoroughbred horses. Two of his brothers were thoroughbred horse trainers who for years had made their living in the feast or famine occupation in which the credo for survival has always been: "Win or go home."

After reviewing his previous two year's tax returns, I agreed to retain him as a client. Once that was out of the way, we talked about horse racing. Some two hours later I was well on my way to becoming an owner and breeder of thoroughbred race horses. The fact that I didn't have a farm on which to board the horses I would acquire was an obstacle easily overcome with money. My new client happened to own a horse farm just south of the city; the following weekend Lillian Louise and I toured the facilities;

two capacious barns with ten stalls, and a training track nearby. As we would be playing the game with fifty cent dollars (net of taxes), we decided to take the plunge. To lay off some of the risk, we entered into a partnership with one of my clients, a good friend for several years. For nearly ten years we raced under the stable name of Prairie Pride Farms, and stood in the winner's circle more than a dozen times in our campaigns on the Nebraska circuit; at the Woodlands in Kansas City; Oaklawn Park in Hot Springs, Arkansas, and Remington Park in Oklahoma City.

It was great fun and good for a middle aged couple's marriage. How invigorating it was to awake just before dawn and get to the track in time to watch our horse work from the gate just as daylight broke; then to head for the track kitchen and a great breakfast among the jockeys, trainers, jockey agents, other owners and the rest of the backstretch community.

About five years after we began to build our stable, dog racing came to the city of Wichita and to Kansas City. A couple years later, attendance started dropping on the Nebraska thoroughbred circuit, exacerbated by the casinos just across the Missouri river in Council Bluffs, Iowa, and Kansas City. The trend was set for horse racing: purses down, expenses up. My partner and I hung on for a few more years before we dispersed our stable of runners. Now, I have nothing but fond memories of my years as an owner and breeder of thoroughbreds; it was an invaluable experience and has served me well in more ways than one.

✵ ✵ ✵

Today the American thoroughbred racing industry is fragmented to a fault. Since that day of beginner's luck at the Fairgrounds some four decades ago, competition for the gambling dollar has grown exponentially, and mostly to the detriment of pari-mutual thoroughbred horse racing. Once the states got into the numbers game with their government sponsored lotteries, it was not long before state-blessed casinos grew like tumbleweeds across the Texas plains. If you wanted to gamble, the states were only too happy to provide the games; for a cut of the action, of course.

Setting aside for the moment the reasonable objections to gambling in general, and notwithstanding the fact that many churches have sponsored raffles and bingo parlors for many years before the lottery was born, surely most reasonable persons would agree that the poor and uneducated bear most of the financial burden of the more avaricious vehicles of gambling that rather easily separate them from their money. But just as the poor have always been with us, so gamblers will continue to be tempted to play at games they do not understand; not only for the money, but for the sheer thrill of winning. Human nature, not having changed since man first crawled out of his cave to stand upright, is the eternal partner of the casino owners.

At the bottom of the barrel of ways to lose your money is the lottery. You have a better chance of being stepped on by an elephant at high noon in the middle of Times Square than you have of winning a lottery. The risk takes absolutely no skill whatsoever. Close behind in the hierarchy of bad bets are the slots. Why do you think there are so many casinos? These glittering castles of excitement where there are always bells and whistles ringing have been built on fool's gold. They require no gambling acumen to win; there are many good systems that can minimize your losses, but they require an iron discipline which few gamblers have. If you are going to play the slots, play them for entertainment and perhaps lightning will strike for there is as much chance of that happening as there is of your hitting a life changing jackpot.

The games of craps and cards are another matter, altogether. While luck is involved with both, you have at least half a chance of winning once you master the intrinsic rules for calculating the odds and measuring the risks of each throw of the dice or deal of the cards. Who could have predicted ten years ago that today Texas Hold'em would be a hit television show on the sports channels? Who can doubt that skill is the most important part of that game, though in all gambling endeavors - as in life itself - luck is always the unseen ghostly player in the game, touching this player and not that one; then that one and not this one.

Most personal tragedies resulting from gambling excesses are the product of a compulsive-obsessive personality of which the great Russian writer Fyodor Dostoyevsky is a perfect example. The author of *The Brothers Karamazov* and *Crime and Punishment* was a manic gambler, nearly ruining his life in the process. To anyone contemplating taking up gambling as a profession I highly recommend his short novel, *The Gambler*; it may give you pause to reconsider.

When greyhound racing came to Wichita it attracted substantial crowds, for the city had never seen anything like it. Today the Wichita Greyhound Park stands empty, but for some twenty years it provided much needed entertainment for this blue collar city - the aircraft building capitol of the world. Lillian Louise and I dabbled at the dogs; gambling on them is similar to horse racing in few respects, yet there are similarities enough to rationalize betting on them for it does take some handicapping experience in order to stand half a chance of winning consistently.

My wife did not care for greyhound racing, though she would occasionally accompany me for dinner at the track. I have to confess that the largest bet I have collected was on the dogs, yet neither skill nor handicapping ability would have anything to do with the cashing of that huge ticket.

When Christmas arrived in 1989 the dog track had been open for all of four months, often to overflow crowds. The fans' appetite for gambling had been fully whetted when the track shut down for a week and did not reopen until the Tuesday after Christmas. On Tuesdays there was both a matinee and an evening program, each with 13 races. My better half asked me to decide which program I wanted to attend; pick either one, but "would I please not go to both." I chose the matinee. That was my first lucky break of that day; the second would be the luck of a lifetime.

Having won the fifth race superfecta of $540 that afternoon, I was determined not to give my winnings back, which is the Achilles heel trait of most gamblers. I made conservative bets for most of the rest of the afternoon. When the twelfth race arrived I was still $500 ahead. I decided to advance bet the evening program for a total of $150, insuring that in a worst case I would be $350 ahead for the entire day. After making a bet on every race except the thirteenth, I prepared my bet for that superfecta. I put $30 into the race, $24 was bet in various combinations on what appeared to be the form of the race. To this day I don't know what possessed me to ask the question: What if the favorites don't get there? On a pure impulse to gamble, I bet the four highest odds dogs in the race in a partial key bet; the 2 to win with the 3, 4, and 5 boxed beneath him for second, third, or fourth in any order, the ticket costing all of $6.

That evening, as we watched from our deck a full moon rising, I felt good about the bet. It had been a good gamble: I had bet from a position of strength, and if it did hit I knew it would be a big one. If it was a loser, I would have still been substantially ahead for the day.

The next morning as I opened the paper to the sports page to read the results of the night before, I started with the first race and gradually worked my way down. As I confirmed the results of each successive race my hopes sank lower and lower until I reached the 13th, the superfecta bet. In 12 races I had not picked one winner. I placed my hand over the results of that last race and slowly lowered it until the winner was uncovered. It was the 2! At 25 to 1. Uncovering the place dog, it was the 4. "Please, please give me the 3 or the 5 for third!" I silently pleaded to the goddess of fortune. It was the 3! It seems to me now that it was a very long time before I uncovered the number of the dog that finished fourth. When I saw the 5 I knew we had hit a big one.

I checked the numbers again then jumped up and ran up the stairs to the master bedroom where the lovely Lillian Louise was finishing her makeup. Grabbing her by the waist I whirled her round and round, accompanied by shouts of: "We did it! We did it! We did it!" She kept repeating: "How much? How much? How much?" The cat ran under the bed. We stopped whirling and kissed in our excitement: "Fifteen thousand!" I whispered. She was late to the office that morning.

It turned out that the evening program had brought out some 4,000 fans and I had the sole winning ticket. Lightning had struck beneath a full December moon. After taxes we were able to apply the $12,000 to the principal of our mortgage, which over its remaining life saved us nearly $8,000 in interest. Looked at in that light; it was really a $20,000 ticket.

A friend who was at the races that evening explained that there was a major pileup at the first turn as the two front running dogs fell and the rest of the field tore into the entanglement. Finally, the 2 dog emerged from the pile and ran on, getting about a 20 length lead before the 3, 4, and 5 dogs got free of the mess.

So it had been pure luck: or had it? Of course the pileup was an accident, but if I had not been winner in the afternoon I would not have advance bet in the evening. The decision to hold back some seventy per cent of my afternoon winnings and wager but $150 in the evening advance betting was a rational decision. Had I not been substantially ahead, I probably would not have had a hunch to swing for the fences with the four longest odds dogs in the 13th race superfecta. In gambling, as in life, one thing leads to another and now and then fortune does favor the brave. Though I went on to cash several low and middle four figure tickets over the next few years, I had no illusions about what happened that full moon night when dame fortune blew me a kiss. I knew that it was a once in a lifetime kiss, sweet in memory nonetheless.

✭ ✭ ✭

Over the years a few of my clients have asked whether or not I thought thoroughbred horse racing is an honest game. After nearly a decade in the sport my experience taught me that for the most part owners are honest; I have made several oral contracts and sealed them with only a handshake, never to regret any deal I have made. I believe that the horse racing community is at least as honest as the accounting, legal, and medical professions. Now and then an individual is tempted to cheat, but that is an aberration as it is in general society for about five percent of the population requires the attention of 100 per cent of the policing authorities.

Unfortunately, the pressures of their profession often lead trainers and their connections to sometimes try to alleviate the tensions of the track by self-medicating with alcohol or various controlled substances; again no more so than in other professions for which we have all too many examples. For the serious handicapper it is wise to confine your wagers to the tracks where the purses are substantial and the quality of trainers and jockeys is high.

This brings us to the subject of this book on handicapping for long shots in pari-mutual thoroughbred horse racing. I will promulgate no "system" that you can follow by rote. The history of thoroughbred handicapping theories is strewn with the failures which are promoted as automatic systems that "require no tedious handicapping on your part." There are no secret methods in learning to isolate winners from the past performances in the racing form; it is all hard work. Yet there are certain variables that can consistently pinpoint candidates that are likely to be competitive at long shot odds. These are the *hidden horses* that you can find by searching in the forest of detail that is in the racing form past performances for certain *variables* that are the "tells" that a particular horse, overlooked by the betting public, will probably run a competitive race that day. Frequently these horses go off at long odds; that is, 10/1 or more. Occasionally, the public lets them get away at extremely long odds of 20/1 and 30/1 and more. When that type of horse wins there are frequently complaints that "it must have been a boat race" and "the race was fixed." More often than not the reasons for the win at long odds were in the form, but hidden to the cursory glance of the unsophisticated player.

Most handicappers, professional and amateur, are form players; that is, they are looking for horses in good current form to repeat that performance in that day's race; however, if you consistently play favorites you will consistently lose for the betting favorite loses two out of three times. If you consistently play nothing but long-shots, you have to carefully pick your spots, for they are the exception. That's why they are called long-shots.

The selection of 10/1 odds as the definition of a long shot is arbitrary. Some handicappers would set the criteria lower, perhaps down to 7/1 which would return a minimum payoff of $16 for each $2 bet. If you use the 10/1 method, you can often spread bet; that is, bet two or three long-shots in the race where the winning return would be at least $22 for each $4 or $6 bet. First you must answer the question: Do any of the horses in a particular race qualify as *hidden horse* competitors?

I use the word "hidden" in the sense that generally a long shot winner's last race was a poor effort. The betting public has extreme difficulty betting a horse whose last race was bad. Much depends on the reason for the poor effort. To find that, we must first go to the "comments" column to the far right of the race chart. Here we will often find *steadied, bumped, traffic, stumbled, between.* Thoroughbred horses will generally shy when bumped. Usually, we will ignore that race. We must then carefully examine previous races in which the horse did not encounter trouble.

One of the most reliable of long shot plays is the "cutback" horse. For instance; suppose today's race is at six furlongs and the horse's previous race was at a mile in which it ran on or close to the lead for at least half way and sometimes to the head of the stretch; but then stopped, getting beat by double-digit lengths. You must check the horse's quarter and half mile times to see if it would have been competitive with today's field had his previous race been at six furlongs. These kinds of horses frequently are let go at long shot odds for the betting public finds it extremely difficult to bet on a horse that stopped badly in its last race, regardless of the distance comparisons.

Another tipoff that a horse is ready to run a big race regardless of his recent past performances is a "monster" work. Perhaps a bullet-work; but in any case an exceptional one. If the last work of the horse is substantially faster than his previous four or five, you may have found a "wake-up" horse. Many a long shot winner has had an exceptional last workout before today's race.

Thoroughbred racing is a contest of numerous variables. In order to locate a long shot candidate you must check for "tells." I usually do it in the following order:

1) Working down the left side of the past performances, check the work times and distances worked of the last two; in special cases and types of races you will need to examine the horse's entire published workout record. The works must have been prior to today's race. If there was an exceptional work before the horse's last race and it finished up the track, ignore that work unless it was an *excuse* race in which the horse was bumped, steadied, or had other traffic trouble. And, of course, work times are relative. A work of :47 2/5 for four furlongs at a New York track is something quite different than the same work of that time at a California track. In two year old races carefully examine the entire pattern of its published works.

2) Examine the back class: Is this horse moving up or down the class ladder? What was its form in previous races in which it was competitive?

3) Is the horse a front runner, a mid-pack closer, or a router usually coming from more than ten lengths behind for its late run? How much front speed is there in the race? Is this horse the sole front speed?

4) Is the horse a "cutback" candidate? For instance; if his last race was at a distance and the current race is at six furlongs, was the horse close to the front to the three-quarters call in the mile or more race?

5) Is the horse coming off a "trouble" race in which he was stead-ied, bumped, checked, forced to alter course, or had general traffic trouble?

6) Was the horse's last race a wakeup call; that is, did it show sudden improvement after several bad races in a row?

7) What are the records of the trainer and the jockey?

8) Is this a first time lasix horse? Have blinkers been added or removed?

9) If today's race is at a distance of a mile or more, is the jockey weight the lowest the horse has carried as shown in the past performances chart?

10) Has this horse been off for more than 46 days? If so, what is the record of its trainer when bringing a layoff horse back to the races?

11) Is this horse going from turf to dirt or dirt to turf? If so, what is the record of its trainer when his horses change running surfaces? What is the horse's record on each surface?

12) Has this horse consistently gone off at short odds but today is at 10/1 or worse? Has the horse consistently gone off at long odds and are his odds long today? If so, has it been bet down moderately from the morning line?

13) Was this horse a badly beaten favorite in its last race?

14) In a maiden claiming race are any of the entries dropping from a maiden special.

15) Was this horse claimed or otherwise changed trainers since its last race?

16) Near post time is this horse an underlay or an overlay?

It has been my experience that the most significant characteristic of a long-shot winner is that it must have run a poor last race prior to the one in which it is entered for today. That prior race has usually been an "excuse" race in which the horse was steadied, bumped, checked, between, had gate trouble, had otherwise traffic trouble, or stumbled. The second most frequent tipoff characteristic is that it is a "cutback" horse, and the third tell that a horse is ready to put in a good effort is the bullet or near bullet workout after modest efforts and mundane workouts, signaling that it is a *wake-up* horse - ready for a suddenly improving race.

All of the examples following are the actual past performances of long-shots that either won or placed at substantial odds. Generally; with few exceptions, I have shown only *that* horse's record prior to the winning effort. From these examples the reader should be able to detect a clear *pattern recognition profile* of long shot candidates. Below each horse's past performance chart I have listed the *tells*; the reasons the author placed a bet on each of them. The Chinese hieroglyphics markings are those of the author; the circles and arrows point to the variables considered in the decision to bet the horse.

Now - let's find the hidden horse!

Chapter 2

Two year old thoroughbreds are the *enfans* terrible of the racetrack; when first brought to the starting gate they are liable to do anything. They pose a particular danger to their jockeys. Upon attempting to lead them into the starting gate they will frequently balk, buck, and otherwise refuse to cooperate. Some of them have to be blindfolded. Once in the gate they will not infrequently buck the jockey off. Sometimes they will just sit down, other times they will flip. They are often scratched from their first start because of their obstreperous behavior. Like their human counterparts at that age, they are the *terrible two's* and they are learning to say "no."

It's a wonder that horseplayers will bet anything more than a dime on two year olds, especially in races where there are three, four, or more than half a dozen first time starters, for the tools in the racing form for handicapping two year olds are slim, indeed. If you just can't sit still and let a race go by without a wager, then you need to carefully examine the non-past performance of the two year old: its breeding; the record of its trainer with first time starters; the times and distances of its works, and the jockey in today's race. The most important tell of a non-raced two year old is the pattern of its workouts. If you find yourself compelled to play a two year old maiden race, study the workouts carefully; note when they were first placed in training, particularly the times of the three workouts prior to the current race.

Usually, when there are more than six first time starters in a race for two year olds it is best to pass that race. When there are three or less first timers and at least four horses who have run at least two races, then perhaps a wager is in order if you just can't resist playing every race on the card, but the odds are very much against you.

There are; nevertheless, long shot tells to be found even in the "baby" races. We will examine several of them in which the long shot winner or place horse was hidden, even though the forest for two year olds is not as dense as the one in which the older horses hide.

Let's begin with a two year old stakes race on September 4, 2009: a Grade 3 stake of $100k for two year olds going a mile and one-sixteenth on the turf at Saratoga. Interactif, trained by Todd Pletcher, a 19% trainer and ridden by Kent Desormeaux, a 19% jockey, had raced twice before today's race. The trainer's record on the grass was 16% while his record from dirt to turf was 18%.

Interactif broke his maiden on July 5, 2009; a five furlong race at Monmouth on the dirt. Winning at odds of 4.10/1, he earned a speed rating of 88. The horse next ran on the dirt in a six furlong Grade 2 stake at Saratoga on July 30, 2009. Near the lead for half way; he pressed - then faltered - finishing up the track.

Interactif worked on the turf at Saratoga on August 28, seven days before the current race, going four furlongs in :48 3/5, the best recent work of any horse in the race. The Saratoga racing secretary set his morning line odds at 6/1. A few minutes into the betting his odds jumped to 15/1, remaining there until post time. Desormeaux rated the horse a couple lengths off the lead, then - in a sweeping burst on the outside on the far turn - led by two lengths at the head of the stretch and widened that margin to the finish.

Interactif was clearly the class of the race, but the betting public could not get past the stakes race of July 30 in which he went halfway at six furlongs then stopped badly. As we will delve into when we get to the three year olds, horses suddenly stop for any number of reasons, not all of them physical. The experienced horseman understands that: the unsophisticated betting public does not.

Interactif paid $33.60, 12.00, and 5.70. Coupled with the second favorite, the $2 exacta paid $152.50. Coupled with the first and second favorite, the $2 trifecta paid $667. The racing secretary gave Interactif fair morning line odds of 6/1. He was correct in his estimation of the horse's chances of winning; the public was not; that is why the horse was a long shot - *hidden* to the inexperienced bettor.

THIRD RACE
Saratoga
September 4th, 2009

$1\frac{1}{16}$ MILES. (Turf) (1.38⁴) STAKES. Purse $100,000 *WITH ANTICIPATION S. (GRADE III)* FOR TWO YEAR OLDS. No nomination fee. A supplemental nomination fee of $1,000 may be made at time of entry. $500 to pass the entry box and an additional $500 to start with $100,000 added. All starters including supplements will be required to pay all fees . The added money and all fees to be divided 60% to the owner of the winner, 20% to second, 10% to third, 5% to fourth, 3% to fifth and 2% divided equally among remaining finishers. Any horse that competes in both the With Anticipation and the Pilgrim atB elmont Park will have their subscription fees waived for the Pilgrim. 120 lbs. Non-winners of a race other than maiden or claiming on the turf allowed 2 lbs.; maidens, 4 lbs. A trophy will be presented to the winning owner. The NYRA reserves the right too transfer this race to the Main Track. In the event that this race is taken off the turf, it may be subject to downgrading upon review by the graded stakes committee. Closed Saturday, August 22, 2009 with 40 Nominations. (If the Stewards consider it inadv isable to run this race on the turf course, Two-Year-Old races will be run at Seven Furlongs and races for Three-Year-Olds and Up will be run at One Mile and One Eighth on the main track.). (Clear 79)

Value of Race: $109,500 Winner $65,700; second $21,900; third $10,950; fourth $5,475; fifth $3,285; sixth $548; seventh $548; eighth $548; ninth $546. Mutuel Pool $566,154 Pick 3 Pool $140,388 Daily Double Pool $91,043 Exacta Pool $476,907 Trifecta Pool $321,191

Last Raced	#	Horse	M/Eqt.	A/S	Wt	PP	St	¼	½	¾	Str	Fin	Jockey	Odds $1
30Jly09 ^{9}Sar^8	8	Interactif	L	2C	118	8	6	6^1	3^1	1^{hd}	$1^{4\frac12}$	$1^{4\frac14}$	Desormeaux K J	15.80
06Aug09 ^{5}Sar^1	7	Jung Man Scott	L	2C	118	7	2	4^1	$5\frac12$	4^1	2^2	2no	Dominguez R A	2.00
05Aug09 ^{4}Sar^2	3	Paddy O'Prado	L	2C	117	2	9	9	9	9	$3\frac12$	$3\frac34$	Albarado R	2.15
05Aug09 ^{4}Sar^1	6	Dean's Kitten	L b	2C	118	6	5	$7^{1\frac12}$	$8^{1\frac12}$	$6\frac12$	$4^{1\frac12}$	4^4	Leparoux J R	9.60
06Aug09 ^{7}Sar^2	2	Zapster	L	2C	116	4	3	$3^{1\frac12}$	$4\frac12$	$5^{1\frac12}$	$5^{1\frac12}$	5^1	Prado E S	b - 4.70
20Aug09 ^{7}Sar^1	2B	Golly Day	L	2G	118	9	8	$8\frac12$	$6^{1\frac12}$	$8\frac12$	$6^{2\frac12}$	6^5	Castellano J	b - 4.70
15Aug09 ^{8}Mth^1	4	Two Notch Road	L	2G	120	3	7	5^{hd}	7^{hd}	7^1	7^4	$7^{8\frac34}$	Uske S	21.00
15Aug09 ^{8}Mth^2	1	Mississippi Hippie	L	2C	118	1	1	$1^{1\frac12}$	1^1	3^1	$8^{2\frac12}$	$8^{3\frac14}$	Velazquez J R	11.30
21Aug09 ^{3}Sar^1	5	Red Rally		2G	118	5	4	2^{hd}	2^1	2^{hd}	9	9	Castanon J L	9.80

b - Coupled:Zapster and Golly Day

OFF AT 3:37 Start Good. Won driving. Track Firm (Rail at 12 ft).

TIME :23^4, :48^4, 1:12^2, 1:35^2, 1:41^2 (:23.87, :48.99, 1:12.54, 1:35.43, 1:41.41)

$2 Mutuel Prices:

8- INTERACTIF	33.60	12.00	5.70
7- JUNG MAN SCOTT		5.20	3.00
3- PADDY O'PRADO			2.70

$2 EXACTA 8-7 PAID $152.50 $2 TRIFECTA 8-7-3 PAID $667.00

Bay Colt, (Feb), by Broken Vow - Broad Pennant by Broad Brush. Trainer Pletcher A. Todd. Bred by Wertheimer & Frere(KY).

INTERACTIF made a sharp middle move from outside along the backstretch, rallied four wide to take the lead leaving the three-eighths pole, shook loose in upper stretch and drew clear under right hand urging. JUNG MAN SCOTT raced in good position between horses, rallied three wide on the turn, but was no match for the winner while holding narrowly for the place. PADDY O'PRADO trailed for a half, moved out on the backstretch, swung five wide on thew turn and closed late in the middle of the track to gain a share. DEAN'S KITTEN steadied in traffic on the first turn, raced well back, gained five wide entering the stretch and closed late from outside. ZAPSTER steadied while rank along the inside for a half mile pole, saved ground to the turn and lacked a strong closing bid. GOLLY DAY was outrun for five furlongs, swung five wide and lacked a late response. TWO NOTCH ROAD was under a firm hold while saved ground, raced in traffic leaving the turn and finished evenly. MISSISSIPPI HIPPIE set the pace on the rail to the far turn and steadily tired thereafter. RED RALLY pressed the pace in the two path to the turn and gave way.

Owners- 8, Wertheimer and Frere ; 7, Winter Park Partners ; 3, Donegal Racing ; 6, Ramsey, Kenneth L. and Sarah K. ; 2, Dogwood Stable ; 2B, Dogwood Stable ; 4, Thompson Glenn R.; 1, Ward Wesley A.; 5, Scherer, Merrill R., Lynch, Dan and Sentel, Ken

Trainers- 8, Pletcher Todd A.; 7, Dutrow, Jr. Richard E.; 3, Romans Dale L.; 6, Maker Michael J.; 2, Pletcher Todd A.; 2B, Weaver George ; 4, Thompson Glenn R.; 1, Ward Wesley A.; 5, Scherer Merrill R.

Breeders- 8, Wertheimer & Frere (KY); 7, Tony Grey (NY); 3, Winchell Thoroughbreds, LLC (KY); 6, Kenneth L. Ramsey & Sarah K. Ramsey (KY); 2, Aaron U. Jones & Marie D. Jones (KY); 2B, Edition Farm (NY); 4, James M. Hackman (VA); 1, BridleOaks Farm, Inc. (FL); 5, Cloyce C. Clark Jr. (LA)

Scratched- Aikenite(09Aug09 ^{7}Sar^1), Strike the Tiger(25 Jly 09 ^{6}Crc^1), Quick Money(31Aug09 ^{5}Sar^4), Turf Melody(08Aug09 ^{11}AP^3)

$2 Daily Double (5-8) Paid $174.50; Daily Double Pool $91,043.
$2 Pick Three (2-5-8) Paid $683.00; Pick Three Pool $140,388.

brisnet.com

[illegible]

brisnet.com
the handicapper's edge

Premium Plus PP's **Saratoga** WAntcpin-G3 $1\frac{1}{16}$ Mile (T) 2yo Friday, September 4, 2009 **Race 3**

E1 E2/LATE SPD
90 96/ 93 96

8 Interactif (E 6)
6/1
Own: Wertheimer Et Frere
B. c. 2
Sire: Broken Vow (Unbridled) $30,000
Dam: Broad Pennant (Broad Brush)
Brdr: Wertheimer & Frere (KY)
Trnr: Pletcher Todd A
Prime Power: 120.6 (1th)
L 118

Fst	(107)	2 1- 0- 0	$23,550 88
Off	(107)	0 0- 0- 0	$0
Dis	(109)	0 0- 0- 0	$0
Trf	(111?)	0 0- 0- 0	$0
AW		0 0- 0- 0	$0

DATE TRK	DIST					RACETYPE	E1	E2/	LP	1c	2c	SPD	PP	ST	1C	2C	Str	FIN	JOCKEY	ODDS	Top Finishers	Comment
30Jly09Sar	6f ft	:22^4	:44^4	:57^1	1:10	Sanford-G2	93	98/	71	-1	-1	77	8	4	$3\frac12$	$2\frac12$			VelazquezJR[119]	L 21.10	BackTalk Enumerate Louisville	Pressed faltered 9
05Jly09Mth	5f	:22^2	:46		:58^2	Mdn 75k		92/	87			88	2	1	$1\frac12$	$1\frac12$	$1\frac12$	1^{hd}	DecarloCP[119]	4.10	Interactif Placitas NarbonaPass	Pace inside,held 7

14Aug Bel tr.t 4f ft :50 B 33/43 ●24Jly Sar 5f ft :59³ H 1/15 17Jly Sar tr.t 5f ft 1:03 B 4/10 29Jun Sar tr.t 4f ft :49⁴ Bg 9/37 22Jun Sar tr.t 4f ft :50³ Bg 27/39
07Jun Sar tr.t 4f ft :51² B 19/34 31May Sar tr.t 3f ft :39 B 43/64 23May Sar tr.t 3f ft :38⁴ B 15/29

TRAINER: 1st on grass (232 16% -0.50) 1st at route (347 23% -0.32) Graded stakes (801 19% -0.49) Dirt to turf (325 18% -0.50) Turf starts (1554 19% -0.45) Sprint-Sprint-Rte (100 22% -0.68)
J/T Meet (2 .00 -$2.00) J/T L365 (6 .17 -$0.77)

W 15/1 WORKS 5 7 D

The tells for Interactif were:

1) He had the best recent work; four furlongs in 48: 3/5.
2) He was the class of the race, dropping from a Grade 2 stake to a Grade 3.
3) His trainer and jockey had superior win percentages.
4) The trainer's dirt to turf record was 18%.

Before examining the next two year old long shot winner, the bettor needs to understand the duties of each track's racing secretary, for they are a considerable influence on the unsophisticated horse player. One of their most important responsibilities is the setting of the *morning line.* It has been my experience that most of them, particularly at the larger tracks, attempt to fairly set the odds line based solely on the past performances of that day's entries; however, I have to admit that there have been a number of times I have been puzzled by what I considered to be unrealistic settings of morning lines; their having been set considerably higher or lower than the horse's past performances objectively justified. Sometimes, when I see certain horses posted as 6/5 or 7/5 morning line favorites, I can't help laughing for what I see from the record is clearly a false favorite. The serious handicapper may ask: Why do I think a particular horse's morning line should be lower or higher than that set by the racing secretary?

I have often questioned the need for the setting of a morning line for any race. After all, why should track management tell the betting patron what the odds on *any* horse should be in *any* race?

What objective criteria could the morning line authority be considering when setting the odds on a first time starter; its works, trainer, jockey, breeding? What purpose does it serve? Why not let the bettors decide what the opening odds should be? Since the chances of eliminating the posting of morning line odds are slim and none, we must deal with their influence on the betting public because the system often works in the sophisticated bettor's favor. Serious handicappers should attempt to set their own morning line, time consuming and tedious though it is, for the bettor should be his or her own racing secretary. It is hard work, but the rewards are great for the discerning player.

A race on point involving two year old first time starters occurred in the second race at Hollywood on December 9, 2009 in a five and a half furlong maiden $35k claimer on the all weather track.

In the field of eight, four horses were first time starters. In examining their workouts, I noted that the 4, Malibu Rum, had worked four furlongs on November 22 in :48 4/5; the best work of the field with the exception of the 6, Deem, another first timer that had equaled Malibu Rum's best work. The rest of the field had posted sub-par workouts. The morning line favorites were the 2, Icey Temper, and the 7, Driveliketiger, at 5/2 and 2/1, respectively.

In spite of Malibu Rum's workout, her line was set at 20/1. It makes you wonder what criteria the Hollywood Park racing secretary was using when he gave long-shot odds to the horse with the fastest workout time of the field, with the exception of the 6 horse, Deem. As we have observed, the betting public bought the racing secretary's estimate of Malibu Rum's chances of winning and sent her from the gate at odds of 49.4/1.

The favorite at 1.3/1 was Icey Temper who was dropping several classes from a maiden special $63k five and a half furlong race on September 6 in which he quit at the head of the stretch, finishing seven lengths out at seventh in a field of eleven. Though he had worked in :59 4/5 at five furlongs on November 22, his two later works on November 29 and December 2 were extremely slow, suggesting to me that the November 22 speedy work should be discounted.

The second favorite at 1.4/1 was the 7, Driveliketiger, a legitimate cutback horse, having finished second in his last race, some three and a half lengths behind the winner after pressing the pace from the start in his last race in a $32k claimer.

The 8 horse, Pat Olcott, was also an obvious contender. He had worked four furlongs on November 14 in a blazing :46 2/5, but his later three works were poor. I thought the morning line of 4/1 was about right. The public, apparently ignoring that work and the fact that Pat Olcott was a beaten favorite at 1.3/1 in his only race, let him leave the gate at 7.3/1 — a mild overlay.

Malibu broke well and hugged the rail to the stretch where he came out to the middle, then closed two and a half lengths to get up by a neck. This obvious contender for the attention of all hidden horse hunters paid $100.80, 34.20, and 11.60. When Pat Olcutt closed for second, the $2 exacta paid $857. The racing secretary's picks finished third and fifth. A *would have, should have, could have* box bet on the four best workout horses would have brought back a $2 trifecta payoff of $2,268.40.

Believe the works!

SECOND RACE
Hollywood
December 9th, 2009

5½ FURLONGS. (1.02) MAIDEN CLAIMING. Purse $15,000 FOR MAIDENS, TWO YEARS OLD. Weight, 120 lbs. Claiming Price $32,000, if for $28,000, allowed 2 lbs. (Clear 57)

Value of Race: $16,300 Winner $9,000; second $3,000; third $1,800; fourth $900; fifth $400; sixth $400; seventh $400; eighth $400.
Mutuel Pool $196,199 Daily Double Pool $72,131 Exacta Pool $165,900 Quinella Pool $9,563 Superfecta Pool $97,649 Trifecta Pool $142,370

Last Raced	#	Horse	M/Eqt.	A/S	Wt	PP	St	¼	½	Str	Fin	Jockey	Cl'g Pr	Odds $1
	3	Malibu Rum	BL	2G	120	3	5	4hd	4½	4½½	1nk	Delgadillo A	32000	49.40
11Jun09 3Hol9	8	Pat Olcott	BL b	2F	115	8	1	3³½	3⁴	3½½	2²	Espinoza V	28000	7.30
19Nov09 6Hol2	7	Driveliketiger	BL b	2C	120	7	2	1hd	2¹½	1½	3nk	Quinonez A	32000	1.40
	6	Deem	BL	2G	120	6	6	6²½	5²	5⁵	4⁴	Bejarano R	32000	9.80
06Sep09 7Dmr7	2	Icey Temper	BL	2G	120	2	3	2²½	1hd	2¹	5¹½	Pedroza M A	32000	1.30
	4	Gold Country	BL b	2G	120	4	7	7¹	7²½	6½	6³½	Valdez F	32000	13.80
19Nov09 4Hol5	5	Golden Boy Mark	BL	2G	118	5	4	5¹	6¹½	7⁸	7¹⁰	Garcia M S	28000	22.80
	1	Jackson's Rainbow	B	2C	118	1	8	8	8	8	8	Amador S R	28000	99.80

OFF AT 1:02 Start Good. Won driving. Track Fast.
TIME :22², :45⁴, :57⁴, 1:04³ (:22.50, :45.92, :57.84, 1:04.79)

$2 Mutuel Prices:	3 - MALIBU RUM	100.80	34.20	11.60
	8 - PAT OLCOTT		8.80	5.00
	7 - DRIVELIKETIGER			2.60

$1 EXACTA 3-8 PAID $428.50 $2 QUINELLA 3-8 PAID $241.00
$1 SUPERFECTA 3-8-7-6 PAID $5,404.60 $1 TRIFECTA 3-8-7 PAID $1,234.20

Bay Gelding, (Apr), by Kela - Moyvane Lass by Dixie Brass. Trainer Capestro S. Paula. Bred by Paula Capestro Bloodstock LLC(KY).

MALIBU RUM chased inside, came out into the stretch, went around a rival in midstretch, angled back and rallied under urging to get up at the wire. PAT OLCOTT stalked off the rail, came three deep into the stretch, bid alongside foes past the eighth pole, gained the lead a sixteenth out and was edged on the line. DRIVELIKETIGER came in at the start, dueled outside a rival, regained the advantage in the stretch, was between foes past midstretch and just held third. DEEM steadied at the start, settled outside a rival or off the rail, angled in on the turn, came out into the stretch and just missed the show. ICEY TEMPER went up inside to duel for the lead, put a head in front on the turn, fought back inside in midstretch and weakened in the final furlong. GOLD COUNTRY broke a bit slowly, settled off the rail, came out a bit wide into the stretch and did not rally. GOLDEN BOY MARK chased outside a rival or off the inside, came out into the stretch and lacked a further response. JACKSON'S RAINBOW broke a bit slowly, saved ground off the pace, came out some into the stretch and was outrun.

Owners- 3, Capestro Paula S.; 8, Liviakis John M.; 7, Barber, Gary and Cecil ; 6, Glen Hill Farm ; 2, Beneto Steve ; 4, Marshall Thane ; 5, Lester Family Racing Stable ; 1, Diaz Jose Romero

Trainers- 3, Capestro Paula S.; 8, Conlon Melody 7, Miller Peter ; 6, Yakteen Tim ; 2, Mullins Jeff ; 4, Mullins Jeff ; 5, Pender Michael ; 1, Herrera Anibal Justo

Breeders- 3, Paula Capestro Bloodstock LLC (KY); 8, Joanne Nor (KY); 7, Maximum Six, LLC. (KY); 6, Glen Hill Farm (FL); 2, Liberation Farm & Stonewall Farm (KY); 4, Mark Parsons (CA); 5, Dr. David Lester (CA); 1, Richard Barton (UT)

$2 Daily Double (1-3) Paid $362.80; Daily Double Pool $72,131.

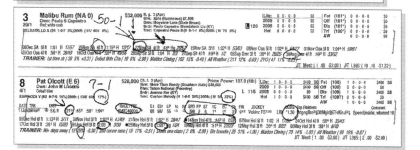

The tells for Malibu Rum were:

1) His work of :48 4/5, the second best of the field.

The tells for Pat Olcutt were:

1) His work of :46 2/5 on November 14, the best work of the field

✳ ✳ ✳

The fifth race at Saratoga on September 3, 2009, was for two year old maiden fillies going five and a half furlongs on the dirt for a purse of $55,000. It was a *maiden special*, meaning none of the horses could be claimed, similar to the conditions of an allowance race.

In a field of ten there were five first time starters. None of the other five horses had raced more than twice. It has been my experience that when there are that many first timers in a two year old race the analytic premium for superior works is extraordinarily high. Better yet, it might be a good time to head for the refreshment stand and pass the race.

If you are compelled to play such a race be sure and examine the two most recent workouts of each horse, methodically working from top to bottom of the form. In the current race the 5, Datt Echo, worked four furlongs on August 27 at Saratoga in :47 flat - a bullet work, the best of 31 horses who worked on that day at that track. The seven, Victoria Lynn, worked five furlongs on August 24 at the same track in :59 2/5, also a bullet work, the best of 29. The 9, Stormandaprayer, worked four furlongs on August 9 in :47 2/5 breezing, then on August 28 worked four furlongs in :48

4/5. None of the other horses in the race had other than average works.

Datt Echo had run two races. Her first was on July 15 in a maiden special at five furlongs with a purse of $43k. She went off at odds of 4.1/1 and finished fourth after being near the lead, running second to the head of the stretch, then gave up four lengths to the finish. Obviously, she tired. Her last start was a maiden $50k on August 13 at Saratoga where she ran on the lead (though closely pressed) to the head of the stretch and finished fourth, beaten four lengths, an improvement over her previous race. Her trainer and jockey were winners at a 13% and 18% clip. The racing secretary set her morning line odds at 12/1; unrealistically high in my view. I pegged the line at about 5/1.

The morning line on the 7, Victoria Lynn, was 20/1; notwithstanding her bullet work of August 24. I eliminated her because of the jockey's record of 7%, though I thought her morning line should have been more like 10/1.

The 9, Stormandprayer, was the morning line favorite at 3/1. She finished third in her first try in a maiden special of $43k, finishing five lengths out after leading to the head of the stretch in a five and a half furlong race. Her next race was in a Grade 3 stakes in which she was on the lead for a half mile, third at the head of the stretch, then tired badly to finish fourth, fifteen lengths back of the winner. I thought she deserved to be the favorite in today's race and that Datt Echo should have been the second morning line favorite.

Datt Echo went off at odds of 22/1. Breaking well, she ran from just off the pace before making her move upon entering the stretch where she pulled away to an easy win, paying $45.60, 14.40, and 6.60. The favorite finished second. The $2 exacta paid $179.50. Apparently, neither the racing secretary nor the betting public were impressed with Datt Echo's pre-race workout of :47 flat for four furlongs: that was, however, a golden *tell* for the hidden horse hunter.

FIFTH RACE
Saratoga
September 3rd, 2009

5½ FURLONGS. (1.03) MAIDEN SPECIAL WEIGHT. Purse $55,000 (UP TO $10,450 NYSBFOA) FOR MAIDENS, FILLIES TWO YEARS OLD. Weight, 119 lbs. (Purse reflects an increase of 10% providing more than eight betting interests leave the paddock.). (Clear 77)

Value of Race: $55,000 Winner $33,000; second $11,000; third $5,500; fourth $2,750; fifth $1,650; sixth $275; seventh $275; eighth $275; ninth $275. Mutuel Pool $387,775 Pick 3 Pool $76,932 Pick 4 Pool $208,188 Daily Double Pool $70,366 Exacta Pool $351,289 Superfecta Pool $82,327 Trifecta Pool $194,570

Last Raced	#	Horse	M/Eqt.	A/S	Wt	PP	St	¼	½	Str	Fin	Jockey	Odds $1
13Aug09 2Sar4	5	Dattt Echo	L	2F	119	5	3	4³	3³	2⁷	1½	Lezcano J	21.80
29 Jly 09 9Sar4	9	Stormandaprayer	L	2F	119	8	4	3¹	1¹	1½	2⁴¾	Castellano J	2.35
13Aug09 2Sar2	6	Happy Week	L	2F	119	6	2	2hd	5½	3²	3²½	Velazquez J R	4.00
	3	Cast Call	L	2F	119	3	9	9	9	5¹½	4⁶¼	Prado E S	10.00
16Aug09 2Sar2	4	Capitalism At Risk	L	2F	119	4	8	6¹	6¹	4¹	5³¼	Desormeaux K J	2.40
	10	Strike It Rich		2F	119	9	6	8⁸	8²	6¹	6⁶¾	Dominguez R A	8.60
	8	How Far to Heaven	L	2F	119	7	7	7hd	7¹	7¹	8½	Maragh R	23.10
	1	Ennis Lady	L	2F	119	1	5	5¹	4½	9	8¹¼	Leparoux J R	8.80
07Aug09 7Sar9	2	Restless Song	L	2F	119	2	1	1¹½	2¹½	7¹½	9	Theriot J	37.00

OFF AT 3:16 Start Good For All But 3,4. Won driving. Track Fast.
TIME :21³, :45¹, :57³, 1:04² (:21.76, :45.25, :57.71, 1:04.48)

$2 Mutuel Prices:

5 - DATTT ECHO	45.60 14.40 6.50
9 - STORMANDAPRAYER	4.30 2.80
6 - HAPPY WEEK	3.10

$2 EXACTA 5-9 PAID $179.50 $2 SUPERFECTA 5-9-6-3 PAID $4,014.00
$2 TRIFECTA 5-9-6 PAID $748.00

Bay Filly, (Mar), by Stormy Atlantic - Rehear by Coronado's Quest. Trainer Hennig A. Mark. Bred by Hermitage Farm LLC(KY).
DATTT ECHO gained from outside on the turn, made a run to challenge in midstretch then edged clear under right urging. STORMANDAPRAYER pressed early from outside, took the lead on the turn, battled into deep stretch and yielded late. HAPPY WEEK pressed the early pace from outside, dropped back on the turn and fought back to gain a share. CAST CALL broke in the air at the start, trailed to the turn, circled five wide and rallied belatedly. CAPITALISM AT RISK reared at the start and failed to threaten with a late five wide rally. STRIKE IT RICH was never a factor. HOW FAR TO HEAVEN failed to mount a serious rally. ENNIS LADY saved ground to no avail. RESTLESS SONG dueled along the rail to the turn and gave way. Following a stewards inquiry into the start there was no change in the order of finish.

Owners- 5, DATTT Stable ; 9, Flay Bobby ; 6, Wertheimer and Frere ; 3, Darley Stable ; 4, Klaravich Stables, Inc. and Lawrence, W.H. ; 10, Waterville Lake Stable ; 8, Pavlish Patricia ; 1, TYB Stable ; 2, Overbrook Farm

Trainers- 5, Hennig Mark A.; 9, Toner James J.; 6, Pletcher Todd A.; 3, Harty Eoin G.; 4, Violette, Jr. Richard A.; 10, Clement Christophe ; 8, Martin Carlos F.; 1, Trombetta Michael J.; 2, Lukas D. Wayne

Breeders- 5, Hermitage Farm LLC (KY); 9, Jaime S. Carrion, Trustee (KY); 6, W. S. Farish &Kilroy Thoroughbred Partnership (KY); 3, Farish and Farish, TGP (KY); 4, Kelly Helen Gregg (FL); 10, Stonestreet Thoroughbred Holdings LLC (KY); 8, Ed H. Pavlish & Patricia Pavlish (KY); 1, Walton Breeders (KY); 2, Overbrook Farm (KY)

Scratched- Victoria Lynn

$2 Daily Double (1-5) Paid $197.50; Daily Double Pool $70,366.
$2 Pick Three (3-1-5) Paid $477.00; Pick Three Pool $78,932.
$2 Pick Four (2-3-1-5) Paid $2,654.00; Pick Four Pool $208,188.

Data provided or compiled by Equibase Company, which includes data from The Jockey Club, generally is accurate but occasionally errors and omissions occur as a result of incorrect data received by others, mistakes in processing and other causes. Equibase Company and Bloodstock Research Information Services, Inc. and Thoroughbred Sports Network disclaim responsibility for the consequences, if any, of such errors, but would appreciate being called to their attention. Copyright 2009.

Datt Echo was not so much a hidden horse as she was simply overlooked.

1) She had the best recent work of the field, yet was ignored by the public.

Ordinarily, I don't pay much attention to weight assignments, especially in sprint races. Occasionally, you can find a long shot play in which the weights are a major factor in a distance race. Such a race was the sixth at Saratoga on August 22, 2009; a maiden special for two year old fillies going a mile on the turf for a purse of $38k. In a field of twelve, there were only three first time starters. The best works horses were the 2 and the 12; the 2 having worked five furlongs at :59 3/5 on August 18, while the 12 had worked four furlongs at a speedy :47 on August 17.

The 1, Sing Sing Cindrela, had raced twice in maiden specials for $28k. In her first race at four and a half furlongs she was made the favorite. Near the front for three quarters, she faded in the stretch to finish fourth, eleven lengths back. She then ran in a seven furlong race on July 15 at Arlington. Bumped at the start, she managed to finish fourth. In those two races she carried 118 pounds. In today's race she carried the apprentice allowance of 108 pounds; every other horse in the race had to give her ten pounds. The morning line odds were set at 12/1, drifting to 16/1 by post time.

The 12 horse - the best works horse - won at 6/1; the 1 placed at odds of 16/1, and the 2 showed at 5/1. Sing Sing Cindrela paid

$15.80 to place and $9.40 to show. The exacta paid $208.40 for $2 and the $2 trifecta 12-1-2 paid four figures. The keys to the race were the two works horses and the horse with 10 pounds less on her back than she had carried in her first two races; Sing Sing Cindrella must have thought there was a feather in the saddle that day. And at those odds the place money was a 7/1 payoff. Sing Sing Cindrela was not so much hidden as she was just overlooked. The telling key was that all eleven horses in the race had to spot her ten pounds for a distance race, and the farther the race the more important the weight differential becomes.

Sometimes in two year old races it is not as complicated as finding three or four tells, but as simple as finding the one dominating variant in a field of twelve, including no less than eight first time starters. In the fifth race at Saratoga on August 2, 2009, that tell was a blazing bullet work by Heavenly Landing on July 15 at Keeneland of a flat :47 breezing for four furlongs (the best of the 45 horses that worked that day at that track).

The race was a maiden special at six furlongs on the dirt for maiden filly two year olds for a purse of $55k. Heavenly Landing had run one race: July 5 at Churchill Downs on a sloppy track in which she was bet down to 10.6/1. She finished sixth by a wide margin in a field of twelve. The chartist's comments were "five wide mid turn."

In the current race the morning line odds were 15/1; the public let her go at 35/1. Her jockey was 12%; her trainer 17%.

From just off the pace, she placed second at $26.80 and 11.80. The key variable was the work of July 15 which was seven lengths better than any of the other fillies, with the exception of the winning favorite who had drilled four furlongs in :47 2/5 on July 26 at Saratoga; the work being a bullet, the best of 42 works that day.

Heavenly Landing coupled with the favorite completed a $2 exacta paying $201. So the race was simple: find the two fastest horses per their current works and box them in an exacta. On a side note, my standard bet on a selected long shot is win and place and to box my long shot with the first and second favorites. You would be surprised at how often a long shot arrives at the finish line either just ahead or just behind a favorite. The bottom line; the key to cashing decent tickets in two year old maiden races where more than half the field consists of first time starters, is to find the naked blazing speed. You find that in the workout times; study them carefully.

FIFTH RACE
Saratoga
August 2nd, 2009

6 FURLONGS. (1.08) MAIDEN SPECIAL WEIGHT. Purse $55,000 (UP TO $10,450 NYSBFOA) FOR MAIDENS, FILLIES TWO YEARS OLD. Weight, 119 lbs. (Purse reflects an increase of 10% providing more than eight betting interests leave the paddock.). (Rainy 73)

Value of Race: $55,000 Winner $33,000; second $11,000; third $5,500; fourth $2,750; fifth $1,650; sixth $184; seventh $184; eighth $184; ninth $184; tenth $184; eleventh $180. Mutuel Pool $581,359 Pick 3 Pool $97,641 Pick 4 Pool $253,267 Daily Double Pool $80,548 Exacta Pool $523,983 Superfecta Pool $134,664 Trifecta Pool $295,586

Last Raced	# Horse	M/Eqt.	A/S	Wt	PP	St	¼	½	Str	Fin	Jockey	Odds $1
01 Jly 09 4Bel2	6 Magic Appeal	L	2F	119	5	4	4²	3hd	1hd	1²	Prado E S	2.35
05 Jly 09 9CD6	10 Heavenly Landing	L	2F	119	9	3	2¹¹⁄₂	1¹¹⁄₂	2³	2¹¹⁄₄	Castanon J L	38.50
	7 Sing My Song	L	2F	119	6	7	7²	7³	5¹¹⁄₂	3³	Lezcano J	6.70
	9 Dynazaper	L	2F	119	8	9	8¹¹⁄₂	9²	7²	4¹	Leparoux J R	9.80
01 Jly 09 4Bel6	12 Rose Catherine	L	2F	119	11	1	3¹¹⁄₂	4⁴	3¹¹⁄₂	5²³⁄₄	Castellano J	6.30
	1 Cape Cod Carrie	L	2F	119	1	8	6¹¹⁄₂	6hd	6¹	6²¹⁄₄	Luzzi M J	24.25
	8 J Z's Revenge	L	2F	119	7	2	1hd	2¹¹⁄₂	4²	7¹¹⁄₂	Maragh R	24.00
	4 Chimayo	L	2F	119	3	11	10³	8¹¹⁄₂	9³	8¹³⁄₄	Garcia A	1.95
21 Jun 09 8CD8	11 Waynetta	Lf	2F	119	10	5	5²	5¹¹⁄₂	8¹¹⁄₄	9¹³⁄₄	Velasquez C H	38.00
	2 La Cloche	L	2F	119	2	10	11	11	10²	10⁹¹⁄₂	Arroyo, Jr. N	26.00
	5 Forest Legacy	L	2F	119	4	6	9²¹⁄₂	10⁴	11	11	Theriot J	26.25

OFF AT 3:16 Start Good For All But CHIMAYO. Won driving. Track Fast.

TIME :22¹, :45², :58, 1:11³ (:22.31, :45.48, :58.14, 1:11.65)

$2 Mutuel Prices:

6- MAGIC APPEAL		6.70	3.80	2.70
10- HEAVENLY LANDING			26.00	11.80
7- SING MY SONG				4.60

$2 EXACTA 6-10 PAID $201.00 $2 SUPERFECTA 6-10-7-9 PAID $7,781.00
$2 TRIFECTA 6-10-7 PAID $1,325.00

Bay Filly, (Apr), by Successful Appeal - Call Her Magic by Caller I. D.. Trainer Hough M. Stanley. Bred by Gulibram Shamrock Stables, LLC(KY).

MAGIC APPEAL tucked in along the rail, saved ground to the turn, angled four wide while launching his move at the quarter pole, made a run to challenge in midstretch then edged clear under steady urging. HEAVENLY LANDING dueled outside on the backstretch, shook loose on the turn, led into midstretch and held well for a two path on the turn and finished with interest to gain a share. SING MY SONG raced in midpack between horses, gained in the two path on the turn and finished with interest to gain a share. DYNAZAPER was outrun for a half, angled four wide at the quarter pole, altered course outside in upper stretch and rallied belatedly. ROSE CATHERINE stalked four wide for a half and weakened. CAPE COD CARRIE was under the while along the rail midway on the turn and lacked a late response. J Z'S REVENGE dueled along the rail for nearly a half and tired. CHIMAYO hesitated then stumbled at the start and failed to threaten while between horses. WAYNETTA raced up close while four wide for a half and gave way. LA CLOCHE checked at the start and failed to menace while wide entering the stretch. FOREST LEGACY steadied in traffic early and was never close thereafter.

Owners- 6, Cobra Farm, Inc. and Hough, Stanley M. ; 10, Lally Stable ; 7, Triple Diamond Stables, Ryan, Michael, J. and Brennan, Niall, J. ; 9, Lakland Farm ; 12, Pompa, Jr. Paul P. ; 1, Braverman, Paul and Lucky Shamrock Stable ; 8, Zayat Stables, LLC ; 4, Darley Stable ; 11, Stewart, Dallas, Andres, Tom and Reynolds, Jeff ; 2, Phillips Racing Partnership ; 5, Marylou Whitney Stables

Trainers- 6, Hough Stanley M. ; 10, Kennealy Eddie ; 7, Klesaris Steve ; 9, Mott William L ; 12, Pletcher Todd A. ; 1, Zito Nicholas P. ; 8, Asmussen Steven M. ; 4, McLaughlin Kiaran P. ; 11, Stewart Dallas ; 2, Toner James J. ; 5, Lukas D. Wayne

Breeders- 6, Gulibram Shamrock Stables, LLC (KY); 10, Gainesway Thoroughbreds Ltd. (KY); 7, Town & Country Farms, Corp. (FL); 9, Stonestreet Thoroughbred Holdings, LLC. (KY); 12, Janavar Thoroughbreds, LLC (KY); 1, Indian Creek, Michael E. Evans,Dr. Chet Blackey, Dr. Robert J. Hun (KY); 8, Lau-Mor Farms, LLC (FL); 4, Stonestreet Thoroughbred Holdings LLC (KY); 11, Robert Keck, Pope McLean,Pope McLean Jr. & Marc McLean (KY); 2, Phillips Racing Partnership (KY); 5, Marylou Whitney Stables (KY)

Scratched- Nonna Mia

$2 Daily Double (8-6) Paid $32.00; Daily Double Pool $80,548.
$2 Pick Three (3-8-6) Paid $72.50; Pick Three Pool $97,641.
$2 Pick Four (4-3/12-2/8/10-6) Paid $474.00; Pick Four Pool $253,267.

The tells on Heavenly Landing were:

1) The blazing work of July 18, less than two weeks before the race.

2) She was bet down to 10/1 in her first race; this frequently indicates barn betting.

3) The trainer was a 13% winner with his second career races; a 14% winner with his two year olds.

The hidden horse handicapper does not always have to find the winner - a place finish at high odds can also bring home the bacon. It is the money we are after, whether our horse finishes first, second, or third.

A good example occurred on November 18, 2009, at Aqueduct in the fifth race; a $16k maiden claimer for two year old fillies going six furlongs on the dirt. In the field of eight two of the horses were first time starters.

Although one of the first timers had a trainer with a 5% winning percentage and an apprentice jockey who had not visited the winner's circle in 49 tries, the 3, Marisadaniele, had the second best works in the race at four furlongs at :48 3/5 at Belmont on October 21. Additionally, all of the other horses were giving the seven pound apprentice allowance to her, while the other first time starter was also being ridden by an apprentice at 113 pounds, but the horse had undistinguished works. The best work in the race belonged to the 6, Artistic Ability, who was fairly made the third morning line favorite at 4/1. At post time the public had bet her down as the favorite at 2.6/1.

In spite of her good work - second only to the favorite - the racing secretary tabbed Marisadaniele at 20/1. She left the gate at 62/1. I backed her with $20 tickets across the board, then coupled her with the first, second, and third favorites in a $5 exacta partial key box.

Marisadaniele, running back to her good work, broke on the lead, was second to Artistic Ability at the half, then placed by a nose, just one and three-quarter lengths back of the winner.

The payoffs on Marisadaniele were $40.80 to place and 12.60 to show. Coupled with the favorite she brought home a $2 exacta of $207.50. It was a nice payoff for this hidden horse hunter of $1,077.75 for the $90 bet. And she had not won the race!

As the great golfer Lloyd Mangrum remarked to an opponent whose blood pressure was dangerously raised by Mangrum's holing out of a ricochet shot: "Are we playing *how* or *how many?*

In the hidden horse hunter game we are not playing *how* but *how much money.*

FIFTH RACE   6 FURLONGS. (1.07²) MAIDEN CLAIMING. Purse $15,000 FOR MAIDENS, FILLIES TWO YEARS OLD.

Aqueduct   Weight, 120 lbs. Claiming Price $16,000. (Clear 53)

November 18th, 2009

Value of Race: $15,000 Winner $9,000; second $3,000; third $1,500; fourth $750; fifth $450; sixth $100; seventh $100; eighth $100.
Mutuel Pool $170,469 Pick 3 Pool $49,986 Pick 4 Pool $90,119 Daily Double Pool $40,809 Exacta Pool $152,963 Trifecta Pool $114,993

Last Raced	# Horse	M/Eqt.	A/S	Wt	PP	St	¼	½	Str	Fin	Jockey	Cl'g Pr	Odds $1
30Sep09 2Bel⁴	6 Artistic Ability	L b	2F	120	5	5	5²	1½	1²	1¹½	Dominguez R A	16000	2.60
	3 Marisadaniele	bf	2F	113	2	6	1hd	2½	2¹½	2no	Peralta A	16000	62.75
05Nov09 2Aqu⁷	1 Lucy N Thunder	L	2F	120	7	4	7¹⁴	6²½	5¹	3¹½	Luzzi M J	16000	2.85
05Nov09 2Aqu⁴	7 Verse Choir		2F	120	6	2	4¹½	4½	3½	4²	Maragh R	16000	2.70
	5 Smokey Eyes	L	2F	113	4	3	2½	5²½	6⁴	5½	Serpa A	16000	11.10
21Oct09 4Bel⁷	4 I've Heard Rumors	L	2F	120	3	8	8	8	7²	6nk	Garcia A	16000	3.20
05Nov09 2Aqu⁸	8 How Cool Is That	L b	2F	120	8	1	3hd	3¹	4½	7⁷	DeSouza N	16000	37.00
02Oct09 9Bel⁸	2 Jazz Performer	L b	2F	120	1	7	6½	7⁸	8	8	Hill C	16000	32.25

OFF AT 2:20   Start Good. Won driving.   Track Fast.

TIME :22², :46¹, :59, 1:13¹   (:22.50, :46.28, :59.14, 1:13.32)

$2 Mutuel Prices:
6- ARTISTIC ABILITY	7.20	4.80	2.70
3- MARISADANIELE		40.80	12.60
1- LUCY N THUNDER			3.00

$2 EXACTA 6-3 PAID $207.50 $2 TRIFECTA 6-3-1 PAID $657.00

Chestnut Filly, (Mar), by City Zip - Micki Michelle by Old Trieste. Trainer Parisella John. Bred by Sarum Farm(KY).
ARTISTIC ABILITY settled just off the early pace, split horses to take the lead on the turn, shook loose in midstretch and edged away under a vigorous hand ride. MARISADANIELE dueled on the rail, drifted out considerably in upper stretch and held well for the place. LUCY N THUNDER was outrun along the rail for a half and closed late to gain a share. VERSE CHOIR chased between horses for a half, altered course a bit in upper stretch and finished evenly. A claim of foul lodged by the rider against MARISADANIELE for interference in the stretch was disallowed. SMOKEY EYES pressed the pace from outside to the turn and tired. I'VE HEARD RUMORS bobbled at the start and was never close thereafter. HOW COOL IS THAT stalked three wide for a half and gave way. JAZZ PERFORMER was never a factor.

Owners- 6, WAJA Racing Stable ; 3, Larinake Stable ; 1, Wolfe Steven ; 7, Hardwicke Stable ; 5, Flying Zee Stable ; 4, Sure Thing Stables LLC ; 8, Mueller David ; 2, Vandervoort-Kumble, Peggy

Trainers- 6, Parisella John ; 3, Ortiz Juan ; 1, Contessa Gary C ; 7, Jerkens H. Allen; 5, Martin Carlos F.; 4, Tagg Barclay ; 8, Lobo Paulo H.; 2, Gullo Gary P.

Breeders- 6, Sarum Farm (KY); 3, Dr. William R. Wilmot, Dr. Joan M.Taylor & Dunn Hill Farms, LLC (NY); 1, John Burns (FL); 7, Elisabeth R. Jerkens (KY); 5, Flying Zee Stables (NY); 4, Sure Thing Stables (KY); 8, Dr. Oscar C. Benavides (KY); 2, Peggy Vandervoort Kumble (NY)

Scratched- Primed to Be Ready, Loveable Lass(30Oct09 9Aqu¹⁰)

$2 Daily Double (7-6) Paid $17.80; Daily Double Pool $40,809.
$2 Pick Three (1-7-6) Paid $355.00; Pick Three Pool $49,986.
$2 Pick Four (3-1-7-6) Paid $5,584.00; Pick Four Pool $90,119.

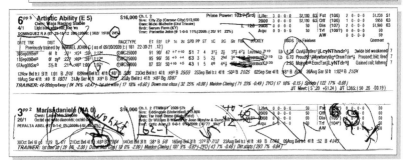

The tell on Marisadaniele was the one overriding variable in a two year old maiden race in which there are first time starters: an excellent pre-race work. The astute handicapper will diligently examine the works of each horse in such a race, and especially the pattern of all the published ones.

Another example of identifying two year old hidden long shots occurred on November 14 at Hollywood Park in a six furlong $40k allowance race on the all weather surface for California bred non-winners of two races. Of the nine entrants, six had at least three past performances; two had competed twice, and one had raced once. The morning line favorite was the 4, Toro Trippi, who had broken his maiden in his last race in a $32k claimer at five furlongs. I thought he was short because of his low last pace rating. Notwithstanding Trippi's remarkable work pattern, I tabbed him as a false favorite because it appeared he would be tested on the front by at least two other horses.

There was one horse in the race with a better current work than Trippi; the 10, Caracortado. His work on November 8, just six days before the race, was a blazing bullet: four furlongs in :47 handily. In his six furlong work on October 22 he posted another bullet of 1:12 4/5. In August, prior to his maiden win on September 24, he worked in :47 2/5 and again at :47 3/5. While his trainer's record was a modest 13% overall, he was 29% when moving from dirt to all weather surfaces and his two year old first time starters had won at a 22% clip.

The negatives were that he had broken his maiden at four furlongs at the bull ring that is Fairplex and that his jockey was an inexperienced rider who had won but two races out of 38 tries. Perhaps that is why his morning line was set at 8/1.

Though he was the most inexperienced horse in the race, he broke well, then attended the pace to the head of the stretch, drawing off to win by an easy two lengths. His backers were well paid with $16.20 for the easy win.

The final example of the technique of identifying two year old hidden horse long shot candidates occurred in the sixth race at Hollywood on December 20, 2009, in a six furlong $25k open claimer for two year old fillies over the all weather track. The field of nine had broken their maidens: the 4, Bye Bye Hollywood, had won two races and placed three times and was made the morning line favorite at 2/1.

I first looked for works horses, but could only find the 1, A Soft Breeze, that had worked four furlongs in :47 4/5 on November 20. None of the other horse's works were exceptional. My attention was drawn to the 6, Right To Work, that was cutting back from a mile and one-sixteenth $40k allowance race in which she gained the lead at the quarter; was a half length from the lead at the half; was still in contention in fourth at the head of the stretch, then weakened to finish fifth, some nine lengths out. Right To Work was dropping considerably in class. Her morning line was 10/1, floating up to 17/1 at post time. Her trainer and her jockey were 15% winners.

The 7, Gambling Pokerface, was also a class dropper, having broken her maiden in a $50k claimer in her last start. She appeared to be a consistent mid-pace closer, having done so in five of her last seven races.

In examining the favorite, Bye Bye Hollywood, the question crossed my mind as to why she was dropping in class after a good second in a $32k claimer in her last race. Normally, the trainer will usually try to move the horse up a bit after a win in a claiming race. In spite of her record of two wins and three seconds for six races, I was suspicious. Additionally, she had not worked since her last race on November 27 – another red flag.

I finally decided to throw out the favorite and bet the 6, Right To Work, to win and place and keyed her in an exacta box with the best works horse, the 1, A Soft Breeze, and the 7, Gambling Pokerface, who was a class dropper with consistent form.

Right To Work closed from mid-pack to win going away; the 7 placed, and the 1 was third. The morning line favorite, the racing secretary's pick, did not hit the board. The cutback winner paid $36.80, 12.80, and 7.00. Coupled with Gambling Pokerface, the $2 exacta paid $218.

The hidden horse hunter must always look for a cutback horse for the public generally lets such a horse get away at long odds.

SIXTH RACE
Hollywood
December 20th, 2009

6 FURLONGS. (1.07²) CLAIMING. Purse $20,000 FOR FILLIES TWO YEARS OLD. Weight, 120 lbs. Claiming Price $25,000, if for $22,500, allowed 2 lbs. (Clear 73)

Value of Race: $21,500 Winner $12,000; second $4,000; third $2,400; fourth $1,200; fifth $400; sixth $400; seventh $400; eighth $400; ninth $400. Mutuel Pool $260,453 Pick 3 Pool $63,561 Daily Double Pool $26,548 Exacta Pool $141,122 Quinella Pool $9,335 Superfecta Pool $97,778 Trifecta Pool $137,939

Last Raced	# Horse	M/Eql	A/S	Wt	PP	St	¼	½	Str	Fin	Jockey	Cl'g Pr	Odds $1
09Dec09 ⁵Hol⁵	6 Right to Work	BL	2F	118	6	6	6²	5½	2½	1¹	Pedroza M A	22500	17.40
05Dec09 ⁴Hol¹	7 Gambling Pokerface	BL f	2F	120	7	5	8²	7³	5²½	2²	Gomez E	25000	5.80
11Oct09 ⁴Fno³	1 A Soft Breeze	BL b	2F	120	1	9	1hd	1½	1hd	3½	Sorenson D	25000	25.90
16Nov09 ⁸Hol⁴	8 My Gal Candy	BL	2F	120	8	4	4¹	3hd	3¹½	4³½	Valdez F	25000	2.00
27Nov09 ¹⁰Hol⁴	9 Hayley's Halo	BL	2F	120	9	1	5hd	6½	6¹½	5nk	Flores D R	25000	7.10
27Nov09 ¹⁰Hol²	4 Bye Bye Hollywood	BL	2F	115	4	2	2½	2hd	4hd	6¹³	Santiago Reyes C	25000	1.90
10Dec09 ⁷Hol⁴	2 Little Dodger	BL b	2F	120	2	7	9	9	7²	7²½	Valdivia, Jr. J	25000	41.10
27Nov09 ¹⁰Hol⁶	3 Gale Schoonover	BL b	2F	120	3	8	7¹½	8½	9	8⁴	Cedeno A	25000	91.80
11Jun09 ⁷Hol⁷	5 Nana Boo	BL	2F	120	5	4	3hd	4½	8¹½	9	Espinoza V	25000	7.50

OFF AT 3:06 Start Good. Won driving. Track Fast.
TIME :21⁴, :45, :57², 1:10³ (:21.83, :45.03, :57.58, 1:10.63)

$2 Mutuel Prices:

6- RIGHT TO WORK	36.80	12.80	7.00
7- GAMBLING POKERFACE		7.40	4.60
1- A SOFT BREEZE			9.40

$1 EXACTA 6-7 PAID $109.00 $2 QUINELLA 6-7 PAID $85.00
$1 SUPERFECTA 6-7-1-8 PAID $8,626.10 $1 TRIFECTA 6-7-1 PAID $1,847.00

Dark Bay or Brown Filly, (Jan), by Marino Marini - Bint Alriyadh by Taj Alriyadh. Trainer O'Neill F. Doug. Bred by Eric Kruljac & Doug Kruidenier(CA).

RIGHT TO WORK chased between horses then inside into and on the turn, split rivals with a bid in midstretch, gained the lead, inched clear under some urging and held. GAMBLING POKERFACE four wide early, angled in and chased off the rail then inside into and on the turn, came out in midstretch and finished with interest while drifting out late. A SOFT BREEZE a step slow to begin, was sent along inside to set a pressured pace, fought back on the turn and until midstretch and held third. MY GAL CANDY prompted the pace between horses then four wide into and on the turn, bid again three deep in midstretch and was edged for the show. HAYLEY'S HALO pressed the pace five wide then stalked outside, angled in off the rail on the turn, came out four wide into the stretch and lacked the needed response. BYE BYE HOLLYWOOD had good early speed and dueled between horses to the stretch, then weakened. LITTLE DODGER allowed to settle inside, saved ground on the turn and into the stretch and did not rally. GALE SCHOONOVER settled off the pace inside then just out from the rail, went outside a rival on the turn and was not a threat. NANA BOO vied for command three deep between foes on the backstretch and turn and weakened in the stretch.

Owners- 6, King Arthur Farms, Master, Robert and O'Neill, Doug ; 7, Arriaga Joy ; 1, Firsthome Thoroughbreds ; 8, Sid and Jenny Craig Trust ; 4, Hoffman Lathrop G.; 4, Meadowbrook Farms, Inc. ; 2, Templeton Horses LLC, Gramer, Robert, Raskey, Jerry, Broguiere, Ray and Solis, ; 3, Stein Stables, Inc. ; 5, Alfonso, Ernie, Jackson, Rick, Pena, Jerry and Snook, Steve

Trainers- 6, O'Neill Doug F.; 7, Shelley Helen ; 1, Kitchingman Adam ; 8, Sise, Jr. Clifford W.; 9, Fanning Jerry M.; 4, La Croix David ; 2, Solis Walther ; 3, Stein Roger M.; 5, Becerra Rafael

Breeders- 6, Eric Kruljac & Doug Kruidenier (CA); 7, Rod Rodriguez & Lorraine Rodriguez (CA); 1, Hidden Point Farm Inc. (FL); 8, Sidney H. Craig & Jenny Craig (KY); 9, Lathrop G. Hoffman (CA); 4, Meadowbrook Farms, Inc. (KY); 2, Thomas H Stonebraker (KY); 3, Stein Stable, Inc.; 5, Special T Thoroughbreds, Inc. (CA)

$2 Daily Double (4-6) Paid $171.40; Daily Double Pool $26,548.
$1 Pick Three (6-4-6) Paid $426.90; Pick Three Pool $63,561.

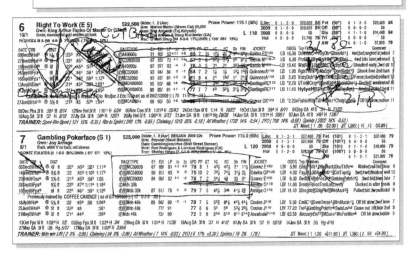

The tells for Right To Work were: her previous race on December 9 in which she ran near the lead to the head of the stretch before weakening in the one and one-sixteenth mile race, and her substantial drop in class for the current race.

These examples of tells predicting superior performances in the races of two year olds are not inclusive; they are representative, for two year old races are the most difficult to handicap because of their inexperience and unpredictability. Generally, I pass the baby races, especially where there are more than four first time starters. Sometimes; however, a couple of simple tells will lead you to the hidden horse that will pay you handsomely for that day's bet. Usually, these tells are most often found in the patterns of its works.

Notwithstanding my general predilection against betting on first time starters – be they two, three, or four year olds – occasionally, there are enough tells in the complete pattern of their works to predict an excellent first time effort. Many times the betting public will overlook the works pattern of a first time starter, especially when the racing secretary posts morning line odds of 10/1 or higher.

An example occurred in the 9th race at Santa Anita on February 21, 2010, in a California bred maiden special $44k race for three year olds going six and a half furlongs on the all weather track. An oversized field of 14, including four first time starters, went to the gate for the last race on the card: I thought it was ripe for a long shot play.

Seven of the competitors – the 1, 4, 6, 7, 8, 9, and 10 - were "works" horses; that is, their pre-race times met my criteria that usually signaled a good effort. I eliminated the 10 because his morning line had been set at 15/1 and he was "dead on the board." The best pre-race work belonged to the 9, My Boy Walsh, with a four furlong work of :46 3/5 on February 15, just six days before the current race; however, in examining the entire pattern of his eleven published workouts, and especially the bullet work of :59 1/5 on January 10 which preceded his poor effort in his only start on January 29, I concluded that he was a "morning glory," a horse that tightens up when confronted with other speedsters in an actual race. Nevertheless, I left him in my superfecta bet.

This left the five other best works horses as obvious contenders; the 1, 4, 6, 7, and 8.

My attention was drawn to the 4, Self Made, a first timer; the sole horse with a six furlong pre-race work, a bullet in 1:13 2/5. Additionally, the track's leading rider, Rafael Bejarano, was up. The trainer was John Sadler, a 21% winner; 18% in maiden special debuts. Self Made's best of his 12 published works was on June 11 when he went four furlongs in :47 4/5, fifth best of 49 working that day at Santa Anita. Two of his 12 works earned bullets.

It is difficult to understand what criteria the racing secretary was using when he set Self Made's morning line at 12/1. I thought the horse should be no more than 7/2; he looked like the winner to me.

In one of the most remarkable stretch runs I have seen, Self Made came from dead last at the head of the stretch – some fifteen lengths back of the leader – to win by a nose. He was followed by the 7, 1, 8, and 6, in that order. The first five horses to the finish line were all "works" horses. The horse with the best work was the 9. As it turned out, he was clearly a "morning glory."

The winner paid $24.80, 10.80, and 6. The two dollar exacta paid $330.20 and the $1 trifecta paid $896.80. The $1 superfecta paid $10,091.90. I had the exacta, the tri, and a dime super. I didn't play the High 5. One ticket wiped out the pool of $51,275.50.

Ah, *if only…would have, could have, should have…*

NINTH RACE
Santa Anita
February 21st, 2010

6½ FURLONGS. (1.13) MAIDEN SPECIAL WEIGHT. Purse $44,000 FOR CALIFORNIA BRED OR CALIFORNIA SIRED MAIDENS, THREE YEARS OLD. Weight, 121 lbs. (Cloudy 64)

Value of Race: $47,600 Winner $26,400; second $8,800; third $5,280; fourth $2,640; fifth $880; sixth $400; seventh $400; eighth $400; ninth $400; tenth $400; eleventh $400; twelfth $400; thirteenth $400; fourteenth $400.   Mutuel Pool $418,547 Pick 3 Pool $179,890 Pick 4 Pool $525,686 Pick 6 Pool $251,547 Daily Double Pool $129,460 Exacta Pool $268,635 Place All Pool $26,896 Superfecta Pool $179,627 Super High Five Pool $63,462 Trifecta Pool $234,266

Last Raced	# Horse	M/Eqt.	A/S Wt	PP	St	¼	½	Str	Fin	Jockey	Odds $1
	4 Self Made	BL	3C 121	4	13	14	14	6hd	1hd	Bejarano R	11.40
29Jan10 ⁸SA⁵	7 Warrens Paddockguy	BL	3C 121	7	4	6½	6²	1hd	2²½	Baze T	19.40
29Jan10 ⁸SA²	1 Circa'sgoldengear	BL	3G 121	1	7	5²½	3hd	2¹	3¹¾	Pedroza M A	3.10
27Jan10 ⁵SA⁴	8 Bold Type	BL	3G 121	8	3	2hd	2¹½	3²½	4¹¼	Talamo J	27.20
	6 Excess Power	BL b	3C 121	6	10	10hd	8hd	5¹	5¹	Rosario J	12.60
	10 Nofty	BL b	3C 116	10	8	7¹	11¹	7½	6½	Santiago Reyes C	38.30
	13 Syncobeat	B	3G 121	13	5	8hd	9½	9¹½	7²¼	Amador S R	210.10
15Jan10 ⁶SA⁷	3 Working Capital	BL b	3C 121	3	14	13¹	13¹½	10²	8hd	Solis A O	7.50
29Jan10 ⁸SA⁸	14 Sky Searcher	BL	3C 121	14	1	4¹	4hd	4hd	9nk	Blanc B	8.00
29Jan10 ⁸SA¹²	11 Full Effect	BL bf	3C 121	11	2	3hd	5¹½	8¹½	10¾	Medina L	185.30
	12 Water Landing	BL	3C 121	12	11	12¹½	12¹	14	11nk	Espinoza V	11.30
29Jan10 ⁸SA¹⁰	9 My Boy Walsh	BL b	3C 121	9	12	11hd	10¹	13hd	12½	Garcia M	2.20
30Jan10 ⁵SA⁷	5 Centrifuge	BL	3C 121	5	9	9¹	7¹	12¹½	13⁷¼	Smith M E	37.90
29Jan10 ⁸SA⁶	2 Camicory	BL b	3C 121	2	6	1¹½	1hd	11hd	14	Baze M C	44.80

OFF AT 4:41   Start Good. Won driving.   Track Fast.
TIME :22, :45¹, 1:10², 1:16⁴   (:22.00, :45.24, 1:10.48, 1:16.83)

$2 Mutuel Prices:

4- SELF MADE	24.80	10.80	6.00
7- WARRENS PADDOCKGUY		18.80	8.60
1- CIRCA'SGOLDENGEAR			3.60

$1 EXACTA 4-7 PAID $165.10 $1 PLACE PICK ALL 8 OF 9 PAID $559.60 8 Correct
$1 SUPERFECTA 4-7-1-8 PAID $10,091.90 $1 SUPER HIGH FIVE 4-7-1-8-6 PAID $50,275.50
$1 TRIFECTA 4-7-1 PAID $896.80

Chestnut Colt, (Mar), by Old Topper - Gender Motors by Mr. Greeley. Trainer Sadler W. John. Bred by Tommy Town Thoroughbreds, LLC(CA).

SELF MADE bumped at the start, settled just off the rail, came out leaving the turn and into the stretch, angled out again in midstretch and rallied under good handling to get up on the wire. WARRENS PADDOCKGUY chased between horses then off the rail, came out on the turn and five wide into the stretch, bid alongside a rival after drifting in, gained the lead, inched away and was caught late. CIRCA'SGOLDENGEAR moved up inside then was in tight on the backstretch, stalked along the rail, split horses leaving the turn, bid inside in the stretch, battled along the fence in midstretch and held third. BOLD TYPE stalked between horses, bid alongside a rival on the turn, came three deep into the stretch and weakened some in the final furlong. EXCESS POWER chased between foes then off the rail, came out five wide into the stretch and lacked the needed rally. NOFTY also chased between horses, came four wide into the stretch and could not summon the necessary response. SYNCOBEAT settled between foes then chased outside, went four wide on the turn and into the stretch and was not a threat. WORKING CAPITAL bumped in a bit of a slow start, settled inside, came out into the stretch and lacked the needed rally. SKY SEARCHER had speed outside then stalked four wide on the backstretch and turn, continued four wide into the stretch and weakened. FULL EFFECT stalked between horses on the backstretch and turn, angled in entering the stretch and also weakened. WATER LANDING settled outside, went four and five wide on the turn, angled inward in the stretch and lacked a further response. MY BOY WALSH broke in and steadied, chased between foes, came out leaving the turn and five wide into the stretch and was not a threat. CENTRIFUGE chased between horses then off the rail, angled in on the turn and lacked a further response. CAMICORY sped to the early lead, inched away inside, dueled on the turn, dropped back in the stretch and had little left for the drive.

Owners- 4, Tommy Town Thoroughbreds LLC ; 7, Warren Benjamin C.; 1, Heap, Blake and Malley, Earle ; 8, Beegle Ron ; 6, Anderson, Dan, Patton, Robert, and Suarez Racing Inc. ; 10, HnR Nothhaft Horse Racing, LLC ; 13, The Hat Ranch ; 3, Double JH Stable, Inc. ; 14, DeRenzo, Dean, Hartley, Randall and Sims, Jack ; 11, Mike Harrington Trustee ; 12, Golden Eagle Farm ; 9, Roberts Tom C.; 5, Freeman, Edward and Reddam, J. Paul ; 2, McBride, Randy and Projump

Trainers- 4, Sadler John W.; 7, Gutierrez Jorge ; 1, Heap Blake R.; 8, McCarthy Sean ; 6, O'Neill Doug F.; 10, Mandella Gary ; 13, Vargas J. Buenaventura; 3, Mandella Gary ; 14, Mollica Michael A.; 11, Harrington Mike ; 12, Cecil Ben D. A.; 9, Sherlock Gary ; 5, Freeman Edward R.; 2, Hajek Ina

Breeders- 4, Tommy Town Thoroughbreds, LLC (CA); 7, Benjamin C. Warren (CA); 1, Earle Malley & Sue Hubbard (CA); 8, Milt A. Policzer (CA); 6, The Merv Griffin Ranch Company (CA); 10, Super Horse Inc. (CA); 13, Hat Ranch West LLC (CA); 3, Double J H Stable, Inc. (CA); 14, Betty L. Mabee & Larry Mabee (CA); 11, Dr. Mikel C. Harrington &Patricia O. Harrington (CA); 12, Betty L. Mabee & Larry Mabee (CA); 9, Tom Roberts, Abrams, Huston, Maities &Nakkashian (CA); 5, J. Paul Reddam (CA); 2, Randy McBride (TX)

$2 Daily Double (3-4) Paid $132.60; Daily Double Pool $129,460.
$1 Pick Three (7-3-4) Paid $285.10; Pick Three Pool $179,890.
$1 Pick Four (2-7-3-4) Paid $2,025.80; Pick Four Pool $525,686.
$2 Pick Six (1-4/8-2-7-3-4) 5 Correct Paid $1,094.40; Pick Six Pool N/A.
$2 Pick Six (1-4/8-2-7-3-4) Paid $69,797.40; Pick Six Pool $251,547.

4	Self Made (NA 0)	Ch. c. 3 (Mar)	Life:	0 0 - 0 - 0	$0	Fst (104)	0 0 - 0 - 0	$0

Own: Tommy Town Thoroughbreds Llc
Silver, gold 'B' on black oval on back
BEJARANO R (208 47-38-35 23%)   2009 (251 1308 21%)

Sire: Old Topper (Gilded Time) $3,900
Dam: Gender Motors (Mr. Greeley)
Brdr: Tommy Town Thoroughbreds, Llc (CA)
Tmr: Sadler John W (90 18-14-14 20%)   2009: (147/ 711 21%)

Another variant in handicapping two year olds has little to do with their works and much to do with odds action. In nearly all other classes of races we are looking for an overlay: in the baby races we are looking for moderate underlays that indicate barn betting; that is, wagers made by the horse's connections that bring mid-price odds of 10/1 to 12/1 down to a range of 5/1 to 7/1 or so. If the horse does not have other than mediocre works, such odds action is a tell that the connections of that horse think it will run a competitive race. Another important variant, of course, is the trainer's record of wins with first time starters.

Generally, I have found that betting two year old races is not a good gamble; they are inconsistent and unpredictable. Often more than half the field in two year old maiden races consists of first time starters. I have found that betting first time starters is an exercise in frustration. Only occasionally should the hidden horse hunter venture into the nearly impenetrable forest of the tells of two or three year old first time starters. With two year old first time starters we must remember that sometimes a shot in the dark hits a bull's eye, but not very often. While I generally pass on betting any first timer, regardless of its breeding or its trainer's record with first timers; or its jockey, there are special cases that have attracted my attention. From time to time and between lengthy intervals some of the following types have won in their first try at huge odds.

In examining a first time starter's pre-race credentials we need to begin with its published workouts. If the last two or three works are mundane, I usually go no further, but if one of those works is exceptional I dig a little deeper, for now we are in the forest of its *tells*. If you find a good workout within the horse's last three works, examine its entire work pattern (sometimes there are as many as a dozen), then note the dates and the tracks.

We must now confront a general misconception among unsophisticated bettors that every trainer works each of their horses at the maximum urging of its jockey – every time. Years of experience as an owner have taught me that is not the case. Sometimes the trainer will have the jockey ask the horse for its top speed in short bursts, usually at three, four, or five furlongs; then alternate with more leisurely works before asking for top speed again. A minority of trainers prefer to work their horses at an easy pace, not wanting to "waste a race in the morning." If the trainer is trying to "put a lot of wind" in his horse, he will stretch out the works to six, seven, and eight furlongs. The hidden horse hunter must learn to read the story that the pattern of a first timer's works will reveal. Unfortunately, some first starters turn out to be *morning glories*; showing blazing speed in their workouts, but in a race they shorten stride and tighten up when pressed.

Once the works of a freshman two year old attracts your attention, you can then go on to what I consider to be tells of lesser importance than the works. You must not let the odds board influence you: remember, we are looking for a long shot, not a substantial bet down underlay of a first time starter. For every time that I have seen that kind of backing on a first timer produce a winner, I have seen twenty that failed to hit the board.

Generally, backing first time starters is a bad bet. We only examine them to spot the occasional long shot that is completely overlooked by the betting public. Look for speed in the works and a consistent pattern of regularly spaced workouts. I want no part of a horse that has not published a work in over a month, and especially if it has not worked in two or more months, no matter the quality of its previous works.

In maiden races the pre-race workouts are the keys to finding the winner, for too often the betting public overlooks the entire pattern of a horse's works after glancing at its most recent one or two. It is difficult to set specific times for particular distances as an absolute for a superior work because speed is relative; that is, a work of :48 2/5 for four furlongs may be the best work in one race while a work of :49 2/5 may be the best work of the field in another race.

At the eastern tracks a four furlong work of :48 4/5 or below will attract my attention, while a work of that time would be ordinary at the California tracks where it takes a four furlong time of :47 4/5 to grab my attention. In any case, workouts are instructive. In maiden races that include first time starters, the astute handicapper will invest some time on the pure analysis of each of the horse's workouts, and especially on those of the first timers.

When you see an exceptional work for a first time starter and a pattern of consistent regular works and the public is letting the horse go at long odds: take a shot — no matter the odds — for this is often the tell of a hidden horse winner. Bet the two year old first starters if you must, but only after searching in the thin-limbed forest of their tells for indications of exceptional speed in the pattern of their works.

Chapter 3

S electing a three year old maiden long shot winner is an entirely different matter than playing the two year olds. A considerable number of owners will not run their horses as two year olds, for many of the fillies and colts do not yet have their knee joints fully closed, nor are they otherwise sufficiently matured - physically or mentally - for the rigors of racing. Even at three a sizable number of colts will shin buck (equivalent to a sprained ankle) in their first or second race. This type of injury can take from six weeks to six months to fully heal. Usually, the injury will cause the horse to suddenly stop; imagine what it would feel like to try to run on a sprained ankle; *no mas*. When those horses return to the races with toughened shins they are frequently excellent long shot candidates because they stopped so abruptly in their last race.

While on the subject of injuries, it has been my experience that the betting public is not well served by the present practice of not reporting the nature of any injury requiring a layoff of more than 30 days. In the interests of fair play, I believe that track management and the state racing authorities should require that all past performance publishers - including the Daily Racing Form and the Bloodstock Research Information Services - note in the past performances that any over 30 day layoff was due to a veterinarian's diagnosis of a *shin buck, bowed tendon, stone bruises, breathing problem* or the like. Sometimes the injury is something as simple as a cold; yes, horses catch colds, too. The betting public has a right to that information which presently is reserved only for the horse's connections. I believe the politically correct word for supporting fair play at the track is *transparency.* The pari-mutual thoroughbred horse racing industry has too often been denigrated for the lack of it.

Lacking the above information, the betting public must at least try to read between the lines. If a horse shows a layoff of 30 days or more, what is the trainer's record of wins at first out when bringing that horse back to the races? When a horse is returning to competition after a year or more layoff, it is imperative that you carefully study the pattern of his works since the layoff. Generally, that situation is a fertile field for finding a long shot for the betting public will ordinarily let that kind of horse go off at long odds.

Finding the hidden horse in a field of three year old maidens requires that no variant in their past performances be overlooked. The *tells* are there: find them and you will be well paid.

✷ ✷ ✷

In analyzing the tells in three year old and up maiden races, let's begin with an extreme example. The sixth race at Del Mar on August 21, 2009, was for three year old fillies and mares going six and a half furlongs on the "all weather" surface for a purse of $19k and a claiming price of $25k. The race contained a full field of 12; all were three year olds with the exception of the 10, Tribal Fire, who was five. This type of race is near if not at the bottom of the barrel at Del Mar.

The best works horses were the 3, 7, 9, 10, and 11. The best work belonged to the 9, Emba U.T.K., who had gone three furlongs on July 23 at Santa Anita in :34 2/5 - a blazing work, even for Santa Anita. The next best work belonged to the 7, Flyinginformation, who had gone four furlongs at Del Mar on August 15 in :47 2/5. The next best work was for the 3, Flashy Traveler, who went five furlongs on August 14 at Del Mar in :58 3/5. The 11, Skim Milk, had worked five furlongs in :59 1/5 on August 15 at Delmar. Finally, the 10, Tribal Fire, had worked four furlongs in :48 2/5 on July 25 at Del Mar. These were, theoretically, the 5 fastest horses in the race.

When I first looked over the race, I thought the 10 and the 11 were long shot possibilities; the 11 because she was well hidden, having finished sixth by five lengths in her last race at today's distance. The 10 horse - the five year old - had run three competitive races in a row, finishing second, fourth, and second; yet the public let her odds drift up to 6/1. The 7, with Garret Gomez up, was the odds on favorite. The 3, Flashy Traveler, was bet down from 15/1 to 8/1.

My attention then turned to the 9, Emba U.T.K. Her trainer and jockey did not have records to write home about; nevertheless, there were several variant tells that indicated this horse was ready to run a competitive race.

The first tell was the pattern of her works. Emba had been off the track for some eight months since November of 2008. Was the injury a shin-buck? Or hoof problems? The public didn't know. My guess was that the injury was a shin-buck. She had started seven times in three months. She was put back in training on May 31, 2009, at Santa Anita; since then she had worked eight times. The first indication that she was rounding into form was the bullet work of :34 2/5 at three furlongs on June 26 at Santa Anita. On July 8 she worked four furlongs in :48 3/5 at Santa Anita; following that decent work with the three furlong work of - again - :34 2/5 on July 23 at Santa Anita. In her first start after the layoff she ran third at Hollywood, going six and a half furlongs with a 72 speed rating. Then on August 2 she ran in a $25k maiden claimer at Del Mar, finishing sixth by seven lengths after being badly bumped at the start.

This horse actually had some back class, having run in a $130k stakes race at Fairplex. In two of her races she had rallied from well back to get a third and a fourth. The public could not get past her last race in which she was bumped at the gate, yet stayed on to beat half the field. The jockey was a problem, having won but 6 races out of 119 mounts, but when a horse is sitting on a big race and has rounded nicely into condition, it will win even if a sack of cement is in the saddle. The horse will, as the old joke goes, win even if it has to drag the jockey, kicking and screaming, across the finish line.

I would like to have been able to report that I played the exacta, trifecta, and superfecta in that race; my modest but heartfelt wager was $20 to win and place on the unusually named Emba U.T.K.

She left the gate at 49/1 - for half of the race it appeared she should have been 100/1 - as she trailed the field until the head of the stretch where she weaved her way through traffic to win on the rail by a head. When they put the numbers up I realized I had let a big one slip through my fingers.

The 10 placed second; the 11 was third; the 7, fourth, and the 3 was fifth. The five best works horses were the first five to cross the finish line. The $2 exacta paid $802, the $2 trifecta paid over $2,900, and the superfecta paid over $20,000 for a $2 ticket. My bet paid $1,000 for the win and $330 for the place. Talk about mixed emotions!

This is an extreme example of tells tipping off long shot plays. It is certainly not going to happen very often, but when it does the astute handicapper must recognize the pattern. To hell with the odds board, keep searching in the forest of detail that is in the past performances for it is only there that you can find the hidden horse.

SIXTH RACE
Del Mar
August 21st, 2009

6½ FURLONGS. (1.15) MAIDEN CLAIMING. Purse $19,000 FOR MAIDENS, FILLIES AND MARES THREE YEARS OLD AND UPWARD. Three Year Olds, 120 lbs.; Older, 124 lbs. Claiming Price $25,000, if for $22,500, allowed 2 lbs. (Cloudy 74)

Value of Race: $21,420 Winner $11,400; second $3,800; third $2,280; fourth $1,140; fifth $400; sixth $400; seventh $400; eighth $400; ninth $400; tenth $400; eleventh $400. Mutuel Pool $395,642 Pick 3 Pool $88,703 Daily Double Pool $33,288 Exacta Pool $230,914 Quinella Pool $12,187 Superfecta Pool $131,334 Trifecta Pool $198,081

Last Raced	#	Horse	M/Eqt.	A/S	Wt	PP	St	¼	½	Str	Fin	Jockey	Cl'g Pr	Odds $1
02Aug09 ²Dmr⁶	9	Emba U. T. K.	BL f	3F	120	8	5	11	10¹½	5²	1hd	Valdez F	25000	49.10
01Aug09 ¹⁰Dmr²	10	Tribal Fire	BL f	5M	122	9	1	1hd	1hd	1½	2no	Baze M C	22500	6.20
25Jly09 ²Dmr⁶	11	Skim Milk	BL b	3F	120	10	3	9¹½	9¹	7¹½	3no	Gryder A T	25000	10.30
25Jly09 ²Dmr⁴	7	Flyinginformation	BL	3F	120	6	4	8hd	7½	4hd	4²½	Gomez G K	25000	1.10
05Jly09 ¹¹Hol⁹	3	Flashy Traveler	BL b	3F	118	3	10	4hd	3¹	2¹½	5hd	Couton J	22500	11.60
24Jly09 ⁹Dmr³	8	Lady Boudicca	BL b	3F	118	7	9	10hd	11	8²½	6⅔	Solis A O	22500	7.20
02Aug09 ²Dmr³	1	Moon Over Malibu	BL	3F	118	1	8	5hd	5½	6hd	7¹½	Baze T	22500	5.70
08Aug09 ¹⁰Dmr⁸	2	Storm'n Marisa	BL	3F	120	2	7	3¹½	2¹	3¹	8¹½	Stra K	25000	35.30
30Jly09 ⁴Dmr¹¹	6	Straight Sue	BL b	3F	120	5	11	7²½	8hd	9¹½	9²¾	Quinonez A	25000	27.90
30Jly09 ⁴Dmr⁹	12	Mystic Trip	BL	3F	118	11	2	6¹	6¹	10hd	10½	Garcia M	22500	35.80
01Aug09 ¹⁰Dmr⁴	5	Cee's Harmony	BL f	4F	124	4	6	2hd	4hd	11	11	Arambula P	25000	26.00

OFF AT 5:39 Start Good. Won driving. Track Fast.

TIME :22³, :45², 1:10¹, 1:16³   (:22.67, :45.54, 1:10.35, 1:16.73)

$2 Mutuel Prices:

9- EMBA U. T. K.	100.20	33.00	15.20
10- TRIBAL FIRE		7.40	5.20
11- SKIM MILK			6.40

$1 EXACTA 9-10 PAID $410.80 $2 QUINELLA 9-10 PAID $317.00
$1 SUPERFECTA 9-10-11-7 PAID $10,821.80 $1 TRIFECTA 9-10-11 PAID $2,906.70

Dark Bay or Brown Filly, (Mar), by The Deputy (IRE) - Marfa's Finale by Marfa. Trainer Ho Herbert. Bred by Margaux Farm LLC(KY).

EMBA U. T. K. settled off the rail then angled in and saved ground off the pace, moved up inside in the stretch then rallied under urging along the fence to gain the lead in deep stretch and held. TRIBAL FIRE dueled three deep then outside a rival on the turn, fought back off the rail in midstretch and continued willingly between foes late. SKIM MILK settled outside or alongside a rival, came out leaving the turn and five wide into the stretch and finished well outside. FLYINGINFORMATION chased off the rail, split horses leaving the turn, came three deep into the stretch and rallied between rivals late. FLASHY TRAVELER broke in and a bit slowly, stalked between horses then outside on the turn, bid three deep into the stretch then outside the runner-up in the drive and weakened late. LADY BOUDICCA a bit slow to begin, settled off the rail, angled in on the turn, came out in midstretch and was not a threat. MOON OVER MALIBU stalked the pace inside, came out into the stretch and did not rally. STORM'N MARISA had good early speed and dueled inside, dropped back in the stretch and weakened. STRAIGHT SUE squeezed at the start, settled off the rail then outside on the turn, came three deep into the stretch and lacked the needed response. MYSTIC TRIP stalked outside then three deep, went four wide leaving the turn and into the stretch and weakened. CEE'S HARMONY broke outward, dueled between horses then stalked on the turn, dropped back between foes leaving the turn and weakened.

Owners- 9, H. D.R. C. Racing and Happy Valley Racing Stable; 10, Mattivi, Albert and Kathleen ; 11, First Run Stable ; 7, La Canada Stables LLC ; 3, Mitchell, Esther, Shedlock, Janine, Swearingen, R. Joe and DeRossi, Daniel ; 8, Reid Gerald ; 1, Reddam J. Paul ; 2, Malette Charles Bud ; 6, Tannyhill, Richard J. and W. Michael and Weeks, Gregory L. ; 12, Cox Lisa ; 5, Four D Stable

Trainers- 9, Ho Herbert ; 10, Knapp Steve ; 11, Stein Roger M. ; 7, Carava Jack ; 3, Powell Leonard ; 8, Gallagher Patrick ; 1, O'Neill Doug F. ; 2, Chew Matthew ; 6, Fanning Jerry M. ; 12, Martin, Jr. Frank ; 5, Shulman Sanford

Breeders- 9, Margaux Farm LLC (KY); 10, Mr. & Mrs. Jay Mitchell, JanineShedlock & R. Joe Swearingen (FL); 8, Gerard Chiusolo (KY); 1, Broodmares Anonymous Partners (KY); 2, Shelley Woodruff (KY); 6, R. Tannyhill, M. Tannyhill & G. Weeks (CA); 12, Donald Valpredo (CA); 5, Four D Stables (CA)

Flyinginformation was claimed by Johnson Stephen E.; trainer, Mitchell Mike R.

Scratched- Cool Spool (16Jly09 ⁶Hol⁸), Warren's High Gear(16Jly09 ⁶Hol⁸), Bonita Birdie(09Aug09 ⁹Dmr⁷)

$2 Daily Double (7-9) Paid $547.80; Daily Double Pool $33,288.
$1 Pick Three (3-7-9) Paid $3,697.50; Pick Three Pool $88,703.

The tells on the well hidden Emba U.T.K were:

1) Returning to the track after an eight month layoff, the pattern of her works clearly indicated that she was rounding into form with the bullet work of :34 2/5 for three furlongs on June 26; her work on July 8 for four furlongs at :48 3/5, and her final pre-race work on July 23 of another :34 2/5 for three furlongs.

2) In her first start after the layoff she was badly bumped at the break, yet finished sixth some seven lengths out; clearly an excusable "throw out race."

3) She had some back class, having run in a $130k stakes race.

4) She was a proven router, having come from well back to finish third in two 25k maiden claiming races.

✫ ✫ ✫

Another example of the hidden cutback horse occurred in the sixth race at Belmont on July 4, 2009. The race was a maiden special $41k for three year old New York breds at five and a half furlongs on the dirt. Eleven were entered, five were first time starters.

The 3, Offensive Attack, had three previous starts. He showed nothing in his maiden effort. In his second start on a muddy track at six furlongs he led through the second call, doing a :22 quarter and a :45 3/5 half mile. At the head of the stretch he was second by a length and a half before stopping badly. The conclusion is that he ran on or near the lead for from five to five and a half furlongs. In his last previous start at six furlongs he was again on the lead to the head of the stretch and this time stayed on to finish fourth, just four lengths out. Again, he slowed at somewhere between five and five a half furlongs.

There did not appear to be front speed from the two horses inside Offensive Attack; the other front appeared to be with the 7, 10, and 11. At five and a half furlongs, Offensive Attack was clearly a horse to be reckoned with.

The morning line was 12/1; for whatever reason the public let him get off at 37/1. On a muddy track he easily wired the field. The "tells" were there in the form, hidden though they were. He had run two similar class races on or near the lead, staying on somewhere between five and five and a half furlongs; today's race was at that distance. The racing secretary and the public made him a long shot; the form made him a solid competitor at a generous price.

SIXTH RACE
Belmont Park
July 4th, 2009

5½ FURLONGS. (1.02¹) MAIDEN SPECIAL WEIGHT. Purse $41,000 FOR MAIDENS, THREE YEARS OLD AND UPWARD FOALED IN NEW YORK STATE AND APPROVED BY THE NEW YORK STATE-BRED REGISTRY. Three Year Olds, 118 lbs.; Older, 123 lbs. (Clear 78)

Value of Race: $41,000 Winner $24,600; second $8,200; third $4,100; fourth $2,050; fifth $1,230; sixth $164; seventh $164; eighth $164; ninth $164; tenth $164. Mutuel Pool $440,054 Pick 3 Pool $66,019 Daily Double Pool $55,882 Exacta Pool $368,916 Superfecta Pool $102,086 Trifecta Pool $233,409

Last Raced	#	Horse	M/EqL	A/S Wt	PP	St	¼	⅜	Str	Fin	Jockey	Odds $1
03Jun09 6Bel4	3	Offensive Attack	L	3G 118	3	1	1¹	1hd	1½	1⅝	Arroyo, Jr. N	35.50
06Jun09 12Bel3	7	African Knight	L b	3C 118	6	2	2½	2½	2³	2³½	Castellano J	1.20
22Nov08 2Aqu2	2	Star of New York	L	3C 118	2	4	5¹	5½	4½	3½	Prado E S	4.20
09May09 5Bel4	1	Hero Figure	L	3R 118	1	3	3hd	3hd	3½	4½	Lezcano J	3.15
	4	Ommadon's Hope		3G 118	4	7	8⁶	8⁴	6½	5⅜	Velazquez J R	28.25
06Jun09 12Bel7	10	Graceful Afleet	L	3G 118	9	5	6³	6³	5²	6²½	Dominguez R A	7.20
	9	Argentinian	L	3G 118	8	10	10	8½	7²½	Maragh R	34.00
30May09 7Bel4	11	Personal Shopper	L b	4G 123	10	8	4¹	4½	7³	8⁵½	Luzzi M J	15.10
	5	Book		3G 118	5	6	7⁴	7½	9⁵	9⁵½	Velasquez C H	44.25
	8	Dance to the Music	L f	3G 111	7	9	9²	9¹	10	10	Casey A J	82.75

OFF AT 3:42 Start Good For All But 8,9. Won driving. Track Fast.
TIME :22², :44³, :56², 1:02⁴ (:22.49, :44.77, :56.58, 1:02.89)

$2 Mutuel Prices:
3- OFFENSIVE ATTACK 73.00 23.20 10.00
7- AFRICAN KNIGHT 3.10 2.40
2- STAR OF NEW YORK 3.70

$2 EXACTA 3-7 PAID $228.00 $2 CONSOLATION PICK 3 10-6/13-2 PAID $291.00 3 Correct
$2 SUPERFECTA 3-7-2-1 PAID $2,178.00 $2 TRIFECTA 3-7-2 PAID $1,142.00

Bay Gelding, (Mr), by Hook and Ladder - Timely Irony by Iron. Trainer Bush M. Thomas. Bred by Chester Broman & Mary R. Broman(NY).

OFFENSIVE ATTACK dueled along the rail, dug in when challenged in midstretch and edged clear under right hand urging. AFRICAN KNIGHT pressed the winner from outside into midstretch but was no match for that one while clearly second best. STAR OF NEW YORK raced in the middle of the pack between horses for a half, checked after lugging in near the eighth pole and finished willingly along the inside. HERO FIGURE steadied along the rail at the half mile pole, waited while saving ground on the turn and finished evenly. OMMADON'S HOPE raced well back for a half, drifted out in upper stretch and lacked a late response. GRACEFUL AFLEET saved ground to the turn, steadied in tight nearing the eighth pole and weakened. ARGENTINIAN never reached contention after breaking poorly. PERSONAL SHOPPER raced in close contention five wide for a half and steadily tired thereafter. BOOK failed to mount a serious rally. DANCE TO THE MUSIC steadied after breaking slowly and was never close thereafter.

Owners- 3, Broman, Sr., Mary and Chester ; 7, M.A.M. Stable ; 2, Lerner Harold ; 1, Flying Zee Stable ; 4, Sorin Stables ; 10, Steel Your Face Stables ; 9, Grant Stuart ; 11, Merrylegs Farm ; 5, Buhr Carl ; 8, Pucker Ridge Racing

Trainers- 3, Bush Thomas M.; 7, Terranova, II John P.; 2, Contessa Gary C.; 1, Serpe Philip M.; 4, O'Brien Leo ; 10, Levine Bruce N.; 9, Dutrow Anthony W.; 11, Kravets Bruce M.; 5, Callejas Bernardo ; 8, Prine David

Breeders- 3, Chester Broman & Mary R. Broman (NY); 7, Castellare di Cracchiolo Stables LLC (NY); 2, Ted Taylor (NY); 1, Flying Zee Stables (NY); 4, Sorin Stables Inc (NY); 10, Steel Your Face Stables, LLC (NY); 9, Gavin Murphy & Catherine Donavan (NY); 11, Merrylegs Farm (NY); 5, Carl Buhr (NY); 8, Lois Engel (NY)

Scratched- Quirk

$2 Daily Double (4-3) Paid $196.00; Daily Double Pool $55,882.
$2 Pick Three (10-4-3) Paid $1,219.00; Pick Three Pool $66,019.

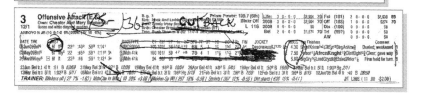

The tells on Offensive Attack were:

1) The horse nicely fit the profile of a cutback long shot prospect.

2) His trainer's record when starting maiden claimers in maiden special races was 20%.

3) In his three previous races, Offensive Attack's odds were 5.9/1, 7.5/1, and 4.3/1. In the current race he was 37/1; hidden to the unsophisticated bettor, yet the clear tells were there for the discerning hidden horse hunter.

On December 4, 2009, an excellent example of a plain tell on a cutback horse occurred in the ninth and final race in a maiden special $50.4k race for New York bred three year olds and up fillies and mares going one mile on the dirt (originally scheduled for the turf).

After the scratch of the morning line favorite, the second lowest morning line odds horse, the 12, Laylaben, was made the favorite. Although I agreed that her record justified her favoritism, I thought the outside post disadvantage would be difficult to overcome.

In an unusual case, the 8 horse, All Sew Smooth, was bet down from a morning line of 12/1 to odds-on at post time of 1.95/1. With the highest last race speed rating and her close of eight lengths from the first call to finish third, just a length out, I agreed that she was a solid contender. I then went looking for a hidden horse contender to hook up with the first two favorites.

First, I eliminated four horses because examination of their records indicated that they were out-classed and out of form. Then I located an obvious hidden horse cutback long shot candidate, the 5, Devilishameye. Her morning line was 20/1, but early in the betting she was being backed at underlay odds of 9/1. She had not hit the board in her ten lifetime tries, the first eight of which were less than stellar efforts. Her last seven races were on the grass; today she was going from turf to dirt.

In her race of October 11 at seven furlongs at Belmont Park she finished fifth, just four and a half lengths out; her best finish to that time. In her last race on November 8 at Belmont at one and one-sixteenth mile on the turf she broke well from the 11 post, closed two lengths from the first call to the head of the stretch where she was second, just a head back of the leader – then gave up three lengths in the last sixteenth, finishing fourth. In the current race she was cutting back one-sixteenth of a mile. She clearly qualified as a cutback contender. She also had the best pre-race work of the field.

Devilishameye, however, did not have the most successful of connections. Her jockey was a 6% winner and her trainer was little better at 7%; no matter, the tells fairly shouted that this horse was ready for a big effort.

I made my normal bets when backing a hidden horse long shot of $20 to win and place, than boxed my pick with the first and second favorites in $10 exacta boxes for a total investment of $80.

When the gates opened I was about to write it off as a bad bet when Devilishameye stumbled badly at the start. She recovered though, and at the three-quarter call was only five lengths back, then rallied down the stretch to win by a head over the favorite, All Sew Smooth.

Devilishameye paid $42.60, 15.40, and 6.60. When the favorite placed, the $2 exacta paid $212. This was another excellent example of the public overlooking another hidden horse cutback candidate. The betting public just can't seem to get by the fact that the horse stopped badly in its last race, no matter the distance of that race and regardless of the point at which the horse weakened. This tell is an invaluable handicapping tool to experienced hidden horse hunters.

NINTH RACE
Aqueduct
December 4th, 2009

1 MILE. (1.35³) (Off The Turf) MAIDEN SPECIAL WEIGHT. Purse $50,400 FOR MAIDENS, FILLIES AND MARES THREE YEARS OLD AND UPWARD FOALED IN NEW YORK STATE AND APPROVED BY THE NEW YORK STATE-BRED REGISTRY. Three Year Olds, 121 lbs.; Older, 122 lbs. (If the Stewards consider it inadvisable to run this race on the turf course, this race will be run at One Mile on the Inner Track.). (Cloudy 46)

Value of Race: $50,400 Winner $30,240; second $10,080; third $5,040; fourth $2,520; fifth $1,512; sixth $252; seventh $252; eighth $252; ninth $252. Mutuel Pool $229,765 Pick 3 Pool $93,480 Pick 4 Pool $152,291 Pick 6 Pool $55,674 Daily Double Pool $151,758
Exacta Pool $218,664 Superfecta Pool $85,528 Trifecta Pool $147,224

Last Raced	#	Horse	M/Eqt.	A/S Wt	PP	St	¼	½	¾	Str	Fin	Jockey	Odds $1
08Nov09 9Aqu⁴	5	Devilishameye	L	3F 121	3	9	9	9	7³	4hd	1hd	Samyn J	20.30
22Nov09 2Aqu³	8	All Sew Smooth	L	3F 121	6	6	7hd	6hd	6¹½	5¹	2³	Castro E	1.95
29Mar09 4Aqu³	10	Best Note	L f	4F 122	8	1	3½	5¹½	2½	1hd	3¹½	Bocachica O	10.70
22Nov09 2Aqu⁴	12	Laylaben	L b	3F 121	9	8	5½	4hd	4¹	6⁹	4¹¼	Cohen D	2.50
04 Jly 08 4Bel⁶	7	Heavenly Pursuit	L	3F 121	5	5	6²	3½	3hd	2½	5nk	Dominguez R A	6.00
11Oct09 10Bel⁶	1	Fairy Wand	L	3F 121	4	2	1²½	1¹	1¹½	3hd	6¹8¼	Fuentes R D	8.60
22Nov09 2Aqu⁹	4	Justify	L b	3F 121	2	3	2½	2¹	5½	7³	7²¾	Rodriguez R R	22.00
22Nov09 2Aqu⁶	9	Deonzion	L	4F 117	7	7	4¹½	8²	9	8³	88¼	Davis J A	16.30
25Nov09 4Aqu³	3	Properlyintroduced	L b	3F 121	1	4	8²½	7½	8½	9	9	Hill C	9.80

OFF AT 4:12 Start Good For All But 5,9. Won driving. Track Fast.
TIME :24, :48¹, 1:13³, 1:40¹ (:24.11, :48.24, 1:13.69, 1:40.24)

$2 Mutuel Prices:

5- DEVILISHAMEYE	42.60	15.40	6.60
8- ALL SEW SMOOTH		4.00	3.30
10- BEST NOTE			6.30

$2 EXACTA 5-8 PAID $212.00 $2 SUPERFECTA 5-8-10-12 PAID $6,941.00
$2 TRIFECTA 5-8-10 PAID $2,358.00

Dark Bay or Brown Filly, (Mar), by Devil His Due - Shambidextress by Sham. Trainer Hertler O. John. Bred by Tri-County Stables(NY).

DEVILISHAMEYE stumbled badly at the start, was outrun for a half, swung four wide and closed steadily to get up in the final strides. ALL SEW SMOOTH lodged a four wide move on the turn, took the lead in deep stretch but couldn't hold the winner safe. BEST NOTE raced in midpack, rallied three wide on the turn, gained a slim lead in midstretch and weakened. LAYLABEN rallied between horses on the turn and flattened out. HEAVENLY PURSUIT saved ground to the turn and tired in midstretch. FAIRY WAND was used setting the early pace. JUSTIFY pressed the pace inside and tired. DEONZION showed only brief speed after stumbling at the start. PROPERLYINTRODUCED was outrun.

Owners- 5, Tri County Stables ; 8, Oil City Stables ; 10, Parker Lightfield Farm, LLC, Curry, Michael ; 12, Five Ways Farm and Sherry Brothers Stable ; 7, Taylor, Ted, Seidman Stables LLC, Team Stallion Racing Corp., Contessa, Jennifer ; 1, Goichman Lawrence ; 4, In The Bag Racing Stable ; 9, Phillips Sean ; 3, Flying Zee Stable

Trainers- 5, Hertler John O.; 8, Brown Bruce R.; 10, Rossi Bobbi ; 12, Schosberg Richard E.; 7, Benzel Seth ; 1, Albertrani Thomas ; 4, Campanella Salvatore ; 9, Pringle Edmund ; 3, Serpe Philip M.

Breeders- 5, Tri-County Stables (NY); 8, McMahon of Saratoga Thoroughbreds, LLC& Robert Forlano (NY); 10, Monhill Farm, LLC (NY); 12, Dr. Herb Sherry (NY); 7, Thomas / Lakin (NY); 1, Larry Goichman (NY); 4, DJJ Racing Ltd. (NY); 9, Pinebourne Farm (NY); 3, Flying Zee Stables (NY)

Scratched- Crystal Galopoff(18Sep09 6Mth⁹), Grace's Valentine(08Nov09 9Aqu³), Es Mia(22Nov09 2Aqu⁸), Point to Royalty(08Nov09 9Aqu²)

$2 Daily Double (1-5) Paid $217.50; Daily Double Pool $151,758.
$2 Pick Three (7-1-5) Paid $3,293.00; Pick Three Pool $93,480.
$2 Pick Four (9-7-1-5) Paid $112,675.00; Pick Four Pool $152,291.
$2 Pick Six (7-4/5/10/12/13-9-7-1-5) 4 Correct Paid $685.00; Pick Six Pool $55,674; Carryover Pool $34,974.

brisnet.com
information at our business

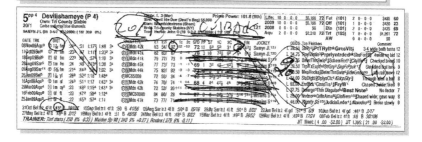

The tells for Devilishameye were:

1) The cutback qualifying race on November 8 at one and one-sixteenth mile.

2) Devilishameye was going from turf to dirt; a positive tell.

3) She had the best pre-race work of the field.

A further example of a cutback long shot occurred in the ninth race at Del Mar on September 2, 2009, in a six furlong three year olds and up maiden $25k claimer for a purse of $19k on the all weather track (a synthetic surface).

The 1, Andrew's Courage, was a layoff horse, having last raced in February of 2008 at Santa Anita. In his maiden attempt on Jan 13, 2008, at Santa Anita he ran for a claiming price of $100k at odds of 31/1, finishing seventh, seven lengths out in a field of 12. His February 14, 2008, try was at a mile and one-sixteenth at Santa Anita in a maiden $75k claimer in which he went something over halfway with some early foot before packing it in somewhere between the half mile marker and the head of the stretch. In that race Andrew's Courage was bet down to 5.2/1.

We have then two long shot tell variants; the cutback angle and the layoff angle. In the current race Andrew's Courage had a 7% trainer, a 12% jockey, and the one post. His trainer's record for bringing layoff horses back to win at first try was 21%. The horse's pattern of works was an excellent tell that he was back in condition. On July 25, 2009, he worked handily from the gate for four furlongs in :48 1/5 and again on August 6 in another four furlong work of :48 4/5. On August 20 he signaled that he was ready to run a big race by working five furlongs in :58 3/5. The racing secretary set his morning line odds at 12/1; I felt his nomenclature called for about half that. The public let him go at 17/1 and he won easily, paying $36.00, 14.80, and 8.20. When the second favorite placed, the $2 exacta paid $243.

The lesson of Andrew's Courage's long shot win is that you have to take a second look at all cutback horses. In his case, the pattern of his works clearly indicated that he was fit to return to the races and that he was ready to win. In my ten years in the sport I often heard both owners and some trainers say that "the works don't mean anything." I am here to tell you that from my experience they frequently mean *everything* - like standing in the winner's circle with a mile wide grin on your face, or cashing an IRS ticket.

The first analysis I do after checking the conditions of the current race is to examine the works. Working from top to bottom, I circle the best works of each horse after checking the two most recent, assuming the horse has not run since those works. (If the horse has been off over 90 days I check the entire pattern of its works since the layoff.) If the horse has run since then and performed poorly, then the works didn't mean anything - *unless in the bad race since the two works the horse had an excuse.* We have talked about "trouble" races and this will take some judgment; some trouble is worse than other trouble. You will have to make a decision as to whether being bumped at the start or encountering traffic trouble later, causing the jockey to *steady* the horse, is worse. If you think there was a sufficient excuse in the horse's last race, then the value of the work before that race is remains intact.

NINTH RACE
Del Mar
September 2nd, 2009

6 FURLONGS. (1.081) MAIDEN CLAIMING. Purse $19,000 FOR MAIDENS, THREE YEARS OLD AND UPWARD. Three Year Olds, 121 lbs.; Older, 124 lbs. Claiming Price $25,000, if for $22,500, allowed 2 lbs. (Clear 82)

Value of Race: $20,820 Winner $11,400; second $3,800; third $2,280; fourth $1,140; fifth $400; sixth $400; seventh $400; eighth $400; ninth $400. Mutuel Pool $340,414 Pick 3 Pool $146,306 Pick 4 Pool $452,983 Pick 6 Pool $1,010,010 Daily Double Pool $101,919
Exacta Pool $196,923 Place Pick All Pool $32,066 Quinella Pool $13,442 Superfecta Pool $127,675 Super High Five Pool $158,328
Trifecta Pool $168,685

Last Raced	#	Horse	M/Eqt.	A/S	Wt	PP	St	¼	½	Str	Fin	Jockey	Cl'g Pr	Odds $1
14Feb08 ⁴SA⁹	1	Andrew's Courage	BL f	4G	124	1	8	7²	7²	4²	1ⁿᵒ	Quinonez A	25000	17.00
06Jun09 ¹⁰Hol²	3	Jamieson	BL	4C	119	3	6	1½	1¹	1¹½	2¹½	Santiago Reyes C	25000	5.10
07Aug09 ⁹Dmr⁴	4	Hotsie	BL	3G	119	4	7	4¹	4¹	3ʰᵈ	3½	Nakatani C S	22500	5.00
12Aug09 ⁹Dmr⁸	2	Good Newsman	BL	3G	121	2	9	9	8ʰᵈ	6¹½	4¹	Espinoza V	25000	3.80
03Jan09 ⁴SA⁵	9	No Pun Intended	BL	5G	124	7	3	5½	6ʰᵈ	5¹	5²½	Pedroza M A	25000	3.00
26 Jly 09 ¹Dmr⁵	10	Eisenheim	BL	4C	122	8	2	3¹	3¹½	2¹	6²½	Talamo J	22500	4.40
12Aug09 ⁹Dmr²	8	Bonkersforbinkers	BL b	3G	119	6	5	6¹½	5ʰᵈ	7²	7²½	Sorenson D	22500	13.40
23 Jly 09 ⁸Dmr¹⁰	12	Gassy Jack	BL b	3G	119	9	1	8½	9	9	8²½	Berrio O A	22500	47.60
20Nov08 ¹Hol⁶	5	Clearly Quiet	BL f	4G	124	5	4	2½	2ʰᵈ	8½	9	Garcia M	25000	12.80

OFF AT 6:05 Start Good. Won driving. Track Fast.
TIME :21⁴, :45, :57³, 1:11¹ (:21.91, :45.07, :57.64, 1:11.25)

$2 Mutuel Prices:	1- ANDREW'S COURAGE	36.00	14.80	8.20
	3- JAMIESON		7.00	4.60
	4- HOTSIE			4.40

$1 EXACTA 1-3 PAID $121.60 $1 PLACE PICK ALL 8 OF 9 PAID $2,816.40 8 Correct
$2 QUINELLA 1-3 PAID $91.20 $1 SUPERFECTA 1-3-4-2 PAID $1,821.10
$1 SUPER HIGH FIVE 1-3-4-2-9 PAID $19,918.80 $1 TRIFECTA 1-3-4 PAID $725.40

Bay Gelding, (Feb), by Jump Start - Sister Hazel by Cahill Road. Trainer Sherman Art. Bred by WinQuest Thoroughbreds,LLC(KY).
ANDREW'S COURAGE saved ground off the pace, moved up inside into the stretch and rallied along the rail under urging to get up late. JAMIESON had good early speed and dueled inside, inched away on the turn, was a bit off the rail in the stretch and was caught alongside the winner late. HOTSIE stalked a bit off the rail then inside, came out leaving the turn and three deep into the stretch and held third. GOOD NEWSMAN at bit slow to begin, settled inside, came out leaving the turn and into the stretch and split rivals late. NO PUN INTENDED stalked outside a rival then a bit off the rail leaving the backstretch and on the turn, was between horses leaving the turn and into the stretch and did not rally. EISENHEIM prompted the pace three deep then stalked outside on the turn and three wide into the stretch and weakened. BONKERSFORBINKERS chased outside then alongside a rival, came out leaving the turn and into the stretch and also weakened. GASSY JACK allowed to settle outside then alongside a rival, came out leaving the turn and four wide into the stretch and did not rally. CLEARLY QUIET dueled inside a rival or between horses on the backstretch, stalked just off the rail on the turn, was between foes in upper stretch and weakened.

Owners- 1, Allred Edward C.; 3, Huston Racing Stable and Johnson, Peggy ; 4, Burns, Mike and Sisemore, Dan ; 2, Blea, Jeff, Morgan, Jocelynn and Peacock, Cecil N. ; 9, De Renzo, Dean and Hartley, Randall ; 10, Moss, Mr. and Mrs. Jerome S. ; 8, Dillon, Tom and Kasparoff, Tim ; 12, McLeod Ross ; 5, Garcia, Juan and Triple M Racing

Trainers- 1, Sherman Art ; 3, Zucker Howard L.; 4, Hess, Jr. Robert B.; 2, Hendricks Dan L.; 9, Mollica Michael A.; 10, Sadler John W.; 8, Kasparoff James M.; 12, Stein Roger M.; 5, Garcia Victor L.

Breeders- 1, WinQuest Thoroughbreds,LLC (KY); 3, Huston, & Johnson-Stoll (CA); 4, Jeanne Mayberry (FL); 2, Mr. & Mrs. J. S. Moss (KY); 9, Lexco Services, Inc. (KY); 10, J. Stuart, P. Bance, J. Amling &C. Noell (KY); 8, Stan Hodge & Fran Hodge (CA); 12, Ross McLeod (CA); 5, Marvin Malmuth (CA)

Scratched- Seany's Story, De Brief Me(12Aug09 ⁹Dmr³), Velikaya(12Aug09 ²Dmr⁵), Downtown Banker(19Jun09 ⁵Hol¹¹), Donthaveatizzy(07Aug09 ⁹Dmr⁷)

$2 Daily Double (1-1) Paid $168.80; Daily Double Pool $101,919.
$1 Pick Three (4-1-1) Paid $386.90; Pick Three Pool $146,306.
$1 Pick Four (2-4/10-1-1) Paid $3,837.00; Pick Four Pool $452,983.
$2 Pick Six (6-8-2-4/10-1-1) 5 Correct Paid $1,878.60; Pick Six Pool N/A.
$2 Pick Six (6-8-2-4/10-1-1) Paid $729,292.20; Pick Six Pool $1,010,010.

The tells on the hidden horse Andrew's Courage were:

1) He qualified as a cutback horse.
2) He was dropping in class to a $25k claimer from $100k and $75k claiming races.
3) His trainer was a 21% winner with layoff horses more than 90 days off.
4) His pattern of works after the layoff, and previous to the current race, were excellent.

Another example of three year old and up maiden hidden long shot winners occurred on August 23, 2009, at Del Mar in the tenth race; a six and a half furlong maiden claimer for $25k on the all weather track.

The 5 horse, Fassnacht, is a representative example of the importance of back class, the freshness from a layoff, and the public's failure to recognize two throw-out trouble races. Fassnacht had been off since his race on July 26, 2008, in which he bobbled at the start and thereafter weakened in a $53k maiden special race, finishing eleventh in a field of twelve. He was not put back in training until May 27, 2009, a layoff of some ten months. His works showed gradual improvement when on July 1 he worked five furlongs handily from the gate in a respectable 1:00 4/5, following that up with a six furlong bullet work on July 17. His final pre-race work of 1:00 3/5 for five furlongs clearly indicated he was rounding into form.

In examining his back class we found that his first race was a maiden special $48k try in which he finished third; the comment was "willingly." In his second race, a $75k stakes, he was bumped at the start and steadied, yet finished third. His next race was a maiden special $48k race in which he was made the favorite and finished with a closing second, only a half length out. His following race was in the Grade 3 Hollywood Juvenile in which Fassnacht finished third, just missing second. His next attempt before the layoff was in a $53k maiden special in which he bobbled at the start, losing all chance. There followed his ten month layoff. My guess was that the injury was probably a shin-buck.

In his first race after the layoff he was entered in a maiden claimer for $25k, a considerable drop in class. In the six furlong race he ran up close half-way then weakened, finishing eighth in a field of ten; the comment was "in between." This usually translates to traffic trouble.

In the current race Fassnacht's trainer was 9%, and his jockey 9%; not the best but certainly not the worst and, as we have seen, when a horse is ready - it is ready. All signs pointed to a big effort in today's race.

The racing secretary set his morning line at 20/1; he went off at 30/1, and won by several lengths from just off the pace.

TENTH RACE
Del Mar
August 23rd, 2009

6½ FURLONGS. (1.15) MAIDEN CLAIMING. Purse $19,000 FOR MAIDENS, THREE YEARS OLD AND UPWARD. Three Year Olds, 120 lbs.; Older, 124 lbs. Claiming Price $25,000, if for $22,500, allowed 2 lbs. (Cloudy 77)

Value of Race: $21,820 Winner $11,400; second $3,800; third $2,280; fourth $1,140; fifth $400; sixth $400; seventh $400; eighth $400; ninth $400; tenth $400; eleventh $400; twelveth $400. Mutuel Pool $401,075 Pick 3 Pool $130,167 Pick 4 Pool $609,645 Pick 6 Pool $347,995 Daily Double Pool $122,096 Exacta Pool $235,009 Place Pick All Pool $36,708 Quinella Pool $14,907 Superfecta Pool $173,740 Super High Five Pool $82,385 Trifecta Pool $218,098

Last Raced	#	Horse	M/Eqt.	A/S	Wt	PP	St	¼	½	Str	Fin	Jockey	Cl'g Pr	Odds $1
29 Jly 09 4Dmr6	5	Fassnacht	BL f	3G	120	5	7	9½	8½	2hd	12¾	Baze M C	25000	29.80
25 Jly 09 10Dmr3	3	Paddy's Magic	BL b	3G	120	3	10	6½	4hd	4hd	2¾	Stra K	25000	13.40
26 Jly 09 1Dmr2	2	Escaping the Storm	BL	3C	120	2	6	51	62	52	3¾	Talamo J	25000	2.20
	4	Tom Bombadil	BL b	3G	120	4	11	101	92½	71	4no	Rosario J	25000	10.80
25 Jly 09 10Dmr12	9	Boo Too	BL b	3G	118	9	2	1hd	1hd	11	51	Pedroza M A	22500	72.40
25Apr09 4Emd4	12	Ry's Not Shy	BL	3G	120	12	1	31½	31½	3½	6¾	Arambula P	25000	2.30
22Oct08 3Osa8	1	What's Important	BL	3G	118	1	12	12	101	61½	7½	Berrio O A	22500	71.40
05Aug09 4Dmr6	6	Blaze of Eminence	BL	3G	120	6	8	81	7hd	8hd	81	Quinonez A	25000	5.40
11May08 5Hol9	11	Irish Weis Man	BL b	4G	124	11	4	41	51	92	95	Solis A O	25000	13.00
07Sep08 11Fpx8	7	Gotham Lights	BL bf	4G	124	7	3	7hd	12	111	102	Kaenel K	25000	84.40
24 Jly 09 6Dmr9	10	Moldy Joe	BL	4G	122	10	9	111	11hd	12	11no	Sorenson D	22500	30.00
26 Jly 09 1Dmr7	8	No Caps No Floors	BL b	3G	120	8	5	2hd	2½	101½	12	Gryder A T	25000	9.80

OFF AT 6:35 Start Good. Won driving. Track Fast.
TIME :22³, :45³, 1:11, 1:17¹ (:22.78, :45.78, 1:11.05, 1:17.37)

$2 Mutuel Prices:

5-FASSNACHT	61.60	23.40	10.80
3-PADDY'S MAGIC		12.00	5.80
2-ESCAPING THE STORM			3.00

$1 EXACTA 5-3 PAID $306.60 $1 PLACE PICK ALL 10 OF 10 PAID $2,949.60 10 Correct
$2 QUINELLA 3-5 PAID $227.20 $1 SUPERFECTA 5-3-2-4 PAID $7,430.70
SUPER HIGH FIVE NO WINNING TICKETS PAID $0.00 Carryover Pool $65,012 $1 TRIFECTA 5-3-2 PAID $1,032.20

Bay Gelding, (Jan), by Johannesburg - Fee Fi Foe by Unbridled. Trainer Harrington Mike. Bred by Patricia A. Youngman(CA).

FASSNACHT chased between horses then a bit off the rail, came out leaving the turn and four wide into the stretch, gained the lead past the eighth pole, drifted in under left handed urging and won clear. PADDY'S MAGIC a bit slow to begin, stalked inside then a bit off the rail leaving the turn, came out three deep between foes into the stretch while bumping a rival, split horses in midstretch and gained the place. ESCAPING THE STORM stalked the pace inside on the backstretch and turn, awaited room into the stretch, split rivals in deep stretch and edged a foe for third. TOM BOMBADIL a bit slow into stride, settled off the rail, came out on the turn and six wide into the stretch and was edged for the show. BOO TOO sped to the early lead off the rail, angled in and dueled inside, inched away briefly in midstretch and weakened late. RY'S NOT SHY wide early, dueled three deep, was bumped four wide into the stretch and weakened some in the final furlong. WHAT'S IMPORTANT broke slowly, settled a bit off the rail, angled in on the turn, came out in upper stretch and was not a threat. BLAZE OF EMINENCE settled off the rail then outside on the backstretch and turn, came three deep into the stretch and did not rally. IRISH WEIS MAN wide between foes early, stalked outside on the backstretch and turn, came out five wide into the stretch and weakened. GOTHAM LIGHTS chased between horses then off the rail, dropped back on the turn and lacked a response in the stretch. MOLDY JOE broke in and steadied, settled outside then off the rail leaving the turn and failed to menace. NO CAPS NO FLOORS went up between horses to duel for the lead, was bumped between foes into the stretch and dropped back.

Owners- 5, Steinmann Heinz; 3, Marks William; 2, Moreno and Corn; 4, Busch, Peter S., Haramoto, Danny and Kawhara, Sheldon; 9, Sandy Weinstock Farm and Herrmann, Jr., Carl L.; 12, McCann Tom J.; 1, Siegel, Howard and Janet; 6, Rubin Barry H.; 11, Abrams, Huston, Matties, Nakkashian and Roberts; 7, Back, Stanley and Sher-Mar Enterprises, LLC; 10, Fisher Derrick; 8, Arbitrage Stables, Avila, Dennis, Rancho San Miguel, et al

Trainers- 5, Harrington Mike; 3, Zucker Howard L.; 2, Hess, Jr. Robert B.; 4, Mitchell Mike R.; 9, Lewis Craig Anthony; 12, Mullins Jeff; 1, Truman Eddie; 6, O'Neill Doug F.; 11, Abrams Barry; 7, Dunham Daniel; 10, Gallagher Patrick; 8, Machowsky Michael

Breeders- 5, Patricia A. Youngman (CA); 3, Anzac LLC (KY); 2, Leverett S. Miller & Linda B. Miller (FL); 4, Peter S. Busch (CA); 9, Carl Herrmann & Sandy Weinstock (KY); 12, Jerry D. Woods & Peggy F. Woods (WA); 1, Cam Ziprick, Larry Falloon & ArnasonFarms (KY); 6, Barry H. Rubin (CA); 11, Nakkashian/Houston, Matties/Roberts &Abrams (CA); 7, Stanley Back (CA); 10, Derrick Fisher (KY); 8, Meralex Farm (KY)

Ry's Not Shy was claimed by O"Neill, Dennis, W. C. Racing and Westside Rentals; trainer, O'Neill Doug F.

Scratched- Saint Chocolate(31 Jly 09 2Dmr6), El Rifle(19Jun09 5Hol5)

$2 Daily Double (5-5) Paid $428.00; Daily Double Pool $122,096.
$1 Pick Three (6-5-5) Paid $1,412.50; Pick Three Pool $130,167.
$1 Pick Four (8-6-5-5) Paid $3,618.90; Pick Four Pool $609,645.
$2 Pick Six (1-7-8-6-5-5) 5 Correct Paid $2,178.20; Pick Six Pool $347,995; Carryover Pool $193,146.

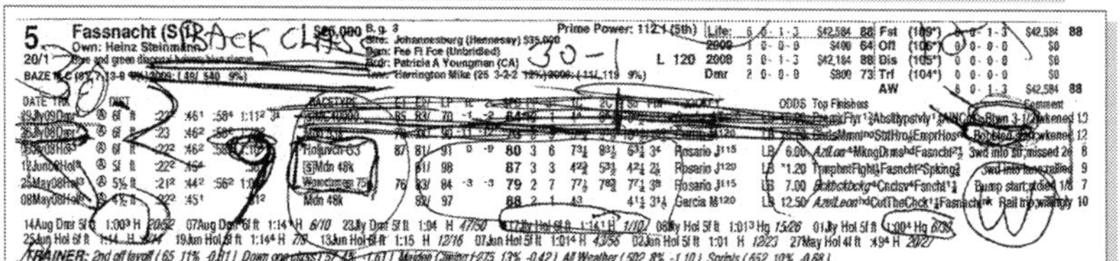

Fassnacht's tells were:

1) He had the best back class in the field.

2) He was a freshened horse with a pattern of works indicating he was in top condition.

3) The public failed to throw out the last two troubled races in which he was bumped at the gate and had traffic trouble down the lane.

The analysis of maiden races for three year olds and up points to the extra importance of checking the workout times of these beginners. I begin by going down the left side of the past performances and checking at least the last two workouts for each horse prior to the current race. I often check the entire works of all first time starters and with three year olds and up who are returning from a layoff. The betting public often pays little attention to their complete works, since they have been so often told that *works don't matter.*

Some good long shot candidates are often found in maidens dropping from a maiden special to a maiden claiming race, though this is a tell that more and more players are beginning to recognize and to bet down.

The cutback horse appears to be the most reliable tell for picking a long shot candidate, as the betting public appears to have a blind spot about it, finding it extremely difficult to bet a horse that stopped badly in its last race, no matter the distance in relation to the current race. And the distance to which the horse is cutting back does not always have to be at five and a half or six furlongs. A horse is also a cutback candidate that is running in a mile race after a mile and one-sixteenth distance. Any race is a *cutback* when it is at least half a furlong shorter than the previous race in which the horse competed. Your cutback analysis time will frequently be generously rewarded; especially in the two and three year old and up maiden races.

Before moving on to examine the sophomore, junior, and senior classes of races and the somewhat different nature of their past performance tells, we must turn to examine the darker side of the sport of kings. Every handicapper has to come to grips with the possibility that their sizable wager - based on the stated form in the past performances - could be lost in a *monkey business* race. In my ten years in the sport, I believe I have had that happen to me perhaps two or three times. I believe, and the records prove out, that at least 98 per cent of pari-mutual thoroughbred races are honest efforts by owners, trainers, and jockeys. I believe that percentage compares favorably with the moguls of Wall Street, politicians, accountants, attorneys, physicians, and the general public at large; nevertheless, when gambling on the horses the player needs to take a double dose of *caveat emptor* - "let the buyer beware."

That is why I confine my wagers to the big time tracks in California, New York, Florida, Kentucky, and the Canadian track, Woodbine. At those tracks the purses are large and the betting pools are huge, while at some of the smaller tracks a $500 win bet will drastically move the odds. Additionally, in the larger states the racing commissions are particularly vigilant as a couple of our leading national trainers will attest to after being ruled off for several months after their horses tested positive for certain prohibited drugs that were alleged to have materially enhanced their horse's performance. It is no secret that there have been a number of times that dishonest connections to any sport on which there is widespread gambling have attempted and occasionally succeeded in fixing the outcomes of college and professional basketball, football, and major league baseball games. (For instance; the infamous *Black Sox World Series* fix, and the recent admission by a National Basketball Association referee that he fixed games by making false penalty calls over several years. And, of course, the persistence controversy about the use of steroid drugs by many professional athletes.)

I persist in believing, however, that thoroughbred pari-mutual horse racing is no more dishonest than any other sport or business. If I thought otherwise I would not have invested substantial sums of money and ten years of my time involved in the sport; not to mention my over forty years as a punter.

I have examined hundreds of past performances of long shot winners; for the most part there have been tells that the horse was ready for a competitive race. Generally, the horse was a long shot because the racing secretary set its morning line odds unrealistically high, and the betting public gave its past performances only a cursory glance; thus the *hidden horse*. Experience has taught me that your best warranty for an honest race is to confine your wagers to the big time tracks.

The twelfth race at Fairplex on September 13, 2009, is an exception that proves the rule. The race was a $25k maiden claimer for three year olds and up going a mile and one-sixteenth on the dirt. Eight runners left the gate; the 7, El Mirage Ranger, was ignored at odds of 74/1. When he crossed the finish line first in the field of eight, my immediate reaction was that it was probably a *monkey business* race; that thought was immediately reinforced when another long shot, the 8, What's Important, closed for second.

The 7 paid $150.80, 67.60, and 9.60. Coupled with the 8, the $1 exacta paid $781; the $2 quinella paid $395; the $1 trifecta paid $4,992, and the super high five was a carryover. I was determined to find out if there was anything I had overlooked that would have made the winner a legitimate competitor in the race. What I found (and what I had missed) in his past performances form was remarkable. El Mirage Ranger was hidden deep in the darkest part of the forest of tells. In this case I had not looked behind every tree, after initially examining his only two races.

In his first race, a $25k maiden claimer at six furlongs on June 27, 2009, at Hollywood, the Ranger finished tenth by eighteen lengths in a field of eleven. The comments were: "Off rail: no menace." In his second attempt in a race with the same conditions, he finished tenth in a field of thirteen - beaten twelve lengths. The comment was: "3 wide into stretch; no threat." After looking at his two races I have to confess that I lost interest in spending much time to further examine his bona fides. After the race I went back and touched all the bases and was amazed by what I found. This horse was actually playable from the tells in his works.

He did have a 16% jockey and 11% trainer, but it was the pattern of his works that qualified him as a competitor in the race. His work of 1:01 2/5 on August 25 at Los Alamitos at five furlongs was the second best pre-race workout of any of the other horses in the current race. In reviewing his entire works pattern, his fifth work since being put into training in January of 2009 was on May 25 at Los Alamitos in which he drilled a "hole in the wind" at :46 3/5 for four furlongs. The Ranger followed that up with a :48 3/5 work at four furlongs at Los Alamitos on June 6.

One last tell, frequently overlooked, was his late pace rating by Brisnet of 91 in his first race. None of the other horses were close to that figure - the closest being an 87 late pace rating - with the exception of the 8 horse, What's Important, who placed and also had a 91 late pace rating. In a distance race the late pace figure is particularly important.

So what at first appeared to me to be a *monkey business* race in which a 74/1 long, long shot came in with no apparent qualifications, turned out to be a playable horse off his well hidden tells. As "the devil is in the details" so too are the long shots frequently hidden in the *forest of their tells.*

While El Mirage Ranger's win is an extreme example, the astute hidden horse hunter should examine a horse's past performance chart from the bottom up, not from the top down, for otherwise the handicapper is too often tempted to give the horse's record only a cursory glance. I have found Fairplex Park a fertile field on which to find hidden long shots, but on the day of the Ranger's improbable win even as careful a hidden horse hunter as the author did not dig deep enough in the tells to find what was there; the clear indication that the horse could compete in that day's race.

Both I and the betting public jumped to conclusions after taking a look at what appeared to be extremely poor efforts by El Mirage Ranger and What's Important in their past performances. Deep in the forest of their previous race figures were the key tells: their Brisnet late pace numbers – the highest of the field – and the pattern of the winner's pre-race works.

In horse racing - as in life - one should not come to a conclusion until all the knowable facts have been determined.

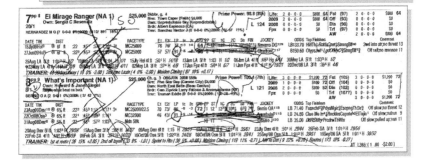

TWELVETH RACE

Fairplex

September 13th, 2009

1 3/16 MILES. (1.413) MAIDEN CLAIMING. Purse $17,000 FOR MAIDENS, THREE YEARS OLD AND UPWARD. Three Year Olds, 121 lbs.; Older, 124 lbs. Claiming Price $25,000, if for $22,500, allowed 2 lbs. (Clear 82)

Value of Race: $18,260 Winner $10,200; second $3,400; third $2,040; fourth $1,020; fifth $400; sixth $400; seventh $400; eighth $400.

Mutuel Pool $127,100 Pick 3 Pool $67,115 Pick 4 Pool $176,109 Pick 6 Pool $82,054 Pick 9 Pool $7,820 Daily Double Pool $38,442

Exacta Pool $65,011 Quinella Pool $4,814 Superfecta Pool $63,354 Super High Five Pool $22,078 Trifecta Pool $76,001

Last Raced	#	Horse	M/Eqt.	A/S Wt	PP	St	1/4	1/2	3/4	Str	Fin	Jockey	Cl'g Pr	Odds $1
18 Jly 09 9Hol10	7	El Mirage Ranger	BL	4G 124	8	9	9	9	5hd	31 1/2	1 5 3/4	Hernandez M	25000	74.40
23 Aug 09 10Dmr7	8	What's Important	BL	3G 121	9	1	8 1	8 2	6 3	4hd	2 2	Berrio O A	25000	8.30
20 Aug 09 5Dmr6	1A	Warren's Allstar	BL	3C 116	4	7	2hd	2hd	2 1/2	2hd	3 1/2	Santiago Reyes C	25000	a - 1.80
03 Sep 09 8Dmr9	3	Truly a Delight	BL	3G 121	3	2	5 1	4 1 1/2	4 3	5hd	4 1 1/2	Garcia M	25000	11.00
20 Aug 09 3Dmr4	6	Mendota Bay	BL f	3C 119	7	5	4hd	3 1	1hd	1hd	5 4	Arambula P	22500	3.00
21 Jun 09 6Hol10	4	Tralee Creek	BL b	3G 119	5	3	1 1/2	1 1/2	3 2 1/2	6 10	6 16 1/2	Valdez F	22500	24.00
03 Sep 09 8Dmr5	1	Warren's Juan	BL b	3G 119	1	6	6 2	5 2	7hd	7hd	7hd	Pedroza M A	22500	a - 1.80
16 Aug 09 6Dmr9	2	Yrunvs M. B.	BL	3G 121	2	9	7 3	6hd	8	8	8	Quinonez A	25000	11.40
02 Sep 09 9Dmr5	5	No Pun Intended	BL	5G 124	6	4	3 1	7 1 1/2	9 DNF	9 DNF	9 DNF	Flores D R	25000	2.50

a - Coupled: Warren's Allstar and Warren's Juan

OFF AT 5:44 Start Good For All But YRUNVS M. B.. Won driving. Track Fast.

TIME :23 1, :47 1, 1:13 1, 1:40, 1:47 (:23.35, :47.22, 1:13.31, 1:40.19, 1:47.17)

$2 Mutuel Prices:

7- EL MIRAGE RANGER	150.80	67.60	9.60
8- WHAT'S IMPORTANT		7.80	5.20
1A- WARREN'S ALLSTAR(a_entry)			2.20

$1 EXACTA 7-8 PAID $781.10 $2 QUINELLA 7-8 PAID $395.00

$1 SUPERFECTA 7-8-1-3 PAID $22,418.60 $1 SUPER HIGH FIVE 7-8-1-3-6 PAID $0.00 Carryover Pool $18,794

$1 TRIFECTA 7-8-1 PAID $4,542.90

Dark Bay or Brown Gelding, (Apr), by Town Caper - Unpredictable Sky by Unpredictable. Trainer Sanchez J. Hector. Bred by Albert Espinoza(CA).

EL MIRAGE RANGER unhurried outside then a bit off the rail, went outside foes leaving the backstretch, split horses on the final turn, came out into the stretch, bid three deep to gain the lead, drifted out and drew clear under some urging. WHAT'S IMPORTANT settled outside then angled in and saved ground, came out into the stretch, found the rail again in the drive and gained the place. WARREN'S ALLSTAR dueled between horses then inside on the last turn, came off the rail in the stretch and held third. TRULY A DELIGHT chased inside, was roused when off the rail leaving the backstretch, came three deep into the stretch and lacked the needed rally. MENDOTA BAY dueled three deep then outside a rival on the final turn, came out some in the stretch and weakened. TRALEE CREEK had good early speed and dueled inside, dropped back on the final turn and also weakened. WARREN'S JUAN bumped at the start, pulled inside then steadied between foes into the first turn, chased outside a rival, dropped back on the backstretch and gave way. YRUNVS M. B. broke in and slowly and bumped a rival, settled outside a foe then angled in and saved ground and also gave way. NO PUN INTENDED stalked three deep, dropped back on the second turn and backstretch, was pulled up and vanned off.

Owners- 7, Resendiz Sergio C.; 8, Siegel, Howard and Janet ; 1A, Warren Benjamin C.; 3, Harris Thomas A.; 6, Johnson, Ellen and Peter O. ; 4, Spindletop Farms ; 1, Warren Benjamin C.; 2, Paranoid Stable ; 5, De Renzo, Dean and Hartley, Randall

Trainers- 7, Sanchez Hector J.; 8, Truman Eddie ; 1A, Gutierrez Jorge ; 3, Bernstein David ; 6, Barba Alexis ; 4, DeLima Jose E.; 1, Lewis Craig Anthony; 2, Becerra Rafael ; 5, Mollica Michael A.

Breeders- 7, Albert Espinoza (CA); 8, Cam Ziprick, Larry Falloon & ArnasonFarms (KY); 1A, Benjamin C. Warren (CA); 3, Tom Harris (CA); 6, Mrs. Arturo Peralta-Ramos (CA); 4, Spindletop Farm (KY); 1, Benjamin C. Warren (CA); 2, Peter McLaughlin (CA); 5, Lexco Services, Inc. (KY)

$2 Daily Double (2-7) Paid $476.60; Daily Double Pool $38,442.

$1 Pick Three (6-2-7) Paid $883.20; Pick Three Pool $67,115.

$1 Pick Four (10-6-2-7) Paid $12,596.70; Pick Four Pool $176,109.

$2 Pick Six (5-2-10-6-2-7) 5 Correct Paid $2,741.80; Pick Six Pool $82,054; Carryover Pool $44,782.

$1 Pick Nine (7-OF-9) 7 Correct Paid $1,520.80; Pick Nine Pool $7,820; Carryover Pool $15,041.

brisnet.com

In four years old and up maiden races the handicapper can be certain that most of the entries will have a history of injuries of varying sorts. In this class of race the hidden horse hunter will do well to spend some extra time in examining their past performances which often have been widely spaced over two, three, or even four years or more.

An example of this type of race occurred in the sixth race at Santa Anita on January 29, 2009, in a five and a half furlong maiden $25k claimer for four year olds and up over the all weather track. In the field of 12 five were five year old maidens, a handicapping challenge if ever there was one.

The morning line favorite was the 1, Motorboat, a thrice in a row beaten favorite. Bejarano was up and the horse was a proven mid-pack closer. Motorboat's four furlong work of :48 4/5 on January 25 was slower than half the field's pre-race workouts and was not an exceptional work for Santa Anita's all weather racing surface.

My attention, however, was drawn to the 5, Seven Below, one of the five year old maidens in the race. The horse raced once at two, once at three, then five times at four. Over that time it had four trainers; the present one's record was five wins out of 153 races. The jockey was a non-winner through 16 tries. It is no wonder that the betting public let Seven Below get away at 24.6/1 after it opened with a morning line of 15/1.

In examining its past performances I noticed the work of 1:00 1/5 for five furlongs on January 8 – the best five furlong work of the field. In its last race at five and a half furlongs it pressed the pace to the head of the stretch where it was forced to steady, then weakened to the wire, finishing out of the money. I noted the first quarter time of :22 1/5 and that Seven Below was just a half length from the lead at the quarter call. In checking his first quarter times in all of his races, I noted that in April of that year he had booked a first quarter :21 3/5 in a front running attempt at six furlongs at Santa Anita. In examining the first quarter times of the field in all of their past performances, I noted that Seven Below had the fastest time. Theoretically, that kind of first quarter would put him two lengths in the lead at the first call.

I could not find indications of front speed for any of the other 11 in the race. In his second race back, a $25k maiden claimer going five and a half furlongs, Seven Below closed from two lengths back at the second call and placed, beaten just a nose. I decided that his last race was a throw out because of the traffic trouble he encountered on entering the stretch. Remembering the trainer's adage that when there is only one front speed horse in a race it will usually stay up, assuming the horse is at class or a dropper, I tapped Seven Below as a hidden long shot candidate.

Notwithstanding the poor records of its trainer and jockey, the hidden horse hunters were well rewarded for their detective work when Seven Below broke on top at the first quarter in :22 2/5, then wired the field by four and a half widening lengths after being sent from the gate at odds of 24.6/1. The payoffs were $51.20, 24.20, and 9.20. When the third favorite placed, the $2 exacta paid $377.20, and when the favorite showed, the trifecta paid $1,193.60.

The often injured five year old had broken his maiden with a big buck bang! The tells were there to be found by hidden horse hunters. Believe what you see in the form, not what the experts and the racing secretary try to tell you about the chances of *any* horse winning *any* race. Remember, the favorite wins but one of three races. Long shots are few and far between; the hidden horse hunter must be patient, but he or she must always ask the question of any race: Is there a long shot candidate hidden in the forest of its tells?

SIXTH RACE
Santa Anita
January 29th, 2009

5½ FURLONGS. (1.01¹) MAIDEN CLAIMING. Purse $15,000 FOR MAIDENS, FOUR YEARS OLD AND UPWARD. Weight, 122 lbs. Claiming Price $25,000, if for $22,500, allowed 2 lbs. (Clear 77)

Value of Race: $17,900 Winner $9,000; second $3,000; third $1,800; fourth $900; fifth $400; sixth $400; seventh $400; eighth $400; ninth $400; tenth $400; eleventh $400; twelveth $400. Mutuel Pool $265,070 Pick 3 Pool $64,984 Daily Double Pool $25,527 Exacta Pool $179,994 Superfecta Pool $117,616 Trifecta Pool $160,184

Last Raced	# Horse	M/Eqt.	A/S	Wt	PP	St	¼	½	Str	Fin	Jockey	Cl'g Pr	Odds $1
19Dec08 ⁸Hol⁶	5 Seven Below	BL f	5G	120	5	4	1¹	1²½	1³½	1⁴²	Rios J M	22500	24.60
02Jan09 ⁹SA⁷	11 Stray Cat	BL b	4G	122	11	1	7¹	5ʰᵈ	2²½	2ⁿᵒ	Rosario J	25000	5.40
02Jan09 ⁸SA²	1 Motorboat	BL	4C	122	1	9	11⁴	10¹½	8½	3¹½	Bejarano R	25000	1.50
02Jan09 ⁸SA⁶	9 Minnie's Boy	BL f	5G	122	9	2	6½	7¹½	6ʰᵈ	4ʰᵈ	Valdivia, Jr. J	25000	9.00
16Jan09 ⁴SA³	12 Cubs Molina	BL	4G	112	12	10	12	12	7¹	5¹	Molina L	25000	32.80
17Sep08 ⁶Fpx⁵	6 Sur Brio	BL	4G	120	6	3	5¹	6¹	4¹½	6²½	Delgadillo A	22500	98.40
10Jan09 ⁵SA⁵	4 Incandescenza	BL f	4C	122	4	12	8½	9¹	9²	7¹	Baze T	25000	20.90
07Jan09 ⁵SA⁹	7 Maria's Cat	BL	5G	122	7	11	10ʰᵈ	11²	12	8ⁿᵏ	Quinonez A	25000	40.60
	3 Bandeira Band	BL	4G	122	3	8	9²	8½	5ʰᵈ	9½	Espinoza V	25000	30.60
13Jan09 ⁶SA³	2 Haggis Macpherson	BL b	4C	122	2	6	3ʰᵈ	3ʰᵈ	3ʰᵈ	10³¹	Gryder A T	25000	2.90
	10 Golden Delight	BL b	4G	122	10	7	4½	4¹½	10¹½	11ⁿᵏ	Talamo J	25000	22.60
25May08 ⁶Hol¹⁰	8 Mort Robbins	BL f	4G	122	8	5	2¹½	2ʰᵈ	11ʰᵈ	12	Vergara O	25000	14.90

OFF AT 3:38   Start Good. Won driving.   Track Fast.
TIME :22², :45¹, :57¹, 1:03²   (:22.52, :45.30, :57.34, 1:03.59)

	$2 Mutuel Prices:			
	5- SEVEN BELOW	51.20	24.20	9.20
	11- STRAY CAT		8.00	4.20
	1- MOTORBOAT			2.60

$1 EXACTA 5-11 PAID $188.60 $1 SUPERFECTA 5-11-1-9 PAID $4,271.10
$1 TRIFECTA 5-11-1 PAID $596.80

Bay Gelding, (Feb), by Six Below - Shewalksinbeauty by Prized. Trainer Mendoza Jesus. Bred by Cardiff Farm Management Corp.(CA).

SEVEN BELOW dueled a bit off the rail then inched away leaving the backstretch, set the pace off the inside, drifted out a bit in the stretch but won clear under urging. STRAY CAT stalked outside then three deep on the turn and into the stretch, drifted in some and just held second. MOTORBOAT settled inside then a bit off the rail, came three deep into the stretch, split rivals in midstretch and finished fast to just miss the place. MINNIE'S BOY had speed between foes then stalked between horses, continued outside on the turn and four wide into the stretch and lacked the needed rally. CUBS MOLINA broke a bit slowly, settled off the rail then angled in on the backstretch, saved ground on the turn, waited off heels then slipped through inside past midstretch and improved position. SUR BRIO between horses early, chased a bit off the rail then inside on the turn and in the stretch and lacked the needed rally. INCANDESCENZA broke a bit slowly, settled three deep then off the rail, came out leaving the turn and five wide into the stretch and was not a threat. MARIA'S CAT also a bit slow to begin, settled outside or off the rail, came five wide into the stretch and did not rally. BANDEIRA BAND chased between horses then angled in for the turn and lacked a response in the stretch. HAGGIS MACPHERSON close up stalking the pace inside on the backstretch and turn, weakened in the stretch. GOLDEN DELIGHT stalked three deep, split rivals on the backstretch, continued three wide on the turn and into the stretch and had little left for the drive. MORT ROBBINS had speed between horses then outside the winner, stalked off the rail then between foes on the turn, dropped back nearing the stretch and weakened.

Owners- 5, H R C Stable, LLC ; 11, Jay Em Ess Stable ; 1, Fosselman, Hollendorfer and Todaro ; 9, Ballena Vista Farm ; 12, Why Knot T. R. S. LLC ; 6, Millard, Marianne and Thompson, Dennis ; 4, Howard Roberts Farm ; 7, Macris, Mr. and Mrs. George and Varelas, Mrs. ; 3, Diamond A Racing Corporation ; 2, MacPherson Shirley ; 10, Sid and Jenny Craig Trust ; 8, Abrams, Barry, Bartlett, Jr., Richard, Robbins, J. and Barath, Carl

Trainers- 5, Mendoza Jesus ; 11, Headley Bruce ; 1, Hollendorfer Jerry ; 9, Puype Mike ; 12, Molina Mark S.; 6, Garcia Victor L.; 4, Knapp Steve ; 7, Eurton Peter ; 3, Mandella Richard E.; 2, Koriner Brian J.; 10, Spawr William ; 8, Abrams Barry

Breeders- 5, Cardiff Farm Management Corp. (CA); 11, Robert D. Nash (KY); 1, Roasting Ear Creek Ranch (KY); 9, Ballena Vista Farm (CA); 12, Brian Valencia (CA); 6, M. Millard (CA); 4, Grousemont Farm (CA); 7, George Macris & Catherine Macris (CA); 3, Diamond A Racing Corp (KY); 2, Morris B. Floyd & Chuck Givens (KY); 10, Sidney H. Craig & Jenny Craig (CA); 8, Abrams, Barth & Robbins (CA)

Scratched- Goodlookindude(02Jan09 ⁸SA⁴)

$2 Daily Double (4-5) Paid $215.40; Daily Double Pool $25,527.
$1 Pick Three (3-4-5) Paid $517.20; Pick Three Pool $64,984.

A final remarkable example of finding a three year old and up hidden long shot winner occurred on January 10, 2010, in the second race at Tampa Bay Downs; a seven furlong $20k maiden special for four year olds and up on the dirt.

In the field of eight only one horse had raced more than six times in three years; indicating, of course, that the entire field was prone to injuries. The premium variant was the evaluation of present form. The racing secretary made the 3, Soda Jerk, the 8/5 favorite apparently on the basis of his two recent good works, the best of the field for four furlongs. I thought, however, that he was short. Nevertheless, I intended to include him in any exacta bet or bets.

Three of the horses had good pre-race workouts: the favorite, Soda Jerk, had drilled four furlongs in :48 4/5 on December 24; the 7, Tisnow Julie, had worked in :49 on December 19, after returning to the track from a seven month layoff; and the 4, Ala Al Din, posted a three furlong work of :35 1/5 on January 2. Both the 4 and the 7 were cutting back in distance from their last race; thus, they met the qualifying requirements of a hidden horse candidate to hit the winner's circle – namely, relative speed and a cutback in distance.

In further examining the tells of the 4, Ala Al Din, I noted that in his first start in March he was bet down to 3.9/1, but was pulled up on the backstretch. His next start was on April 7 at one mile on the turf in a maiden special for $20k. In that race (under a new trainer) Ala Al Din was eleven lengths back of the leader at the first call, then closed some eight lengths to finish third, just three lengths from the front. Thereafter, he was away from the track until November 7, when he started in a seven furlong race on the turf in another $20k maiden special at Calder. In that race he finished far up the track after being in contention to the half. Following that less than stellar effort, he next started in a one and one-sixteenth mile race on the turf at Tampa Bay Downs on December 23. In that race he was just four lengths from the front at the half, then stopped somewhere between the second call and the head of the stretch. My guess was that he stopped, or was pulled up, at about the six and a half furlong mark of the race. For all of the above reasons I thought he was an excellent hidden horse candidate.

Ala Al Din's morning line was 20/1. When I made my bet he was 35/1 and at post time was 66.3/1. The favorite, the 3, Soda Jerk, was bet down to odds-on. No doubt, only a few other hidden horse hunters saw what I had seen in the forest of Ala Al Din's tells: a $20 win and place and a $5 exacta box that included the winner and the 1, 3, 7, and 8 would have returned a tidy $3,292 for an investment of $80.

Always cover legitimate cutback horses that are on class and have exceptional pre-race works; they frequently go off at more than generous odds. Their *tells* are nuggets of gold.

SECOND RACE
Tampa Bay
January 10th, 2010

7 FURLONGS. (1.22) MAIDEN SPECIAL WEIGHT. Purse $20,000 (Includes $3,000 FOA - Florida Owners Awards) FOR MAIDENS, FOUR YEARS OLD AND UPWARD. Weight, 120 lbs. (Preference Will Be Given To Horses Which Have Not Started For Less Than $25,000. The Same Preference Will Be Given To Horses Which Have Started For Less Than $25,000 And Since Then Have Finished 2 nd Or 3rd For $25,000 Or More.)(Registered Florida Breds Preferred). (Clear 42)

Value of Race: $20,000 Winner $13,200; second $3,230; third $2,040; fourth $850; fifth $170; sixth $170; seventh $170; eighth $170.
Mutuel Pool $66,469 Daily Double Pool $31,920 Exacta Pool $69,391 Trifecta Pool $76,366

Last Raced	# Horse	M/Eqt.	A/S	Wt	PP	St	¼	½	Str	Fin	Jockey	Odds $1
23Dec09 7Tam8	4 Ala Al Din	L f	4C	120	4	7	8	6³	2⁶	1no	Schwartz J D	66.30
08May09 2Cro³	7 Tisnow Julie	L b	4C	120	7	2	5½	5¹½	1hd	2¹³½	Cotto, Jr. P L	9.30
16Dec09 10Tam³	8 Coast to Coast	L b	4G	120	8	1	3½	2hd	3hd	3²³	Centeno D	4.50
16Dec09 10Tam²	1 Powerhouse	L	5H	121	1	5	2hd	3¹	5²½	4¹½	Bush V	3.70
24Nov09 10CD⁴	3 Soda Jerk	L	4G	120	3	3	4³	1hd	4¹	5⁶	Goncalves L R	0.50
	5 Gilded Hero	L	4G	120	5	8	7½	8	6⁴	6⁸	Felix J E	28.40
16Dec09 10Tam⁵	2 Favorite Prank	L	4G	110	2	4	1hd	4¹	7³	7⁸½	Gutierrez C L	103.10
16Dec09 10Tam⁷	6 Fancyfreeeverett	L	4C	120	6	6	6¹½	7²	8	8	Lopez J	41.60

OFF AT 12:54 Start Good. Won driving. Track Fast.
TIME :23¹, :47³, 1:13³, 1:26⁴ (:23.30, :47.63, 1:13.77, 1:26.90)

$2 Mutuel Prices:

4- ALA AL DIN	134.60	39.40	15.00
7- TISNOW JULIE		10.20	6.60
8- COAST TO COAST			3.60

$2 EXACTA 4-7 PAID $621.00 $2 TRIFECTA 4-7-8 PAID $5,418.40

Dark Bay or Brown Colt, (Ma), by Repent - Prized Prospect by Prized. Trainer Boileau Robert. Bred by Brent Fernung(FL).

ALA AL DIN saved ground, rushed to the lead inside leaving the turn, held on well when headed in the drive then showed strong stamina to come again and prove narrowly best. TISNOW JULIE made a four wide middle move to challenge into the stretch, gained a short lead a furlong out then continued well to just miss. COAST TO COAST dueled four wide to the stretch then gave way. POWERHOUSE was hard used disputing the pace inside and faded after five furlongs. SODA JERK was also hard used three wide and gave way. GILDED HERO showed little. FAVORITE PRANK was used up. FANCYFREEEVERETT showed little.

Owners- 4, Shoukry Robert B.; 7, De Mora Julian ; 8, USA Thoroughbreds ; 1, Walton Bob ; 3, Humphrey, Jr., Louise I. and G. Watts ; 5, Lageman William J.; 2, Ham, Sr. Bill ; 6, Larsen, Carl and Pentheny, Everett

Trainers- 4, Boileau Robert ; 7, Harvatt Charles R.; 8, Shaw John E.; 1, Francy Kate ; 3, Arnold, II George R.; 5, Reed Eric R.; 2, Sexton Edward C.; 6, Pittman Donald M.

Breeders- 4, Brent Fernung (FL); 7, Sez Who Thoroughbreds (NY); 8, University of Florida Foundation (FL); 1, Phipps Stable (KY); 3, G. Watts Humphrey Jr. &Louise I. Humphrey (KY); 5, Shelby Parrott & Jane Parrott (KY); 2, Ute F. Ham (FL); 6, Everett Pentheny (FL)

$2 Daily Double (2-4) Paid $159.00; Daily Double Pool $31,920.

Data provided or compiled by Equibase Company, which includes data from The Jockey Club, generally is accurate but occasionally errors and omissions occur as a result of incorrect data received by others, mistakes in processing and other causes. Equibase Company and Bloodstock Research Information Services, Inc. and Thoroughbred Sports Network disclaim responsibility for the consequences, if any, of such errors, but would appreciate being called to their attention. Copyright 2010.

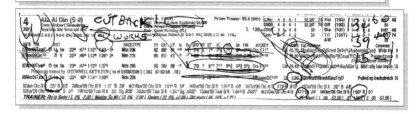

Chapter 4

O nce a horse breaks its maiden its connections have an important decision to make. The trainer must decide what class of race in which to enter the new winner for its next race. If the trainer thinks the horse is something special it will be entered in a stakes race; usually, the progression is to an allowance race for non-winners of a race other than maiden, claiming, or starter. Sometimes lower class horses will be entered in an allowance race restricted to non-winners of two races. Horses with varying talent will be entered in straight or optional claiming races for prices at the major tracks of from $5,000 to $100,000.

In our analysis of long shot prospects in the claiming ranks we will be examining the middle range of claimers. Once you get to the bottom of the barrel with $5,000 claiming races it's a crap shoot, and the best recent works angle is not as effective as it is with better class horses. I'm assuming that the reader is familiar with the claiming system in which any licensed owner or trainer can enter a claim for any horse entered in a non-restricted claiming race. Sometimes more than one claim is entered for the same horse with its new owner decided by straws or a roll of the dice. The claiming system tends to level the playing field.

My partner and I claimed one horse in ten years as we preferred to buy two year olds or raise our own foals as we owned two promising broodmares. The one time we claimed a horse makes for an unusual (perhaps not so unusual, after all) story that nearly ended with my partner having to physically defend himself against the distraught former owner and angry trainer of the horse we had moved to our barn legitimately pursuant to the rules of the Nebraska State Racing Commission. Our answer to the former owner and trainer of the horse we then owned was: "If you didn't want your horse claimed, you shouldn't have put him in a claiming race!" The comment was not appreciated, but we escaped without bodily harm as the two of them were mostly bluff and bluster. They were really ticked when we won with "their" horse in his first try. The stable bet of $200 to win returned $28.60. Our share of the purse was nearly what we had paid to claim the gelding.

The day of the claim the former connections tried to be too shifty by half. They had claimed the gelding off a win in a $5k claimer at Oaklawn Park. Under the claiming rules and regulations then in effect they were required to enter the horse in a claiming race for a price at least 35% higher than the race in which he had been claimed. An exception to that rule allowed them to enter for the same price as the race in which the horse was claimed if they did not race again for at least 30 days from the date of the claim; thus, the aptly named "get out of jail" rule.

When they brought the horse to the saddling stall they had wrapped his forelegs from chest to hooves in bright orange leggings. When they were removed our trainer saw that there was no indication that there was anything wrong with the horse's forelegs so he gave us the high sign to drop the claim in the claiming box.

The horse ran a close up second then was brought to our barn. We paid $5,000 for him; as it turned out he was worth every penny. For his next try we moved him up to a $7,500 claiming race at six furlongs. I had studied the racing form and his past performances and noted that he had gone six and a half furlongs on the front at Arlington in the slop a few races back, losing by a nose at the wire.

On the day of the race his morning line odds were 10/1, and floated up to 13/1 at post time. Our trainer looked at the Arlington race and discussed putting him on the front. A few minutes before post time, a cloudburst quickly turned the track from fast to sloppy. Out of the 11 post our jockey guided him to the front; our horse held on by a head at the wire. Fortunately, I had bets down for most of the family and a celebration was in order. Unfortunately, we chose the same restaurant as the former owner and trainer of the horse who had just won a big race at generous odds for someone else, and were commiserating over their bad luck. We explained to the waiter that we had changed our mind and wouldn't be having our steak and beer at his establishment that evening.

A year later we found ourselves on the other end of the claiming system when we lost through the claim box a horse that had brought us three wins and several substantial purses. We bought the mare for $10k in a private transaction, having watched her finish a fast closing fourth after being blocked in the stretch. She won at double digit odds in her next out, recovering some 75% of our investment. After a successful fall season we looked forward to the spring and the anticipated dividends our roan filly with the silver tail would return to the stable.

After performing poorly in her first out in the spring, our trainer suggested we drop her from a $10k claiming race to a $5k claimer. She did not hit the board in that race and was claimed. We had lost our money making mare.

At first my partner and I were disappointed, yet the mare did not owe us any money: we had bought her for $10k, though she was claimed for half of that after winning purses of over $22k for the stable. The new connections were able to win a $4k claimer with her - the last win of her racing career. As it turned out, her new connections did us a favor. Such are the vicissitudes of the claiming game.

Human nature being what it is, the connections who have lost their horses through the claim box too often bemoan the loss of "their" horse, yet claimers are entirely fair game, for the claiming connections own the horse once it is in the starting gate, though any purse money won belongs to the former owner. The new owner takes title no matter if the horse wins, loses, breaks a leg, or does not finish the race - that's the gamble of the claiming box.

If you are a substantial barn, however, you can keep claiming losses at a minimum. One of the more noted tactics is to let it be known that should one of your horses be claimed, you will claim every horse entered for a claiming price in the barn of the claimer.

One of the most noted and successful trainers in the Midwest used this tactic in the late 60s to protect his stable of claiming horses.

Generally, it is easier to determine relative class in straight claiming races than in allowance races. On the other hand, the lower rungs of the claiming ladder produces races that are long on guess work and short on form. The works of cheap horses are generally unreliable and their past performances particularly inconsistent. As a handicapper, the lower the claiming price the less I am interested in playing that race as I prefer a minimum $10k tag before tackling a claiming race in the pursuit of a hidden horse.

Let's begin at Belmont on September 17, 2009, with a $25k claiming race on the turf at six furlongs for fillies and mares three and up which have never won three races and for a purse of $25k.

The favorite was the 7, Sweet Madness, who was a class dropper; having previously run in a five and a half furlong race on the turf in an optional $50k claimer, finishing fourth by three lengths. None of the rest of the field of eight was particularly noteworthy. The favorite's morning line was 7/2 and was bet down to 5/2 at post time.

In searching for a hidden horse I found two that qualified; the 6, Risky Gamble, and the 9, For Free. Both had encountered trouble in their last race. Risky Gamble was cutting back from a mile on the turf at Suffolk Downs, an optional claiming race for $20k in which he was in contention half-way, but was forced wide on the second turn, finishing sixth by nine lengths in a field of nine. His Brisnet late pace rating was 88, third best of the field. Risky Gamble's owners changed trainers after the August race. The new trainer's record with a first starter was 16% - 11% overall; the jockey 15%. This is an angle too often overlooked by the betting public; a change in trainer. Risky Gamble was a shipper from Suffolk Downs (sometimes known as "Sufferin' Downs"), and his new trainer's record with shippers was 15%.

The 9, For Free, was hidden because of his last race, a straight claimer for $35k in which he was checked at the start, finishing a well beaten fifth in a field of ten. His trainer was 14%; his jockey, 12%. I eliminated him because of his post position and his slow works.

I landed on Risky Gamble as the hidden horse that I felt had a good chance at a price. His morning line was 15/1; when I placed my bet of win and place and boxed him in an exacta with the first and second favorites, his odds were 23/1. He left the gate at 45/1. Breaking second, he collared the leader at the head of the stretch and held on to win over the favorite, paying $93.50 to win and $24.80 to place. The two dollar exacta paid $553; the trifecta paid boxcars. The betting public just couldn't get past Risky Gamble's poor last race, and that he was a shipper from Suffering Downs.

SECOND RACE
Belmont Park
September 17th, 2009

6 FURLONGS. (Inner Turf) (1.07) CLAIMING. Purse $25,000 INNER TURF FOR FILLIES AND MARES THREE YEARS OLD AND UPWARD WHICH HAVE NEVER WON THREE RACES OR THREE YEAR OLDS. Three Year Olds, 119 lbs.; Older, 123 lbs. Non-winners of two races on the turf since July 11 Allowed 2 lbs. Such a race since then Allowed 3 lbs. Claiming Price $25,000 (Races where entered for $20,000 or less not considered in allowances) (Winners Preferred). (Cloudy 62)

Value of Race: $25,000 Winner $15,000; second $5,000; third $2,500; fourth $1,250; fifth $750; sixth $125; seventh $125; eighth $125; ninth $125. Mutuel Pool $176,275 Daily Double Pool $129,365 Exacta Pool $150,629 Quinella Pool $15,643 Trifecta Pool $108,948

Last Raced	#	Horse	M/Eqt.	A/S	Wt	PP	St	1/4	1/2	Str	Fin	Jockey	Cl'g Pr	Odds $1
12Aug09 8Suf6	6	Risky Gamble	L	3F	116	5	4	2¹	2½	1½	1hd	Bocachica O	25000	45.75
27Aug09 8Sar3	7	Sweet Madness	L b	4F	120	7	6	5hd	5hd	4hd	2¹½	Velasquez C H	25000	2.55
24Aug09 4Sar3	5	Dressed to Win	L	5M	121	2	5	4½	4½	3hd	3¾	Castellano J	25000	3.20
04Sep09 8Sar6	2B	My Anna Rose	L	4F	120	8	1	3hd	3¹	6½	4hd	Luzzi M J	25000	b - 8.20
04Sep09 8Sar7	2	Sweet Bama Breeze	L b	4F	120	4	3	1¹	1½	2¹½	5no	Desormeaux K J	25000	b - 8.20
04Sep09 6Sar5	9	For Free	L	4F	120	9	2	6¹	6hd	7¹½	6¹	Prado E S	25000	4.60
23Aug09 6Sar7	4	Zip by You	L	5M	120	1	9	7¹	7¹	5½	7¹	Dominguez R A	25000	7.70
07Sep09 8Sar12	3	Kitty Nip	L b	6M	120	6	7	8hd	8hd	8¹	8½	Coa E	25000	25.50
20Aug09 10Sar1	1	Beso Del Sur	L b	3F	117	3	8	9	9	9	9	Leparoux J R	25000	3.65

b - Coupled: My Anna Rose and Sweet Bama Breeze

OFF AT 1:32 Start Good For All But ZIP BY YOU. Won driving. Track Firm.
TIME :23, :463, :58, 1:094 (:23.08, :46.70, :58.11, 1:09.90)

$2 Mutuel Prices:

6- RISKY GAMBLE	93.50	24.80	9.80
7- SWEET MADNESS		4.00	3.40
5- DRESSED TO WIN			3.40

$2 EXACTA 6-7 PAID $452.00 $2 QUINELLA 6-7 PAID $132.50
$2 TRIFECTA 6-7-5 PAID $2,284.00

Bay Filly, (Mar), by During - Risky Kitten by Formal Gold. Trainer D'Alessandro Ralph. Bred by Sez Who Thoroughbreds & Aron Yagoda(NY).

RISKY GAMBLE pressed the pace under a firm hold, surged to the front in midstretch and prevailed under right hand urging. SWEET MADNESS raced in midpack,. was behind horses leaving the turn, rallied between rivals in upper stretch and closed steadily but could not get up. DRESSED TO WIN was rated in hand just off the early pace, steadied along the rail on the turn, angled out in upper stretch then finished willingly between horses to gain a share. MY ANNA ROSE stalked three wide for a half, lagged behind in upper stretch and fought back late between rivals. SWEET BAMA BREEZE set the pace on the rail into midstretch and weakened. FOR FREE was reserved early, advanced four wide on the turn and lacked a late response. ZIP BY YOU stumbled at the start, moved up along the rail, made and inside run in upper stretch and flattened out. KITTY NIP failed to threaten while six wide at the quarter pole. BESO DEL SUR trailed throughout.

Owners- 6, Glenridge Stable ; 7, Parting Glass Stable ; 5, Dubb, Michael, High Grade Racing Stables, and Joscelyn, Robert ; 2B, Fertile Acres Farm ; 2, Gumpster Stable LLC ; 9, Jacobson Racing Stable ; 4, HorsePartners Stable ; 3, Imperio, Michael and Joseph ; 1, Ostrager Barry R.

Trainers- 6, D'Alessandro Ralph ; 7, Bush Thomas M.; 5, Brown Chad C.; 2B, Sciacca Gary ; 2, Sciacca Gary ; 9, Jacobson David ; 4, Grennan George J.; 3, Imperio Joseph ; 1, Rice Linda

Breeders- 6, Sez Who Thoroughbreds & Aron Yagoda (NY); 7, Joe W. Gerrity, Jr. (NY); 5, Padua Stables (FL); 2B, Barry Ostrager (NY); 2, Barry R. Ostrager (NY); 9, Bryant H. Prentice III (KY); 4, Gus Schoenborn Jr. (NY); 3, Pegasus Farms Inc. (NY); 1, Ocala Horses, LLC (KY)

Scratched- Skip Away Belle (24Aug09 4Sar2), Read the Post (09Sep09 4Pen1), O'Sotopretty (03Aug09 1Sar2), Gentle Ride (05Sep09 12Sar1), Gin Tango (05Aug09 1Sar5), Way to Karakorum (05Aug09 9Sar2).

$2 Daily Double (1-6) Paid $158.50; Daily Double Pool $129,365.

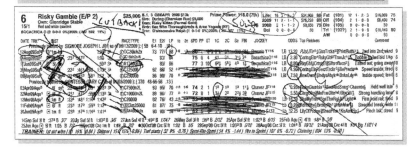

Risky Gamble's tells were:

1) The trainer change.
2) His third race back win on the turf in a $17k allowance race of five furlongs in which he broke tenth, was five lengths back at the head of the stretch and won going away, earning the third best late pace rating of 88.
3) He was 50% in the money in his 16 starts and winner of three.
4) His trainer was a 15% winner with shippers.
5) He was a cutback horse.

✡ ✡ ✡

Another example of a playable hidden horse occurred in the ninth race at Del Mar on August 30, 2009, where eight three year old fillies went six furlongs on the all weather track in a $32k claiming race for a purse of $37k.

There appeared to be no less than five front runners in the race which usually results in a just off the pace closer prevailing. The 9 horse, High Note, had gone six and a half furlongs on the front in breaking her maiden on Feb 15 at Santa Anita. In her most recent race at six and a half furlongs she led for a half mile, was two lengths out at the head of the stretch, then weakened down the lane in an optional $25k claimer. High Note had been away from the track from July 3 until the current race.

Her six works since her layoff were exceptional, concluding with one of :58 4/5 for five furlongs ten days before the current race. The racing secretary once again cooperated with the long shot players when he set her morning line at 15/1, apparently ignoring her exceptional four superior works in her last six tries.

Her trainer was a 12% winner with layoff horses for from 46 to 90 days and was 11% overall. The jockey's winning percentage was 7%; but, as we have seen, when the horse is ready it will generally bring the jockey along.

High Note left the gate at 25/1, a generous tab to be sure, and won in a drive from just off the pace paying $52.80, 22.20, and 9.40, anchoring the exotic bets to box car figures.

The tells were clear: superior works (not just one, but five of six since her last race of July 3) fairly screamed at the long shot player to tab High Note, but the tells fell upon the deaf ears of the average public bettor. This hidden horse was found by a few sophisticated hidden long shot hunters, for the tells could not have been more clear.

NINTH RACE
Del Mar
August 30th, 2009

6 FURLONGS. (1.08⅟) CLAIMING. Purse $37,000 FOR FILLIES THREE YEARS OLD. Weight, 124 lbs. Non-winners of two races since May 30 Allowed 2 lbs. A race since then Allowed 4 lbs. Claiming Price $32,000, if for $28,000, allowed 2 lbs. (Maiden races and Claiming races for $25,000 or less not considered) . (Cloudy 85)

Value of Race: $38,200 Winner $22,200; second $7,400; third $4,440; fourth $2,220; fifth $740; sixth $400; seventh $400; eighth $400.
Mutuel Pool $341,319 Pick 3 Pool $76,252 Daily Double Pool $34,344 Exacta Pool $170,162 Quinella Pool $11,925 Superfecta Pool $95,070 Trifecta Pool $140,303

Last Raced	# Horse	M/Eqt.	A/S	Wt	PP	St	¼	½	Str	Fin	Jockey	Cl'g Pr	Odds $1
03 Jly 09 ⁵Hol⁷	9 High Note	BL f	3F	120	6	4	6½	5½	2¹	1¹½	Valdivia, Jr. J	32000	25.40
26 Jly 09 ⁴Dmr³	10 Ashee	BL	3F	120	7	2	8	8	6¹	2¾	Rosario J	32000	3.10
21 Aug 09 ⁷Dmr⁵	3 Nine to Dine	BL f	3F	120	2	5	1¹	1²	1²½	3ⁿᵏ	Baze M C	32000	8.20
16 Aug 09 ¹Dmr¹	12 Steam Iron	BL b	3F	120	8	1	7ʰᵈ	7ʰᵈ	4ʰᵈ	4²¾	Solis A O	32000	2.10
22 Aug 09 ²Dmr⁶	8 Ten Churros	BL b	3F	120	5	3	4¹½	4¹	7½	5¹¾	Talamo J	32000	6.90
22 Aug 09 ²Dmr⁴	7 Bagels N Bones	BL	3F	115	4	6	2ʰᵈ	3ʰᵈ	3ʰᵈ	6¾	Santiago Reyes C	32000	4.20
06 Apr 09 ¹Tup⁷	5 Elegant Miss	BL 2	3F	120	3	7	3ʰᵈ	2ʰᵈ	5¹	7¹	Gryder A T	32000	26.70
12 Aug 09 ⁵Dmr⁷	2 Multitasker	BL b	3F	120	1	8	5¹	6¹½	8	8	Bejarano R	32000	6.90

OFF AT 6:10 Start Good. Won driving. Track Fast.
TIME :22, :45¹, :57⁴, 1:11   (:22.19, :45.34, :57.89, 1:11.15)

$2 Mutuel Prices:

9- HIGH NOTE	52.80	22.20	12.40
10- ASHEE		4.20	3.00
3- NINE TO DINE			6.20

$1 EXACTA 9-10 PAID $117.30 $2 QUINELLA 9-10 PAID $73.00
$1 SUPERFECTA 9-10-3-12 PAID $2,415.30 $1 TRIFECTA 9-10-3 PAID $912.10

Dark Bay or Brown Filly, (Feb), by In Excess (IRE) - Salty Steph by Salt Lake. Trainer Hendricks L. Dan. Bred by Legacy Ranch, Inc.(CA).

HIGH NOTE chased outside, went three deep on the turn and four wide into the stretch, drifted in and rallied to the front under urging in deep stretch to prove best. ASHEE settled off the rail, came out leaving the turn, lacked room off heels three deep into the stretch, was blocked behind rivals in midstretch then split horses and finished well for the place. NINE TO DINE had good early speed and dueled inside, inched away on the backstretch, kicked clear, held on well to deep stretch, could not match the winner, lost second late but held third. STEAM IRON chased outside on the backstretch and turn, came out five wide into the stretch, finished with some interest and just missed the show. TEN CHURROS was in a good position stalking the pace three deep to the stretch and lacked the needed response. BAGELS N BONES close up stalking the pace between horses to the stretch, weakened. ELEGANT MISS had speed between horses then stalked a bit off the rail or inside, continued along the rail in the stretch and also weakened. MULTITASKER saved ground chasing the pace to the stretch and lacked a further response.

Owners- 9, Thor-Bred Stable LLC ; 10, Chandler Bruce ; 3, Knapp, Steve and Mikesell, Pam and Nute ; 12, Black Diamond Racing LLC ; 8, Earnhardt, III, Patti and Hal J. ; 7, Capen, Dan and Ustin, Steve, Charlene and Jeff ; 5, Firsthome Thoroughbreds and Stanley, W. Don ; 2, Warren, Deanne and Craig

Trainers- 9, Hendricks Dan L ; 10, Sherlock Gary ; 3, Knapp Steve ; 12, Stute Gary ; 8, Baffert Bob ; 7, Mitchell Mike R.; 5, Kitchingman Adam ; 2, Sherlock Gary

Breeders- 9, Legacy Ranch, Inc. (CA); 10, Bruce Chandler (CA); 3, Six-S Racing Stable (CA); 12, Lathrop G Hoffman (CA); 8, Harris Farms Inc. (CA); 7, Liam Benson (FL); 5, John James Revocable Trust (KY); 2, Pam and Martin Wygod (CA)

Scratched- Martini Mixer(16Aug09 ¹Dmr⁴), Good Night Gyrene(02Aug09 ⁴Dmr⁶), Costa Marta(26 Jly 09 ⁴Dmr⁶), Epitome of a Lady(22Jan09 ³GG⁵)

$2 Daily Double (8-9) Paid $215.60; Daily Double Pool $34,344.
$1 Pick Three (4-8-9) Paid $482.60; Pick Three Pool $76,252.

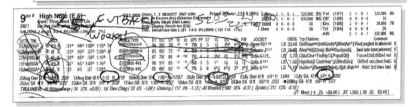

The tells for High Note were:

1) She was a cutback horse.
2) She had the best works of the field.
3) She had won her maiden race at six and a half furlongs.

Another example of the importance of the tell of a cutback horse occurred on August 5, 2009, at Del Mar in a seven furlong race for four year olds and up for $12.5k claimers over the all weather surface.

The field included four cutback horses: the 6, Will O Wisp; the 11, Doriprize; the 12, Raingear; and the 13, Grafton. In the field of eleven, six were stretching out to seven furlongs; the lone exception being the second favorite, Warren's Pepe.

The 6 was a layoff horse, having been away from the track since May 23, 2009. On that day Will O Wisp went a mile and a half at Lonestar in an optional claimer for $30k, finishing fourth, just four lengths out after being bumped at the start. His works were only fair, but compared favorably with the rest of the field. He returned to the track for the current race with a new trainer. Not only was he a cutback horse, he was cutting way back; at seven furlongs he was cutting back five furlongs from a twelve furlong race. Additionally, the horse had substantial back class as the seven year old had won over $700k in purses.

The horse's new trainer was an 18% winner when returning his horses from a 46 to 90 day layoff. When adding first time blinkers, the trainer was a 21% winner; as a shipper he was 24%.

The trainer was a 14% winner overall; the jockey, 18%. The morning line on Will O Wisp was 12/1.

The 11, Doriprize, was another cutback horse, having gone a mile in its previous race, a $32.5k claimer. He was also a layoff horse, having raced last on May 23 at Hollywood Park in which he put in a dull effort and was thereafter freshened. His trainer's record with layoff horses of from 46 to 90 days was 19%. The jockey was 16%; the trainer, 12% overall. Doriprize's morning line odds were 20/1.

Raingear was the 12 horse, another class dropper, having last raced at a mile on the turf at Hollywood Park on July 2 in which he turned in an even effort, finishing fifth, some seven lengths back of the winner. His previous race was also at a mile on the turf in an open $40k claimer in which Raingear finished seventh, but only two lengths back of the winner. He also had a new trainer since his last race, having been claimed in that effort for $25k. The trainer was a 12% winner; the jockey, 8%. The trainer's record when going to all weather from turf was 18%. Raingear's morning line was 10/1.

The fourth Cutback horse was Grafton, the 13, who had not raced since August of 2008. Though he was also a substantial class dropper, his trainer's record with layoff horses was 5%. Because of the sub-par records of his owner and trainer, I could not find anything to recommend Grafton, whose morning line odds were 20/1.

Will O Wisp broke sharply at 17/1, and promptly wired the field by five lengths with the 12, Raingear, closing late to be second and the 11, Doriprize, closing very late to be third. The winner paid $37.40, 16.40, and 7.80. The $2 exacta paid $343 and the "cutback horse trifecta" paid $7,340. The superfecta paid box car figures when the favorite finished off the board.

When you find a hidden horse or horses after correctly reading the tells, believe what the racing form is telling you. Don't succumb to the herd mentality which leads its followers to back the "sure thing." In pari-mutual thoroughbred horse racing there is no such thing as a "mortal lock" certainty as one of my dog racing friends was fond of calling his winner picks. Have the courage of your convictions. Back your conclusions; for when betting on long shots you don't have to bet the farm to cash some huge tickets. It's a challenge to your attention for detail, but the rewards can be life changing.

NINTH RACE
Del Mar
August 5th, 2009

7 FURLONGS. (1.21) CLAIMING. Purse $19,000 FOR FOUR YEAR OLDS AND UPWARD. Weight, 124 lbs. Non-winners of two races since May 5 Allowed 2 lbs. A race since then Allowed 4 lbs. Claiming Price $12,500, if for $10,500, allowed 2 lbs. (Maiden races and Claiming races for $10,000 or less not considered). (Clear 80)

Value of Race: $21,020 Winner $11,400; second $3,800; third $2,280; fourth $1,140; fifth $400; sixth $400; seventh $400; eighth $400; ninth $400; tenth $400. Mutuel Pool $326,478 Pick 3 Pool $132,698 Pick 4 Pool $412,389 Pick 6 Pool $180,139 Daily Double Pool $109,330 Exacta Pool $176,871 Place Pick All Pool $26,946 Quinella Pool $11,642 Superfecta Pool $106,954 Super High Five Pool $41,867 Trifecta Pool $144,206

Last Raced	#	Horse	M/Eqt.	A/S	Wt	PP	St	¼	½	Str	Fin	Jockey	Cl'g Pr	Odds $1
23May09 ^{8}LS^{4}	6	Willow O Wisp	BL b	7G	120	4	3	$1^{\frac{1}{2}}$	$1^{1\frac{1}{2}}$	$1^{2\frac{1}{2}}$	1^{2}	Espinoza V	12500	17.70
02 Jly 09 ^{5}Hol^{5}	12	Raingear	BL b	4C	120	9	2	$6^{\frac{1}{2}}$	5^{hd}	$2^{1\frac{1}{2}}$	$2^{1\frac{3}{4}}$	Delgadillo A	12500	8.40
23May09 ^{6}Hol^{9}	11	Doriprize (ARG)	BL b	5G	120	8	9	10	10	5^{hd}	3^{1}	Quinonez A	12500	22.10
22 Jly 09 ^{5}Dmr^{8}	2	Spot the Diplomat	BL b	5G	120	2	10	8^{2}	7^{hd}	$6^{\frac{1}{2}}$	4^{2}	Garcia M	12500	15.50
12 Jly 09 ^{7}Hol^{6}	3	Warren's Pepe	BL b	5H	120	3	7	$4^{1\frac{1}{2}}$	$4^{1\frac{1}{2}}$	7^{2}	$5^{1\frac{3}{4}}$	Rosario J	12500	3.60
03Aug08 ^{3}Dmr^{4}	13	Grafton	BL bf	9G	118	10	1	9^{hd}	8^{hd}	$8^{1\frac{1}{2}}$	$6^{\frac{3}{4}}$	Valdez F	10500	32.30
10 Jly 09 ^{4}Hol^{3}	9	Bullya	BL	5G	111	6	4	2^{1}	2^{1}	4^{hd}	7^{nk}	Santiago Reyes C	10500	3.90
05Jun09 ^{3}Hol^{3}	1	Western Comment	BL bf	5G	120	1	8	3^{hd}	3^{1}	3^{1}	$8^{3\frac{1}{4}}$	Gomez G K	12500	2.90
23May09 ^{4}Hol^{4}	8	Elusive Pleasure	BL f	4G	120	5	6	5^{2}	$6^{1\frac{1}{2}}$	$9^{2\frac{1}{2}}$	$9^{4\frac{1}{2}}$	Gryder A T	12500	6.40
22 Jly 09 ^{6}Dmr^{7}	10	Swift Demand	BL	5G	120	7	5	7^{hd}	9^{2}	10	10	Valdivia, Jr. J	12500	10.10

OFF AT 6:20 Start Good. Won driving. Track Fast.
TIME :23^{1}, :46^{1}, 1:10^{2}, 1:23 (:23.36, :46.29, 1:10.49, 1:23.09)

$2 Mutuel Prices:

6- WILLOW O WISP	37.40	16.40	7.80
12- RAINGEAR		10.40	7.40
11- DORIPRIZE (ARG)			13.80

$1 EXACTA 6-12 PAID $171.50 $1 PLACE PICK ALL 7 OF 9 PAID $1,215.60 7 Correct
$2 QUINELLA 6-12 PAID $195.40 $1 SUPERFECTA 6-12-11-2 PAID $16,046.70
SUPER HIGH FIVE NO WINNING TICKETS PAID $0.00 Carryover Pool $33,066 $1 TRIFECTA 6-12-11 PAID $3,670.70

Bay Gelding, (Apr), by Misnomer - Willow Woodman by Woodman. Trainer Kitchingman Adam. Bred by Fred W. Pace(FL).

WILLOW O WISP had good early speed and dueled a bit off the rail, inched away into the turn, kicked clear and held on gamely under urging. RAINGEAR chased outside, went four wide leaving the turn and three deep into the stretch and was second best. DORIPRIZE (ARG) angled in and saved ground off the pace, rode the rail on the turn, split horses in midstretch and picked up the show. SPOT THE DIPLOMAT bumped between horses at the start, settled inside, came out leaving the turn and three deep into the stretch and bested the others. WARREN'S PEPE broke in and bumped a rival, stalked outside a foe then off the rail, was in a bit tight three deep into the stretch and weakened. GRAFTON broke outward, angled in and settled alongside a rival, went three deep leaving the turn and four wide into the stretch and did not rally. BULLYA prompted the pace outside the winner then stalked off the rail on the turn and weakened. WESTERN COMMENT bumped at the start, went up inside to stalk the pace to the stretch and also weakened. ELUSIVE PLEASURE between horses early, tracked the pace a bit off the rail then inside, came out into the stretch and had little left for the drive. SWIFT DEMAND chased between horses on the backstretch and turn, came three deep into the stretch and lacked a further response.

Owners- 6, Harris Kirk ; 12, Tom Grether Farms, Inc. ; 11, Batchelor Family Trust ; 2, Catalan Hugo E.; 3, Hollendorfer, Jerry and Todaro, George ; 13, Miller Michael J.; 9, Flintridge Stable and STD Racing Stable ; 1, Risoli, Ralph and Brackin, Doug ; 8, Berta, Peter and Julie, Koriner, Brian and Lyons, Janet ; 10, Cusimano, Eagles Mate Partnership, Mundt et al

Trainers- 6, Kitchingman Adam ; 12, Sherlock Gary ; 11, Becerra Rafael ; 2, Sierra Cirilo M.; 3, Hollendorfer Jerry ; 13, Knapp Steve ; 9, O'Neill Doug F.; 1, Mullins Jeff ; 8, Koriner Brian J.; 10, Ellis Ronald W.

Breeders- 6, Fred W. Pace (FL); 12, Paul Boghossian (CA); 11, Jose Ignacio Hurtado Vicuna (ARG); 2, Harris Farms Inc. (CA); 3, Benjamin C. Warren (CA); 13, Glen Hill Farm (FL); 9, Adena Springs (FL); 1, Mill Ridge Farm, Ltd. & Troy Rankin (KY); 8, Dapple Bloodstock (KY); 10, Betty L. Mabee & Larry Mabee (CA)

Warren's Pepe was claimed by Isom Lamonte ; trainer, Morey William E.

Scratched- Make Mine Vodka(22 Jly 09 ^{6}Dmr^{6}), Taint That a Cat(13 Jly 09 ^{7}Yav^{2}), Kaffeinator(22 Jly 09 ^{1}Dmr^{9})

$2 Daily Double (9-6) Paid $864.40; Daily Double Pool $109,330.
$1 Pick Three (10-9-6) Paid $3,502.70; Pick Three Pool $132,698.
$1 Pick Four (9-10-9-6) Paid $40,804.40; Pick Four Pool $412,389.
$2 Pick Six (1-3/11/14-9-10-9-6) 5 Correct Paid $6,119.20; Pick Six Pool N/A.
$2 Pick Six (1-3/11/14-9-10-9-6) Paid $99,947.60; Pick Six Pool $180,139.

The tells for Will O Wisp were:

1) He was a cutback horse from his previous race of a mile and a half to the current race of seven furlongs.

2) He had considerable back class, having won over $700k.

3) He was dropping from a $30k optional claiming race to a straight $12.5k claiming race, a considerable drop in class.

4) He had a new trainer for the current race whose record with returning horses from a 46 to 90 day layoff was 18%. When adding first time blinkers he was a 21% winner, 18% per cent as a shipper. The jockey was an 18% winner.

The tells for Doriprize were:

1) Another class dropper and cutback horse.

2) His trainer's record with 46 to 90 day layoff horses was 19% and the jockey was a 16% winner.

Raingear's tells were:

1) Another class dropper and cutback horse.

2) This was his first race since being claimed for $25k by his new trainer.

3) The trainer was 12%, but 18% when going from all weather to turf.

Another hidden horse was found in the ninth race at Aqueduct on December 28, 2008, when twelve horses that had not won a race in six months competed on the dirt in a six furlong $10k claimer for a purse of $19k. (For whatever reason, the last race on the program seems to yield an inordinate number of long shot winners.)

The 5, Undocumented, had not raced since July 19, 2008, at Finger Lakes in Canada. His works were not exceptional except for his November 12, 2008, four furlong work at :48 3/5, indicating that by then he was fit. New York punters generally discount the form on an "inferior track." (Trust me that New Yorkers consider Finger Lakes to be inferior to the Empire State's racing circuit.)

However, Undocumented was the class of the race; the only horse that had not run for a claiming price in his last ten races. Seven of these were for purses ranging from $18k to $21k and three were optional claiming races where he was not entered for a claiming price, making them the equivalent of allowance races. He was cutting back in distance to six furlongs; he had been the favorite three times and had won two with a close second in the other. His longest odds in those ten races had been 6.6/1. The trainer was unknown to me and probably to most of New York; however, he was a 16% winner and the jockey had won with 15% of his mounts. Additionally, the trainer was a 12% winner with more than 90 day layoff horses. Undocumented had won twice, placed twice, and showed once in his six races in 2008. He had won five times, placed six times, and was third four times in 20 lifetime starts. Over all, Undocumented was 75% in the money.

Why did the betting public let him get off at odds of 32/1? Because the general racing fan finds it difficult to bet on a horse whose last race was non-competitive; in short, a clunker in which he "barely lifted his hoofs." The public bettor will also usually shun a horse returning to the races after a layoff of more than 90 days, no matter his pre-layoff form. In view of the length of the layoff, my guess was that Undocumented had shin-bucked; an injury that is usually good for a two to six month layoff. The racing secretary obligingly set his morning line at 20/1.

I was fortunate in this race for I was able to find the other class horse, Lights of Broadway, apparently the second best class of the race. He was also covered up by a poor last race in which he was in the ninth post position and got hung out wide for the whole trip. In the current race he went off at 8/1, completing a $272 exacta with Undocumented who easily won at 32/1.

Both of these horses stood out to the experienced horse player; both were hidden to the general race fan who did not dig deep enough into the details for tells in their past performances. Long shot tip offs are frequently there, but a cursory view of the race will usually put you on a favorite who will lose two out of three times.

For the hidden horse hunter, a poor last race following previous races in which the horse was in good form; followed by a layoff of more than 90 days; often points to a tell that the horse has been freshened and is rounding into his previous form, especially when accompanied by a superior pattern of workouts. These types of horses are frequently sent off at more than generous odds and often win, sometimes at huge prices.

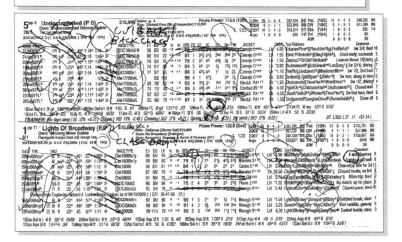

The tells for Undocumented were:

1) He was cutting back from a mile to six furlongs.
2) He was the class of the race, dropping into a straight claimer from optional claiming and allowance races.
3) He had run seven straight races, finishing no worse than third, before throwing in his clunker before his five month layoff.
4) His trainer was 16% and his jockey was 15%
5) He had not started at odds of more than 6.6/1 in his last ten races.

One of the more remarkable cutback long shot winners occurred on July 5, 2009, at Churchill Downs in the sixth race for fillies and mares three years old and up going six and a half furlongs on the dirt for $16k claimers over a sloppy track.

The 2, No Image, had raced at one mile ten days before at Churchill for the same claiming price. She was second at the start; second at the half mile; third some eight lengths out at the head of the stretch before stopping badly, finishing sixth in the field of seven. The comment was: "Chased 3 wide; tired." In her prior race on May 6 at Churchill, she was entered in a starter allowance $7.5k race at six furlongs, and finished a distant fourth in a field of 7 over a sloppy track. The comment was: "4 wide, improved position."

In her seven races prior to May 6; however, she was competitive in each race, her odds never exceeding 5.8/1. On March 9 at Turfway Park she was beaten by a nose in a one mile $16k claimer at the same conditions of the current race. In her lifetime she was in the money in 20 of 36 tries. Her trainer was 12%; her jockey, 18%. The racing secretary set her morning line odds at 15/1. What raised my eyebrows was that she had not shown a published workout since October 27 in 2008. As a former owner, I knew that could not be correct for she had run eleven races since then. She looked like a hidden horse competitor to me but was ignored by the betting public who let her leave the gate at odds of 60.4/1.

Leaving the gate third, she soon improved at the half to be second by a length, gradually improved, and at the head of the stretch led by a length and a half, then held that margin to the wire.

She was an excellent example of a playable cutback horse, and the hidden horse hunters were rewarded with boxcar payoffs. When I find a horse like this, my usual bet is to win and place the long shot candidate, then box it with the first and second favorites in an exacta.

SIXTH RACE
Churchill
July 5th, 2009

6½ FURLONGS. (1.14¹) CLAIMING. Purse $23,000 FOR FILLIES AND MARES THREE YEARS OLD AND UPWARD. Three Year Olds, 118 lbs.; Older, 123 lbs. Non-winners Of Two Races Since May 5, 2009 Allowed 2 lbs. A race since then Allowed 4 lbs. Claiming Price $16,000 (Races where entered for $12,500 or less not co nsidered). (Showery 67)

Value of Race: $22,885 ($115 reverts) Winner $13,800; second $4,600; third $2,300; fourth $1,150; fifth $690; sixth $115; seventh $115; eighth $115. Mutuel Pool $207,854 Pick 3 Pool $15,750 Daily Double Pool $15,113 Exacta Pool $164,589 Superfecta Pool $68,096 Trifecta Pool $127,556

Last Raced	# Horse	M/Eqt.	A/S Wt	PP	St	¼	½	Str	Fin	Jockey	Cl'g Pr	Odds $1
26Jun09 ¹CD⁶	2 No Image	LA bf	5M 119	2	3	3¹	2¹	1¹½	1¹½	Goncalves L R	16000	60.40
30May09 ³CD²	7 Mylilmoneymaker	LA bf	6M 119	6	6	6¹	6¹½	3¹½	2ⁿᵒ	Court J K	16000	2.30
18Jun09 ¹CD¹	8 Archmani	LA b	4F 123	7	8	8	7⁵	4²	3ⁿᵒ	Castanon J L	16000	3.30
31May09 ³CD⁶	1 Sneak a Drink	LA b	4F 119	1	7	5⁴	3½	2⁴	4⁹	Borel C H	16000	5.30
22Jun09 ⁷Ind¹	6 Blue Satin Sash	L b	5M 121	5	5	4½	5¹½	5¹½	5²¼	Theriot L	16000	2.20
06Jun09 ¹CD³	9 C J's Nannie	LA b	4F 119	8	2	7⁴	8	7¹½	6⁴¾	Hernandez, Jr. B J	16000	23.70
14Jun09 ⁶CD⁸	3 Thundering Jill	LA b	5M 119	3	1	1¹½	1½	6⁴	7⁸	Albarado R	16000	15.40
17Jun09 ⁶Pid⁴	5 Tactical Candy	L bf	6M 119	4	4	2½	4½	8	8	Rojas C	16000	12.00

OFF AT 3:26 Start Good. Won driving. Track Sloppy (sealed).
TIME :22⁴, :46³, 1:12¹, 1:19 (:22.94, :46.69, 1:12.21, 1:19.12)

$2 Mutuel Prices:
2- NO IMAGE..................	122.80	32.00	12.00
7- MYLILMONEYMAKER..........		4.40	3.00
8- ARCHMANI.................			3.00

$2 EXACTA 2-7 PAID $467.20 $2 SUPERFECTA 2-7-8-1 PAID $17,172.60
$2 TRIFECTA 2-7-8 PAID $3,728.40

Dark Bay or Brown Mare, (Jan), by Stone Bridge - Inaccessible by Private Terms. Trainer Gray L. Gary. Bred by Ralph Sessa(FL).

NO IMAGE close up from the start, challenged three wide on the turn, drew clear into the stretch and stayed clear under steady urging. MYLILMONEYMAKER bumped out at the start, was outrun early, commenced her rally three wide on the turn, angled out for the drive and closed well late. ARCHMANI bothered at the start, was outrun early, raced three wide on the turn, came to the outside for the drive and closed fast. SNEAK A DRINK close up along the inside, failed to respond in the stretch. BLUE SATIN SASH bumped out at the start, raced within striking distance five wide and tired. C J'S NANNIE carried out at the start, was no factor. THUNDERING JILL bumped TACTICAL CANDY at the start, set the pace off the inside and tired in the drive. TACTICAL CANDY bumped out at the start, pressed the early pace four wide and stopped.

Owners- 2, Marsch Mitchell B.; 7, Hays Billy J.; 1, No Joke Stables ; 6, Carl R. Moore Management LLC ; 9, Schickel Robert L.; 3, Bolerjack, James and Bridwell, Glenn ; 5, Tango Stable-Verdis Corp.

Trainers- 2, Gray Gary L.; 7, Woodard Joe ; 8, Kenneally Eddie ; 1, O'Connor, II Robert R.; 6, Calhoun W. Bret; 9, Jackson Christopher J.; 3, Larue Benjie ; 5, Seglin Luis E.

Breeders- 2, Ralph Sessa (FL); 7, Paul Sharp (FL); 8, Joe King (KY); 1, Hargus Sexton & Sandra Sexton (KY); 6, Elizabeth P. Whelan & David J. Whelan (KY); 9, James T. Hines Jr. (KY); 3, Hal Snowden Jr. (ON); 5, Don & Pam Mattox (FL)

Blue Satin Sash was claimed by L. T. B., Inc. and Childers, Miles ; trainer, Flint Bernard S.,
Archmani was claimed by Tomlinson Michael A.; trainer, Tomlinson Michael A.

Scratched- On Your Knees(23Jun09 ⁶RD⁵)

$2 Daily Double (4-2) Paid $160.60; Daily Double Pool $15,113.
$2 Pick Three (4-4-2) Paid $2,148.60; Pick Three Pool $15,750.

brisnet.com

Data provided or compiled by Equibase Company, which includes data from The Jockey Club, generally is accurate but occasionally errors and omissions occur as a result of incorrect data received by others, mistakes in processing and other causes. Equibase Company and Bloodstock Research Information Services, Inc. and Thoroughbred Sports Network disclaim responsibility for the consequences, if any, of such errors, but would appreciate being called to their attention. Copyright 2009.

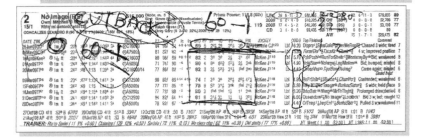

The tells for No Image were:

1) She was cutting back from a mile to six and a half furlongs.

2) Her jockey was 18%.

3) She had hit the board in 20 of her 36 lifetime races.

4) She had some back class at the current race conditions.

The final example of finding hidden long shot candidates in claiming races occurred in the sixth race at Churchill Downs on November 18, 2009, in a six furlong $15k claimer on the dirt for three year olds and up that had never won two races.

In a field of twelve the morning line favorite was the 8, Cognito. The racing secretary liked him at 7/2 and the public made him the post time favorite at 1.8/1. The horse was making a steep drop from his previous class in four consecutive $50k allowance races for non-winners of a race other than maiden, claiming, or starter. The only question I had was whether or not its connections were running for the purse of $14k or were trying to sell an injured horse via the claim box. If not, then I thought Cognito should easily win.

When I examined the last three works of each horse prior to the current race, I landed on the 10, Bonboni, whose morning line was 30/1. His work of 1:00 4/5 for five furlongs on October 27 was by far the best current work of the field. He had last run on September 23, 2009, at Turfway Park, an all weather track, in a six furlong $15k claimer for non-winners of two. Steadied at the half, he lost all chance. Prior to that race he had competed at Turfway at six and a half furlongs in a $24k allowance race for non-winners of two. Up close to the half, he stopped. Prior to that race he had broken his maiden in a $6.5k maiden special at River Downs. That is probably why the betting public thought he was too cheap to compete in the current race.

On the positive side (aside from his good work) the field had to give him from seven to ten pounds. I thought his excellent work on his layoff return was tell enough to tab him as a hidden horse long shot candidate, although I didn't think he could beat the favorite.

There was another long shot candidate in the race, the 1, Buddha Can Dance. In his last race he was bumped at the start, losing all chance. In his second race back, however, he broke his maiden in a driving finish of a five and a half furlong $10k maiden claimer at Ellis Park. While his works were mundane, his trainer was a15% winner; 17% with all weather to dirt starts, and his jockey was a 17% winner. At post time his odds were 23.8/1.

The long shot play was $20 to place and show on Bonboni and a $10 exacta box of the favorite with Bonboni and Buddha Can Dance. For the hidden horse trifecta players the bet, of course, was to box the favorite with these two hidden horse long shot candidates.

Cognito closed from fourth at the half to win easily by two and a half lengths; Bonboni, after leading at the half, held on for second; Buddha Can Dance danced home from tenth at the half to place third.

The $2 exacta paid $139.80; the $2 trifecta paid $3,078; Bonboni paid $26.80 to place and $18.20 to show: the payoff for the $92 investment would have been $4,136.

Ah, *if only*!

SIXTH RACE
Churchill
November 18th, 2009

6 FURLONGS. (1.072) CLAIMING. Purse $14,000 FOR THREE YEAR OLDS AND UPWARD WHICH HAVE NEVER WON TWO RACES. Three Year Olds, 122 lbs.; Older, 124 lbs. Non-winners Of A Race Since October 18 Allowed 3 lbs. Claiming Price $15,000, if for $10,000, allowed 2 lbs. (Clear 56)

Value of Race: $14,210 Winner $8,400; second $2,800; third $1,400; fourth $700; fifth $420; sixth $70; seventh $70; eighth $70; ninth $70; tenth $70; eleventh $70; twelveth $70. Mutuel Pool $138,054 Pick 3 Pool $16,206 Daily Double Pool $12,784 Exacta Pool $130,498 Superfecta Pool $53,686 Trifecta Pool $90,268

Last Raced	# Horse	M/Eqt	A/S Wt	PP	St	¼	½	Str	Fin	Jockey	Cl'g Pr	Odds $1
29Oct09 7Kee10	8 Cognito	L A	3C 119	8	9	7½	4	4½	1½	12½	Albarado R	15000	1.80
23Sep09 8TP9	10 Bonboni	L b	3G 112	9	2	3½	1¹	2⁴	2³½	Creed B	15000	47.10
28Oct09 9Kee8	1 Buddha Can Dance	LA b	3G 119	1	11	10½	10³	4½	3³½	Torres F C	15000	23.80
08May09 7RD1	2 The Big Highroller	LA b	3C 119	2	12	12	11⁵	7¹	4½	De La Cruz F	15000	81.00
12Jly09 6Elp10	7 Dookie Duck	L b	3C 119	7	8	9½	7hd	5½	5hd	Gonzalez, Jr. S	15000	41.10
04Oct09 8TP8	11 Go Getem	L	3C 119	10	4	4½	2hd	3¹½	6⁴½	Woods, Jr. C R	15000	9.80
04Oct09 8TP9	4 Ridge Royale	LA b	4C 119	4	7	6¹½	6¹½	6¹	7¾	Leparoux J R	10000	3.30
02Oct09 7TP7	3 Sabago	LA	3G 119	3	5	8⁴	9¹	9⁵	8¹½	Ocampo I	15000	90.60
06Nov09 2CD7	12 Grasmere Park	LA b	4G 121	11	3	5hd	3½	8½	9⁵¾	Lopez J	15000	7.40
03Nov09 6Beu1	13 Well Bred Boy	LA b	7G 122	12	10	11²	12	12	10²½	Court J K	10000	62.30
18Sep09 9TP6	6 Forchtenberg	LA	3G 119	6	1	2hd	5½	10¹	11¹	Lanerie C J	15000	3.90
30Oct09 3Kee8	5 Full Curtain	LA	3G 119	5	6	1hd	8½	11¹	12	Goncalves L R	15000	11.90

OFF AT 3:06 Start Good. Won driving. Track Muddy (sealed).

TIME :22¹, :46¹, :58³, 1:11⁴ (:22.38, :46.33, :58.63, 1:11.84)

$2 Mutuel Prices:
8- COGNITO	5.60	4.00	3.60
10- BONBONI		26.80	18.20
1- BUDDHA CAN DANCE			12.00

$2 EXACTA 8-10 PAID $139.80 $2 CONSOLATION PICK 3 5-2-8 PAID $18.20 3 Correct
$2 CONSOLATION PICK 3 5-4-8 PAID $18.20 3 Correct $2 SUPERFECTA 8-10-1-2 PAID $57,753.80
$2 TRIFECTA 8-10-1 PAID $3,078.00

Gray or Roan Colt, (May), by Langfuhr - Coral Sea by Rubiano. Trainer Asmussen M. Steven. Bred by W. S. Farish, E.J. Hudson, Jr.Irrevocable Trust, et al(KY).

COGNITO moved up from between horses for a contending position three wide, angled in leaving the turn, got through and opened clear, was kept to task and maintained a safe advantage. BONBONI disputed the issue three deep from between horses, edged clear leaving the turn, continued on willingly but was unable to match strides with the winner. BUDDHA CAN DANCE was allowed to settle, made a late rally circling six wide and was along for the show. THE BIG HIGHROLLER was void of early speed, angled out entering the stretch and improved his position. DOOKIE DUCK was allowed to settle, came four wide to make a mild rally but failed to seriously threaten. GO GETEM pressed the pace four wide from between horses, but weakened during the drive and gave way. RIDGE ROYALE attended the pace along the inside, shifted out entering the stretch but lacked a response when called upon. SABAGO saved ground to no avail. GRASMERE PARK chased the pace five wide for a half and gave way. WELL BRED BOY passed only his tiring rivals. FORCHTENBERG contested the pace from between

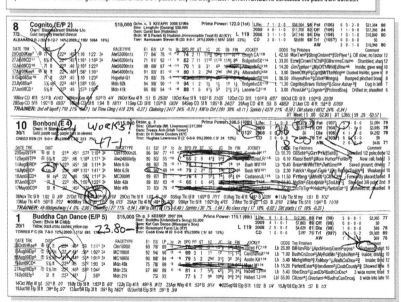

Nearly all of the claiming race long shot winners we have examined were cutback horses. That particular tell appears to be the most reliable variant tipoff of a long odds hidden horse candidate, at least in the claiming ranks. The unsophisticated betting public just can't bring themselves to bet on a horse that stopped badly in its last race; no matter the difference in distances of that race compared to the current race's shorter distance.

A horse suddenly stops for any number of reasons, not all of them physical. Over the years only three of our horses stopped badly after being on the lead to the stretch; two of them bled and were treated with lasix in their next starts; the other one shin-bucked and was returned to the races after a four month layoff. Having toughened up his shins, he won on the lead at 10/1 in his return race. The past performance form will note bleeding, but not a shin-buck injury.

Sometimes a horse will have spent so much energy that it is spinning its wheels, which the jockey recognizes, and just as it is idiocy to "beat a dead horse," it is foolish to persevere with a horse who has obviously lost his action. When it is obvious to the jockey (who usually "asks the question" for more drive at the head of the stretch) that the tank is near empty, he will not abuse the horse to get a minor check. Is this honest? Put yourself in the position of the owner. The high strung thoroughbred, who takes nearly ten days to recover from the stress of an all out effort, only has so many races to run. The owner does not want to waste any of them in uselessly expended energy.

There are reasons other than physical that cause a horse to quit trying in any given race, and we will confront them honestly from the author's experience as an owner and handicapper. How often have you heard a disgruntled fan holding a worthless ticket on a favorite that suddenly stopped, complain: "Aah, they pulled him up! The jockey quit on my horse. Didn't even try." Let me reassure the bettor that that there is usually a good and sufficient reason for the abrupt shortening of stride.

In the early days of building our stable, we purchased a two year old in training filly out of a Jaipur mare. In her first race she exhibited front speed and held on for fourth, bringing home a modest check. In her second race she again ran on the front and held on again for fourth. In her next race we had high hopes and were lucky enough to draw the one post. We were with the trainer at our horse's pre-race stall when the call for "Jockey's up!" came. One of the Midwest's better riders approached us, but did not speak to our trainer as the jockey was boosted onto the saddle. Oh-oh! We asked the trainer why the jock was so cool to him. He explained that the jock was to have exercised one of the trainer's other horses that looked ready to win, but the present jock had not shown up in time to work that horse; the trainer then obtained another jock who rode that horse to a win. Our trainer explained that the jockey on our horse was: "a little hot tempered."

As the field stood in the gate, I trained my field glasses on our horse. The bell rang: the hot tempered jockey had a choke hold on our horse; the field got five lengths down the track before our horse - usually a front runner - left the gate. The jockey then rushed our filly to catch the field, but at the head of the stretch she was hopelessly beaten. The hot tempered jockey then beat our horse all the way down the stretch to finish sixth; our horse bowed a tendon in what turned out to be her last race. The jock had got even with our trainer, ruining our promising horse in the bargain.

It is unrealistic of the racing fan to believe that the jockey should apply constant urging when he recognizes that there is little gas left in the horse's tank of energy. That is why when you see in the past performances a horse badly stopping after half way into the race that you have to ask the question: Is it a physical problem or was the horse pulled up for strategic reasons; that is, was the horse too far behind at that point in the race to have a reasonable chance to bring home a check?

A notable example of asking that question happened many years ago that involved Thunder Gulch, a top Kentucky Derby contender after the spring pre-derby races. His last race before the Derby was in the Pacific Classic which offered a decent six figure purse, but small potatoes compared to the Derby. The field was small - Pat Day was the rider - and the horse was made the odds on favorite. A speed duel developed for three fourths of the race between Thunder Gulch and two other horses; at the head of the stretch barely a head separated the three. Halfway down the stretch the other two horses pulled ahead of the Gulch, who finished third after Pat discontinued persevering with him to the wire and at the finish was five lengths out. The racing press then pontificated that there must have been something physically wrong with Thunder Gulch, and generally down played his chances in the weeks before the Derby, so much so that the Gulch went off at 27/1 in the Run for the Roses.

I didn't think anything was physically wrong with the horse, especially after following his workouts since the third place finish in the Pacific. It seemed clear from his works since the Classic that he had been eased by Day after the experienced jockey recognized that the other two horses were determined to speed duel all way down the stretch. My conclusion was that Pat and Thunder Gulch's connections decided to save the horse's energy for another day - Kentucky Derby day! Put yourself in the owner and trainer's position. What would you have instructed Pat to do under the circumstances he found himself in during the stretch run of the Pacific Classic: punish his horse for *all* of the final half a furlong?

The racing press and the public criticized the Gulch's connections and his trainer, D. Wayne Lukas, after the horse won the Derby at 27/1. (I had a nice bet of $200 to win and place on him.) "They must have 'pulled' him in the Pacific Classic," was the general complaint of his non-backers in the Derby. Of course they eased him when Pat Day found his horse involved in a suicidal speed duel with two other horses. Would it have been better - more fair - to have killed their horse to win the much lower purse at the cost of losing the Derby? The betting public so often fails to consider one of the most important variants in handicapping analysis; the horse's connections and the irrevocable constants of basic human nature. In pursuing hidden long shot plays, that factor should always be considered as one of the most important variables in evaluating a horse's chances of winning.

A case in point was the seventh race at Arlington on September 25, 2009; an open $25k claimer at five and a half furlongs on the turf for a purse of $31.95k for fillies and mares three years old and up.

The 1, Ride Em Cowgirl, was installed as the morning line favorite at 2/1. She had lifetime earnings in excess of $260k and was obviously the back class of the race. The astute handicapper and hidden horse pursuer should ask: Is she a false favorite? An important factor in finding a long shot candidate is the determination that the morning line favorite is *false*; that is, that the horse's past performances do not justify the racing secretary's posting of unrealistically low morning line odds. On June 6 at Piedmont, Ride Em Cowgirl ran in a $100k stakes race at five and a half furlongs, and threw in a clunker, finishing seventh, some thirteen lengths out in a field of nine. Then on July 24, 2009, she finished second, just a nose back in an optional claiming race for $62.5 at five furlongs on the turf at Arlington. Her last race on September 5 was at Mountainer in a $37.5k allowance race at 5 furlongs in which she finished sixth, beaten five lengths in a field of nine. What was she doing now in a claiming race where she could be bought for $25k after running in nine straight races that were either stakes or allowance races?

My conclusion was that her connections were either desperate for a win or knew that there was something physically wrong with the horse and were trying to get another owner or trainer to take her off their hands for $25,000. I tabbed the reason to be the latter and marked her as a false favorite. While I eventually passed the race because I couldn't find a long shot candidate, Ride Em Cowgirl finished last. A lot of bettors lost a lot of money on this false favorite. Her connections were following one of the most primordial instincts of human nature - the pursuing of one's own self-interest. What the Cowgirl's connections had tried is legal;

yes, of course it is: but was it fair? Let the buyer beware, *caveat emptor* in spades, when it comes to claiming thoroughbred race horses, and for the bettor who is a slave to the morning line odds. Decide for yourself. Don't be influenced by those "experts" with years of experience from which they have apparently learned so few lessons. Most of the tracks in this country have "handicappers" who attempt to give the bettors an analysis of each race in the period just before the horses come out for their post parade. My experience has been that they are all strictly form players and that most of the time they just list the reasons they think the favorite will win. Since favorites lose two of every three races, the astute handicappers will do their own analysis. Everything you need to know to pick winners is in the past performances; nowhere else. Keep looking at the form, keep looking and searching, for it will give you "tells" that the professional handicapping "experts" never can – nor will.

Chapter 5

Once a horse breaks its maiden, the usual progression of class is to an allowance race restricted to non-winners of two races other than maiden, claiming, or starter allowance. It is in this type of race that the question of class comes to the fore. The first time winner's connections will have a better idea of its class after the horse's first try against other winners.

For whatever reason, this type of race appears to be the most difficult of the classes to handicap for it produces more than its share of hidden long shot winners. Much depends on the class of the maiden win. We seldom find class droppers in this type of race unless the horse went directly from its maiden win to stakes competition, then dropped back down to an allowance race.

All too often maiden race winners that post an exceptional speed rating in their first win will be installed as morning line favorites in their next race. Frequently, these horses bounce off the form of their maiden win, especially if they were involved in

long and hotly contested drives down the stretch. Astute handicappers will be on the lookout for bouncing candidates and seek
the winner elsewhere; possibly a hidden long shot.

Before examining our next class of races, we need to pause to
reflect on an often overlooked tell that is one of the first steps in
determining the probability of a long shot competing in the current race; that is, the identifying of a "false favorite."

The favorite is established by the setting of the morning line
by the track's racing secretary. It is simply the secretary's opinion
of which horse the betting public will likely make the favorite. It is
sort of a "catch 22" situation: the secretary sets the morning line
which the betting public then establishes as the favorite because
the track "expert" thinks they will make that horse the favorite.
The proposition is something like "which came first, the chicken
or the egg?"

Again, it is difficult to define the rationale for the universal
practice of the racing secretary setting a morning line. Of what
benefit is it to the betting public? I guess I should not complain
about the practice for it is an invaluable tool for the experienced
handicapper in locating hidden long shot winners, as too often it
appears that the morning line is set from little more than a quick
glance at the past performances. And too often the public bets
from a quick glance at the same information. The herd instinct is
another handy tool for the hidden long shot hunter, for the most
likely top finishers in a race are predictive in the past performances, not on the odds board.

If you can learn to identify a false favorite (and restrain yourself
from being stampeded by the crowd) you are a giant step closer to

locating a competitive horse at a decent overlay price. Not infrequently, the false favorite will finish second or third; that does not make the horse a "true" favorite, for our definition in making it false is that it will probably not stand in the winner's circle at the conclusion of that race. The astute handicapper is always aware that *there is no such thing as a sure thing in thoroughbred pari-mutuel horse racing.*

On October 3, 2009, an example of a false favorite occurred in the fourth race at Belmont; a $45k allowance for three year olds and up non-winners of two races, going six and a half furlongs on the dirt.

The 5 horse, Captain Rio, was established as the 2/1 morning line favorite. At first glance at his past performances he appeared to be the logical choice, however, on closer inspection I thought he was probably short; that is, that his staying power was questionable. First, his works were mediocre; second, he was returning from over a two month layoff. In examining his four lifetime starts, we find that he broke his maiden in his first start, a $40k maiden special at Gulfstream going six furlongs on the dirt. In his second race, a six and a half furlong $43k allowance race over a sloppy track, he was on the lead at the first call, second by a half length at the half, then gradually faded to finish fourth, some five lengths out. The current race was at the same distance of six and a half furlongs.

His next two races were competitive efforts at six furlongs in which he ran evenly to finish second. I thought that he probably would not win the race but could easily hit the board for second or third, so I began my search for a long shot competitor. Finding two hidden horse candidates, I bet them in a trifecta box with Captain Rio, who finished second.

Sangre Frio was pegged with a morning line of 12/1. In his previous race at six and a half furlongs he was steadied and pinched at the break, losing all chance of competing, finishing next to last in a field of twelve. In our hidden horse handicapping methodology, that race was a non-starter; a throw out as if the race never happened, because - having been left behind after being pinched and steadied at the break - it would have been wasted effort for the jockey to persevere with his horse just to finish ninth or tenth. In Sangre Frio's prior race he finished a close up second at Oaklawn Park on Feb 1, after closing two lengths from the first call to the finish in an optional $62k claiming race at six furlongs. He had come to New York with a new trainer and jockey, whose winning percentages were 15% and 18%, respectively. The key race for the horse was the six and a half furlong try on November 22, 2008, at Churchill Downs; a maiden special $42k which he won by nearly four lengths. In the current race Sangre Frio got up to win after being last at the head of the stretch, paying $33.00, 10.80, and 7.60.

The 6 horse in the current race was Trigger's Missile, whose morning line was set at 30/1. His last race was on August 30, 2009, at Saratoga in a $50k allowance in which he finished fifth, some four lengths out after being a close up third at the head of the stretch and on the lead at the second call on a muddy track at six furlongs. In his race prior to that he finished second, just four lengths back in a six furlong $35k claiming race for non winners of two races. He had broken his maiden at Belmont on July 22,

2009, in a $16k maiden claiming race at six and a half furlongs. In the current race the racing secretary thought his odds should be 30/1. The Trigger left the gate at 43/1 and finished third, just a head back of the winner, completing a $1 trifecta box of $913.50. Special thanks go to the racing secretary for setting the morning line odds of the winner at 12/1 and the show horse at 30/1: the crowd believed him; the hidden horse hunters did not.

FOURTH RACE
Belmont Park
October 3rd, 2009

6½ FURLONGS. (1.14²) ALLOWANCE. Purse $45,000 (UP TO $6,550 NYSBFOA) FOR THREE YEAR OLDS AND UPWARD WHICH HAVE NEVER WON TWO RACES. Three Year Olds, 119 lbs.; Older, 123 lbs. Non-winners of $24,000 since August 2 Allowed 2 lbs. Non-winners of a race since then Allowed 3 lbs. (Races where entered for $50,000 or less not considered in allowances). (Cloudy 69)

Value of Race: $45,000 Winner $27,000; second $9,000; third $4,500; fourth $2,250; fifth $1,350; sixth $300; seventh $300; eighth $300. Mutuel Pool $446,496 Pick 3 Pool $62,108 Daily Double Pool $68,026 Exacta Pool $373,605 Quinella Pool $28,027 Trifecta Pool $284,948

Last Raced	#	Horse	M/Eqt.	A/S	Wt	PP	St	¼	½	Str	Fin	Jockey	Odds $1
05Sep09 6Sar10	2	Sangre Frio	L	3C	116	1	8	8	7½	4¹½	1hd	Garcia A	15.50
29Jly09 8Sar2	5	Captain Rio	L	3C	117	3	1	1½	1½	1¹½	2no	Desormeaux K J	1.90
30Aug09 5Sar5	6	Trigger's Missile	L bf	3G	116	5	2	2½	2hd	2½	3no	Espinoza J L	43.75
29Aug09 3Sar1	1A	Schneerson	L	4C	123	4	4	6²½	6¹	5²	4¹	Prado E S	3.45
05Sep09 8Sar5	4	Redding Colliery	L	3C	116	2	6	4hd	5¹	3½	5⁷½	Maragh R	3.40
17Sep09 8Bel7	7	Charlott Humor	L f	3G	116	6	7	7¹	8	7¹½	6nk	Luzzi M J	11.20
05Sep09 11Sar9	9	Perfect Easter	L	3C	116	8	5	5½	4¹	6²	7³½	Castellano J	4.60
20Jun09 6Bel6	8	Prince Charming	L	3C	116	7	3	3¹	3hd	8	8	Velazquez J R	15.40

OFF AT 2:14 Start Good. Won driving. Track Fast.

TIME :22¹, :45, 1:09², 1:16   (:22.28, :45.12, 1:09.54, 1:16.07)

$2 Mutuel Prices:

2- SANGRE FRIO	33.00	10.80	7.60
5- CAPTAIN RIO		3.60	3.00
6- TRIGGER'S MISSILE			10.80

$2 EXACTA 2-5 PAID $114.50 $2 QUINELLA 2-5 PAID $44.00
$2 TRIFECTA 2-5-6 PAID $1,827.00

Chestnut Colt, (Apr), by More Than Ready - Miss Cap by Capote. Trainer Harty G. Eoin. Bred by Respite Farm, Inc.(KY).

SANGRE FRIO checked in tight at the start, trailed for a half, made a strong move along the rail to reach contention in midstretch then finished well while slipping through on the fence to get up in the final strides. TRIGGER'S MISSILE pressed the pace between horses into upper stretch, exchanged bumps with REDDING COLLIERY while battling heads apart into midstretch and yielded late. SCHNEERSON was reserved early, raced behind a wall of horses while in traffic at the quarter pole and rallied belatedly. REDDING COLLIERY waited along the inside while boxed in on the turn, raced behind horses lacking room in upper stretch, exchanged bumps with TRIGGER'S MISSILE while attempting to split rivals in midstretch, clipped heels and stumbled a sixteenth out then steadied in deep stretch. CHARLOTT HUMOR failed to mount a serious rally. PERFECT EASTER stalked five wide for a half and tired. PRINCE CHARMING chased four wide between horses and gave way. Following a stewards inquiry into the stretch run there was no change in the order of finish.

Owners- 2, Gold Mark Farm LLC ; 5, Zabeel Racing International, Corp ; 6, Lotruglio Edward ; 1A, Zayat Stables, LLC ; 4, Hay Mrs. Fitriani ; 7, E. Paul Robsham Stables LLC ; 9, Garner David E.; 8, Moore, Susan and M and M Thoroughbred Partners.

Trainers- 2, Harty Eoin G.; 5, Albertrani Thomas ; 6, Lotruglio Edward ; 1A, Asmussen Steven M.; 4, McLaughlin Kiaran P.; 7, Hough Stanley M.; 9, Nicks Ralph E.; 8, Jerkens James A.

Breeders- 2, Respite Farm, Inc. (KY); 5, Gulf Coast Farms, LLC (KY); 6, White Otter Farm (KY); 1A, Fred W. Hertrich III (KY); 4, Gainesway Thoroughbreds Ltd. & 707Stables (KY); 7, Fortress Pacific Equine, LLC (KY); 9, Mr. & Mrs. David Garner (KY); 8, Takahiro Wada (KY)

Scratched- B Z Warrior(05Sep09 8Sar9), Great Debater(19Jan09 3Aqu4)

$2 Daily Double (3-2) Paid $146.50; Daily Double Pool $68,026.
$2 Pick Three (7-3-2) Paid $357.00; Pick Three Pool $62,108.

brisnet.com

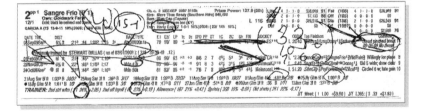

The tells on Sangre Frio were:

1) His key race of the six and one half furlong $42k maiden special win at Churchill Downs on November 8, 2008.

2) His new trainer was a 15% winner; his jockey, 18%.

3) His works pattern was good.

4) His trainer was a 24% winner with his second race off a claim, and a 23% winner with horses in their second race off a layoff.

There were no tells on the place horse, Captain Rio, he was clearly competitive at the level of this race.

The tells on Trigger's Missile were:

1) His maiden win on July 22, 2009 at the same distance as the current race, six and a half furlongs.

✵ ✵ ✵

The tenth race at Belmont on September 26, 2009, is an example of two overlays combining for a substantial exacta payoff; in that case at odds of 104/1 for a $2 bet or 52/1 for a $4 box. The race was at six furlongs on the turf for fillies and mares three years old and up foaled in New York State and which had never won two races.

No doubt the reader has begun to notice that a substantial number of these long shot overlay winners occur in the last race of the day. I make no aspersions as to the reason therefore; it could very well be that the racing secretary simply wishes to card a mixed class and difficult to handicap race just to make it more interesting for the bettor. We do not need to know the reason that so many long shot winners and place horses dominate the last race on the card, we just need to know that the statistic is demonstrably valid. The lesson is clear; beware of betting the favorite in the last race of the day. With that in mind, I searched for hidden horses in the above race.

The 4, Runfromthestorm, was the morning line favorite at odds of 3/1, and was bet down to an underlay of 1.55/1 at post time. She had run three races; her first a maiden special of $41k at five furlongs on the turf at Gulfstream Park in which she finished seventh, some five lengths out. Her next race was at the same five furlong distance for the same conditions on the turf in which she closed some two lengths in the stretch to finish third, a length out. Her last race was a maiden special $44k on the turf at five and a half furlongs at Saratoga; she was up close from the start and won by three lengths, posting a respectable speed rating of 90. The winning percentages of her trainer and her jockey were 21% and 19%. I thought there was a good chance that she would bounce in the current race. All of the other horses except the 3, Kaz Dear, had run at least one race against winners since breaking their maiden, most of them had more experience in this class of race than the favorite, Runfromthestorm. It has been my experience that the percentages are against the morning line favorite and underlay horse winning the last race of the day - at any track, at any time.

There were two horses in the race that qualified as overlays; the 2, Meese Rocks, and the 5, Fiona Freud. Their morning line odds had been set at 9/2 and 12/1, respectively: they left the gate at odds of 7.9/1 and 15/1 - both overlays. The morning line favorite was an underlay, bet down from 3/1 to 1.55/1. *While not all underlays are losers, not all overlays are hidden horse winners, but all hidden horse winners are overlays after winning at odds greater than their morning line.*

Fiona Freud had run five races in 2009, three at six furlongs and two at five and a half. Prior to her last race her record for the year was one win, one second, one third, and one close up fourth, only a length and three-quarters out. In her last race on August 23, 2009, at Saratoga she finished sixth, some eight lengths out after being pushed eight wide on the far turn. In her last ten races her odds never exceeded 8.3/1; four times she was the favorite, finishing first once, second once, and third twice. In her lifetime she had hit the board in 14 of 27 races. She had the best last workout of the entire twelve horse field, going four furlongs in :48 4/5 on September 16 at Belmont, just four days before the current race. She had a 12% jockey, though her trainer was a sub-par winner at 9%. My view of the proper morning line on Fiona Freud was 5/1, qualifying her as a hidden horse winner candidate overlay.

The 2, Meese Rocks, had finished third by a neck in her last race at five and a half furlongs on the turf at Saratoga on September 7, after exhibiting front speed at each call, then losing by a neck, finishing third. She appeared to be able to easily get to the front out of the gate for her quarter call in her last three sprints was :21 1/5; :21 4/5; and a flat :22. The horse inside her was a router and the horse in the three post outside her could not match Meese Rocks at the quarter calls. I thought the Meese deserved a morning line of 7/2.

The favorite got out third at the first call and gradually faded to fifth, while Meese Rocks sprinted to an early lead, then led to the wire where Fiona Freud nipped her to win by a neck, paying $32.20, 12.80, and 7.00. The exacta paid $210; the favorite bounced.

TENTH RACE
Belmont Park
September 26th, 2009

6 FURLONGS. (Inner Turf) (1.07) ALLOWANCE. Purse $43,000 INNER TURF FOR FILLIES AND MARES THREE YEARS OLD AND UPWARD FOALED IN NEW YORK STATE AND APPROVED BY THE NEW YORK STATE-BRED REGISTRY WHICH HAVE NEVER WON A RACE OTHER THAN MAIDEN, CLAIMING, OR STARTER OR WHICH HAVE NEVER WON TWO RACES. Three Year Olds, 119 lbs.; Older, 123 lbs. Non-winners of $24,000 on the turf since July 26 Allowed 2 lbs. Non-winners of a race on the turf since then Allowed 3 lbs. (Races where entered for $35,000 or less not considered in allowances.) (Cloudy 63)

Value of Race: $43,000 Winner $25,800; second $8,600; third $4,300; fourth $2,150; fifth $1,290; sixth $123; seventh $123; eighth $123; ninth $123; tenth $123; eleventh $123; twelfth $122. Mutuel Pool $453,098 Pick 3 Pool $181,805 Pick 4 Pool $380,806 Pick 6 Pool $92,572 Daily Double Pool $245,786 Exacta Pool $389,077 Superfecta Pool $172,732 Trifecta Pool $282,047

Last Raced	#	Horse	M/Eqt.	A/S	Wt	PP	St	¼	½	Str	Fin	Jockey	Odds $1
23Aug09 8Sar6	5	Fiona Freud	L b	5M	120	5	5	5²½	5¹½	2½	1nk	Velasquez C H	15.10
07Sep09 8Sar3	2	Meese Rocks	L	4F	123	2	1	1½	1½	1³	2nk	Chavez J F	7.90
23Aug09 8Sar3	9	More Oats Please	L	3F	116	9	10	8¹½	8¹½	7¹½	3¹	Maragh R	6.00
07Sep09 8Sar2	10	Hold the Cruiser	L	3F	116	10	9	10½	9¹½	6½	4hd	Garcia A	2.50
06Sep09 11Sar1	4	Runfromthestorm	L	3F	119	4	3	3²	3½	3½	5¹½	Desormeaux K J	1.55
12Jly09 10Bel1	3	Kaz Dear	L	4F	120	3	11	7¹	7½	5½	6¹½	Studart M	66.75
23Aug09 8Sar4	12	Miss Dolan's Rose	L	4F	120	12	8	9²½	11¹	9½	7½	Lezcano J	24.50
13Sep09 6Bel5	11	Punt's Kitty	L	4F	120	11	7	11²	10¹	10²	8no	Coa E	34.25
10Aug09 9FL5	7	Fast Footnote	L	3F	116	7	2	2²½	2²½	4¹	9²	Rodriguez R R	56.00
13Sep09 6Bel6	8	Hookin the Goods	L	3F	116	8	4	4½	4²½	8½	10no	Fuentes R D	136.75
30Apr09 5Bel7	1	Adastraperaspera	L	4F	116	1	12	12	12	11½	11¹⁸	Velasquez J R	11.60
03Aug09 1Sar5	6	A Girl Named Maria	L	5M	120	6	6	6½	6½	12	12	Samyn J	49.25

OFF AT 5:48 Start Good. Won driving. Track Firm (at 18 ft).
TIME :214, :443, :562, 1:082 (:21.90, :44.62, :56.42, 1:08.55)

$2 Mutuel Prices:

5- FIONA FREUD	32.20	12.80	7.00
2- MEESE ROCKS		9.70	5.50
9- MORE OATS PLEASE			4.90

$2 EXACTA 5-2 PAID $210.00 $2 SUPERFECTA 5-2-9-10 PAID $4,140.00
$2 TRIFECTA 5-2-9 PAID $1,379.00

Bay Mare, (Apr), by Freud - Grozny by Shananie. Trainer Ritvo Timothy. Bred by Anthony Grey(NY).

FIONA FREUD saved ground for a half, angled out in upper stretch and closed steadily to get up in the final strides. MEESE ROCKS dueled along the rail, shook loose in midstretch but couldn't hold the winner safe. MORE OATS PLEASE checked at the start, advanced three wide and rallied belatedly. HOLD THE CRUISER raced well back for a half and finished strongly along the inside. RUNFROMTHESTORM saved ground for a half, angled out and lacked a late response. KAZ DEAR saved ground after breaking slowly and lacked a strong closing response. MISS DOLAN'S ROSE never reached contention. PUNT'S KITTY was never a factor. FAST FOOTNOTE bumped at the start, pressed the pace from outside for a half and tired. HOOKIN THE GOODS was bumped at the start, chased four wide for a half and gave way. ADASTRAPERASPERA was outrun after breaking slowly. A GIRL NAMED MARIA faded after going a half.

Owners- 5, O'Connor Darrin ; 2, Terranova Henry ; 9, Waterville Lake Stable ; 10, Fingleton, Donall and Moloney, Joseph ; 4, New Day Racing and Lynn, William ; 3, Kazamias Peter ; 12, Freeman Willard C. ; 11, Marjac Pino Stable and Bommarito, Vincent ; 7, Winter Park Partners ; 8, Custard Stable ; 1, Behrendt John T. ; 6, Boice Brook Stable

Trainers- 5, Ritvo Timothy ; 2, Barker Edward R. ; 9, Bush Thomas M. ; 10, Duggan David P. ; 4, Weaver George ; 3, Kazamias Peter ; 12, DiSanto Glenn B. ; 11, Miceli Michael ; 7, Dutrow, Jr. Richard E. ; 8, Pringle Edmund ; 1, Donk David G. ; 6, Figueroa David A.

Breeders- 5, Anthony Grey (NY); 2, Robert W. Misa Jr. (NY); 9, Waterville Lake Stables Limited LLC (NY); 10, John Hettinger (NY); 4, Elsway LLC & Partners (NY); 3, Peter Kazamias (NY); 12 W.C. Freeman (NY); 11, James Pino & Lisa Pino (NY); 7, Tony Grey (NY); 8, Thomas Flakin (NY); 1, Dr. William B. Wilmot &Dr. Joan M. Taylor (NY); 6, Mr. & Mrs. Michael Spielman (NY)

Scratched- Mercy's Delight(13Sep09 6Bel2), Way to Karakorum(05Aug09 5Sar9)

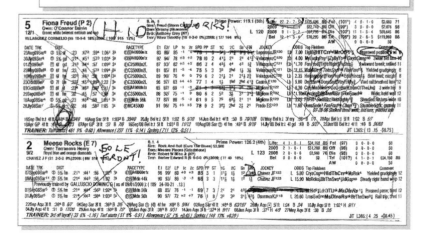

The tells for Fiona Freud were:

1) Her work at Belmont of :48 4/5 for four furlongs on September 16, 2009, four days before the current race.

2) In ten previous consecutive races she had never left the gate at odds higher than 8.3/1. At the morning line odds of 12/1, she was a clear overlay in the current race.

The tells for Meese Rocks were:

1) She was clearly the front speed of the race, having posted quarters of :21 1/5 and :21 4/5 in her last two races.

2) Her trainer and jockey were 18% and 13% winners.

An excellent example of finding the tells of a hidden horse contender occurred on August 12, 2009, in the tenth at Saratoga in a $35k claimer at a mile and one-eighth on the turf for three year olds and up which had never won two races.

The public established the 10, D'Wildcard, as the 1.45/1 favorite, making him an underlay to his morning line odds of 4/1. He was dropping in class from three straight $50k allowance races in which he finished fourth by five; steadied and finished ninth in a field of twelve; and in his previous race finished third, beaten four and a half lengths in a field of eight. I thought his outside post was a disadvantage as is usually the case with outside posts on the turf at both Saratoga and Belmont.

The 1, Wild Way, had finished third five straight times in $35k claiming non-winners of two, and then three times in $25k claiming races with the same conditions. His morning line odds were 9/2 and by post time had floated up to 9/1, clearly an overlay, for in his last four races his highest odds at post time were 6.5/1. I thought he had a good chance to hit the board for second or third. Wild Way had a trainer and jockey with winning percentages of 18%.

The 8, New York Holiday, had the best work of the field, having worked four furlongs in a flat :48 on August 2, just ten days before the current race. He had broken his maiden in his last race in a maiden claiming one mile turf race for $35k, earning an 84 speed rating and a late pace score of 100. His jockey and his trainer were winning at clips of 17% and 13%. His morning line odds were 10/1. He was bet down by post time to 8/1, an indication that he was "live on the board."

The 2, Masterofthehouse, had never run past seven furlongs. In his last race he was checked at the break and forced four wide, finishing fifth, some seven lengths back of the winner. His second race back was at seven furlongs on the turf where he finished fourth, just four lengths out. His third race back was at six furlongs on the dirt; after being pinched between, he finished sixth by five lengths. The Master had broken his maiden in his fourth race back, going six furlongs on the turf in a maiden $35k claiming race, closing from some six lengths back at the first call, winning by a nose. Throwing his two troubled races out revealed him to be a logical hidden horse winner candidate. His morning line odds of 20/1 floated up to 32/1 at post time.

Masterofthehouse broke well in the current race, was never more than a length and a half back of the pace; gave up a length entering the stretch, then came on again to win by a half length. New York Holiday ran second at every call and Wild Way closed from sixth to finish third. The exacta paid $738; the trifecta $3,420, and the superfecta paid $11,779 for a $2 ticket when the favorite 10 horse finished fourth. (It is remarkable how many times the favorite in a superfecta race finishes fourth.) In this case, the winner was a huge overlay; the place horse, a mild underlay, and the show horse a mild overlay. The beaten favorite was a notable underlay. Again, the racing secretary and the betting public overlooked several tells that should have tipped them to further examine the three hidden horses that hit the board together. Believe what the racing form is telling you and you will be well rewarded.

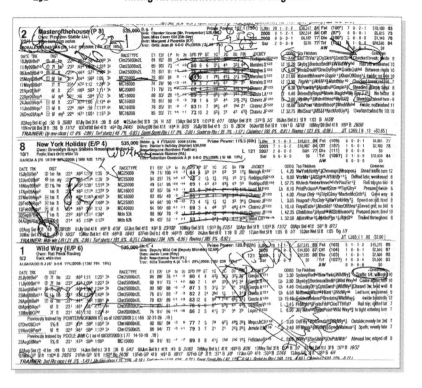

TENTH RACE
Saratoga
August 12th, 2009

$1\frac{1}{16}$ MILES. (Inner Turf) (1.39^{4}) CLAIMING. Purse $30,000 INNER TURF (UP TO $5,700 NYSBFOA) FOR THREE YEAR OLDS AND UPWARD WHICH HAVE NEVER WON TWO RACES. Three Year Olds, 119 lbs.; Older, 123 lbs. Non-winners of a race at a mile or over on the turf since June 12 Allowed 2 lbs. Claiming Price $35,000 (Races whe re entered for $25,000 or less not considered) (Winners Preferred). (Clear 78)

Value of Race: $30,000 Winner $18,000; second $6,000; third $3,000; fourth $1,500; fifth $900; sixth $120; seventh $120; eighth $120; ninth $120; tenth $120. Mutuel Pool $369,993 Pick 3 Pool $114,585 Pick 4 Pool $294,596 Pick 6 Pool $83,774 D ily Double Pool $228,980 Exacta Pool $340,393 Superfecta Pool $160,231 Trifecta Pool $257,436

Last Raced	#	Horse	M/Eqt.	A/S	Wt	PP	St	¼	½	¾	Str	Fin	Jockey	Cl'g Pr	Odds $1
18 Jly 09 ^{5}Bel^{5}	2	Masterofthehouse	L f	5G	121	2	1	7^{1}	$7^{1\frac{1}{2}}$	$6^{1\frac{1}{2}}$	$3^{2\frac{1}{2}}$	$1^{\frac{1}{2}}$	Morales S	35000	32.25
15 Jly 09 ^{7}Bel^{1}	8	New York Holiday	L	4G	121	8	5	$2^{1\frac{1}{2}}$	2^{1}	$2^{1\frac{1}{2}}$	$1^{\frac{1}{2}}$	2^{2}	Garcia A	35000	8.90
25 Jly 09 ^{7}Bel^{3}	1	Wild Way	L b	4G	121	1	2	$6^{\frac{1}{2}}$	6^{2}	3^{1}	4^{2}	3^{1}	Albarado R	35000	8.10
17 Jly 09 ^{1}Bel^{3}	10	D' Wildcard	L bf	4G	121	10	8	8^{2}	8^{2}	$7^{1\frac{1}{2}}$	$5^{\frac{1}{2}}$	4^{nk}	Maragh R	35000	1.75
25May09 ^{11}Bel^{2}	5	Hint	L a	4G	121	5	10	$9^{\frac{1}{2}}$	$9^{\frac{1}{2}}$	8^{2}	$6^{1\frac{1}{2}}$	5^{nk}	Castellano J	35000	4.30
23 Jly 09 ^{2}Bel^{5}	3	Bold Vindication	L	3C	117	3	3	$1^{1\frac{1}{2}}$	$1^{\frac{1}{2}}$	1^{hd}	$2^{\frac{1}{2}}$	$6^{7\frac{1}{2}}$	Dominguez R A	35000	3.15
11 Jly 09 ^{10}Bel^{9}	7	Kick Up Your Heels	L b	6G	121	7	4	$3^{\frac{1}{2}}$	4^{hd}	5^{1}	7^{4}	$7^{1\frac{1}{4}}$	Arroyo, Jr. N	35000	54.25
26 Jly 09 ^{4}Bel^{1}	9	Interference	L	4C	121	9	9	10	10	9^{8}	9^{20}	$8^{\frac{1}{2}}$	Espinoza J L	35000	49.50
12 Jly 09 ^{5}Bel^{5}	6	Victory March	L b	3G	117	6	7	5^{1}	5^{hd}	4^{hd}	8^{1}	$9^{27\frac{1}{4}}$	Velazquez J R	35000	8.30
29 Jly 09 ^{10}Sar^{11}	4	Sergeant Karakorum	L	3C	117	4	6	$4^{\frac{1}{2}}$	$3^{\frac{1}{2}}$	10	10	10	Wilsey J A	35000	41.50

OFF AT 6:05 Start Good. Won driving. Track Firm (Rail at 9 ft).
TIME :24^{1}, :48^{4}, 1:13, 1:37^{2}, 1:43^{3} (:24.27, :48.91, 1:13.06, 1:37.42, 1:43.62)

$2 Mutuel Prices:

2- MASTEROFTHEHOUSE	66.50	29.80	10.60
8- NEW YORK HOLIDAY		9.90	6.70
1- WILD WAY			6.40

$2 EXACTA 2-8 PAID $738.00 $2 SUPERFECTA 2-8-1-10 PAID $11,779.00
$2 TRIFECTA 2-8-1 PAID $3,420.00

Bay Gelding, (My), by Chester House - Miss Cover Girl by Oh Say. Trainer Ortiz Juan. Bred by Margaret J Picarello(KY).

MASTEROFTHEHOUSE steadied sharply between horses in the first turn, raced well back for a half, rallied along the rail on the turn, got through along the inside while gaining a sixteenth out then wore down the runner-up in the final strides. NEW YORK HOLIDAY pressed the pace in the two path, gained a slim lead in midstretch and was nipped by the winner in deep stretch. WILD WAY checked in traffic on the first turn, raced in hand to the turn and finished willingly to gain a share. D' WILDCARD raced well back for six furlongs and rallied belatedly. HINT was in hand soon after the start, raced well back to the turn, swung five wide at the quarter pole then closed late to no avail. BOLD VINDICATION set the pace inside into midstretch and tired. KICK UP YOUR HEELS raced up close along the rail to the turn and gave way. INTERFERENCE was never a factor. VICTORY MARCH lodged a move three wide on the turn and flattened out. SERGEANT KARAKORUM raced up close for a half and gave way on the urn.

Owners- 2, Picwynn Stable LLC ; 8, Brooklyn Boyz Stables, Rosenthal, Robert D. and O'Connor, Claudia ; 1, Rat Pack Racing ; 10, Castletop Stable ; 5, Tucker, Jeffrey and Very Un Stable ; 3, Winpress Stables, Saggio, John, Manorwood Stables ; 7, Team Jomar Stable ; 9, Greeley Richard ; 6, Moore, Susan and M and M Thoroughbred Partners ; 4, Karakorum Farm

Trainers- 2, Ortiz Juan ; 8, Schettino Dominick A.; 1, Hills Timothy A.; 10, Penna, Jr. Angel J.; 5, Morrison John ; 3, Gullo Gary P.; 7, Martin, Sr. Frank ; 9, Friedman Mitchell E.; 6, Jerkens James A.; 4, Odintz Jeff

Breeders- 2, Margaret J Picarello (KY); 8, Keswick Stables (VA); 1, Newchance Farm (FL); 10, Jaswinder Grover (KY); 5, Everest Stables, Inc. (KY); 3, Gulf Coast Farms LLC (KY); 7, Flying Zee Stables (NY); 9, Sanford Robertson & Judy Hicks (KY); 6, Grade I Bloodstock, Inc. & Halcyon Farm (KY); 4, Debra S. Divito & John Lemmens (NY)

Scratched- Smart Enuf(25 Jly 09 ^{1}Bel^{8}), Good Question(04Jun09 ^{4}CD^{5}), Memorized(29 Jly 09 ^{4}Mth^{1}), Stroll for Acure(17 Jly 09 ^{1}Bel^{4}), Ninth Client(29 Jly 09 ^{4}Sar^{9}), Spartan King(29 Jly 09 ^{10}Sar^{10})

$2 Daily Double (5-2) Paid $292.50; Daily Double Pool $228,980.
$2 Pick Three (11-5-2) Paid $2,476.00; Pick Three Pool $114,585.
$2 Pick Four (9-11-5-2) Paid $9,273.00; Pick Four Pool $294,596.
$2 Pick Six (4-3-9-11-5-2) 5 Correct Paid $1,458.00; Pick Six Pool $83,774; Carryover Pool $52,505.

The tells on Master of the House were:

1) The ignoring of his key race win of May 25, in which he closed six lengths from the first call to the finish.

2) The failure to throw out the races of June 6 and July 18 in which he encountered traffic trouble, having been checked at the gate in his last race.

The tells on New York Holiday were:

1) He had the best work of the field on August 2 when he worked four furlongs in :48 flat.

2) He had broken his maiden handily, earning an 84 speed rating and a 100 late pace score, third best of the field of eleven.

3) His jockey was a 20% winner at Saratoga.

4) He was a mild underlay; "live on the board" as they say in the broadcast booth.

The tells on Wild Way were:

1) His trainer was 18% and his jockey was 18%.

2) In his last five races he finished third in each, never more than five lengths out.

3) He was a mild overlay; his morning line odds were 9/2; he left the gate at odds of 8.1/1.

Sometimes the connections of the winner in a maiden race will reach for the stars in their optimism over their first time winner's potential, often placing the horse in a stakes race, thereby skipping the usual progression ladder of non-winners of two or non-winners of a race other than maiden, claiming, or starter allowance.

An example of this occurred at Saratoga on August 28, 2009, in a $52k allowance at six furlongs on the dirt for fillies and mares three years old and up which had never won a race other than maiden, claiming, starter, or restricted, or which had never won two races. The field of seven included two previous race maiden winners. There were three "works" horses, one of which was the 4, Moontune Missy, who was returning to the track after a nine and a half month layoff.

In Missy's first race at Del Mar on an all weather track in August of 2008, she broke a bit slow yet closed three lengths from the second call to finish sixth, out seven lengths in an eleven horse field. After nearly a three month layoff she broke her maiden at Santa Anita in a maiden special $44k race on another all weather track, earning a respectable speed rating of 95, closing some six lengths from the second call.

In her next race on November 16, 2008 she was ambitiously entered in the seven furlong Moccasin Stakes at Hollywood Park. She finished eleventh of eleven horses, no doubt being eased at the head of the stretch because of what later turned out to be an obvious injury, for after that race a layoff of some nine and a half months ensued.

I was familiar with her trainer's reputation for producing winners from layoffs; his winning percentage with over 90 day layoff horse's first time out was 18%. With shippers, Eoin Harty was a 20% winner and a remarkable 41% winner when moving horses from all weather to dirt tracks. The jockey was a 19% winner. An analysis of Missy's pattern of works over the layoff period revealed that she had produced no less than four bullet works; two in July of 2009, one of which was on July 4th when she worked four furlongs in an excellent :47 3/5 breezing. The racing secretary - apparently not giving much weight to Moontune Missy's chances - obliged the hidden horse hunters by setting her morning line at 12/1. By post time her odds had floated up to 17/1.

Moontune Missy's past performances chart was filled with tells that she was primed for a big effort. She did not disappoint; breaking on the lead, she was head and head for the front at the second call, increased that margin to the head of the stretch, and maintained it to the wire.

This hidden horse long shot paid $36.00, 12.60, and 4.40, anchoring an exacta of $198 when the second favorite placed second. The trifecta paid $589 when the odds-on favorite was third.

The racing secretary's setting of Moontune Missy's morning line at 12/1 led the public away from this horse; running her into the arms of the hidden horse hunters, rewarding them with a solid overlay return.

THIRD RACE
Saratoga
August 28th, 2009

6 FURLONGS. (1.08) ALLOWANCE. Purse $52,000 (UP TO $9,880 NYSBFOA) FOR FILLIES AND MARES THREE YEARS OLD AND UPWARD WHICH HAVE NEVER WON A RACE OTHER THAN MAIDEN, CLAIMING, STARTER, OR RESTRICTED OR WHICH HAVE NEVER WON TWO RACES. Three Year Olds, 119 lbs.; Older, 123 lbs. Non-winners of $25,000 since June 28 Allowed 2 lbs. Non-winners of a race since then Allowed 3 lbs. (Races where entered for $50,000 or less not considered in allowances). (Clear 66)

Value of Race: $52,000 Winner $31,200; second $10,400; third $5,200; fourth $2,600; fifth $1,560; sixth $520; seventh $520. Mutuel Pool $393,648 Pick 3 Pool $88,276 Daily Double Pool $67,027 Exacta Pool $374,340 Superfecta Pool $65,584 Trifecta Pool $200,747

Last Raced	#	Horse	M/Eqt.	A/S	Wt	PP	St	¼	½	Str	Fin	Jockey	Odds $1
16Nov08 ⁸Hol¹¹	4	Moontune Missy	L	3F	116	4	1	1hd	1hd	1²	1¹½	Leparoux J R	17.00
14Aug09 ²Sar¹	3	East Breaks	L	3F	119	3	5	7	3¹	2½	2³¾	Lezcano J	3.60
11Jly09 ⁷Crc⁸	7	Underground	L	3F	116	7	2	3¹½	2½	3²½	3¹½	Maragh R	1.25
31Jly09 ⁶Sar²	1	Diamond Song	L b	4F	120	1	7	5½	4½	4½	4nk	Theriot J	6.40
04Jly09 ²Mth¹	2	Powder Princess	L	3F	117	2	6	6½	6⁴	6¹⁶	5²½	Dominguez R A	6.00
31Jly09 ⁶Sar⁹	5	Heavenly Vision	L b	3F	116	5	4	4¹	5²	5²	6³⁵½	Bridgmohan S	7.20
31Jly09 ⁶Sar³	6	Dulcet Tone	L	4F	120	6	3	2½	7	7	7	Velazquez J R	11.40

OFF AT 2:08 Start Good. Won driving. Track Fast.
TIME :22, :45, :57½, 1:10 (:22.16, :45.10, :57.29, 1:10.14)

$2 Mutuel Prices:
4- MOONTUNE MISSY	36.00	12.60	4.40
3- EAST BREAKS		4.50	2.70
7- UNDERGROUND			3.00

$2 EXACTA 4-3 PAID $198.00 $2 SUPERFECTA 4-3-7-1 PAID $1,949.00
$2 TRIFECTA 4-3-7 PAID $589.00

Bay Filly, (Mar), by Forest Wildcat - Moonsong by Deputy Minister. Trainer Harty G. Eoin. Bred by Gaines-Gentry Thoroughbreds & S&HThoroughbreds, LLC(KY).

MOONTUNE MISSY dueled along the rail for a half, shook loose in midstretch and edged away under steady left hand urging. EAST BREAKS bobbled at the start, moved out on the backstretch, circled four wide while rallying at the quarter pole then finished willingly to best the others. UNDERGROUND pressed three wide into upper stretch and weakened. DIAMOND SONG was reserved to the turn, rallied along the rail entering the stretch then closed mildly while drifting out in the late stages. POWDER PRINCESS failed to mount a serious rally while swinging five wide at the quarter pole. HEAVENLY VISION settled in good position between horses for a half and lacked a further response. DULCET TONE pressed the winner between horses, gave way on the turn and was eased late.

Owners- 4, Gold Mark Farm LLC ; 3, Strazzanti, Joseph and Randolph, Gary ; 7, Hill n Dale Equine Holdings, Inc. ; 1, Fipke Charles E.; 2, Virginia Kraft Payson LLC ; 5, Bolton, George, Bonsal, Jr., Frank, A., Di Pietro, David and Pesch, Alan ; 6, Juddmonte Farms, Inc.

Trainers- 4, Harty Eoin G. ; 3, Shuman Mark ; 7, Baffert Bob ; 1, Stewart Dallas ; 2, Clement Christophe ; 5, Asmussen Steven M.; 6, Frankel Robert J.

Breeders- 4, Gaines-Gentry Thoroughbreds & S&HThoroughbreds, LLC (KY); 3, Dr. & Mrs. R. Smiser West (KY); 7, Richard Nip & BDP Holdings (KY); 1, Charles Fipke (KY); 2, Payson Stud, Inc. (KY); 5, Richard L. Elam & Katherine H. Elam (KY); 6, Juddmonte Farms Inc. (KY)

$2 Daily Double (3-4) Paid $231.00; Daily Double Pool $67,027.
$2 Pick Three (8-3-4) Paid $1,109.00; Pick Three Pool $88,276.

brisnet.com

Data provided or compiled by Equibase Company, which includes data from The Jockey Club, generally is accurate but occasionally errors and omissions occur as a result of incorrect data received by others, mistakes in processing and other causes. Equibase Company and Bloodstock Research Information Services, Inc. and Thoroughbred Sports Network disclaim responsibility for the consequences, if any, of such errors, but would appreciate being called to their attention. Copyright 2009.

The tells on Moontune Missy were:

1) Her four bullet works during her layoff, including two in the month before the current race.

2) She was dropping in class from a stakes race.

3) Her jockey was a 19% winner and her trainer won at 18% with layoff horses, and an amazing 41% when moving horses from all weather surfaces to dirt.

The first race at Saratoga on August 5, 2009, was an example of a long shot that was not, strictly speaking, hidden, but was discounted because the horse was moving up one grade. The race was a one and one-eighth mile $20k claimer for fillies and mares three years old and up which had never won two races. The additional conditions were that races where the horse was entered for $16k or less were not considered.

Three of the field of eight had not won after breaking their maiden. The racing secretary gave the 4, Madison Avenue, a morning line of 5/2; the horse left the gate at odds-on of 1.05/1. I thought she was a false favorite as I viewed with suspicion the drop in class from a $50k claiming race to three grades down. In her second race back at Charlestown she wired the field on the front in a $31k allowance race at a mile and one- eighth for non-winners of three; however, Charlestown is not exactly in the same league as Saratoga. After throwing in a clunker in the $50k claiming race on the turf, I thought the connections might be trying to get her claimed and suspected an injury sustained in the Charlestown race.

The 8, Driven By Seattle, was made the morning line favorite at 2/1 and was a slight overlay at post time with odds of 2.6/1. I thought she was a legitimate favorite, while the public went for Madison Avenue with the drop in class and Ramon Dominguez up - the leading rider of the meet.

In analyzing the race my attention was drawn to the 7, Disco Diva. She was returning from a six week layoff freshener, having last raced on June 19 at Belmont in a non-winner of two races $15k claimer at seven and a half furlongs on the dirt. The chart writer's comment was: "pace in 2p, *strong* drive." As the 1.45/1 favorite, she had broken on top and wired the field by five lengths after never being headed.

Her trainer was a 25% winner, 16% when returning freshened horses from a layoff of from 46 to 90 days. Disco Diva had two of the best works in the race, having worked five furlongs on July 4 at Belmont in 1:00 1/5; following that on July 14 with a four furlong work at Belmont of :48 4/5 breezing.

I thought her morning line should be about half of the racing secretary's posting of 12/1. The betting public followed the expert's ignoring of her clear tells and floated her odds up to 25.5/1 as the field left the gate.

The Diva again broke on top and was never headed, winning by a comfortable one and one-quarter length. The second favorite, Driven by Seattle, finished second and another overlay, Saarlandisourland, finished third at odds of 17.5/1.

The winner paid $53.00, 17.60, and 8.80; coupled with the second favorite the exacta paid $210.50, while the trifecta paid $2,483.

In spite of having won her previous race impressively with a late pace rating of 94, the racing secretary and the betting public ignored the several tells in her past performances which pointed to a big effort in the current race. When the hidden horse hunter finds such a not so hidden horse as Disco Diva, a substantial wager is mandatory. Believe your eyes, for the money is in the details of the hidden horse long shot winner's past performances.

FIRST RACE
Saratoga
August 5th, 2009

1⅛ MILES. (1.46³) CLAIMING. Purse $30,000 FOR FILLIES AND MARES THREE YEARS OLD AND UPWARD WHICH HAVE NEVER WON TWO RACES OR THREE YEAR OLDS. Three Year Olds, 119 lbs.; Older, 123 lbs. Non-winners of a race at a mile or over since June 5 Allowed 2 lbs. Claiming Price $20,000 (Races Where Entered for $16,000 Or Less Not Considered). (Cloudy 79)

Value of Race: $30,000 Winner $18,000; second $6,000; third $3,000; fourth $1,500; fifth $900; sixth $300; seventh $300. Mutuel Pool $243,424 Exacta Pool $230,217 Trifecta Pool $152,429

Last Raced	# Horse	M/Eqt.	A/S Wt	PP St	¼	½	¾	Str	Fin	Jockey	Cl'g Pr	Odds $1
19Jun09 ⁵Bel¹	7 Disco Diva	L	3F 117	5 1	1½	1¹	1½	1½	1¹½	Luzzi M J	20000	25.50
12Jly09 ¹Bel²	8 Driven by Seattle	L bf	3F 117	7 4	2³	3½	2²	2²	2nk	Lezcano J	20000	2.60
26Jun09 ⁶Bel¹	5 Saarlandisourland	L b	3F 117	3 2	4³	4⁴	3⁴	3hd	3nk	Velazquez J R	20000	17.50
12Jly09 ¹Bel⁴	3 Touchof Perfection	L f	3F 118	1 5	5³	5¹½	5³	4⁵	4⁹½	Velasquez C H	20000	4.40
26Jun09 ²Bel¹	6 Gin Tango	L b	3F 117	4 6	7	7	6hd	5½	5nk	Castanon J L	20000	16.50
17Jun09 ⁴Bel¹	1A Truly Divine	L	3F 119	6 7	6¹	6hd	7	6⁷	6²⁰½	Castellano J	20000	8.80
28Jun09 ⁹Mth⁸	4 Madison Avenue	L f	3F 119	2 3	3½	2½	4¹	7	7	Dominguez R A	20000	1.05

OFF AT 1:00 Start Good. Won driving. Track Fast.

TIME :23³, :47⁴, 1:12¹, 1:39¹, 1:53¹ (:23.76, :47.90, 1:12.39, 1:39.22, 1:53.35)

$2 Mutuel Prices:	7- DISCO DIVA	53.00	17.60	8.80
	8- DRIVEN BY SEATTLE		4.00	3.50
	5- SAARLANDISOURLAND			7.30

$2 EXACTA 7-8 PAID $210.50 $2 TRIFECTA 7-8-5 PAID $2,483.00

Dark Bay or Brown Filly, (Feb), by Roaring Fever - Disco Vixen by Key Contender. Trainer Galluscio G. Dominic. Bred by Mrs. Tracy Egan(NY).

DISCO DIVA sprinted clear, raced uncontested on the lead while saving ground, dug in when threatened on the turn, shook loose in midstretch and held off the runner-up under good handling. DRIVEN BY SEATTLE rushed up three wide, stalked outside for five furlongs, lodged a move to threaten on the turn, but was no match for the winner while holding for the place. SAARLANDISOURLAND steadied entering the backstretch, gained three wide on the turn and finished willingly. A claim of foul lodged by her rider against the runner-up for interference entering the backstretch was disallowed. TOUCHOF PERFECTION was under a firm hold along the rail for a half, swung five wide while gaining on the turn and rallied belatedly. GIN TANGO failed to mount a serious rally. TRULY DIVINE was outrun after breaking slowly. MADISON AVENUE pressed between horses to the far turn and gave way.

Owners- 7, Sanford H. Robbins LLC and P and D Kaplan Racing LLC ; 8, Repole Stable ; 5, Cushny, Van and Michel, Alix ; 3, SBW Birthstone Stables ; 6, Pegasus Dream Stable ; 1A, Bilinski, Darlene, Contessa, Jennifer and Magis Thoroughbreds ; 4, Ruby Stables and Klesaris, Steve

Trainers- 7, Galluscio Dominic G.; 8, Brown Bruce R.; 5, O'Brien Keith ; 3, Levine Bruce N.; 6, Badgett, Jr. William ; 1A, Contessa Gary C.; 4, Klesaris Steve

Breeders- 7, Mrs. Tracy Egan (NY); 8, Coronach Farm (NY); 5, Rojan Farms Inc. (NY); 3, Tracy Egan (NY); 6, Bruno Hofmann (NY); 1A, Glen Avon Farm (NY); 4, Sarum Farm (KY)

Driven by Seattle was claimed by J and R Racing Stable ; trainer, Barbara Robert

Scratched- Sage the Rage(17 Jly 09 ⁷Bel⁶), Lady Valiant(18 Jly 09 ⁷Bel⁸)

brisnet.com

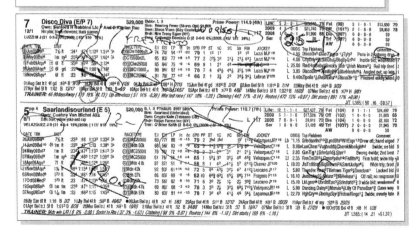

The tells for Disco Diva were:

1) Her trainer was a 25% winner, 16% with freshened horses from a 46 to 90 day layoff.

2) Her exceptional works on July 4 and July 14 of five furlongs in 1:00 1/5 and four furlongs in :48 4/5, breezing. These were two of the best works in the race.

3) The ease with which she won her last race at seven and a half furlongs, with the chart writer's comment: "strong drive," indicating that she could probably get the added distance of the current race.

While most of the long shot winners analyzed in this chapter were well hidden, the astute handicapper should always be on the lookout for the horse with a good record moving up in class for the racing secretary and the betting public often turns this type of horse into an overlay. While I will rarely bet on such a horse at short odds, I usually bet such a horse if it is at odds above 10/1.

Horses are constantly moving up or down the class ladder; few remain at the same class level for long unless they are at the bottom of the barrel which is the $5k claiming price at major tracks. It is extremely important that the handicapper correctly assess the relative class of each horse in the race. The general rule is: first you find the class then you find the form *at* the class. Class droppers without current form are generally not good bets.

The hidden horse hunter must always examine the recent works of each horse for recent form includes recent works. When next you see a horse that last ran in a Grade 3 race, now dropping into a $30k claimer, always ask yourself the question: Does this horse have decent recent form or are its connections trying to sell an injured animal?

And if a horse is dropping in class *after* a win, heed the Latin: *caveat emptor* – let the buyer beware.

Chapter 6

What a rush it is to see your horse break on top, then wire the field on the front all the way! What a downer it is to see your horse break on top, lead the field until the last hundred yards from the wire, then shorten stride and finish off the board. As hall of fame jockey Angel Cordero and hall of fame trainer Woody Stephens acknowledged: "Speed is always dangerous: it depends on where you use it." Without a rider, a thoroughbred horse - once loose - will give in to its instincts and run until it drops. Jockeys learn to control that speed with the whip and the bit and trainers attempt to teach the horse to use its speed in a tactical way.

It is extremely difficult to win on the front all the way. There have been a selective few that have won any of the classic races on the front from gate to wire, a notable exception being the giant filly, Winning Colors, and the recently troubled, Big Brown. The shorter the race, of course, the better the chance that the front runner can wire the field. On the other hand, some of my best bets have been in distance races on dirt or grass in which there was only one front speed horse that held off the pacers and the routers and the deep closers. That doesn't happen often, but it is the kind of race the hidden long shot hunter needs to search for; though, of course, in those races the winner is certainly not hidden. Sometimes the speed of a horse is hidden in the sense that it is a cutback horse that has demonstrated speed on the front in the past and is coming off a distance race to run at a shorter distance after running on or near the lead in the distance race before quitting, usually at the top of the stretch. Frequently the public will let that kind of horse leave the gate as an overlay at remarkably generous odds.

An excellent example of sole front speed holding at a distance occurred on August 9, 2009, at Saratoga in the eighth race, an optional $25k claimer for three year olds and up going a mile and one-eighth on the dirt for a purse of $76.6k for New York State breds. The betting public let the 7, Freddy the Cap, get away at 32/1, after which he promptly wired the field, winning by a head and leaving the wise guys shaking their heads. Yet the indications that he would run a competitive race were clearly printed in his past performances; the tells were there.

Freddy had won the same type of race, an optional claiming state bred $25k, at six and a half furlongs on May 9, 2009. Prior to that race, he won at a mile under the same conditions on March 14, 2009, wiring the field. Since his May 3rd win he ran in an open $40k claiming race at six furlongs, stopping after being on or near the lead for a half mile. Prior to that he tried a

$10k handicap starter at seven furlongs and again went half way before stopping. His race on July 4 at Piedmont found him in a $5k starter allowance at a mile and seventy yards in which he finished second by five lengths after contending the front from the break. His race prior to the current one was at the same track under the same conditions as the July 5th race, finishing fourth by fourteen lengths on July 18.

Freddy the Cap woke up on August 3, 2009, when he worked at Finger Lakes in :59 4/5, breezing - a bullet and the best of his previous three works. He was, in my judgment, a wake-up horse

Though his odds in his last four races had not exceeded 9/1, the public - apparently not being able to see past his last two cheap allowance races - let him leave the gate at 32/1. Perhaps the fact that he hadn't raced at that day's distance influenced the odds, though he had been competitive at a mile and seventy yards. As the sole front speed, he wired the field despite being struck by a seagull at the first turn. The second favorite finished second, completing a $330.50 exacta. Several tells were in Freddy the Cap's past performances; neither the racing secretary nor the betting public saw them. The hidden long shot hunters saw them clearly and were well paid for the clarity of their vision.

EIGHTH RACE
Saratoga
August 9th, 2009

1⅛ MILES. (1.46^{3}) ALLOWANCE OPTIONAL CLAIMING. Purse $76,650 FOR THREE YEAR OLDS AND UPWARD FOALED IN NEW YORK STATE AND APPROVED BY THE NEW YORK STATE-BRED REGISTRY WHICH HAVE NEVER WON TWO RACES OTHER THAN MAIDEN, CLAIMING, OR STARTER OR WHICH HAVE NEVER WON THREE RACES OR OPTIONAL CLAIMING PRICE OF $25,000. Thre e Year Olds, 119 lbs.; Older, 123 lbs. Non-winners of $26,000 at a mile or over since June 7 Allowed 2 lbs. Non-winners of a race at a mile or over since then Allowed 3 lbs. (Races where entered for $20,000 or less not considered in allowances) (Purse ref lects an increase of 15% providing more than eight betting interests leave the paddock. Plus an additional $6000.00 for each betting interest over six that leaves the paddock.)). (Showery 70)

Value of Race: $76,650 Winner $45,990; second $15,330; third $7,665; fourth $3,833; fifth $2,300; sixth $307; seventh $307; eighth $307; ninth $307; tenth $304. Mutuel Pool $494,697 Pick 3 Pool $93,687 Daily Double Pool $72,345 Exacta Pool $423,137 Trifecta Pool $299,320

Last Raced	#	Horse	M/Eqt.	A/S	Wt	PP	St	¼	½	¾	Str	Fin	Jockey	Cl'g Pr	Odds $1
18 Jly 09 ^{3}Pid^{4}	7	Freddy the Cap	L bf	7H	120	7	5	1^{1}	1^{1}	1^{1}	1½	1^{hd}	Morales S	25000	32.50
08 Jly 09 ^{3}Bel^{5}	1A	Groomedforvictory	L	4G	120	10	3	5½	4^{1}	$4^{1\frac{1}{2}}$	3½	2^{nk}	Dominguez R A		a - 3.10
05Jun09 ^{6}Bel^{5}	9	A Zero Trap	L b	4G	120	9	4	$2^{1\frac{1}{2}}$	$2^{1\frac{1}{2}}$	$2^{1\frac{1}{2}}$	$2^{1\frac{1}{2}}$	$3^{1\frac{3}{4}}$	Leparoux J R	25000	14.10
16 Jly 09 ^{8}Bel^{5}	1	Tall Poppi	L b	3C	119	5	7	3½	$6^{1\frac{1}{2}}$	$5^{2\frac{1}{2}}$	4½	4½	Coa E		a - 3.10
22 Jly 09 ^{3}Bel^{1}	8	Pretty Boy Freud	f	3C	119	8	6	6^{3}	3½	3½	5^{2}	$5^{1\frac{1}{4}}$	Velazquez J R		2.20
03 Jly 09 ^{5}CD^{2}	2	Almighty Silver	L	4G	120	1	1	8^{3}	10	$8^{1\frac{1}{2}}$	$6^{1\frac{1}{2}}$	$6^{4\frac{3}{4}}$	Borel C H	25000	4.40
17 Jly 09 ^{2}Bel^{3}	3	Stopbluffing	L b	5G	120	2	2	$7^{1\frac{1}{2}}$	7^{3}	$6^{1\frac{1}{2}}$	7^{6}	$7^{10\frac{1}{2}}$	Luzzi M J		15.40
17 Jly 09 ^{2}Bel^{4}	5	That'srightofficer	L f	4C	120	4	9	9^{2}	8½	9^{4}	$8^{1\frac{1}{2}}$	$8^{2\frac{3}{4}}$	Prado E S		3.10
19 Jly 09 ^{1}Bel^{5}	6	Goldispretty	L b	5G	120	6	10	10	9^{1}	7^{2}	9	9	Espinoza J L	25000	32.25
03 Jly 09 ^{7}Bel^{6}	4	Western Deed	L bf	5G	120	3	8	$4^{1\frac{1}{2}}$	5^{1}	10	10^{DNF}	10^{DNF}	Maragh R	25000	39.00

a - Coupled:Groomedforvictory and Tall Poppi

OFF AT 4:48 Start Good. Won driving. Track Fast.

TIME :23^{2}, :48, 1:13^{3}, 1:39^{2}, 1:53 (:23.48, :48.11, 1:13.73, 1:39.51, 1:53.07)

$2 Mutuel Prices:

7- FREDDY THE CAP	67.00	22.00	11.60
1A- GROOMEDFORVICTORY(a_entry)		4.60	3.50
9- A ZERO TRAP			8.30

$2 EXACTA 7-1 PAID $330.50 $2 TRIFECTA 7-1-9 PAID $3,292.00

Chestnut Horse, (Mar), by Precise End - Farma Speech by Farma Way. Trainer Barrera, Jr. S. Oscar. Bred by Sez Who Thoroughbreds, Inc.(NY).

FREDDY THE CAP was struck by a seagull when setting the pace on the first turn, set the pace along the rail into upper stretch, dug in when challenged in midstretch and prevailed late. GROOMEDFORVICTORY stalked three wide for a half, angled in on the turn, swung out in midstretch and closed steadily but could not get up. A ZERO TRAP pressed three wide to the top of the stretch and weakened. TALL POPPI steadied along the inside on the first turn, raced between horses for a half, swung four wide on the turn then lacked a strong closing bid. PRETTY BOY FREUD stalked three wide to the turn and tired. ALMIGHTY SILVER raced well back to the turn, swung five wide and failed to threaten. STOPBLUFFING saved ground to no avail. THAT'SRIGHTOFFICER was never a factor. GOLDISPRETTY was outrun after breaking slowly. WESTERN DEED raced in midpack and gave way on the far turn and was eased.

Owners- 7, Sosa-Barrera Clery L.; 1A, Sure Thing Stables LLC ; 9, Anstu Stables, Inc. ; 1, Yurch Michael ; 8, Bobley Suzann ; 2, Patton's Creek Farm ; 3, Our Eyes Wide Open Stable ; 5, Clear Stars Stable ; 6, Giorgi Stable ; 4, Imperio Michael

Trainers- 7, Barrera, Jr. Oscar S.; 1A, Tagg Barclay ; 9, Pletcher Todd A.; 1, Tagg Barclay ; 8, O'Brien Leo ; 2, Baker James E.; 3, Carroll, II Del W.; 5, Schosberg Richard E.; 6, Ortiz Paulino O.; 4, Schettino Dominick A.

Breeders- 7, Sez Who Thoroughbreds, Inc. (NY); 1A, Sure Thing Stables, LLC & Michael JMcGuire (NY); 9, Robert C. Baker & Sugar Maple Farm (NY); 1, Philip Trowbridge (NY); 8, Mr. & Mrs. Richard Powers (NY); 2, Kenneth L. Ramsey & Sarah K. Ramsey (NY); 3, Barbara Cross Graham (NY); 5, William Ammann Trust (NY); 6, Carmine Telesca & John Guerrera (NY); 4, Flying Zee Stables (NY)

A Zero Trap was claimed by Me You and Magoo Stable ; trainer, Imperio Joseph ,

Almighty Silver was claimed by Giorgi Stable ; trainer, Ortiz Paulino O.

$2 Daily Double (10-7) Paid $666.00; Daily Double Pool $72,345.

$2 Pick Three (3-10-7) Paid $3,013.00; Pick Three Pool $93,687.

brisnet.com

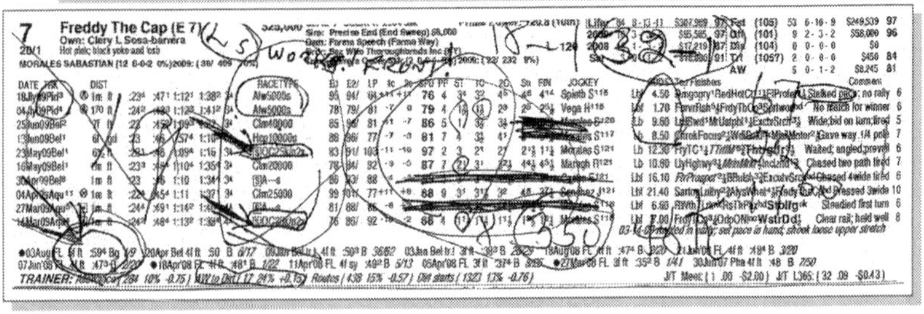

The tells in Freddy the Cap's past performances were:

1) His :59 4/5 work just six days before the current race, a wake up work.

2) His competitive back class efforts at the current race's conditions, winning on March 14, 2009, at a mile at Aqueduct and May 9, 2009, at Belmont at six and a half furlongs.

3) His trainer's record when switching from a synthetic surface to dirt was 24%.

4) In sixty-four lifetime efforts he had hit the board at a 50% clip.

5) He appeared to be the sole front speed in the race, the others being pacers or routers.

More than mileage distance separates the Saratoga and Fairplex race tracks, but often there are equally rewarding long shot payoffs at each. Fairplex is a five-eighths mile bull ring where front speed is at a premium and routers are handicapped by the tight turns on which many young horses bear out, losing valuable lengths. If a front running horse can't stay up at Fairplex it can't stay up anywhere, according to the track's community of trainers.

A remarkable opportunity presented itself on September 27, 2009, the closing day of the meet. In the eleventh race, the one and one-eighth mile Ralph M. Hinds Invitational Handicap for a purse of $100k for three year olds and up, a field of nine went to the post. The 1, Acclamation, and the 2, Z Humor, were the only front runners facing seven pace horses and routers. Remembering the dictum that when there is only one front runner in a distance race (all other factors being equal) the front will usually stay up, I determined that Z Humor had the better chance of beating Acclamation to the first turn. Acclamation's best split time for the quarter was :22 3/5 and :46 3/5 for the half mile; Z Humor's best quarter time was :22 1/5 and :44 1/5 for the half. None of the other horses could come close to those splits. It looked like a cold 1-2 exacta box.

When I looked at the odds board I was incredulous that Z Humor was 13/1, even more so when I saw that his morning line was 8/1. What an overlay! Perhaps the reason was that Acclamation was being bet down to 1.9/1 as the favorite. I was determined, nevertheless, to make my maximum single race bet by loading up on Z Humor to win and place and to bet my maximum exacta box bet, using the 1 and the 2. What I had seen in the past performances was enough to tempt me to "bet the farm," but, of course, you can never do that because there is no such thing in pari-mutuel thoroughbred horse racing (or any other gamble, for that matter) as a "mortal lock," as my friend the dog track tip sheet writer was overly fond of calling his picks.

I could see why Acclamation was made the favorite, even though Z Humor was the class of the race, having run in the 2008 Run for the Roses, though finishing far down the track. He was pure front speed, knowing no other gear. Fairplex was built for a horse like him, with its short distance to the first turn and its relatively short stretch run.

As a four year old he had accumulated lifetime earnings of $662,705. Yet 2009 had not been a glory year, for he had run seven times and had one place finish and $7,390 to show for his efforts.

Since his race of August 16, 2009, he had changed trainers, moving into the hands of noted California veteran trainer, Mike Mitchell, who was a 23% trainer for the year and a 27% winner at Fairplex. Mitchell brought Z Humor up to the current race with a decent pattern of works which were topped with one on August 31 of :48 3/5 handily at four furlongs. Mitchell was also a 21% winner with horses new to his barn.

When the gates opened, Z Humor sprang to the lead, never to relinquish it. Acclamation ran second, never getting closer than a length to the winner; the rest of the field never got within three and a half lengths of the top two. The exacta paid $99.60 - 24 to 1 on a box. Z Humor paid a generous $28.40, 11.00, and 5.00.

Yes, Angel and Woody, "front speed *is* always dangerous." Especially at the bull ring that is Fairplex.

ELEVENTH RACE
Fairplex
September 27th, 2009

About 1¼ MILES. (1.48²) STAKES. Purse $100,000 *RALPH M. HINDS INVITATIONAL H.* FOR THREE YEAR OLDS AND UPWARD BY INVITATION. $100,000 Guaranteed with $55,000 to the winner, $18,000 to second, $12,000 to third, $6,000 to fourth, $4,000 to fifth, $2,000 to sixth, $1,000 to seventh and eighth, $500 to ninth and tenth. d Wednesday, September 23, 2009. Horsemen wishing to have their horse(s) considered for invitation please contact Racing Secretary Tom Knust no later than Saturday, September 19, 2009. (Clear 101)

Value of Race: $99,000 ($1,000 reverts) Winner $55,000; second $18,000; third $12,000; fourth $6,000; fifth $4,000; sixth $2,000; seventh $1,000; eighth $1,000. Mutuel Pool $166,063 Pick 3 Pool $27,839 Daily Double Pool $14,038 Exacta Pool $90,598 Quinella Pool $6,859 Superfecta Pool $56,293 Trifecta Pool $84,437

Last Raced	# Horse	M/Eqt.	A/S Wt	PP	St	¼	½	¾	Str	Fin	Jockey	Odds $1
16Aug09 ⁷Emd⁷	2 Z Humor	BL	4C 115	2	1	1½	1½	1²	1½	1¹	Garcia M	13.20
06Sep09 ⁶Dmr³	1 Acclamation	BL f	3C 110	1	2	3ʰᵈ	3ʰᵈ	2¹½	2⁵	2³½	Talamo J	1.90
09Sep09 ⁵Dmr⁷	5 Racketeer	BL b	6H 117	4	8	6½	6ʰᵈ	6½	5½	3¹½	Espinoza V	4.40
18Sep09 ⁵Fpx¹	6 Trevor's Clever	BL b	4G 113	5	6	8	8	7½	4½	4¹½	Santiago Reyes C	11.90
06Sep09 ⁸Dmr¹	7 Quarter Moon	BL	4G 118	6	4	5³	5¹½	4ʰᵈ	3¹	5⁴½	Delgadillo A	7.90
15Aug09 ⁹Evd⁵	3 Overbid	BL	4R 116	3	3	4²	4¹½	5²	6⁵	6²½	Gryder A T	12.10
09Sep09 ⁵Dmr⁶	10 No Dream	BL	5H 117	8	5	2¹	2¹	3ʰᵈ	7⁴	7⁸½	Flores D R	7.60
30Aug09 ⁴Dmr¹	8 Cigar Man	BL b	4G 116	7	7	7ʰᵈ	7²	8	8	8	Quinonez A	3.30

OFF AT 5:37 Start Good. Won driving. Track Fast.

TIME :24¹, :47⁴, 1:12², 1:38, 1:51²   (:24.32, :47.83, 1:12.52, 1:38.07, 1:51.43)

$2 Mutuel Prices:

2- Z HUMOR	28.40	11.00	5.00
1- ACCLAMATION		3.60	3.00
5- RACKETEER			2.80

$1 EXACTA 2-1 PAID $49.80 $2 QUINELLA 1-2 PAID $30.40
$1 SUPERFECTA 2-1-5-6 PAID $1,629.60 $1 TRIFECTA 2-1-5 PAID $245.90

Bay Colt, (Feb), by Distorted Humor - Offtheoldblock by A.P. Indy. Trainer Mitchell R. Mike. Bred by Jayeff "B" Stables(KY).

Z HUMOR quickly sent to the lead, rated from along the rail, moved away before leaving second turn, under strong asking on final turn and when challenged into the stretch then determinedly held under vigorous handling. ACCLAMATION settled inside then bit off the rail while stalking the pacesetter, moved up into final bend, loomed outside winner entering the stretch, battled gamely in the drive but got no closer in the lane. RACKETEER settled inside, saved ground chasing the pace to the final turn, angled out some, between foes in the drive and pulled away late to best others. TREVOR'S CLEVER lagged back from the inside, saved ground around two turns, shifted out, caught three wide into and around the final turn and failed to threaten. QUARTER MOON caught three wide early, chased on same path into the stretch and lacked needed late response. OVERBID settled from between foes, chased outside runner-up in the early stages, later secured the rail, remained inside and weakened. NO DREAM three wide on the first turn, moved up to pressure the pacesetter then settled off the leader, dropped back nearing final bend and faded. CIGAR MAN reserved while bit off the rail, chased two then three wide, also lost contact and gave way.

Owners- 2, Zayat Stables, LLC ; 1, Johnston, E. W. and Judy ; 5, Abrams, Barry, David and Dyan, M. Auerbach, LLC and McCauley, Ron ; 6, O'Neill, Dennis, Sarno, Russell and Westsiderentals.com ; 7, Stute Annabelle M.; 3, Southern Equine Stable LLC ; 10, Wertheimer and Frere ; 8, Manzani, Ron and Sarno, Russell

Trainers- 2, Mitchell Mike R.; 1, Warren Donald ; 5, Abrams Barry ; 6, O'Neill Doug F.; 7, Stute Melvin F.; 3, Guillot Eric J.; 10, Mandella Richard E.; 8, Cerin Vladimir

Breeders- 2, Jayeff "B" Stables (KY); 1, Old English Rancho (CA); 5, Adena Springs (KY); 6, Donna M. Wormser (FL); 7, Robert C. Henderson (KY); 3, Farfellow Farms Ltd. (KY); 10, Wertheimer & Frere (KY); 8, Charles Spence (FL)

Scratched- On Fire(19Sep09 ⁷Fpx¹), Generalito Nain (ARG)(31Jly 09 ⁸Dmr⁹)

$2 Daily Double (5-2) Paid $142.20; Daily Double Pool $14,038.
$1 Pick Three (3-5-2) Paid $492.70; Pick Three Pool $27,839.

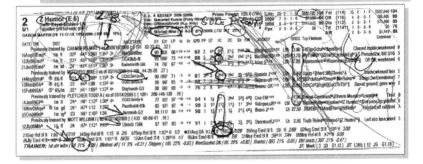

The tells on Z Humor were:

1) He was clearly the back class of the race.

2) With the exception of Acclamation, he was the front speed.

3) His fractional split times at the quarter and half were considerably faster than Acclamation's.

4) His trainer was an overall 23% winner, 27% at Fairplex.

5) His work on August 31 of :48 3/5 for four furlongs was the best recent work of the field.

As we have seen, your horse doesn't have to win for you to make a good hit; frequently a second place finish will do if the odds are long enough. An example occurred on August 7, 2009, at Del Mar in a $10k claiming race for fillies and mares four and up going six furlongs on the all weather track for a purse of $16k.

This race is an example of hidden front speed in a back class horse being overlooked by the public. With the favorite leaving the gate at odds of 3.45/1, it was a good bet that the race was wide open. In searching for front speed we examined the 7, Saint's Crown, who had won her last race at Hollywood on the front at seven and a half furlongs. But with a first quarter of :22 4/5 in that try she did not figure to be the front in the current race; that position appeared to belong to the 12, Heavenly N' Free. She had booked her first quarter in her last race at :22 1/5. Additionally, she had considerable superior back class, as did the favorite.

Though Heavenly's trainer had not won a race in 11 tries, the jockey was an apprentice and would carry seven pounds less than any of the other horses. Normally, weight difference is not much of a factor in a sprint, but seven pounds is a lot of weight to give another horse at any distance. It was the lowest weight by far than the horse had carried in her last ten races. In the current race Heavenly N' Free must have felt like there was a feather in the saddle.

Though the horse had wired the field in a $40k allowance race at a mile and one-sixteenth at Hollywood on December 8, 2008, her form had faltered since then. In her last race at six furlongs on July 19 at Hollywood, she contested the lead for a half with good splits for the quarter and half of :22 1/5 and :45 2/5. At the quarter pole she was squeezed between and finished fourth by six lengths. Her workout prior to that race was a flat :47 for four furlongs, preceded by a blazing work of :46 2/5 on June 28, the best of 54 horses working that day. The troubled race of July 19 disguised her readiness to put in a big effort. Then on August 2 at Santa Anita she worked five furlongs in 1:00 2/5, fourth best of twenty-four, signaling that she was again ready for a big effort.

Again the racing secretary obliged the hidden horse hunters by setting her morning line at a generous 30/1. My handicapping analysis tabbed her as a long shot play: a bet of win and place was called for. As I felt the tepid favorite was the class of the race, I boxed her in an exacta with Heavenly N' Free.

To my surprise, Heavenly N' Free broke eighth, but was second by two lengths at the half and closed to within a length and a half of the leader, then was dead heated by the 8, Snow on Christmas, for the place. This knocked place money down considerably, but the exacta paid $144.80.

A cursory glance at Heavenly N' Free's past performances would have clearly caused the average public bettor to look elsewhere for a decent bet, but a careful analysis of her record pulled her out of the forest of past performances details to reveal another hidden horse long shot winner.

FIFTH RACE
Del Mar
August 7th, 2009

6 FURLONGS. (1.081) CLAIMING. Purse $16,000 FOR FILLIES AND MARES FOUR YEARS OLD AND UPWARD. Weight, 124 lbs. Non-winners of two races since May 7 Allowed 2 lbs. A race since then Allowed 4 lbs. Claiming Price $10,000, if for $9,000, allowed 2 lbs. (Maiden races and Claiming races for $8,500 or le ss not considered). (Clear 77)

Value of Race: $18,880 Winner $9,600; second $2,560; second $2,560; fourth $960; fifth $400; sixth $400; seventh $400; eighth $400; ninth $400; tenth $400; eleventh $400; twelveth $400. Mutuel Pool $413,385 Pick 3 Pool $82,982 Daily Double Pool $28,069 Exacta Pool $223,829 Quinella Pool $15,101 Superfecta Pool $128,838 Trifecta Pool $202,254

Last Raced	#	Horse	M/Eqt.	A/S	Wt	PP	St	¼	½	Str	Fin	Jockey	Cl'g Pr	Odds $1
27Jun09 8Hol7	10	Kiss the Cooke	BL	5M	120	10	1	2¹	2²	1½	1½	Gryder A T	10000	3.40
19 Jly 09 2Hol4	12	DH Heavenly n' Free	BL f	4F	113	12	8	7½	4hd	3¹	2	Santiago Reyes C	10000	31.60
17 Jly 09 3Hol2	8	DH Snow On Christmas	BL	4F	120	8	11	11²½	10hd	5½	2½	Talamo J	10000	6.90
19Dec08 5Hol5	1	Stuttgart	BL b	4F	120	1	9	5½	5½	4¹½	4½	Rosario J	10000	5.90
27Jun09 3Hol1	6	Threat	BL	4F	122	6	6	9¹½	9²	6¹	5hd	Baze T	10000	4.20
19 Jly 09 2Hol5	4	Paddlin Mud	BL f	4F	118	4	4	3hd	6½	8¹½	6hd	Pedroza M A	9000	39.40
12 Jly 09 4Hol1	7	Saint's Crown	BL b	5M	122	7	5	1½	1hd	2hd	7¾	Arambula P	10000	28.10
22 Jly 09 9Dmr7	3	Kneeling's Pride	BL f	5M	120	3	10	10hd	8hd	9¹½	8½	Delgadillo A	10000	3.50
25Jun09 5Hol7	11	No Cream Or Sugar	BL b	4F	120	11	2	4hd	3hd	7hd	9¹½	Sorenson D	10000	45.10
26Apr09 9Hol3	5	Winky	BL	4F	120	5	7	8¹	11⁴	10½	10¹	Berrio O A	10000	12.80
16 Jly 09 1Hol3	9	Oakhill Girl	BL f	5M	120	9	3	6¹½	7¹½	11³	11³¼	Espinoza V	10000	12.40
23 Jly 09 5Dmr10	2	Starstruck Kristen	BL bf	4F	118	2	12	12	12	12	12	Blanc B	9000	54.40

DH-Dead Heat.

OFF AT 5:03 Start Good. Won driving. Track Fast.
TIME :22⁴, :46, :58¹, 1:11 (:22.83, :46.07, :58.22, 1:11.06)

$2 Mutuel Prices:

10- KISS THE COOKE	8.80	5.20	4.20
8- DH SNOW ON CHRISTMAS		4.00	4.60
12- DH HEAVENLY N' FREE		11.40	11.20

$1 EXACTA 10-12 PAID $72.90 $1 EXACTA 10-8 PAID $17.30
$2 QUINELLA 10-12 PAID $116.60 $2 QUINELLA 8-10 PAID $24.20
$1 SUPERFECTA 10-12-8-1 PAID $3,295.60 $1 SUPERFECTA 10-8-12-1 PAID $2,853.10
$1 TRIFECTA 10-12-8 PAID $750.60 $1 TRIFECTA 10-8-12 PAID $470.10

Dark Bay or Brown Mare, (Jan), by Kessem Power (NZ) - Zealed With a Kiss by Unreal Zeal. Trainer Koriner J. Brian. Bred by James R. Wilson(CA).

KISS THE COOKE angled in and dueled outside a rival, gained the advantage nearing the stretch, kicked clear under urging in the drive and proved best. SNOW ON CHRISTMAS settled outside a rival then a bit off the rail, angled to the inside in the stretch and rallied for a share of the place. HEAVENLY N' FREE hopped at the start, chased outside, went four wide on the turn and into the stretch, drifted in some and held a share of second. STUTTGART saved ground stalking the pace, came out in upper stretch and split horses at the wire. THREAT chased off the rail then outside on the turn, came five wide into the stretch and missed a minor award four wide on the line. PADDLIN MUD stalked a bit off the rail then between horses on the backstretch and turn, found the fence in the stretch and weakened. SAINT'S CROWN broke in the air, had speed between horses then dueled just off the rail or inside and weakened in the stretch. KNEELING'S PRIDE chased outside a rival then a bit off the rail on the backstretch and turn and lacked the needed response in the stretch. NO CREAM OR SUGAR stalked four wide on the backstretch and turn, came three deep into the stretch and weakened. WINKY chased a bit off the rail, went between horses and was in a bit tight midway on the turn, came out into the stretch and did not rally. OAKHILL GIRL stalked between horses on the backstretch and turn, was in a bit tight nearing the quarter pole and weakened in the stretch. STARSTRUCK KRISTEN broke a bit slowly, settled inside, came out leaving the turn and into the stretch and was outrun.

Owners- 10, Legacy Ranch ; 12, Hedrick, William L. and Kango Racing ; 8, Lindo, David and Spawr, Bill ; 1, Desert Sun Stables ; 6, Batchelor Family Trust ; 4, Murillo Jose Luis; 7, Sherlock Gary ; 3, Kasparoff Tim ; 11, Omnia Racing Stable ; 5, L-Bo Racing, Baldi, Mark, Pyle, Monte and Tahmasebi, Kourosh ; 9, Han Moon S.; 2, Knapp Steve

Trainers- 10, Koriner Brian J.; 12, Rodriguez Suzanne Kane; 8, Spawr William ; 1, Sadler John W.; 6, Becerra Rafael ; 4, Martinez Silverio ; 7, Sherlock Gary ; 3, Kasparoff James M.; 11, Piccioni Gerard ; 5, Avila A. C.; 9, Han Moon S.; 2, Knapp Steve

Breeders- 10, James R. Wilson (CA); 12, Gus Rodriguez Sr. & Suzanne Rodriguez (CA); 8, Albert Frassetto (KY); 1, Sycamore Hall Farm, LLC (MD); 6, Brereton C. Jones (KY); 4, Special T Thoroughbreds, Inc. (CA); 7, WinStar Farm, LLC (KY); 3, Dinesh Maniar & Getaway Farms (CA); 11, Winning Ways Farm (KY); 5, Midhurst Farm Inc. & Teresa McWilliams (FL); 9, Moon Suk Han (KY); 2, St. George's Farm (CA)

Kneeling's Pride was claimed by Altamira Racing Stable and Campochiaro ; trainer, Miller Peter ,
Stuttgart was claimed by Dizney Donald R.; trainer, Baffert Bob

Scratched- Ju Ju Baby(23 Jly 09 5Dmr12), Dine At Nine(23 Jly 09 5Dmr3)

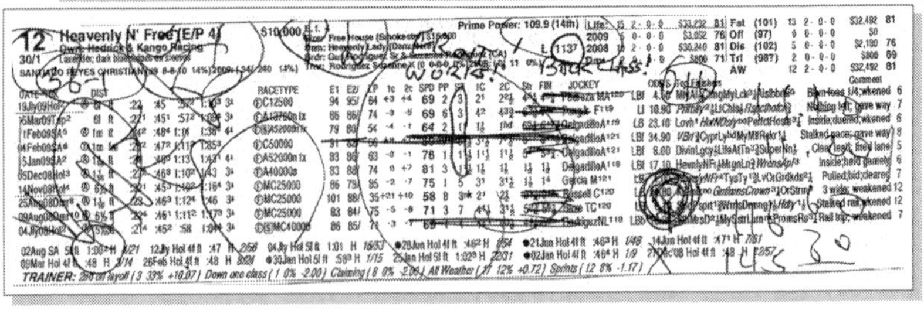

The tells for Heavenly N' Free were:

1) She was the front speed of the race.
2) She was the back class of the race, with the exception of the winner.
3) She was getting a seven pound weight allowance.
4) She was a "wakeup" horse with her work of 1:00 2/5 on August 2nd, just five days before the current race.

The eighth and last race on the card at Hollywood Park on November 19, 2009, was clearly an on point example of - at first glance - a front running horse that looked short at the six furlong distance over the all weather track. The race was an $8k claimer with a purse of $10k.

The racing secretary made the 7, Usually Hot, the 5/2 favorite; probably because she was a 50% class dropper. I thought she was a false favorite and considered with suspicion the deep class drop. In addition, her two pre-race works were undistinguished.

The second favorite at 3/1 was the 3 horse, Msty Aly, who was also dropping in class by 25%. In her last race at five and a half furlongs she was second, only a head back from the winner then gave up two lengths to finish third. She had not worked since that race; a red flag in itself. Always view with suspicion the present condition of a horse that has not worked since its last race.

As I thought that the first and second morning line favorites were false, I went looking for hidden horse long shots, landing on a cutback horse and one that appeared at first glance to be short at six furlongs.

The 5 horse, Kneeling's Pride, caught my eye when she was bet down from a morning line of 8/1 to an underlay of 5/1. The horse's previous race was a $10k claimer at Santa Anita on the all weather track at a distance of one mile in which she turned in a clunker. At that distance she appeared to be short. The second race back, however, indicated that she would be competitive in the current race as a cutback horse. In a six and a half furlong $12.5k claimer, Kneeling's Pride closed three lengths from the first call to win by three-quarters of a length. The board action indicated she was live for the current race.

I then examined the 2 horse, Company Secret, whose morning line odds were 30/1, floating up to 56/1 at post time. Once I determined that she would probably be on the front at the first call, I debated with myself whether or not she could stay up to the wire. There were several pros and cons and it was evident that the betting public had decided she was short at the distance.

In examining the past performances of Company Secret I was struck by the unusual formulation of her running line in her last race on November 6 at Los Alamitos. The call columns were considerably offset to the left. Perhaps that was because that last race was for quarter horses at 870 yards, and that racing line set-up is normal for quarter horse races. In any case it drew my attention as peculiar. That race was an allowance condition for a purse of $13.1k in which the Secret finished fourth, three lengths out. The chart writer's comments were: *inside, evenly late.*

In examining her other nine races, I thought she could and probably would get the lead at the first call and would probably have the lead at the half. Her best time for the half was :44 4/5, compared to the :45 2/5 of the front runner to the outside of her, the 3, Msty Aly, the second favorite. The question was: could Company Secret stay up for the six furlongs? That question was answered when I looked at her record for that distance; she had won one six furlong race and was third twice. At that distance, the only other question was the other front speed in the race in the 10 post. I felt that if the 10 did not break, Company Secret would get an easy lead and that if she got that kind of lead, she could hold on to the wire.

Another tell was that with an 85 in her last race she held the best speed rating of the field. Additionally, only the favorite had won more money for her lifetime than the Secret. She had hit the board in 50% of her 2009 races and her record at Hollywood Park was 1-1-1 in seven starts.

On the negative side, her jockey, Maggie Carter, a Los Alamitos regular, had won four races in 73 tries: her trainer had an 11% record with eight wins in 74 tries. As we have shown, however, when a horse is ready for a big effort, it will drag its connections along and, unless the jockey falls off, will bring home the bacon.

You may ask: how does a jockey fall off his mount unless there is traffic trouble? I saw it happen once at small Midwestern track years ago. This horse had a three length lead at the head of the stretch, maintaining it to about 100 yards from the wire, when the jockey turned to look back and fell off his mount. This jockey had a reputation for being a little goofy and I can't say with any certainty that when he saw his horse was going to be first to the wire he *jumped* off, for that was the only way his mount could lose. Just as, some days, a horse is meant to win; some days a certain horse just isn't meant to win because the stars are out of alignment. A contributing factor could have been that the riderless mount was the odds-on favorite.

Though Company Secret's modest connections probably contributed to the sizable overlay, it seemed clear to me that the reason for her box car odds was that the Hollywood betters look askance at Los Alamitos and Fairplex Park runners and that, at first glance, it did not appear the mare could get the distance. A complete reading of the form said that she could because she had.

I made my usual long shot bet of $20 to win and place, then boxed her in $5 exactas with the modest underlay I had spotted, the 5, Kneeling's Pride, and the second favorite, the 3, Msty Aly, for a total hidden horse long shot play investment of $60.

The 10 horse, Puddlin Mud, broke on top; but at the first call Company Secret had a length lead and widened it to four at the half, then coasted to a length and a half win after holding on against the closing 5 horse, Kneeling's Pride. There was hushed silence at Hollywood Park as Company Secret crossed the finish line.

The Secret paid $114.80, 46.00, and 14.60; the exacta paid $827.80. When the second favorite, Msty Aly, finished third the $1 trifecta paid $1,025.60. When the $1 superfecta paid $7,512 I found myself muttering the inevitable bettor's lament: *If only; would have; could have, should have.*

Believe the tells in the form. Don't let the odds board put doubt into your bet. When you find such a remarkable set of tells, bet them with conviction for they are generally golden.

EIGHTH RACE
Hollywood
November 19th, 2009

6 FURLONGS. (1.07²) CLAIMING. Purse $10,000 FOR FILLIES AND MARES THREE YEARS OLD AND UPWARD. Three Year Olds, 122 lbs.; Older, 124 lbs. Non-winners Of Two Races Since June 1 Allowed 2 lbs. A Race Since Then Allowed 4 lbs. Claiming Price $8,000. (Clear 74)

Value of Race: $11,800 Winner $6,000; second $2,000; third $1,200; fourth $600; fifth $400; sixth $400; seventh $400; eighth $400; ninth $400. Mutuel Pool $192,739 Pick 3 Pool $70,347 Pick 4 Pool $259,856 Pick 6 Pool $106,715 Daily Double Pool $53,563 Exacta Pool $130,215 Place Pick All Pool $17,539 Quinella Pool $6,985 Superfecta Pool $92,127 Super High Five Pool $38,412 Trifecta Pool $122,914

Last Raced	#	Horse	M/Eqt.	A/S Wt	PP	St	¼	½	Str	Fin	Jockey	Cl'g Pr	Odds $1
06Nov09 4LA4	2	Company Secret	BL bf	5M 122	2	3	1¹	1⁴	1⁵	1¹½	Carter M	8000	56.40
24Oct09 5Osa8	5	Kneeling's Pride	BL f	5M 122	5	9	9	8²½	5¹½	2¹½	Quinonez A	8000	5.00
08Nov09 4Osa3	1	Msty Aly	BL b	4F 124	3	4	4¹	3½	2¹	3¹½	Valdez F	8000	2.20
30Oct09 4Osa3	4	No Cream Or Sugar	BL	4F 120	4	5	6¹	6¹½	4hd	4½	Talamo J	8000	8.20
08Nov09 4Osa4	8	Sararah Jr.	BL bf	5M 122	8	2	5⁴	5²	6²	5²½	Cedeno A	8000	11.20
30Oct09 3Osa3	10	Paddlin Mud	BL f	4F 124	9	1	2½	4hd	8²	6¹	Blanc B	8000	7.60
16Oct09 1Osa3	7	Unusually Hot	BL y	4F 115	7	6	7hd	7¹½	7hd	7nk	Santiago Reyes C	8000	2.40
04Feb09 6SA1	6	Field of Joy	B f	6M 120	6	8	8²½	9	9	8½	Berrio O A	8000	18.10
01Nov09 6Osa8	1	Bouncer	BL bf	4F 122	1	7	3hd	2¹½	3hd	9	Garcia M	8000	22.60

OFF AT 4:08 Start Good. Won driving. Track Fast.
TIME :22, :44³, :56⁴, 1:10   (:22.18, :44.67, :56.86, 1:10.10)

$2 Mutuel Prices:

2- COMPANY SECRET	114.80	46.00	14.60
5- KNEELING'S PRIDE		6.80	4.00
3- MSTY ALY			3.20

$1 EXACTA 2-5 PAID $413.90 $1 PLACE PICK ALL 8 OF 8 PAID $257.50 8 Correct
$2 QUINELLA 2-5 PAID $307.40 $1 SUPERFECTA 2-5-3-4 PAID $7,512.00
$1 SUPER HIGH FIVE 2-5-3-4-8 PAID $30,439.90 $1 TRIFECTA 2-5-3 PAID $1,025.60

Dark Bay or Brown Mare, (Mar), by Sea of Secrets - Company B by Lost Soldier. Trainer Martinez A. Rafael. Bred by Victory Racing LLC.(KY).

COMPANY SECRET had good early speed and set the pace inside, opened a clear lead on the turn, continued clear past midstretch and held under some urging and good handling. KNEELING'S PRIDE threw her head in a bit of a slow start, angled in and saved ground off the pace, moved up along the rail into and through the stretch and closed the gap to the winner. MSTY ALY stalked between horses, was shuffled back a bit into the turn, went around a rival into the stretch, came out and bested the others. NO CREAM OR SUGAR saved ground chasing the pace, came out a bit in upper stretch and lacked the needed rally. SARARAH JR. chased outside then off the rail, came four wide into the stretch and did not rally. PADDLIN MUD stalked three deep then outside a rival into the turn, continued outside on the bend, came three wide into the stretch and weakened. UNUSUALLY HOT allowed to settle outside then three deep, continued off the rail on the turn and alongside a rival into the stretch and was not a threat. FIELD OF JOY a bit slow to begin, settled outside a rival then off the rail, came out into the stretch and failed to menace. BOUNCER also a bit slow into stride, went up inside to stalk the pace, was just off the rail in the stretch and weakened.

Owners- 2, Urbina Antonia ; 5, Altamira Racing Stable and Campochiaro ; 3, Youkhanna, Joette and Joel ; 4, Omnia Racing Stable ; 8, Aquino Angela Maria; 10, Murillo Jose Luis; 7, Edwards, Craig and Karen, O'Riordan, Michael and Walsh, Kathy ; 6, Martinez Rafael A.; 1, Double JH Stable, Inc.

Trainers- 2, Martinez Rafael A.; 5, Miller Peter ; 3, DeLima Jose E.; 4, Piccioni Gerard ; 8, Aquino Angela M.; 10, Martinez Silverio; 7, Walsh Kathy ; 6, Martinez Rafael A.; 1, Mandella Gary

Breeders- 2, Victory Racing LLC. (KY); 5, Dinesh Maniar & Getaway Farms (CA); 3, River Edge Farm (CA); 4, Winning Ways Farm (KY); 8, Abrams & Robbins (CA); 10, Special T Thoroughbreds, Inc. (CA); 7, Edie Leone (CA); 6, Myung Kwon Cho (CA); 1, Mr. & Mrs. F. Gill Aulick (KY)

Unusually Hot was claimed by Dominguez Henry ; trainer, Solis Walther
Scratched- Starstruck Kristen(07Aug09 5Dmr12)

$2 Daily Double (4-2) Paid $199.20; Daily Double Pool $53,563.
$1 Pick Three (10-4-2) Paid $188.40; Pick Three Pool $70,347.
$1 Pick Four (1-10-4-2) Paid $361.40; Pick Four Pool $259,856.
$2 Pick Six (6-9-1-10-4-2) 5 Correct Paid $126.60; Pick Six Pool N/A.
$2 Pick Six (6-9-1-10-4-2) Paid $14,803.00; Pick Six Pool $106,716.

The tells for Company Secret were:

1) She appeared to be the tactical front speed; a half in :44 4/5, best of the field.

2) She had won at six furlongs.

3) She had the highest speed rating in her last race of the current race's field.

4) She was 1-1-1 at Hollywood out of seven races.

5) Her pattern of works was excellent.

6) Her post position was particularly favorable for a front runner.

7) Her lifetime earnings were second only to the favorite.

An example of both hidden front speed and a cutback horse occurred in the ninth race at Belmont on September 30, 2009. Fillies and mares three years old and up that had never won two races were going six furlongs on the turf for $25k claimers and a purse of $22k. The 1, Private Battle, was tabbed the probable favorite by the racing secretary and, for once, I agreed. By post time, however, he was an underlay at odds of 1.45/1 so I looked for a promising long shot or two.

After my analysis, two horses appeared to fit the profiles of hidden horse long shots; the 4, Judge's Pride, and the 7, Hello Gold. Judge's Pride had just completed a losing effort at five and a half furlongs on the turf at Saratoga in a $35k claimer for non-winners of two. In a field of eleven, she finished seventh: ordinarily a performance not worth spending much time on; however, I noticed that she had closed some six lengths from the top of the stretch to the finish. Looking back, I noted that in the previous race the chart writer's comments were: *reared; ducked in*. I threw that race out as if it hadn't happened.

That brought me to the third race back; seven furlongs on the turf for three and up in a $25k claimer at Belmont on July 9. In that effort she grabbed the lead with a quarter of :22 3/5, led by a length to the half mile; at the head of the stretch was second by three and a half lengths, finishing third by five. The comments were: *hustled; rapid pace*. Looking back even farther in her past performances, I noted that she had twice thrown quarters of :21 4/5 in five furlong sprints on the grass, only to fade in the stretch. I thought the key race for her was the seven furlong run in which she stayed up to the head of the stretch, indicating that she could probably get the distance in the current race.

Her morning line was 12/1, but at post time floated up to 28/1. When the New York crowd lets a horse go, they let it go. In spite of that, I thought she was a promising candidate to hit the board.

My attention next turned to the 7, Hello Gold, whose morning line was also 12/1. The fact that Jorge Chavez was up caught my eye, for I have won several good bets with his ability to keep front runners up. Hello Gold was a cutback horse, having run in eight straight distance races before the current sprint. At the half mile pole she had been either on or no more than a length from the front in seven of those races. In her last three races the comments were: *pace; tired*. The key race; however, came in the fourth race back, a one and one-sixteenth mile turf try for $25k claimers and non-winners of two. In that race Hello Gold broke on top;

led at the half; was a half length back at the top of the stretch and finished second by two and a half lengths. The comment was: *held well for second.* In the current race the bettors let her get off at odds of 19.1/1.

In the structuring of my usual long shot plays I bet both Judge's Pride and Hello Gold to win and place. (With those odds I only needed one of them to win or place.) As I thought the favorite was legitimate, I boxed Private Battle up and back with both my long shot candidates in an exacta. I then played a single ticket trifecta with the three of them boxed.

I watched with some trepidation when the gates opened and my long shots broke seventh and eleventh. At the quarter Hello Gold was ninth and far back; Judge's Pride was only four lengths from the leader and closing. At the head of the stretch, Hello Gold began to close and finished second to Private Battle, only one and three-quarter lengths out, while Judge's Pride was a half length back in third after leading at the half. My long shot plays hit the board, but for the wrong reasons; but what did reason matter when I saw the tote board light up with the exacta price of $82.50 and the trifecta payoff of $1,058. And that was with the 1.45/1 underlay favorite winning! When Hello Gold paid $15.80 to place I actually profited on my straight bets. It's a race like that which keeps you coming back for more.

Speed on the Lead

165

NINTH RACE
Belmont Park
September 30th, 2009

6 FURLONGS. (Inner Turf) (1.07) CLAIMING. Purse $22,000 INNER TURF FOR FILLIES AND MARES THREE YEARS OLD AND UPWARD WHICH HAVE NEVER WON TWO RACES. Three Year Olds, 119 lbs.; Older, 123 lbs. Non-winners of a race on the turf since July 27 Allowed 2 lbs. Claiming Price $25,000 (Races where entered for $15,000 or less not considered) (Winners Preferred). (Clear 58)

Value of Race: $22,000 Winner $13,200; second $4,400; third $2,200; fourth $1,100; fifth $660; sixth $63; seventh $63; eighth $63; ninth $63; tenth $63; eleventh $64; twelveth $61. Mutuel Pool $274,877 Pick 3 Pool $79,679 Pick 4 Pool $183,670 Pick 6 Pool $42,325 Daily Double Pool $141,956 Exacta Pool $249,220 Superfecta Pool $116,526 Trifecta Pool $190,328

Last Raced	#	Horse	M/Eqt.	A/S	Wt	PP	St	¼	½	Str	Fin	Jockey	Cl'g Pr	Odds $1
16Aug09 ^{11}Sar^{3}	1	Private Battle	L	4F	121	1	4	3^{1}	3^{1}	1^{2}	$1^{1\frac{3}{4}}$	Maragh R	25000	1.45
11Sep09 ^{7}Bel^{8}	7	Hello Gold	L f	4F	121	7	7	$9^{\frac{1}{2}}$	9^{1}	$4^{\frac{1}{2}}$	$2^{\frac{1}{2}}$	Chavez J F	25000	19.10
05Sep09 ^{12}Sar^{7}	4	Judge's Pride	L b	5M	121	4	11	$4^{\frac{1}{2}}$	$1^{\frac{1}{2}}$	$2^{2\frac{1}{2}}$	3^{1}	Rodriguez R R	25000	28.25
16May09 ^{3}WO^{2}	2	Naughty Kitty	L	3F	117	2	12	12	11^{1}	8^{2}	4no	Lezcano J	25000	4.90
05Sep09 ^{12}Sar^{6}	6	Stayawaystella	L	3F	117	6	3	6^{1}	$4^{\frac{1}{2}}$	3^{hd}	$5^{\frac{1}{2}}$	Dominguez R A	25000	3.45
11Sep09 ^{7}Bel^{9}	9	Hier Encore	L	3F	117	9	9	$10^{\frac{1}{2}}$	10^{1}	7^{1}	6^{1}	Garcia A	25000	13.40
05Sep09 ^{12}Sar^{5}	8	Lady Wynne	L	3F	117	8	5	7^{1}	$7^{\frac{1}{2}}$	6^{1}	7^{2}	Studart M	25000	18.10
05Sep09 ^{12}Sar^{8}	3	Sinister Deance	L bf	6M	121	3	1	$1^{1\frac{1}{2}}$	$2^{\frac{1}{2}}$	$5^{\frac{1}{2}}$	$8^{2\frac{1}{4}}$	Morales S	25000	118.50
05Sep09 ^{12}Sar^{11}	11	Belonged to Sy	L f	3F	117	11	8	$5^{\frac{1}{2}}$	$6^{1\frac{1}{2}}$	$10^{3\frac{1}{2}}$	9^{2}	Luzzi M J	25000	24.00
18Jly09 ^{7}Bel^{7}	10	Justinline	L	4F	121	10	6	8^{hd}	$8^{1\frac{1}{2}}$	9^{hd}	$10^{6\frac{1}{4}}$	Samyn J	25000	16.80
18Sep09 ^{2}Bel^{6}	5	Mocha Shake	L b	3F	117	5	2	$2^{1\frac{1}{2}}$	5^{1}	11^{6}	$11^{5\frac{3}{4}}$	Fuentes R D	25000	113.25
05Aug09 ^{5}Sar^{6}	12	Im a Mosaic Rocker	L b	3F	117	12	10	$11^{1\frac{1}{2}}$	12	12	12	Velasquez C H	25000	12.70

OFF AT 5:18 Start Good. Won driving. Track Yielding (Rail at 18 ft).
TIME :23, $:46^{4}$, $:58^{3}$, 1:11 (:23.18, :46.87, :58.66, 1:11.01)

$2 Mutuel Prices:				
	1- PRIVATE BATTLE	4.90	3.40	2.90
	7- HELLO GOLD		15.80	7.60
	4- JUDGE'S PRIDE			9.00

$2 EXACTA 1-7 PAID $82.50 $2 SUPERFECTA 1-7-4-2 PAID $6,005.00
$2 TRIFECTA 1-7-4 PAID $1,058.00

Bay Filly, (May), by Military - Energica by Affirmed. Trainer Levine N. Bruce. Bred by Kenny Ackerman & Saratoga Glen Farm, LLC(NY).

PRIVATE BATTLE stalked three wide for a half, shook loose after taking the lead in upper stretch and held off the runner-up under good handling. HELLO GOLD was outrun for a half then finished strongly along the rail to gain the place. JUDGE'S PRIDE checked at the start, steadied inside at the half mile pole, slipped through along the rail to gain the lead on the turn, battled into midstretch and held well to gain a share. NAUGHTY KITTY was outrun for a half after breaking slowly and rallied belatedly. STAYAWAYSTELLA saved ground to the turn, steadied along the rail in upper stretch and failed to threaten thereafter. HIER ENCORE failed to mount a serious rally while four wide. LADY WYNNE saved ground to no avail. SINISTER DEANCE set the pace to the turn and gave way. BELONGED TO SY raced up close between horses for nearly a half and tired. JUSTINLINE failed to menace. MOCHA SHAKE pressed the early pace from outside and tired on the turn. IM A MOSAIC ROCKER was outrun.

Owners- 1, Harvey Robert ; 7, D'Amelio, III Frank S.; 4, Mi Star Stables, Inc. ; 2, Ruby Stables and Klesaris, Steve ; 6, Grier Mark B.; 9, Montilli, Anthony and Juckiewicz, Thomas E. ; 8, Clemmens Judy K.; 3, Tortora Sally L.; 11, Delehanty Stable ; 10, Cohen Robert B.; 5, Lotruglio Edward ; 12, Script R Farm, Mazur, Edward, Olson, Donald, W., Teitel, Robert, Alleva, Vincent

Trainers- 1, Levine Bruce N.; 7, D'Amelio Michael Vincent; 4, DiPrima Gregory ; 2, Klesaris Steve ; 6, Hennig Mark A.; 9, Nieminski Richard S.; 8, Galluscio Dominic G.; 3, Reiff Eugene ; 11, Morrison John ; 10, Cedano Heriberto ; 5, Lotruglio Edward ; 12, Miceli Michael

Breeders- 1, Kenny Ackerman & Saratoga Glen Farm, LLC (NY); 7, Frank S. D'Amelio, Frank D'Amelio II &Michael V. D'Amelio (NY); 4, Sez Who Thoroughbreds (NY); 2, B. M. Kelley & B. P. Walden (KY); 6, Wind Hill Farm (KY); 9, Pontchertain (KY); 8, Nelson Clemmens (NY); 3, Clarke Whitaker (PA); 11, Eugene Melnyk (KY); 10, Rebecca E. Schroeder (NY); 5, Henry G. Freebern & Lance Freebern (NY); 12, Leslie Roncari Marconi (NY)

Scratched- Worth a Shot(13Sep09 ^{8}Bel^{9}), Roger's Julie(14Feb09 ^{5}GP^{9}), Vaughndidit(25Sep09 ^{3}Bel^{1}), Imandra(05Sep09 ^{12}Sar^{9})

$2 Daily Double (3-1) Paid $18.80; Daily Double Pool $141,955.
$2 Pick Three (3-3-1) Paid $47.60; Pick Three Pool $79,679.
$2 Pick Four (4-3-3-1) Paid $155.50; Pick Four Pool $183,670.
$2 Pick Six (2-14-4-3-3-1) 5 Correct Paid $51.50; Pick Six Pool N/A.
$2 Pick Six (2-14-4-3-3-1) Paid $4,422.00; Pick Six Pool $42,325.

Hello Gold's tells were:

1) She was a cutback horse, running in a six furlong sprint after eight straight mile or more races.

2) She was on the lead at the first quarter in five of those eight distance races.

3) Her jockey, Jorge Chavez, was known for being able to keep front running horses up.

The tells for Judge's Pride were:

1) Her work of :47 2/5 on August 9, 2009.

2) Though decisively beaten in her race of September 5, she closed six lengths from the top of the stretch to the finish.

3) She was dropping from a $35k claimer to a $25k claimer.

Another exceptional example of a front speed cutback hidden long shot horse occurred on October 21, 2009, at Hawthorne in a six furlong optional claiming $30k race for three year olds and up which had never won two races other than maiden, claiming, starter, state bred allowance, or which had never won three races.

The pretty young woman track handicapper spent a considerable amount of time promoting the 1, Foxie's Boy, and the 8, Hurta, as the probable favorites and the crowd obliged by making the 1 the favorite at odds of 1.9/1 and the 8 the second favorite at odds of 2.6/1. I thought they were both false favorites. Both horses had proven front speed, but Foxie's Boy had faded in the stretch in his last three races; giving up a length in his last; then four lengths after leading at the top of the stretch in the second race back; then gave up three lengths down the stretch in his third race back.

Hurta, the 8, was also a proven front runner but had given up a length and a half in the stretch in his last race after leading entering the stretch. I thought the record showed that both the touted favorites were short.

In searching for a hidden long shot candidate in the nine horse field, I landed on the 6, Big Boy Charlie. He was the only horse cutting back from a route to a sprint, having completed three consecutive one mile turf races. In his third race back at Canterbury - a $50k stakes - he ducked out and lost his rider at the quarter pole; a throw out race. In his second race back, an optional $50k claiming for non-winners of a race other than, he was on the lead and being pressed to the head of the stretch then finished fourth by four and a half lengths. The important tell was that at the six furlong call he was second by a head in 1:12 2/5. In his last race at a mile he was again close to the pace, finishing fifth by two and a quarter lengths for it all.

Big Boy Charlie had a 25% trainer and a 26% jockey; additionally, his trainer was a 27% winner in route to sprint starts, and an amazing 32% in turf to dirt starts. After breaking his maiden at Canterbury, Charlie had won two straight optional $25k claimers, showing front speed in both races. His last work, while not exceptional, was the sixth best of 56 on October 18, just three days before the current race. Clearly, the tells pointed to a big effort for Big Boy Charlie.

Again the Racing Secretary obliged the hidden long shot hunters by setting the horse's morning line at a generous 12/1. After reserving his speed for the close, Big Boy Charlie rallied from seventh at the half mile to win by a neck. He returned $26.60, 10.60, and 5.30. When the third favorite placed the exacta paid $149.80. The first two favorites that the track handicapper had spent so much screen time on finished fourth and seventh.

EIGHTH RACE
Hawthorne
October 21st, 2009

6 FURLONGS. (1.07¹) ALLOWANCE OPTIONAL CLAIMING. Purse $28,000 FOR THREE YEAR OLDS AND UPWARD WHICH HAVE NEVER WON TWO RACES OTHER THAN MAIDEN, CLAIMING, STARTER, OR STATE BRED ALLOWANCE OR WHICH HAVE NEVER WON THREE RACES OR CLAIMING PRICE $30,000, IF FOR $25,000 ALLOWED 2 LBS. Three Year Olds, 121 lbs.; Older, 124 lbs. Non-winners of a race since September 21 Allowed 2 lbs. (Claiming races for $20,000 or less not considered in estimating allowances) (Preference By Condition Eligibility). (Clear 59)

Value of Race: $28,000 ($15,288 reverts) Winner $16,800; second $5,600; third $3,080; fourth $1,680; fifth $840. Mutuel Pool $84,974 Pick 3 Pool $4,092 Exacta Pool $69,901 Superfecta Pool $32,321 Trifecta Pool $51,329

Last Raced	#	Horse	M/Eqt.	A/S Wt	PP	St	¼	½	Str	Fin	Jockey	Cl'g Pr	Odds $1
18Sep09 8AP5	6	Big Boy Charlie	L bf	3G 119	6	7	86½	7½	3½	1nk	Sukie D	30000	12.30
20Sep09 9AP5	10	Prestidigitation	L	4G 122	9	6	61½	4½	2¹	22¾	Thornton T		4.20
02May09 9Prm6	9	Hold That Broad	L b	3C 119	8	4	4½	3¹	1½	3½	Smith A		18.90
02Oct09 7Haw4	8	Hurta	L f	6G 122	7	5	5½	5½	5²	4no	Ocampo I		2.60
02Oct09 7Haw5	5	Caruso	L b	5G 122	5	2	2¹	2¹	4¹	58½	Silva C H		7.90
27Aug09 5AP4	4	Big Red Ranger	L	6G 122	4	8	7¹	84½	7hd	6²	Razo, Jr. E	30000	12.90
23May09 1AP4	1	Foxie's Boy	L f	7G 122	1	1	1¹	1¹	6³	7nk	Ferrer J C		1.90
04Oct09 9Haw3	2	Next Adventure	L bf	5G 122	2	9	9	9	9	84 86½	Riggs T		16.40
14Sep09 2Prm4	3	Getchamotorrollin	L	3G 119	3	3	3hd	6¹	9	9	Molina T		29.10

OFF AT 4:52   Start Good For All But NEXT ADVENTURE. Won driving. Track Fast.
TIME :21⁴, :45², :57⁴, 1:10³   (:21.98, :45.59, :57.80, 1:10.65)

$2 Mutuel Prices:	6- BIG BOY CHARLIE	26.60	10.60	5.20
	10- PRESTIDIGITATION		6.20	4.40
	9- HOLD THAT BROAD			8.40

$2 EXACTA 6-10 PAID $149.80 $1 SUPERFECTA 6-10-9-8 PAID $3,138.90
$2 TRIFECTA 6-10-9 PAID $1,296.80

Bay Gelding, (Apr), by Include - Lake Huron by Salt Lake. Trainer Robertson McLean. Bred by Brereton C. Jones(KY).

BIG BOY CHARLIE reserved early, swung six wide into the stretch, rallied and was up in time. PRESTIDIGITATION settled well, moved five wide into the stretch, finished well, late but was caught. HOLD THAT BROAD raced in striking position while four wide, continued four wide into the stretch, led at the furlong marker but was worn down. HURTA outpaced early, entered the stretch three wide and lacked the needed rally. CARUSO stalked the pace and weakened. BIG RED RANGER was outrun. FOXIE'S BOY gained the lead, was headed the leaving turn and gave way. NEXT ADVENTURE was unprepared at the start and lost all chance. GETCHAMOTORROLLIN raced forwardly along the inside and faded.

Owners- 6, Jer-Mar Stable LLC ; 10, R. M. Living Trust ; 9, Auglyn Stables, Burlingham, Ruffolo, Jackson, Osterland, and Cherrywood Racing ; 8, Clarizio, III Louis ; 5, Asiel Stable ; 4, Thunderhead Farms ; 1, Scarlet Stable ; 2, Bruner Terry ; 3, Lafoy Jeff

Trainers- 6, Robertson McLean ; 10, Catalano Wayne M.; 9, Boyce Michele ; 8, Tomillo Thomas F.; 5, Hazelton Richard P.; 4, Von Hemel Don ; 1, Brueggemann Roger A.; 2, Zavash Kerry ; 3, McShane David D.

Breeders- 6, Brereton C. Jones (KY); 10, Calumet Farm (KY); 9, Karl M. Hohensee (FL); 8, Craig L. Wheeler (FL); 5, Asiel Stable (IL); 4, Gilbert G. Campbell (FL); 1, William P Stiritz (IL); 2, Respite Farm (KY); 3, Paul Tackett (KY)

Scratched- Biglie Smallworld(16Sep09 9Hoo²), Last Wompus(25Sep09 9AP¹)

$2 Pick Three (1-9-6) Paid $613.40; Pick Three Pool $4,092.

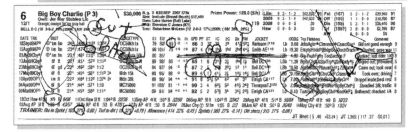

The tells on Big Boy Charlie were:

1) He was a cutback horse, having shown speed to the head of the stretch in three route races.

2) His trainer was a 25% winner; a 27% winner when moving his horses from route to sprint; an amazing 32% winner when moving his horses from turf to dirt. His jockey was a 26% winner.

3) His work of :49 for four furlongs on October 18, three days before the race, which would ordinarily be a humdrum effort was; nevertheless, the second best work of the field.

Early foot was the dominant factor in the seventh race at Tampa Bay on December 16, 2009. Ten entries went to the post in the seven furlong $8k claimer on the dirt for three year olds and up that had never won three races.

No less than six horses were bet down to odds of less than 8.4/1. I thought the 10, Slievenamon, was a fair pick by the racing secretary as the 5/2 favorite, but the betting indicated that the race was wide open.

In looking for "best works" horses my attention was drawn to the 8, Exchange The Limit, a shipper from Suffolk Downs. The horse's works of :48 4/5 for four furlongs on November 28 and :48 3/5 on December 4 were the best works of the field by a considerable margin. They were the horse's best works in the last year and a half. The gelding was cutting back from a mile and seventy yards race in which he was close to the front at the second call then weakened somewhere between the half mile post to the head of the stretch, finishing seventh in a field of nine. I was struck by the fact that he was on the lead at the first call in nine of his last ten races.

Unfortunately, Exchange The Limit also badly quit in six of those tries. Could he be the only front speed in the race? I then examined the first quarter times of the field in all of their published past performances. On the 14th and 29th of September, he had booked consecutive quarters of :21 4/5 and :21 2/5, respectively. No other horse in the current race had booked less than a :22 2/5 first quarter in any of their published past performances.

His trainer was a 13% winner; 14% when moving a horse up one class, while his jockey had won at a rate of 14%. It appeared that Exchange The Limit was the sole front speed of the race. He was also cutting back in distance in addition to having the fastest pre-race workout times.

The Limit's morning line was 15/1 but the bettors thought he should be more like 50/1 and let him leave the gate at that price, after which he gained an easy one and a half length lead at the half in :45 3/5, then coasted to the finish to win by over two lengths.

He paid $102.60, 31.40, and 15.40. When the second favorite placed, the $2 exacta paid $1,218. The betting public was sure he would stop again, but the tells were clear: if he gained the easy lead that his works and prior races indicated he could, there would be no stopping him this time. The clear tells were there for the finding by the hidden horse hunters.

The placing of the minimum hidden horse long shot candidate bet of $10 to win and place and a $5 exacta box with the first two favorites would have returned $3,715 for the investment of $40. Don't join the crowd in lamenting: *If only, would have, could have, should have,* for there's gold in them there tells!

SEVENTH RACE
Tampa Bay
December 16th, 2009

7 FURLONGS. (1.22¹) CLAIMING. Purse $9,300 FOR THREE YEAR OLDS AND UPWARD WHICH HAVE NEVER WON THREE RACES. Three Year Olds, 120 lbs.; Older, 122 lbs. Non-winners of a race since October 16 Allowed 2 lbs. A race since September 16 Allowed 4 lbs. Claiming Price $8,000 (Races Where Entered For $6,25 0 Or Less Not Considered In Weight Allowances). (Cloudy 73)

Value of Race: $9,300 Winner $5,580; second $1,674; third $1,023; fourth $465; fifth $93; sixth $93; seventh $93; eighth $93; ninth $93; tenth $93. Mutuel Pool $144,261 Daily Double Pool $16,704 Exacta Pool $132,849 Superfecta Pool $45,548 Trifecta Pool $91,859

Last Raced	#	Horse	M/Eqt.	A/S	Wt	PP	St	¼	½	Str	Fin	Jockey	Cl'g Pr	Odds $1
27Oct09 ^{9}Suf^{7}	8	Exchange the Limit	L b	3G	116	8	1	2½	$1^{1\frac{1}{2}}$	$1^{3\frac{1}{2}}$	$1^{2\frac{1}{4}}$	Amiss D D	8000	50.30
24Nov09 ^{10}Pha^{4}	10	Slievenamon	L b	3G	118	10	8	5½	4^{1}	3^{1}	2½	Gonzalez L A	8000	3.00
13Nov09 ^{2}Pen^{5}	9	Timeoutforthejudge	L	3C	111	9	4	3½	3^{hd}	2^{1}	3½	Rincon G	8000	4.40
08Nov09 ^{1}Crc^{4}	5	Misfit Manny	L b	5G	118	5	7	$7^{1\frac{1}{2}}$	5½	4½	4^{nk}	Bernal O	8000	2.90
04Nov09 ^{7}Suf^{5}	7	Capulet	L b	3G	116	7	2	4½	$6^{1\frac{1}{2}}$	5½	$5^{1\frac{1}{4}}$	Ramgeet A R	8000	3.90
19Oct09 ^{6}FE^{6}	3	Buck Cash	L f	3G	120	3	6	6^{hd}	8^{5}	6^{3}	$6^{9\frac{3}{4}}$	Bush V	8000	6.70
26Apr09 ^{8}Tam^{5}	6	Whip the Groom	L b	4G	118	6	9	9½	7^{1}	7^{1}	7¾	Galviz W	8000	59.70
04Jan09 ^{6}Tam^{6}	2	Raleigh Express	L bf	7G	118	2	10	10	9^{1}	9^{4}	$8^{3\frac{3}{4}}$	Feliciano R	8000	80.70
15Nov09 ^{7}Crc^{8}	4	Atsatsuki	L b	3G	116	4	3	$1^{1\frac{1}{2}}$	2^{2}	8^{2}	9^{5}	Allen, Jr. R D	8000	8.40
24Aug09 ^{5}Del^{5}	1	Holy Limerick	L b	3G	116	1	5	8½	10	10	10	Ortiz F L	8000	20.50

OFF AT 3:41 Start Good. Won driving. Track Fast.
TIME :22², :45³, 1:11¹, 1:25² (:22.59, :45.63, 1:11.30, 1:25.53)

$2 Mutuel Prices:

8- EXCHANGE THE LIMIT	102.60	31.40	15.40
10- SLIEVENAMON		5.40	3.40
9- TIMEOUTFORTHEJUDGE			4.40

$2 EXACTA 8-10 PAID $604.00 $1 SUPERFECTA 8-10-9-5 PAID $7,176.10
$2 TRIFECTA 8-10-9 PAID $2,310.00

Dark Bay or Brown Gelding, (Feb), by Exchange Rate - Beyond the Limit by Unbridled. Trainer McCarthy Brenda. Bred by Patricia Generazio(FL).

EXCHANGE THE LIMIT chased the leader early, took over in the turn, drew off to mid stretch then had enough left to prevail late under pressure. SLIEVENAMON was hung wide much of the trip, fanned five wide into the stretch then was slowly gaining while outfinishing the rest. TIMEOUTFORTHEJUDGE came in a bit in the turn, angled to the rail for the drive then gained some ground late. MISFIT MANNY steadied in the turn then lodged a mild rally late. CAPULET was shuffled back in the turn, angled outside then lodged a mild rally. BUCK CASH made a mild gain late. WHIP THE GROOM raced evenly. RALEIGH EXPRESS failed to menace. ATSATSUKI sprinted clear early but gave way after five furlongs. HOLY LIMERICK showed little. A claim of foul by the rider of MISFIT MANNY against TIMEOUTFORTHEJUDGE for interference in the turn was disallowed.

Owners- 8, George David C.; 10, Wisteria Lane Stable ; 9, Pecoraro Racing Stable ; 5, Van Worp Robert E.; 7, Surya Avatar Racing LLC ; 3, Cummins Leslee ; 6, Gardea Adela ; 2, Moreland Annie ; 4, Blackacre Farms, Inc. ; 1, Vina Del Mar Thoroughbreds LLC

Trainers- 8, McCarthy Brenda ; 10, Ryan Derek S.; 9, Pecoraro Matteo ; 5, Behrens Ronald P.; 7, Wilson Tony ; 3, Burns David R.; 6, Behrens Ronald P.; 2, Jeffries Robert A.; 4, O'Connell Kathleen ; 1, Wasiluk, Jr. Peter

Breeders- 8, Patricia Generazio (FL); 10, Clover Leaf Farms II, Inc. (FL); 9, Jo Halleck Finley & Joe McMahon (NY); 5, Robert Van Worp (FL); 7, Padua Stables (FL); 3, Charles A. Woodson Jr. (WV); 6, Dr. Alfonso E. Martinez (FL); 2, Donald Wilson (FL); 4, Joseph Barbazon & Helen Barbazon (FL); 1, Rosebrook Farms, LLC (FL)

$2 Daily Double (1-8) Paid $807.00; Daily Double Pool $16,704.

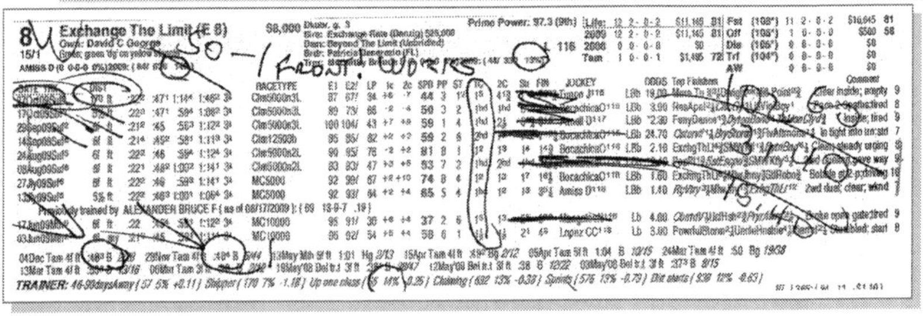
8 Exchange The Limit (E 8) $8,000
15/1
Own: David C George
Prime Power: 97.3 (9th)
Life: 12 2 - 0 - 2 $11,145 81
2009 12 2 - 0 - 2 $11,145 81
116
Previously trained by ALEXANDER BRUCE F
TRAINER: 46-90daysAway (57 5% +0.11) Shipper (170 7% -1.18) Up one class (55 14% 0.25) Claiming (632 13% -0.38) Sprints (576 13% -0.73) Dirt starts (930 12% -0.63)

Front speed is always dangerous, but tactical speed is golden. The best jockeys are those who have sound judgment in knowing at just what point in the race to ask for that extra burst of speed, for most thoroughbreds can only maintain their top speed for a half mile or so. It has been my experience that proven front speed in a cutback horse is one of the most reliable tells of a hidden long shot candidate. When a horse like Big Boy Charlie exhibits front speed in a route race and carries it to six furlongs near or on the lead before fading, and the time is 1:12 2/5 for that interior call, then he will probably run a competitive race when he is then entered in a sprint race. That's exactly what Charlie did, bringing home a huge payoff. The surprise was that he closed from off the pace to win. But then, in this game, we are not playing *how* but - *how much!*

Each of the seven horses examined in this chapter had the same tells: exceptional, if not the best of the field pre-race workouts and were consistent front runners. Additionally, three of the winners were cutback horses.

Consistent front speed in a horse's past performance is tempting. The years have taught me never to bet a front speed horse that is a substantial underlay. Many times; however, there is hidden front speed in cutback races that the public lets go at substantial overlay odds. This kind of value bet is worth the time it takes to thoroughly analyze the quality of a hidden horse's speed and to turn that information into a value bet on a long shot competitor. A horse with tactical speed (that is, the ability to use it in short bursts at appropriate points in the race) is always dangerous, especially at the break. Generally, though, the rule is that when there is only one front speed horse in the race that horse will usually carry his speed to the wire (especially if Jorge "chop-chop" Chavez is in the irons), assuming the horse is on class. When there are two or more consistent front runners in the race, look elsewhere for the winner. Don't bet that a horse that has won on the front at six furlongs can carry its speed beyond that distance until it has proven that it can.

Always look for the proven front runner that appears to be the only front speed in the race, for sole speed on the lead is a joy to behold for the punter. Be wary of front speed when there are two or more front speed horses in the race. And remember that front speed is often concealed within a *cutback* race.

Chapter 7

Pace Makes the Race on the Green

There is something about a turf race that is missing from the dirt and synthetic surface races. Yes, you might reply - grass. To which I answer: of course, hastening to add that in addition there is the matter of consistency of form. In over 40 years of handicapping - which includes 10 years of owning, breeding, and racing thoroughbred horses - I have found turf runners, and especially route turf runners, consistently perform more true to form than those that run on dirt and the synthetic surfaces.

The question naturally arises: how does the percentage of hidden long shot winners on the grass compare with the other running surfaces? It has been my experience that there is little difference; tells are tells whether on grass or dirt or synthetic tracks. Many handicappers teach that you should learn all about grass breeding sires but I have found that to be wasted time. How do you know if a first time starter can run on the grass? Has it run on the grass? If it hasn't then the bettor is foolish to bet that a horse can handle the turf on its first try. It is a foolish bet to wager on first time starters – period; whatever the racing surface.

Most turf courses are narrow and the turns are tight, generally giving the advantage to inside post runners, especially at Belmont and Saratoga. On those courses outside post runners are at a distinct disadvantage. Frequently, the betting public will overlook a good effort from a horse whose previous race was from an outside post on the grass and who finished some four or five lengths back. Give that same horse an inside post and considerable improvement can be expected, assuming the class of the race and the distance are similar to the previous race.

One of the problems with the handicapping of foreign turf runners is that when they ship to this country and are first time starters here there are few and far between tells, for the reason that foreign chart writers have their own peculiar style which provides precious little information on their past performances in Europe or Great Britain. They disdain giving the times of the fractions of the race, such as at the one-quarter and half-mile posts. You get their position at the finish and the time of the winner of the race and the names of the second and third place finishers; that's about it, except for some often nearly unintelligible comments describing a particular horse's positions during the race. Because of that, the works of a foreign horse in this country prior to its first race here are especially important as is the record of the trainer with grass horses.

The Breeder's Cup turf races are particularly difficult to handicap because so many foreign turf horse's connections are attracted to the huge purses and the prestige a Breeder's Cup win brings. If we want to bet on foreign turf horses, we have to make do with the information that is in their past performances; including their recent works; the records of their trainers and jockeys, and how the turf horse has performed from various post positions.

This is an example of a foreign turf chart writer's comments: *Chsd ldrs; hmpd ov 1f out; sn rdn & wknd.* What are we to make of this? We can only guess that the writer meant: *Chased leaders; hampered over one furlong out; (surely the word wasn't "humped") soon ridden and weakened.* The American handicapper can probably assume from these tortured comments that the horse did not run on the front.

Another example from the same past performance of the same foreign runner: *Trkd ldr; hdwy 2f out; chs wnr & ev ch 1f out; ; drvn; one pc fnl f.* How can we make sense of these confusing abridging attempts at describing how that horse ran in that race? Did the chart writer mean: *Tracked leaders; headway 2 furlongs out; chased winner & even chased (even chance?)1 furlong out; driven; one paced final furlong.* Call me dense if they wish; but what do they mean by "one paced" and "even chance?" Was the horse head and head with the leader or just close about?

Nevertheless, if you are going to bet on foreign horses you must learn to read these comments. We can assume that when the chart writer comments: *tracked leaders,* the horse was near the front; not at the back of the pack. Sometimes, if we try hard, we can even deduce that the horse was a stretch runner.

Here are some other remarkable examples: *raced keenly*; (don't all thoroughbreds race keenly? Generally, they just don't lollygag around the track); *held up*; (In American English we call it - *reserved*); *stayed on strongly*; (on this side of the pond we use:

driving). At least there is enough information in the foreign turf chart writer's comments to determine if the horse is a front runner, deep router, or mid-pack closer.

Like it or not, we must become proficient in interpreting these abbreviations if we are to wager successfully on foreign horses who have not run in this country. The lack of information provided by the chart writers for the past performances of foreign runners will apparently always be with us: it is tradition, perhaps going as far back as Eclipse. As Kenny Rogers was fond of saying: (or, if he didn't, he should have) "We have to play with the cards we are dealt, once we have made our draw."

One variable that foreign and American chart writers have in common is in the descriptions of the conditions of the running surfaces. We are all familiar with the standard descriptions of the conditions of dirt and synthetic tracks: *ft, gd, sy, and my* - fast, good, sloppy, and muddy. The correlating track condition descriptions for races on the grass are: *fm, gd, yl, and sf* - firm, good, yielding, and soft. Generally, there are not a lot of turf races bearing the track condition description as soft as most tracks in this country take their races off the turf in what would be sloppy conditions for a dirt or synthetic track surface. In handicapping the turf races it is important to note which horses have performed well on a good or yielding surface and which have failed to handle that track condition.

While many handicappers prefer to back deep routers in distance races on the grass, the records reveal that most of these races are won by mid-pace closers; that is, horses that get out no worse than five or six lengths from the lead, then gradually close. The pace must break just right for the deep closer to win; too often they finish a closing third or fourth.

The following example illustrates the difficulty of correctly determining the form of the past performances of foreign turf runners who are making their first try on the grass in this country. The past performance recap is that of a false underlay co-favorite that failed.

In an optional $40k turf race for three year olds and up going one mile at Oaktree-Santa Anita on October 28, 2009, the 1, Bombina, was bet down from a morning line of 6/1 to an underlay of 3/1. Bombina had not raced in this country; her last race was in Great Britain on August 6, 2009, at Yarmouth in which she finished fifth, six lengths back, in a mile $7,592 allowance race on the turf. In seven starts the filly had won twice, placed once, and showed once; her lifetime winnings were all of $14,757. Yet the public cut her morning line odds in half. Why?

The foreign chart writer's comments were of little help. What is the American handicapper to make of the comments regarding Bombina's last race in Great Britain before shipping to Santa Anita? We know that she finished fifth, six lengths behind the winner that posted a time of 1:37 3/5 for the mile over a good track. By using a little inverse deduction (a favorite of Sherlock Holmes: the punter has to be a little like Sherlock if he is to consistently pull hidden horse candidates out of the forests of their tells), we can deduce that Bombina ran the mile in 1:38 4/5. We don't know how she broke from the gate, nor do we know her position at the quarter or half mile posts, nor her position on entering the stretch.

What we know is this: *Chsd ldrs; hmpd ov 1f out; sn rdn & wknd.*
In English we must assume the meaning was: Chased leaders; hampered over 1 furlong out; soon ridden and weakened. When the commenter says "chased leaders" what did he mean? All horses in all races chase the leaders. Is "hampered" the same as "steadied?" As you can see, the lack of intermediate position calls is anyone's guess. As far as the comments of the foreign chart writers are concerned, they might as well be written in French or Latin, for it is all Greek to me.

I thought the racing secretary set a fair morning line on Bombino at 6/1, though mine was closer to 10/1. The betting public bet her down to near favoritism. I searched for a reason to justify that kind of backing. My guess was that it was probably because of the three consecutive good works preceding this race. On October 11 she worked four furlongs in :47 3/5; on October 17 she worked five furlongs in 1:00; and on October 23, five days before this race, she worked five furlongs in :59 3/5. These are indisputably superior works; however, they were not on the grass. Bombina finished sixth in a field of seven, after trailing for most of the race. It is probably not a good bet to wager on a foreign horse's first start in this country, no matter the quality of the horse's pre-race workouts. If you decide to make the bet, it's a good idea to make sure the superior works were on the turf.

SEVENTH RACE
Oak Tree
October 28th, 2009

1 MILE. (Turf) (.00) ALLOWANCE OPTIONAL CLAIMING. Purse $40,000 FOR FILLIES AND MARES THREE YEARS OLD AND UPWARD WHICH HAVE NEVER WON $10,000 OTHER THAN MAIDEN, CLAIMING OR STARTER OR WHICH HAVE NEVER WON TWO RACES OR OPTIONAL CLAIMING PRICE OF $40,000. Three Year Olds, 120 lbs.; Older, 124 lbs. Non-winners of a race other than Maiden, Claiming or Starter since November 2, 2008 Allowed 2 lbs. A race since August 29 Allowed 4 lbs. (Maiden and Claiming races for $32,000 or less not considered) (Rail at 30 feet). referred). (Rail at 30 feet). (Clear 71)

Value of Race: $43,200 ($9,600 reverts) Winner $24,000; second $10,400; third $4,800; fourth $2,400; fifth $800; sixth $400; seventh $400. Mutuel Pool $212,905 Pick 3 Pool $31,363 Daily Double Pool $18,696 Exacta Pool $118,121 Superfecta Pool $62,944 Trifecta Pool $92,546

Last Raced	#	Horse	M/Eqt.	A/S Wt	PP	St	¼	½	¾	Str	Fin	Jockey	Cl'g Pr	Odds $1
07Oct09 4Osa3	3	Mohaka	BL	4F 120	3	3	31	31	32	2½	1½	Gomez G K		2.70
09Oct09 5Osa2	2	My Maloof Rocker	BL b	4F 124	2	1	11	12	12	1½	22	Bejarano R	40000	7.20
02Oct09 7Osa1	6	Dextera (GER)	BL b	3F 118	6	7	62½	61	61½	51	3½	Flores D R		4.60
30Sep09 7Osa3	4	Andalacia (IRE)	BL	3F 116	4	4	51	51½	5½	41½	41	Solis A O		3.40
07Oct09 4Osa5	7	Malibu Win	BL b	3F 112	7	5	2½	2hd	2hd	3½	5hd	Santiago Reyes C		9.30
06Aug09 YAR5	1	Bombina (GB)	BL	3F 120	1	6	7	7	7	7	61	Espinoza V		3.00
08Oct09 7Osa5	5	Fire n' Brimstone	BL	4F 120	5	2	4½	4hd	41	6½	7	Blanc B		18.20

OFF AT 4:09 Start Good. Won driving. Track Firm (Rail at 30 ft).
TIME :243, :483, 1:114, 1:231, 1:344   (:24.61, :48.70, 1:11.92, 1:23.30, 1:34.86)

$2 Mutuel Prices:

3- MOHAKA	7.40	4.20	2.40
2- MY MALOOF ROCKER		6.40	3.60
6- DEXTERA (GER)			3.60

$1 EXACTA 3-2 PAID $19.60 $1 SUPERFECTA 3-2-6-4 PAID $261.40
$1 TRIFECTA 3-2-6 PAID $80.00

Bay Filly, (Feb), by Belong to Me - Beauty Queen by Fighting Fit. Trainer Semkin Sam. Bred by Wakefield Farm(KY).

MOHAKA stalked the pace inside, came out into the stretch, bid alongside the runner-up under a left handed crack of the whip, gained the lead in deep stretch and gamely prevailed under energetic handling. MY MALOOF ROCKER sped to the early lead, set the pace a bit off the rail then came out a bit into the stretch, fought back inside the winner in the final furlong and continued willingly. DEXTERA (GER) pulled a bit and chased outside a rival or just off the rail, came out three deep into the stretch and edged a foe for the show. ANDALACIA (IRE) was in a good position stalking the pace inside to the stretch, remained along the rail and was outfinished for third. MALIBU WIN close up stalking the pace outside a rival, came three deep into the stretch and could not offer the necessary late kick. BOMBINA (GB) saved ground off the pace, came out a bit into the stretch, angled back in, was in a little close of heels past midstretch and lacked the needed rally. FIRE N' BRIMSTONE stalked outside a rival, was between horses into the stretch and could not summon the needed response.

Owners- 3, Kelly Jon S.; 2, Giordano, Lou, Featherston, Roger and Miller, Tom and Lynne ; 6, Fontana Racing LLC and Pearson, Deron ; 4, Team Valor International ; 7, Martin Racing Stable LLC, Capestro, Paula and England, Greg ; 1, M Racing ; 5, A and R Stables LLC and Class Racing Stable

Trainers- 3, Semkin Sam ; 2, Troeger Robert ; 6, Cassidy James M.; 4, Gallagher Patrick ; 7, Capestro Paula S.; 1, Walsh Kathy ; 5, Hofmans David E.

Breeders- 3, Wakefield Farm (KY); 2, Winfield S. Tuttle (CA); 6, Gestut Ebbesloh (GER); 4, Mountarmstrong Stud (IRE); 7, Paula Capestro Bloodstock LLC (PA); 1, Dukes Stud & Overbury Stallions Ltd (GB); 5, Hinkle Farms (KY)

$2 Daily Double (1-3) Paid $26.60; Daily Double Pool $18,696.
$1 Pick Three (6-1-3) Paid $47.40; Pick Three Pool $31,363.

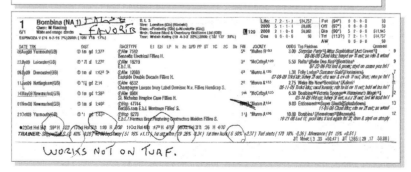

WORKS NOT ON TURF.

Turf handicapping can be rewarding, even if a hidden horse long shot is difficult to find because of the high percentage of grass races that run to form. The tells are more subtle than those for horses running on dirt or synthetic tracks, and there are slightly more variables. The handicapper must carefully check a trainer's record on the turf and his record when moving a horse from dirt or synthetic surfaces to the grass. For whatever reasons, there are more front speed winners on the dirt and synthetic surface races than on the turf. It seems to me that the jockeys must be more patient on the turf, and must be able to negotiate the tight turns without losing valuable ground.

One of the most important variables to be considered in handicapping turf route races is the Brisnet late pace rating, an invaluable tool in determining the relative stamina of the distance runners. While the Beyer numbers in the *Daily Racing Form* are equally important in determining whether or not a horse can carry its speed for the distance, the Brisnet late pace number is just as predictive: both of these variables are invaluable tells too often overlooked by the betting public.

An example occurred on February 21, 2010, in a one and a half mile turf stakes at Santa Anita. The eighth race was the $150k San Luis Obispo Handicap for four year olds and up.

The racing secretary spent a considerable amount of pre-race air time in touting his morning line favorite, the 1, Dynamic Range. At first glance at the past performances it appeared he could make a decent case for his tout: the horse had finished a close up fourth in his last race, the Grade 2 San Marcos at one and one quarter mile on the turf. After examining the seven other entries, I concluded that Dynamic Range was probably a false favorite.

My attention was drawn to the 3, Bourbon Bay. He had won his last race, an optional claiming $40k at a mile and a half on the turf, earning a 104 Brisnet late pace rating, second best of the field and two points higher than the 1. Rafael Bejarano was up; a "money" jockey if ever there was one. The 8, Sudden War, appeared to be the only front speed but it appeared that Bourbon Bay had enough early speed to lay just off the pace.

Since late pace would be crucial at this distance, I examined the past performances of each entry and marked the best late pace figure of the last three races. The 3, Bourbon Bay, was at 104; the 4, Romp, was 107; the 5, Unusual Suspect, was at 104, and the 8, was at 103. The 1, Dynamic Range, was close by at 102; I eliminated him for entirely different reasons.

I decided to box the 3, 4, 5, and 8 in a $2 exacta and then bet a $1 trifecta and $1 superfecta box. In a well judged ride, Bejarano stalked the 8, Sudden War, to the head of the stretch then turned Bourbon Bay loose to win by half a dozen lengths going away. Clearly, one of the more important variables in a distance race is that of the late pace rating. It is another tell that should not be overlooked

EIGHTH RACE
Santa Anita
February 21st, 2010

1¼ MILES. (Turf) (2.224) STAKES. Purse $150,000 *SAN LUIS OBISPO H. (GRADE II)* FOR FOUR-YEAR-OLDS AND UPWARD. By subscription of $150 each to accompany the nomination. Closed February 11th, 2010 with 13. $1,500 additional to start, with $150,000 guaranteed.of which $90,000 to second, $30,000 to second, $18,000 to third, $9,000 to fo urth and $3,000 to fifth. A trophy will be presented to the owner of the winner. (Rail at 15 feet.) t 15 feet). (Cloudy 64)

Value of Race: $150,000 Winner $90,000; second $30,000; third $18,000; fourth $9,000; fifth $3,000. Mutuel Pool $395,459 Pick 3
Pool $67,033 Daily Double Pool $37,537 Exacta Pool $211,092 Superfecta Pool $138,982 Trifecta Pool $196,675

Last Raced	# Horse	M/Eql	A/S	Wt	PP	¼	½	1m	1¼	Str	Fin	Jockey	Odds $1
06Jan10 7SA1	3 Bourbon Bay	BL b	4G	114	3	2¹	2¹	2½	2¹	1½	1⁴¼	Bejarano R	3.80
30Jan10 8SA6	5 Unusual Suspect	BL b	6H	115	5	7⁴½	7⁴	7⁴	6¹½	3²	2¹½	Quinonez A	12.30
31Dec09 7SA3	8 Sudden War (ARG)	BL	5G	116	7	1¹½	1¹½	1¹½	1¹½	2²½	3¹³½	Solis A O	2.70
06Jan10 7SA3	4 Romp (ARG)	BL b	6G	114	4	8	8	8	8	8	4rk	Sutherland C	25.00
19Dec09 3Hol6	6 Obrigado (FR)	BL b	7G	116	6	6²	6¹	6hd	4hd	4½	5⁵½	Rosario J	7.50
24Jan10 8SA7	9 Porfido (CHI)	BL b	8H	116	8	4²	4¹½	4²	5hd	7²	6¹½	Talamo J	8.40
24Jan10 8SA4	1 Dynamic Range	BL b	4G	117	1	5¹½	3hd	3hd	3¹	6¹	7³¼	Espinoza V	2.10
14Jan10 7SA6	2 Sir Dave	BL	5G	116	2	3½	5¹½	5½	7½	8	8	Flores D R	15.50

OFF AT 4:08 Start Good. Won driving. Track Firm (Rail at 15 ft).
TIME :25, :49⁴, 1:15, 1:41, 2:05², 2:284   (:25.03, :49.89, 1:15.14, 1:41.12, 2:05.53, 2:28.89)

$2 Mutuel Prices:

3- BOURBON BAY	9.60	5.20	4.20
5- UNUSUAL SUSPECT		10.00	6.00
8- SUDDEN WAR (ARG)			4.20

$1 EXACTA 3-5 PAID $63.50 $1 SUPERFECTA 3-5-8-4 PAID $3,172.00
$1 TRIFECTA 3-5-8 PAID $317.80

Bay Gelding, (Feb), by Sligo Bay (IRE) - Coral Necklace by Conquistador Cielo. Trainer Drysdale D. Neil. Bred by Adena Springs(KY).

BOURBON BAY stalked the pace just off the rail, bid alongside SUDDEN WAR in the stretch to gain the lead and drew clear in the final furlong under a left handed crack of the whip and a brisk hand ride. UNUSUAL SUSPECT saved ground chasing the pace, came out into the stretch and gained the place. SUDDEN WAR (ARG) took the early lead, set the pace a bit off the rail then inside, fought back into the stretch and until past the eighth pole and held third. ROMP (ARG) settled off the pace inside, saved ground, came out into the stretch, split rivals in midstretch and could not summon the needed late kick. OBRIGADO (FR) settled off the rail then outside a rival, went three deep into and on the second turn and four wide into the stretch and lacked the needed rally. PORFIDO (CHI) close up stalking the pace outside a foe three deep into and on the second turn and into the stretch, weakened. DYNAMIC RANGE saved ground tracking the pace to the stretch and also weakened. SIR DAVE pulled his way along inside then hopped onto the main track crossing and again onto the course proper, chased off the rail then outside a rival, came out into the stretch and had little left for the drive. Rail on hill at 7 feet.

Owners- 3, Heerensperger, David and Jill ; 5, Abrams, Barry, David and Dyan ; 8, Magdelena Racing, Frazier, Bruce and Hughes, Bill ; 4, Sisters in Racing Stable and Siskin, Jeff ; 6, Seidler, Gary and Vegso, Peter ; 9, Sumaya Us Stables ; 1, Mercedes Stables LLC ; 2, La Canada Stables LLC

Trainers- 3, Drysdale Neil D.; 5, Abrams Barry ; 8, McPeek Kenneth G.; 4, Mulhall Kristin ; 6, Drysdale Neil D.; 9, Ascanio Humberto ; 1, Canani Julio C.; 2, Carava Jack

Breeders- 3, Adena Springs (KY); 5, David Abrams (CA); 8, San Francisco De Pilar (ARG); 4, John T. Behrendt (ARG); 6, M. Didier Blot & M. Christian De Asis Irsen (FR); 9, Haras Sumaya (CHI); 1, Mercedes Stables, LLC (KY); 2, Gilbert G. Campbell (FL)

Scratched- Troubletimesthree(31Jan10 6SA8)

$2 Daily Double (7-3) Paid $39.20; Daily Double Pool $37,537.
$1 Pick Three (2-7-3) Paid $178.10; Pick Three Pool $67,033.

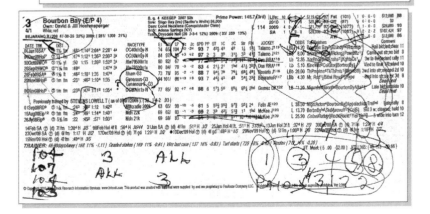

With all of the complications that come with turf racing, I have to admit; nevertheless, that it's my favorite racing surface for the grass is an especially fertile field in which to find hidden horse long shot candidates, and a race on the turf is a thing of beauty and a sight to behold for thoroughbred horse racing fans.

Chapter 8

Hidden in Plain Sight

Too often the betting public is inordinately influenced by the morning line odds set by the track racing secretary. Handicappers - especially the hidden horse hunters - would be better off if they never saw the morning line odds. To their detriment, the form players too often believe the line on an odds-on horse. Experience has taught me never to bet on a horse going off at 4/5 or less. Be patient: there will be races aplenty; no harm is done in passing a race or two. Besides, underlays often create overlays.

Not all long shot winners are concealed in cutback races or run under the cover of a poor performance in their last race or two: some are hidden in plain sight; but, for whatever reasons, the public discounts their good past performances. This is often aided by the racing secretary's setting of unrealistically high morning line odds. When you find a race like that believe what you see in the past performances and not anyone else's opinion of what the odds should be, expert or not.

An example of this phenomenon occurred at Arlington on September 27, 2009, in the tenth and final race of the day and the season in a maiden special for $38k for fillies and mares three years old and up going a mile and one-sixteenth on the turf.

The 6, Mattieandmorgan, was the morning line favorite at 2/1. I discounted her due to her slow workouts. The 7 had not raced in two years, but the trainer was William Mott and my experience has taught me that he does not bring a horse to the track unless he thinks it has a chance to win.

When I looked at the 4, Krista's Quick Chic, I was struck by the fact that the racing secretary set her morning line at 15/1 in spite of the horse having run three straight seconds at a mile at Piedmont. I confess that I had no idea of the location of that track nor of the quality of its purses; nevertheless, Krista's Quick Chic had placed second in three consecutive races in maiden special $38k races there. Additionally, in her last four races she had never gone off at odds of more than 6/1. The Arlington season champion was in the saddle for the current race. It was puzzling that the Chicago crowd let her get off at nearly 15/1. Frequently in thoroughbred racing you have to take the past performances as you find them. Believe what you see in the form. Don't let the odds makers dissuade you.

Krista's Quick Chic won easily after overcoming traffic trouble in the stretch, paying $29.60 to win and 11.40 to place. She was a long shot at the urging of the racing secretary, but was certainly not hidden to the astute handicappers who ignored the ratings of the experts. Apparently they didn't think she could run on the turf.

How any one reasonably sophisticated handicapper, much less the great majority of the betting public wagering at Arlington that day, could have ignored the plain tells of the Chic's four consecutive good efforts, not to mention the fact that the track's just crowned leading rider was up, boggles the mind of the experienced punter. It is remarkable that the crowd bought the racing secretary's ridiculous setting of the morning line on this horse of 15/1. Prior to post-time, the beautiful young woman track handicapper was busy touting the morning line favorite. If I remember correctly, she didn't have much to say about Krista's Quick Chic. The favorite has surely crossed the finish line by the time you read this recap of the race.

Wagering on a horse for the reason that "everyone is betting it down" is giving in to the herding instinct by acknowledging that the crowd "must know something." You, as a hidden horse hunter, must think for yourself. I recommend to every serious handicapper the reading of Charles Mackay's classic study: *Extraordinary Popular Delusions and the Madness of Crowds.* His premise is as valid at the race track as it is in the stock or real estate markets. Always examine the past performances with critical eyes; never come to a conclusion about a race until you have carefully scrutinized the past performances of each horse. In handicapping analysis it is not the "devil" that is in the details, it is the "tells" that will reveal the truth that will often light your way to a long shot winner.

TENTH RACE
Arlington
September 27th, 2009

1¹⁄₁₆ MILES. (Turf) (1.41) MAIDEN SPECIAL WEIGHT. Purse $28,000 FOR MAIDENS, FILLIES AND MARES THREE YEARS OLD AND UPWARD. Three Year Olds, 121 lbs.; Older, 123 lbs. Lane 5. (If the management considers it inadvisable to run this race on the Turf Course, it will be run on the main track at One Mile and One Sixteenth) . (Clear 75)

Value of Race: $28,000 ($15,288 reverts) Winner $16,800; second $5,600; third $3,080; fourth $1,680; fifth $840.   Mutuel Pool $148,429 Pick 3 Pool $22,134 Pick 4 Pool $47,169 Pick 6 Pool $8,023 Daily Double Pool $26,143 Exacta Pool $107,198 Superfecta Pool $61,063 Trifecta Pool $99,358 Z-5 Super Hi-5 Pool $8,500

Last Raced	# Horse	M/Eqt.	A/S Wt	PP St	¼	½	¾	Str	Fin	Jockey	Odds $1
04Sep09 ¹Pid²	4 Krista's Quik Chic	L b	3F 121	3 2	6³	6³	6³	5½	1²	Alvarado J	13.70
05Sep09 ¹ºAP²	9 Here Oui Go Again	L	3F 121	8 9	9	9	8⁴	2½	2²	Graham J	4.20
08Sep07 ⁵Bel³	7 Show 'Em All	L	4F 123	6 6	5¹	5²	5³	3²	3¾	Albarado R	3.30
	11 Liz Hunter	L b	3F 121	9 8	7²	7²	7½	7²	4½	Sterling, Jr. L J	10.40
05Sep09 ¹ºAP¹⁰	5 Betty Lou	L b	3F 121	4 3	1²	1²	11½	1hd	5⁴¾	Campbell J M	13.90
26Aug09 ⁴Mth⁴	6 Mattieandmorgan	L	4F 123	5 4	2½	2½	2½	4hd	6⁴½	Castanon J L	2.50
05Sep09 ¹ºAP³	8 Sensational Gold	L b	3F 121	7 5	3½	3¹	3½	8³	7¹½	Razo, Jr. E	9.70
05Sep09 ¹ºAP⁶	1 Sweet Ariette	L b	3F 121	1 1	4²	4²	4¹	6¹	8³¾	Sanchez D	4.80
27Aug09 ³Cby⁶	2 Minnetonka Melody	L	3F 121	2 7	8²	8½	9	9	9	Riggs T	66.40

OFF AT 5:14 Start Good. Won driving. Track Good.

TIME :23², :48, 1:12², 1:38², 1:44⁴   (:23.53, :48.06, 1:12.54, 1:38.53, 1:44.90)

$2 Mutuel Prices:

4- KRISTA'S QUIK CHIC	29.40	11.40	7.00
9- HERE OUI GO AGAIN		5.00	3.20
7- SHOW 'EM ALL			3.80

$2 EXACTA 4-9 PAID $153.60 $2 SUPERFECTA 4-9-7-11 PAID $7,936.20
$2 TRIFECTA 4-9-7 PAID $827.00 $1 Z-5 SUPER HI-5 4-9-7-11-2 PAID $6,831.70

Dark Bay or Brown Filly, (Apr), by Forestry - Geisha Girl (GB) by Nashwan. Trainer Reed R. Eric. Bred by FEM Management Corporation(KY).

KRISTA'S QUIK CHIC rated early, lacked room and altered course in the lane then ran down the leader and got up in time. HERE OUI GO AGAIN made a bold move in the stretch, took the lead late but weakened in the last furlong. SHOW 'EM ALL was unhurried early, drew even in the lane but was not good enough. LIZ HUNTER was void of early speed then ran on late while widest. BETTY LOU set the pace, led to mid stretch and gave way. MATTIEANDMORGAN had good early speed and flattened out. SENSATIONAL GOLD chased the pace, was used up and stopped. SWEET ARIETTE broke sharply, was placed forwardly and lacked a late response. MINNETONKA MELODY was through early and always outrun. RACE RUN 10 FEET INSIDE OF LANE 1.

Owners- 4, Jamgolchian Jerry ; 9, Keith Lazarz LLC ; 7, Cox Nellie Mae ; 11, Wyn Racing ; 5, Bonnie Heath Farm ; 6, Dell Ridge Farm ; 8, Maier Kenneth ; 1, Darley Stable ; 2, Nicol, Susan and Bona Fortuna, Ltd.

Trainers- 4, Reed Eric R.; 9, Janks Christine K.; 7, Mott William I.; 11, McKeever Andrew ; 5, Thornbury Jeffrey D.; 6, Catalano Wayne M.; 8, Block Chris M.; 1, Stidham Michael ; 2, Ramwick, Jr. Bobby

Breeders- 4, FEM Management Corporation (KY); 9, Brandywine Farm, LLC & Stephen Upchurch (KY); 7, Nellie M. Cox (KY); 11, John Glenney & Kim Glenney (KY); 5, Bonnie Heath Farm, LLC (KY); 6, Dell Ridge Farm (KY); 8, White Fox Farm (KY); 1, Eldon Farm Equine, LLC (KY); 2, Susan Nicol & Bona Fortuna, Ltd (MN)

Scratched- Storm Pocket (29Aug09 ⁴Cby⁶), Katie the Lady (19Aug09 ¹AP²)

$2 Daily Double (4-4) Paid $96.00; Daily Double Pool $26,143.
$2 Pick Three (8-2/4/8-4) Paid $396.60; Pick Three Pool $22,134.
$1 Pick Four (1-8-2/4/8-4) Paid $2,222.50; Pick Four Pool $47,169.
$2 Pick Six (2-4-1-8-2/4/8-4) 5 Correct Paid $12,033.80; Pick Six Pool $8,023.

Data provided or compiled by Equibase Company, which includes data from The Jockey Club, generally is accurate but occasionally errors and omissions occur as a result of incorrect data received by others, mistakes in processing and other causes. Equibase Company and Bloodstock Research Information Services, Inc. and Thoroughbred Sports Network disclaim responsibility for the consequences, if any, of such errors, but would appreciate being called to their attention. Copyright 2009.

Another example of this phenomenon occurred on the same day at Keeneland in the fourth race, a $25k claimer at 7 furlongs on the synthetic surface for three year olds and up which had never won two races.

The 10, Cape San Blas, had won his last race, a $16k open claimer for three and up going a mile and one-sixteenth at Keeneland. The racing secretary set his morning line at 8/1, possibly because that day's race was for $25k and at first glance Cape San Blas appeared to be attempting to win at a higher class. I thought a fair line would be 7/2 after complete examination of his ten past performances revealed that he had competed at considerably higher class levels than the current $25k claimer. Six races back he had finished second in an optional $40k claimer for non-winners of two. Additionally, his work of :47 breezing on September 19 was the best work of the twelve horses in the current race as was his speed rating of 92 in his last race, and the trainer was a 17% winner. Cape San Blas left the gate at odds of 9.7/1. After being ninth at the three-quarter pole, he rallied to win by three-quarters of a length. This hidden in plain sight long shot paid $21.40, 11.20, and 6.80; another example of the betting public being influenced by an unrealistic setting of the morning line.

FOURTH RACE
Keeneland
October 25th, 2009

1¹⁄₁₆ MILES. (1.41³) CLAIMING. Purse $29,000 FOR THREE YEAR OLDS AND UPWARD. Three Year Olds, 121 lbs.; Older, 124 lbs. Non-winners of two races over a mile since August 25 Allowed 2 lbs. A Race At A Mile Or Over Since Then Allowed 4 lbs. Claiming Price $25,000 (Races where entered for $20,000 or le ss not considered). (Clear 56)

Value of Race: $29,000 Winner $17,400; second $5,800; third $2,900; fourth $1,450; fifth $870; sixth $116; seventh $116; eighth $116; ninth $116; tenth $116. Mutuel Pool $230,686 Pick 3 Pool $19,464 Daily Double Pool $22,109 Exacta Pool $159,051 Superfecta Pool $67,229 Trifecta Pool $107,925

Last Raced	#	Horse	M/Eqt.	A/S	Wt	PP	St	¼	½	¾	Str	Fin	Jockey	Cl'g Pr	Odds $1
10Oct09 ¹Kee¹	10	Cape San Blas	L A	5G	120	8	5	9¹½	10	9hd	2hd	1¾	Graham J	25000	9.70
01Oct09 ⁶Bel¹	12	Whirling Thunder	L A b	4G	122	10	2	3hd	2hd	1hd	1¹	2½	Lanerie C J	25000	11.20
26Sep09 ⁹AP⁶	7	King of Speed	L A	10G	122	6	6	5hd	7²	8¹	4¼	3¹	Mena M	25000	6.40
26Sep09 ⁹AP¹	5	Eighteenthofmarch	L A b	5G	122	4	7	8²	8¹½	7½	5hd	4nk	Albarado R	25000	3.80
27Aug09 ⁹Sar⁴	6	Inti (URU)	L A	4C	120	5	10	10	9½	10	8³	5³⁄₈	Torres F C	25000	8.80
23Sep09 ⁸Bel⁵	2	Richland Creek	L A b	5H	120	2	4	2¹	3¼	3hd	6hd	6²	Leparoux J R	25000	1.40
05Oct09 ⁷Del⁴	3	Templar's Cup	L A b	6G	120	3	9	7²	6¹	6¹½	7¹½	7nk	Borel C H	25000	13.80
25Sep09 ⁵AP¹	11	Paster's Bad Habit	L	3C	119	9	8	6½	5¹	4¹	3hd	8³	Thompson T J	25000	35.70
03Oct09 ⁹TP¹	8	U D Ghetto	L A b	5G	120	7	1	4²	4hd	5hd	9¹	9²¼	Lopez J	25000	18.30
11Oct09 ¹Kee⁶	1	T. C. Champ	L A	5G	120	1	3	1¹	1½	2¹	10	10	Theriot J	25000	38.80

OFF AT 2:39 Start Good For All But INTI (URU). Won driving. Track Fast.
TIME :24, :48², 1:12², 1:37², 1:43³ (:24.15, :48.46, 1:12.57, 1:37.48, 1:43.71)

$2 Mutuel Prices:

10- CAPE SAN BLAS	21.40	11.20	6.80
12- WHIRLING THUNDER		11.40	7.20
7- KING OF SPEED			4.80

$2 EXACTA 10-12 PAID $169.60 $2 SUPERFECTA 10-12-7-5 PAID $271.28
$2 TRIFECTA 10-12-7 PAID $1,939.80

Bay Gelding, (My), by Royal Academy - Defining by Miswaki. Trainer Thornbury D. Jeffrey. Bred by Bonnie Heath Farm, LLC(KY).

CAPE SAN BLAS was unhurried into stride and tucked in to save ground, ranged into striking distance through the second turn, angled out and split horses four wide entering the stretch, struck the front nearing the sixteenth marker and gamely held sway. WHIRLING THUNDER was away alertly and dropped to the inside mid way through the first turn, prompted the pace along the rail, edged clear entering the stretch, kept on well through a prolonged drive but was grudgingly gave way late. KING OF SPEED settled in hand, swung seven wide to make a bold bid, loomed large inside the final furlong but was unable to reach. EIGHTEENTHOFMARCH was allowed to settle, advanced from between horses, angled out six wide to make his bid from between horses but lacked the needed late response. INTI (URU) broke a step slow, was unhurried into stride, made his rally six wide but found his best stride too late. RICHLAND CREEK tracked the pace three deep, drew even leaving the second turn between horses, but failed to sustain the drive. TEMPLAR'S CUP attended the pace along the inside, got through to make a mild bid but faltered. PASTER'S BAD HABIT made a middle move five wide, loomed a danger entering the stretch but came up empty in the final furlong. U D GHETTO contended between horses three wide for six furlongs and dropped out. T. C. CHAMP opened clear to set the early pace, was collared after a half, disputed the issue to the stretch and stopped.

Owners- 10, Bonnie Heath Farm ; 12, Avalon Farms, Inc. ; 7, Carl R. Moore Management LLC ; 5, R. M. Living Trust ; 6, Smith Brook T.; 2, Ramsey, Kenneth L. and Sarah K. ; 3, Gilliam James William; 11, Phelps G. James; 8, Lucky Seven Stable ; 1, Mounts David G.

Trainers- 10, Thornbury Jeffrey D.; 12, Kennealy Eddie ; 7, Calhoun W. Bret; 5, Catalano Wayne M.; 6, Romans Dale L.; 2, Brown Chad C.; 3, O'Connor, II Robert R.; 11, Booker, Jr. John A.; 8, Pitts Helen ; 1, Hiles Rick

Breeders- 10, Bonnie Heath Farm, LLC (KY); 12, Avalon Farms, Inc. (KY); 7, Carl Hurst, Fred Bradley & WilliamBradley (KY); 5, Mr. Gabriel Dixon (FL); 6, Haras Don Alfredo (URU); 2, Robert Lapenta (KY); 3, Roger Browning (KY); 11, Stony Oak Farm, LLC (KY); 8, Lucky Seven Stable (KY); 1, B. E. Howerter (KY)

Richland Creek was claimed by Urwelling, Al and Bill ; trainer, Scherer Merrill R.
Scratched- Incalzando(10Oct09 ¹Kee²), Cajun Prize(11Oct09 ¹Kee²)

$2 Daily Double (7-10) Paid $145.60; Daily Double Pool $22,109.
$2 Pick Three (5-7-10) Paid $787.60; Pick Three Pool $19,464.

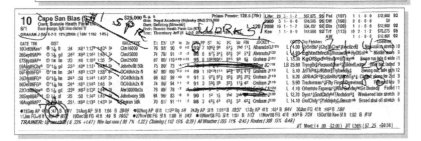

Another excellent example of a hidden in plain sight long shot occurred on December 16, 2009, in the ninth race at Tampa Bay Downs; a six furlong $6.25k claimer on the dirt for fillies and mares three year olds and up.

The racing secretary made the 5, Excellent Rate, the morning line favorite at 2/1. The horse had last run in a six furlong open $10k claiming race at Mountaineer, finishing fourth by three and three-quarters in a field of nine. It had not won a race in a year. Its works were mundane, although its trainer was a 27% winner and her jockey was the track leader; nevertheless, I thought Excellent Rate was a false favorite.

The 6, Real Place, had easily won her last race in the mud in a $5k claimer at Suffolk Downs - known to its punters as: "Sufferin' Downs." In her second race back she finished third, just three-quarters of a length out. Her morning line was 8/1, but by post time had risen to 16/1. Her trainer was a 14% winner; her jockey was winning at a 19% rate. Additionally, Real Place had the best pre-race workout of the field.

Influenced by what I considered to be the racing secretary's unrealistically low setting of the odds for Excellent Rate, the betting public bet her down to even money. She finished a badly beaten sixth, while Real Place stalked the pace and closed in the stretch to win by a comfortable length.

This hidden in plain sight long shot paid $34.40, 12.80, and 6.20, though she had won her previous race by a length and one-quarter, driving. Apparently the Tampa Bay punters didn't think she could move up to the $6.25k class, overlooking the fact that on July 18 she had won a $12.5k claimer at six furlongs at Sufferin' Downs in another driving finish.

Not only must the hidden horse hunter be constantly on the lookout for a long shot candidate that possesses several hidden tells, but also to be eternally vigilant in recognizing a horse that is obviously *hidden in plain sight*.

NINTH RACE
Tampa Bay
December 16th, 2009

6 FURLONGS. (1.09) CLAIMING. Purse $10,000 (Includes $500 FOA - Florida Owners Awards) FOR FILLIES AND MARES THREE YEARS OLD AND UPWARD. Three Year Olds, 120 lbs.; Older, 122 lbs. Non-winners of a race since November 16 Allowed 2 lbs. A race since October 16 Allowed 4 lbs. Claiming Price $6,250 (Races Where Entered For $5,000 Or Less Not C onsidered). (Cloudy 73)

Value of Race: $10,000 Winner $6,200; second $1,805; third $1,140; fourth $475; fifth $95; sixth $95; seventh $95; eighth $95.
Mutuel Pool $111,559 Daily Double Pool $18,106 Exacta Pool $92,314 Superfecta Pool $41,324 Trifecta Pool $82,014

Last Raced	#	Horse	M/Eqt.	A/S	Wt	PP	St	¼	½	Str	Fin	Jockey	Cl'g Pr	Odds $1
24Oct09 9Suf1	6	Real Place	L b	3F	116	6	1	5²½	2½	2½	1¹	Gonzalez P	6250	16.20
28Oct09 1Suf4	1	New Day Rising	L b	3F	111	1	7	7¹	8	7⁶	2nk	Schorr F	6250	24.40
29Aug09 9Del5	4	Hands Wavering	L b	6M	118	4	8	8	7¹	5½	3¹	Cotto, Jr. P L	6250	5.30
18Oct09 4Kee9	2	Once Is Enough	L	4F	118	2	6	6⁵	5½	3½	4²½	Lopez J	6250	3.40
24Nov09 4Med4	8	Talking Flirt	L f	5M	118	8	3	1hd	1¹½	1hd	5¹½	Rivera, Jr. L R	6250	4.10
15Nov09 7Mnr4	5	Excellent Rate	L b	4F	118	5	2	3hd	3½	4½	6²½	Feliciano R	6250	1.00
04Nov09 1Suf1	3	Beautiful Insight	L b	4F	118	3	5	4hd	4½	6½	7⁸	Medina J C	6250	26.50
22Nov09 3Crc6	7	Going On Again	L b	7M	118	7	4	2¹½	6²½	8	8	Garcia J J	6250	38.70

OFF AT 4:38 Start Good. Won driving. Track Fast.
TIME :224, :463, :593, 1:12² (:22.84, :46.66, :59.65, 1:12.53)

$2 Mutuel Prices:

6- REAL PLACE	34.40	12.80	6.20
1- NEW DAY RISING		21.00	9.60
4- HANDS WAVERING			4.80

$2 EXACTA 6-1 PAID $538.40 $1 SUPERFECTA 6-1-4-2 PAID $5,526.50
$2 TRIFECTA 6-1-4 PAID $3,947.80

Chestnut Filly. (Apr), by Real Quiet - Heathers Chillan by Out of Place. Trainer Camilo Juan. Bred by L & D Farms, Inc.(FL).
REAL PLACE was hustled along to challenge for the lead from the outside into the stretch then after driving clear leaving the furlong grounds, lasted late. NEW DAY RISING bobbled at the break, was void of speed for a half, fanned seven wide into the stretch then closed fast from the outside late. HANDS WAVERING was also void of early foot, got through along the inside in the drive and was also going well late. ONCE IS ENOUGH made a middle move to challenge a furlong out but was outkicked late. TALKING FLIRT dueled to the final furlong then weakened. EXCELLENT RATE pressed the issue into the furlong grounds then weakened. BEAUTIFUL INSIGHT was through after a half. GOING ON AGAIN stopped.

Owners- 6, L and D Farm ; 1, Gomez Nancy ; 4, Dougherty, Raymond and Wasiluk, Jr., Peter ; 2, Lossen Richard ; 8, Suscavage Michael G.; 5, Tallisman Bruce N.; 3, Boyd Anthony ; 7, Odom Lisa

Trainers- 6, Camilo Juan ; 1, Gomez Alejandro ; 4, Wasiluk, Jr. Peter ; 2, McQuade Owen ; 8, Harvatt Charles R.; 5, Feliciano Benny R.; 3, Poxon, Jr. Ernest ; 7, Mora Myra

Breeders- 6, L & D Farms, Inc. (FL); 1, The Answer LLC (KY); 4, Stanley M. Ersoff (FL); 2, J. D. Squires & J. T. L. Jones Jr. (KY); 8, Ro Parra MD (NY); 5, Bruce Tallisman (FL); 3, Kris Thurmond (FL); 7, Richard O'Neill & Douglas Peterson (KY)

Excellent Rate was claimed by Ingram, Mike and O'Connor, Robb R., II ; trainer, O'Connor, II Robert R.

$2 Daily Double (6-6) Paid $53.80; Daily Double Pool $18,106.

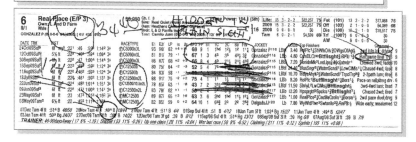

Chapter 9

Most stock market players will probably describe themselves as "investors" while most horse players like to describe themselves as "handicappers." Whatever they call themselves, both are gamblers who are willing to take risks for high rewards. None of us can take the gamble out of life; risk is an integral part of living. The decisions we make have costs and sometimes unwelcome conclusions in both our personal relationships and in our pursuit of the greenback; yet sometimes the bets we make return to us more than we deserve and sometimes more than we could have dreamed of because, for a few brief moments, dame fortune smiled in our direction. Though Lady Luck is fickle, it is the fortunate player who recognizes early in a roll that momentum is with him or her and can capitalize upon it by increasing the size of their wagers. It is the doubly fortunate player who recognizes that momentum has departed the scene and reduces his or her bets until the mighty magic Mo returns.

Surely the best movie on thoroughbred horse race gambling is *Let It Ride!*, with Richard Dreyfuss as the manic gambler on a roll in a day at the track. Anyone who has been on such a roll will identify with him.

Theory is fine, but putting it into practice is the payoff - or not. Let me share with you a remarkable afternoon in which the author practiced the principles that this book preaches. While we have spent considerable space on elucidating the techniques of finding a hidden horse long shot candidate, we have not yet discussed in detail how to bet the hidden horse, once found.

On the afternoon of October 25, 2009, I loaded $100 into my online betting account and printed the cards for Keeneland and Santa Anita. After placing a few conservative bets at Keeneland, my stake increased to $246. Then came the fourth race which we have previously discussed and in which the hidden horse tells landed me on the 10, Cape San Blas.

Once I find a long shot candidate, my standard bet is usually $10 to win and place. If I feel strongly about the horse I will usually run it up and back with the field in an exacta wheel. In this case I decided to use a $2 exacta base, costing $36 for the field of ten. My total wager cost $56. My money management rule is that I won't bet more than 40% of my current stake in any one race.

Cape San Blas paid 21.40 to win and 11.20 to place, returning $158 for my straight bets. Luckily, a long shot placed at odds of 11.2/1; the exacta payoff was $169.60. The profit on the race was $271.60, bringing my winnings for the day to $417.

In the remaining races at Keeneland I was unable to find another long shot so I played the apparent form. By the time I

switched to Santa Anita my stake was up to $378. I had no premo-
nition of what was about to happen at one of my favorite tracks, but
I knew that I was concentrating clearly and felt confident; the same
feeling I had experienced just before some previous hot streaks.

In the sixth race my attention was first drawn to the 7, Mark
The Bend, a Golden Gate invader. His morning line was 12/1 in
spite of his two wins, two places, and two shows in his last seven
races. His highest odds in his last six races had been 6.9/1. In his
last race at Golden Gate he had won at the same class and distance,
a $40k allowance race for California breds. At 21/1 he was the hid-
den horse in plain sight that the southern California crowd apparently disdained in spite of his excellent record; probably because
he was a shipper from Golden Gate, the San Francisco track. No
matter the reason, the form said he was a player.

I bet $10 to win and place and a $4 exacta partial key with
the 1, Kalookan Storm, that I thought to be the class of the race,
and with the favorite, the 8, Unbridled Story. Mark The Bench
placed at $17.20. When Kalookan Storm won, the exacta paid
$269.80 for $2. After collecting $86.00 for the Bench's place and
$539.60 for the exacta, my profit for the day climbed to $867.60.
My pulse quickened as I examined the past performances of the
next race. Had I had any inkling of what was about to happen,
I *would have, could have, should have* increased the size of my bets.

SIXTH RACE
Oak Tree
October 25th, 2009

1 MILE. (Turf) (.00) ALLOWANCE. Purse $40,000 FOR CALIFORNIA BRED OR CALIFORNIA SIRED THREE YEAR OLDS AND UPWARD WHICH HAVE NEVER WON $10,000 OTHER THAN MAIDEN, CLAIMING OR STARTER OR WHICH HAVE NEVER WON TWO RACES. Three Year Olds, 120 lbs.; Older, 124 lbs. Non-winners of a race other than Maiden, Claiming or Starter at a mile or over Allowed 2 lbs. A race at a mile or over since September 10 Allowed 4 lbs. (Races where entered for $20,000 or less not considered) (Rail at 15 feet). Rail at 15 feet). (Clear 84)

Value of Race: $40,800 Winner $24,000; second $8,000; third $4,800; fourth $2,400; fifth $800; sixth $400; seventh $400. Mutuel Pool $274,407 Pick 3 Pool $49,906 Daily Double Pool $25,003 Exacta Pool $157,109 Superfecta Pool $85,467 Trifecta Pool $144,061

Last Raced	# Horse	M/Eqt.	A/S Wt	PP	St	¼	½	¾	Str	Fin	Jockey	Odds $1
23Aug09 6GG6	1 Kalookan Storm	BL b	3G 116	1	1	4½	3hd	3²	2½	1²	Berrio O A	9.20
26Sep09 3GG1	7 Mark the Bench	BL f	4C 122	6	2	1½	1¹	1¹	1¹	2¹	Garcia M	21.00
23Aug09 4Dmr²	8 Unbridled Story	BL	3C 116	7	3	2¹½	2¹	2hd	3²	3²½	Talamo J	1.00
22Jly09 7Dmr5	6 Unbridled Roman	BL	3C 116	5	5	5⁴½	5⁴	4hd	4²	4½	Smith M E	5.40
26Sep09 11Fpx4	3 Premiere Flyer	BL	3G 111	3	6	7	6hd	6³	6²	5¹½	Santiago Reyes C	5.40
02Sep09 7Dmr5	2 Renegade Storm	BL b	3C 116	2	4	6¹	7	7	7	6½	Bejarano R	3.60
18Oct09 9Osa8	4 Complexity	B f	5G 120	4	7	3hd	4½	5²	5hd	7	Delgadillo A	40.80

OFF AT 3:11   Start Good. Won driving.   Track Firm   (Rail at 15 ft).
TIME :24¹, :48, 1:11¾, 1:23², 1:35¹   (:24.36, :48.19, 1:11.75, 1:23.42, 1:35.38)

$2 Mutuel Prices:

1- KALOOKAN STORM	20.40	10.40	4.80
7- MARK THE BENCH		17.20	3.80
8- UNBRIDLED STORY			2.60

$1 EXACTA 1-7 PAID $134.90 $1 SUPERFECTA 1-7-8-6 PAID $3,233.90
$1 TRIFECTA 1-7-8 PAID $336.20

Gray or Roan Gelding, (May), by Storm Boot - Chautauqua by With Approval. Trainer Avila C. A.. Bred by Betty L. Mabee & Larry Mabee(CA).

KALOOKAN STORM stalked the pace inside, steadied off heels into the stretch, bid along the fence under urging past midstretch to gain the lead nearing the wire and gamely prevailed. MARK THE BENCH pulled his way to the front and set a pressured pace inside, inched away a half mile out, came a bit off the fence on the second turn, fought back alongside the winner in deep stretch and continued willingly to the wire. UNBRIDLED STORY prompted the pace outside the runner-up, stalked off the rail a half mile out and outside the winner on the second turn and into the stretch and clearly bested the others. UNBRIDLED ROMAN bumped at the break, chased outside a rival then between horses, continued a bit off the rail on the second turn and lacked the needed late kick. PREMIERE FLYER came off the rail on the first turn and settled outside a rival, angled out into the stretch and did not rally. RENEGADE STORM settled off the pace inside, came out into the stretch and was not a threat. COMPLEXITY bumped at the start, pulled his way along to stalk the pace three deep then outside a rival, came a bit wide into the stretch and weakened.

Owners- 1, L-Bo Racing and Putnam, James ; 7, Brook Joseph ; 8, Traver, Thomas J. and Webb, Priscilla ; 6, Rodriguez, Lorraine and Rod ; 3, Johnston, E. W. and Judy, Portolesi, Mike and Riggio, Dolores ; 2, Conquest Racing ; 4, Campbell Stephen R.

Trainers- 1, Avila A. C.; 7, Brook Joseph ; 8, Hendricks Dan L.; 6, Homans David E.; 3, Warren Donald ; 2, Jones Martin F.; 4, Caldwell William R.

Breeders- 1, Betty L. Mabee & Larry Mabee (CA); 7, Joseph Brook (CA); 8, Jim & Michelle Gustafson (CA); 6, Rod Rodriguez & Lorraine Rodriguez (CA); 3, Old English Rancho (CA); 2, Dale Pyle Jr. (CA); 4, Mr. & Mrs. Martin J. Wygod (CA)

Scratched- Atticus Jack(26Dec08 6SA³)

$2 Daily Double (5-1) Paid $75.20; Daily Double Pool $25,003.
$1 Pick Three (4-5-1) Paid $277.20; Pick Three Pool $49,906.

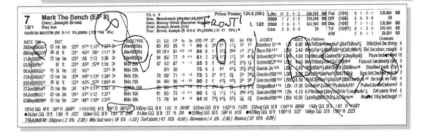

The seventh race was a $25k claimer for fillies and mares three years old and up which had never won two races, going seven furlongs on the all weather track. After a scratch the field was reduced to six entries. The 1, I Swear, was bet down to 1.4/1 as the favorite; a false one I thought because of the suspicious class drop.

In looking for a long shot I landed on the 5, Angel Of Mystery. By post time her odds had climbed to 21/1 from her morning line of 15/1. She was a genuine cutback horse, having run in a mile turf race in her last effort in which she was competitive to the head of the stretch before fading. Now she was cutting back one-eighth of a mile to seven furlongs. The public let her go at 21/1, completely overlooking the clear cutback angle.

I decided to increase my bet on the race to $90, which would leave my account ahead by $777 even if I lost that race. So I bet $20 to win and place and wheeled Angel of Mystery up and back in a $5 exacta.

Angel placed at $13.40; when the third favorite won the exacta paid $120. After collecting $134 for the straight bet and $300 for the exactas, my winnings for the day climbed to $1,311. I *could have* bet more: I *should have* bet more.

SEVENTH RACE   7 FURLONGS. (1.20⁴) CLAIMING. Purse $16,000 FOR FILLIES AND MARES THREE YEARS OLD AND UPWARD WHICH HAVE NEVER WON TWO RACES. Three Year Olds, 121 lbs.; Older, 124 lbs. Claiming Price $25,000. (Clear 84)

Oak Tree

October 25th, 2009

Value of Race: $16,480 Winner $9,600; second $3,200; third $1,920; fourth $960; fifth $400; sixth $400.   Mutuel Pool $229,732 Pick 3 Pool $55,980 Daily Double Pool $22,643 Exacta Pool $129,630 Superfecta Pool $69,922 Trifecta Pool $118,561

Last Raced	# Horse	M/EqL	A/S Wt	PP	St	¼	½	Str	Fin	Jockey	Cl'g Pr	Odds $1
15Oct09 ⁷Osa⁴	7 Dominadora	BL f	7M 124	6	2	2ʰᵈ	3½	1¹	1²¾	Arambula P	25000	3.40
08Oct09 ⁶Osa⁶	5 Angel of Mystery	BL	3F 121	4	1	1¹½	1½	2ʰᵈ	2ⁿᵏ	Delgadillo A	25000	21.20
09Oct09 ³Osa¹	3 Anundeniablyhappy	BL f	3F 121	2	4	3²	2²	3²½	3ⁿᵏ	Baze M C	25000	10.20
09Sep09 ⁶Dmr⁴	4 Morgan Lane	BL	5M 124	3	3	4ʰᵈ	4¹	4½	4¹½	Gomez G K	25000	3.10
12Oct09 ⁷Osa⁵	1 I Swear	BL	3F 121	1	5	5ʰᵈ	5	5⁵	5¹⁶½	Rosario J	25000	1.40
01Oct09 ⁵Osa¹	6 Hot Summer Breeze	BL b	3F 121	5	6	6	5ʰᵈ	6	6	Flores D R	25000	4.80

OFF AT 3:41   Start Good. Won driving.   Track Fast.

TIME :24², :47⁴, 1:11³, 1:23³   (:24.45, :47.91, 1:11.78, 1:23.75)

$2 Mutuel Prices:

7- DOMINADORA	8.80	4.60	3.80
5- ANGEL OF MYSTERY		13.40	6.40
3- ANUNDENIABLYHAPPY			5.20

$1 EXACTA 7-5 PAID $60.40 $1 SUPERFECTA 7-5-3-4 PAID $1,366.10

$1 TRIFECTA 7-5-3 PAID $296.20

Chestnut Mare, (Mx), by Benchmark - Pleasure Bought by Marfa. Trainer Martinez Silverio. Bred by Granja Vista Del Rio(CA).

DOMINADORA had speed outside then stalked alongside a rival, bid three deep into the stretch, gained the lead, inched away under urging in midstretch, drifted in and proved best. ANGEL OF MYSTERY sped to the early lead a bit off the rail, angled in and dueled inside leaving the backstretch and on the turn, fought back into the stretch, could not match the winner in the final furlong but gamely held second. ANUNDENIABLYHAPPY stalked just off the inside, bid alongside the runner-up into and on the turn, battled between horses into the stretch and edged a rival for the show between foes late. MORGAN LANE was in a good position stalking the pace inside, came out into the stretch and was edged for a minor award three deep on the line. I SWEAR taken off the rail early, chased between horses then just off the fence on the turn, swung three deep into the stretch and did not rally. HOT SUMMER BREEZE settled three deep chasing the pace, dropped back off the rail on the turn, gave way in the stretch and was not persevered with late.

Owners- 7, K and K Stables ; 5, Cannon Nevada and Weinstein, Judy ; 3, Redwood Racing, Perlberg, Bob, Rykoff, Tom, et al ; 4, Whitham Janis R.; 1, Madison Stewart Mather; 6, Hicks, Judy and Robertson, Sanford

Trainers- 7, Martinez Silverio ; 5, Marquez Alfredo ; 3, Knapp Steve ; 4, McAnally Ronald L.; 1, Sadler John W.; 6, Walsh Kathy

Breeders- 7, Granja Vista Del Rio (CA); 5, Madera Thoroughbreds & Dr. JackWeinstein (CA); 3, Douglas Arnold (KY); 4, Janis R. Whitham (KY); 1, Kim Nardelli, Rodney Nardelli & JohnClarke (KY); 6, Sanford Robertson & Judy Hicks (KY)

Scratched- Morning Frost(25Jly08 ⁶Dmr⁹), Life by R R(05Aug09 ⁷Dmr⁹).

$2 Daily Double (1-7) Paid $97.00; Daily Double Pool $22,643.

$1 Pick Three (5-1-7) Paid $166.40; Pick Three Pool $55,980.

I was in a state of high excitement; momentum was with me; my concentration was point on; I knew I was on a roll, and when you are on a roll the rule is: increase your bets until you lose a race.

I could not find a credible long shot candidate in the eighth race until I landed on the 4, Bert's Law. I thought he was the class of the race, having run decent races in two stakes with purses of $125k and $100k. Additionally, he was a cutback horse, having stayed up to the stretch in a September 6 mile and one-eighth race. In his previous race he had stayed up to the head of the stretch in a mile and three-eighths route. His morning line was 8/1 and he left the gate at 8.6/1. His trainer was 14%; his jockey, a 19% winner.

The 5, Fire Break, was a proven deep closer. He had closed seven lengths in his previous race to finish just two lengths out in a six and a half furlong sprint in a $42k allowance race. Rafael Bejarano was up, a 22% jockey. I structured my wagers with $20 to win on Bert's Law, and boxed him with Fire Break in a $3 exacta. Never headed, Bert's law wired the field in a one length win; Fire Break closed well, and Dynamic Range, the false favorite at 1.6/1, finished a weakening fourth.

The winner paid $19.20, 8.80 to place, and 6.60 to show. The exacta paid $101. I collected $280 for the straight bets and $151.50 for the exacta box. After deducting my investment of $50, I netted $381 for the race, bringing my profit for the day to $1,692.

I know: I *could have, should have, would have* bet more, if only I had recognized earlier in the streak that I was on a roll.

EIGHTH RACE
Oak Tree
October 25th, 2009

1 MILE. (Turf) (.00) ALLOWANCE. Purse $40,000 FOR THREE YEAR OLDS AND UPWARD WHICH HAVE NEVER WON $10,000 OTHER THAN MAIDEN, CLAIMING OR STARTER OR WHICH HAVE NEVER WON TWO RACES. Three Year Olds, 120 lbs.; Older, 124 lbs. Non-winners of a race other than Maiden, Claiming or Starter at a mile or over Allowed 2 lbs. A race other than Claiming, or Starter at a mile or over Allowed 4 lbs. (Rail at 15 feet). (Clear 84)

Value of Race: $40,000 ($4,800 reverts) Winner $31,200; second $8,000; third $4,800; fourth $2,400; fifth $800; sixth $400; seventh $400. Mutuel Pool $275,432 Pick 3 Pool $53,428 Daily Double Pool $31,217 Exacta Pool $144,287 Superfecta Pool $82,083 Trifecta Pool $126,851

Last Raced	# Horse	M/Eqt.	A/S Wt	PP	St	¼	½	¾	Str	Fin	Jockey	Odds $1
03Oct09 9Osa4	4 Bert's Law	BL bf	4G 124	3	2	1½	22½	11	12	11	Rosario J	8.60
04Oct09 7Osa4	5 Fire Break	BL b	4G 120	4	4	4hd	4hd	41½	42	2hd	Bejarano R	6.70
21Aug09 5Dmr4	7 Blazing Spirit	BL	3R 118	6	6	7	7	7	5½	3¾	Solis A O	4.80
30Sep09 4Osa2	8 Dynamic Range	BL b	3G 118	7	5	53	3hd	31½	2hd	42	Espinoza V	1.60
04Oct09 2Osa1	6 Shelter Island	BL b	4G 120	5	7	62	61½	6½	61	5hd	Quinonez A	32.00
21Aug09 5Dmr8	3 Nitro Active	BL b	4G 124	2	3	24	1½	22	31	62	Talamo J	4.20
11Oct09 5Osa3	1 Unbridled Papillon	BL	5G 120	1	1	3hd	54½	51½	7	7	Gomez G K	4.40

OFF AT 4:10 Start Good. Won driving. Track Firm (Rail at 15 ft).

TIME :23¹, :46¹, 1:10, 1:22², 1:34³ (:23.27, :46.38, 1:10.00, 1:22.58, 1:34.61)

$2 Mutuel Prices:	4- BERT'S LAW	19.20	8.80	6.60
	5- FIRE BREAK		8.20	4.80
	7- BLAZING SPIRIT			4.80

$1 EXACTA 4-5 PAID $50.50 $1 SUPERFECTA 4-5-7-8 PAID $638.00
$1 TRIFECTA 4-5-7 PAID $220.90

Dark Bay or Brown Gelding, (Ma), by Bertrando - Digby by Pirate's Bounty. Trainer Moger, Jr. Ed. Bred by Mr. & Mrs. Martin J. Wygod(CA).

BERT'S LAW had speed outside a rival then angled in approaching the first turn and dueled inside, regained the advantage into the second turn, inched away a quarter mile out, came off the rail into the stretch, angled back in and kicked clear and held under left handed urging. FIRE BREAK chased between horses a bit off the rail on the second turn, came out in the stretch, was three deep past midstretch and edged a foe for second between rivals late. BLAZING SPIRIT settled inside, went outside a rival on the second turn and three deep into the stretch and just missed the place. DYNAMIC RANGE stalked three deep, angled to the inside on the second turn, came out a bit in the stretch and was outfinished late for a minor award. SHELTER ISLAND a bit slow to begin, settled off the pace inside, split horses into the stretch and lacked the needed rally. NITRO ACTIVE had speed inside then dueled outside the winner, gained a short advantage on the backstretch, battled alongside that one on the second turn, was between horses past midstretch and weakened. UNBRIDLED PAPILLON was in a good position chasing the pace inside, fell back some on the second turn and weakened in the stretch.

Owners- 4, Lanning, Curt and Lila ; 5, Onsurez, David, Polanco, Marcelo and Ungaro, Evelyne ; 7, Burnett, Steve, CRT Stables, LLC, Terrana, John and Burnett, Terry ; 8, Mercedes Stables LLC ; 6, Cappelli, Anthony and Sebold Racing, LLC ; 3, Flintridge Stable and Decker Racing and Venneri Racing ; 1, Diamond A Racing Corporation

Trainers- 4, Moger, Jr. Ed ; 5, Polanco Marcelo ; 7, Troeger Robert ; 8, Canani Julio C.; 6, Eurton Peter ; 3, Machowsky Michael ; 1, Mandella Richard E.

Breeders- 4, Mr. & Mrs. Martin J. Wygod (CA); 5, Everest Stables, Inc. (KY); 7, TLC Farms, LLC (KY); 8, Mercedes Stables, LLC (KY); 6, Tim James Mawhinney &Karen Faye Mawhinney (FL); 3, B n D Chase Thoroughbreds, Inc. (CA); 1, Diamond A Racing Corporation (KY)

Scratched- Structural(04Oct09 7Osa5)

$2 Daily Double (7-4) Paid $92.00; Daily Double Pool $31,217.
$1 Pick Three (1-7-4) Paid $476.90; Pick Three Pool $53,428.

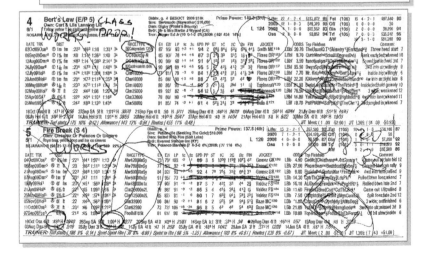

One more race on the card; could I really win four in a row? After looking over the ninth race past performances, I decided to bet $200 or so. If I lost I would still have been up over $1,492. I was playing from a position of strength, and found myself eerily calm.

The race was a one mile $25k maiden claimer for fillies and mares three year olds and up, over the all weather track. After scratches there remained a field of ten. For once, I agreed with the racing secretary that the 2, First Queen, should be the morning line favorite. She was clearly the class of the race in addition to being a credible cutback candidate. The crowd, however, did not agree and made the 4, Prophetise, the 1.8/1 favorite at post time. I thought she was "pushing class" and was too cheap to run with First Queen.

In searching for a hidden long shot candidate, I landed on the 5, Acute Velocity, who had finished fifth in her last race at a mile and one-sixteenth, but was only five lengths out and was cutting back for the current race. Just five days before, Acute Velocity worked :47 2/5 for four furlongs - the best work of her career of four starts and easily the best of that day's field.

My first bet was to box Acute Velocity in a $10 exacta with the first three favorites. While I didn't think Velocity could beat the Queen, I thought she was a good bet to hit the board, so I bet $100 to place and show on her. Her morning line was 15/1; she left the gate at 20/1.

First Queen beat Acute Velocity by a neck in a driving finish in which both horses closed several lengths from the half mile post. Acute Velocity paid $16.60 to place and 5.60 to show; the exacta paid $87.40, netting me $1,267 for the race.

NINTH RACE
Oak Tree
October 25th, 2009

1 MILE. (1.343) MAIDEN CLAIMING. Purse $14,000 FOR MAIDENS, FILLIES AND MARES THREE YEARS OLD AND UPWARD. Three Year Olds, 120 lbs.; Older, 124 lbs. Claiming Price $25,000, If for $22,500, allowed 2 lbs. (Clear 64)

Value of Race: 515,720 Winner $8,400; second $2,800; third $1,680; fourth $840; fifth $400; sixth $400; seventh $400; eighth $400; ninth $400. Mutuel Pool $273,109 Pick 3 Pool $136,073 Pick 4 Pool $324,657 Pick 5 Pool $100,528 Pick 6 Pool $173,689 Daily Double Pool $75,850 Exacta Pool $151,849 Place Pick All Pool $22,409 Superfecta Pool $120,831 Super High Five Pool $77,015 Trifecta Pool $157,397

Last Raced	# Horse	M/Eqt.	A/S Wt	PP St	¼	½	¾	Str	Fin	Jockey	Cl'g Pr	Odds $1
04Oct09 4Osa4	2 First Queen (GB)	BL	3F 120	1 7	8³	5hd	3hd	2hd	1nk	Sorenson D	25000	2.70
08Oct09 8Osa5	5 Acute Velocity	BL f	3F 118	4 8	9	9	6¹	3²½	2no	Valdez F	22500	20.20
23Sep09 12Fpx3	4 Prophetise	BL b	3F 120	3 5	4²½	3¹	1¹	1½	3⁴½	Talamo J	25000	1.80
08Oct09 8Osa6	3 Warrens Sweetheart	BL	3F 120	2 6	7²	8³	7¹½	4¹½	4⁴	Quinonez A	25000	27.10
25Sep09 5GG6	12 Lucy Got Lucky	BL b	3F 120	9 9	6hd	7½	4¹	6¹	5nk	Baze M C	25000	3.50
16Oct09 4Osa7	11 Switch It Up	BL	3F 120	8 2	5¹	6¹	5hd	7⁸	6³½	Valdivia, Jr. J	25000	8.10
08Oct09 8Osa3	8 Dee Dee's Flight	BL	5M 124	6 3	2½	2²½	2½	5hd	7¹⁵	Atkinson P	25000	9.60
09Oct09 3Osa7	9 Cee's Harmony	BL f	4F 122	7 1	3³½	1hd	8¹⁰	8²⁰	8⁴⁹½	Delgadillo A	22500	32.10
11Oct09 3Osa8	7 Californiarockstar	BL	4F 124	5 4	1hd	4hd	9	9	9	Puglisi I	25000	41.80

OFF AT 4:43   Start Good. Won driving.   Track Fast.

TIME :22⁴, :46³, 1:12³, 1:25¹, 1:38   (:22.86, :46.77, 1:12.66, 1:25.27, 1:38.14)

$2 Mutuel Prices:

2- FIRST QUEEN (GB)	7.40	4.60	3.20
5- ACUTE VELOCITY		16.60	5.60
4- PROPHETISE			2.60

$1 EXACTA 2-5 PAID $43.70 $1 PLACE PICK ALL 9 OF 9 PAID $2,959.50 9 Correct
$1 SUPERFECTA 2-5-4-3 PAID $794.40 $1 SUPER HIGH FIVE 2-5-4-3-12 PAID $2,662.90
$1 TRIFECTA 2-5-4 PAID $127.00

Bay Filly, (Feb), by Rock of Gibraltar (IRE) - Orange Blossom (IRE) by Sadler's Wells. Trainer Lloyd James. Bred by Gainsborough Stud Management Ltd(GB).

FIRST QUEEN (GB) settled inside, split rivals on the backstretch, moved up inside then steadied off heels early on the second turn, came out between foes leaving the turn and three deep into the stretch, bid between horses in the drive, gained the advantage in deep stretch and gamely prevailed under urging. ACUTE VELOCITY unhurried a bit off the rail early, advanced outside leaving the second turn and five wide into the stretch, bid three deep in the drive and continued willingly to the wire. PROPHETISE chased just off the inside, advanced outside a rival on the backstretch, went up three deep to gain the lead on the second turn, inched away and angled in some leaving the turn, fought back inside in the stretch and also continued willingly late. WARRENS SWEETHEART saved ground chasing the pace, came a bit off the rail on the second turn and bested the others. LUCY GOT LUCKY broke slowly, went three deep on the first turn then chased outside, moved up four wide on the second turn, was in a bit tight four wide into the stretch and weakened. SWITCH IT UP chased outside a rival or a bit off the rail, advanced between horses leaving the second turn, came three deep into the stretch, had the rider lose the whip in midstretch and lacked a further response. DEE DEE'S FLIGHT dueled between horses then inside, dropped back leaving the second turn and into the stretch and weakened. CEE'S HARMONY had good early speed and dueled three deep then outside a rival, dropped back fast between foes on the second turn and gave way. CALIFORNIAROCKSTAR angled in and dueled inside, dropped back leaving the backstretch and on the second turn, also gave way and was eased in the stretch.

Owners- 2, Newmarket Thoroughbred Racing, LLC ; 5, Murkidjanian, Diane, Sana, Lynn and Zennedjian, Heather ; 4, Lanni Family Trust ; 3, Warren Benjamin C.; 12, Maryanski, John and Janene ; 11, Amerman Racing Stables LLC ; 8, Ocegueda Alfredo ; 9, Four D Stable ; 7, Holder Anna Maria

Trainers- 2, Lloyd James ; 5, French Neil ; 4, Baffert Bob ; 3, Gutierrez Jorge ; 12, Wright Blaine D.; 11, Periban Jorge ; 8, Zamora Ricardo ; 9, Shulman Sanford ; 7, Chew Matthew

Breeders- 2, Gainsborough Stud Management Ltd (GB); 5, Gary Howard, Marlene Howard, Bruce Dunmore & Jim & Michelle Gustafson (CA); 4, Robert P. Levy (KY); 3, Benjamin C Warren (KY); 12, Lucky Shamrock (KY); 11, Amerman Racing LLC (FL); 8, Matthew Rasich (CA); 9, Four D Stables (CA); 7, Anna Holder (CA)

Lucy Got Lucky was claimed by Tarma Corporation ; trainer, Canani Julio C.
Scratched- With Respect(06Oct09 8Osa4), New Citizen(09Oct09 3Osa6), Asturias (GB)(24 Jly 08 8Dmr7)

$2 Daily Double (4-2) Paid $83.00; Daily Double Pool $75,850.
$1 Pick Three (7-4-2) Paid $169.50; Pick Three Pool $136,073.
$1 Pick Four (1-7-4-2) Paid $2,026.20; Pick Four Pool $324,657.
$1 Pick Five (5-1-7-4-2) Paid $6,632.50; Pick Five Pool $100,528.
$2 Pick Six (4-5-1-7-4-2) 5 Correct Paid $923.20; Pick Six Pool N/A.
$2 Pick Six (4-5-1-7-4-2) Paid $96,416.80; Pick Six Pool $173,689.

It is difficult enough to hit two consecutive races; three wins in a row is formidably daunting; four is exceptional. I was paid well with a profit of $2,959. The most remarkable thing about this streak was that in three of the races my backed horse finished second. Again, it's not *how* but *how much*. The post time odds on my four picks were 21/1, 21/1, 9/1, and 20/1. Three of the winners were hidden long shot candidates overlooked by the public because they did not go deep enough into the forest of their past performances to find the tells.

The winner of the sixth, Mark The Bench, was a long shot hidden in plain sight, disdained by the southern California crowd and the Santa Anita racing secretary who apparently discounted his excellent past performances at class because he was a Golden Gate invader. The betting public completely discounted his record in his previous seven races in which he finished first twice, second twice, and third twice. His last three races were at the same class as the current one and he had won his last race at the same class; therefore, he was truly "hidden in plain sight." When you spot that kind of horse, don't hesitate to bet it. Don't think that the crowd must know something that you don't just because the racing secretary posts the horse as a long shot.

Angel of Mystery, who left the gate at odds of 21/1, was a genuine cutback and class dropping horse. Bert's Law was the "works" horse of his race, possessing the fastest pre-race four furlong work of :47 1/5 and was a substantial class dropper. Acute Velocity was a cutback and a "works" horse, having drilled four furlongs in :47 2/5 just six days before the race.

Thinking I had found a horn of plenty, I couldn't wait to play the next day. Try as I might, I couldn't hit the broad side of a barn for I couldn't concentrate. And *pure analytic concentration* is the key to finding a hidden horse winner.

Search for the tells; when you find them have the courage of your convictions and bet the hidden horse for it will always be an overlay. It will not always win, but it will always go off at delicious odds.

Chapter 10

n theory, the betting favorite in any race is set by the betting public; in practice, the racing secretary exerts a huge influence when he sets the morning line. The public generally follows that lead, often to their detriment. Usually, the morning line favorite leaves the gate as an underlay. As we have seen, consistently betting an underlay is not a profitable system of play for the value is in the overlay; that is, a horse going off at odds higher than its past performance record deserves. Astute handicappers will take the time to set their own morning line, for finding a *false favorite* is half of finding a hidden long shot overlay candidate.

A large number of false favorites are horses with a number of front running efforts in their past performances. The unsophisticated bettor loves front speed, yet it is only the occasional race in which the field is wired by a front runner. Too many shorten their stride in the last hundred yards to the wire; the majority of them finish off the board. It is the mid-pack pace runner with some stretch kick that wins the majority of sprint races.

It is even more difficult for front runners to carry their speed beyond seven furlongs. Yet, as we have discussed, when there is only one front speed horse in the race there is a good chance it can stay up to the wire. This does not often occur, as in any race there are usually at least two front runners to knock heads with each other. In the recent 14 race Breeder's Cup just one front runner wired the field; that race was the one of a kind peculiar downhill six and a half furlong turf sprint at Santa Anita. In the other 13 races just three front runners held on to be second, while one was third.

You may fairly ask: when do we know that a favorite is false? The simple answer is: when the favorite fails to win. Remembering that the betting favorite fails to win in two of three races, we are left with a lot of false favorites. It is not as elementary as that; however, for the favorite either places or shows in a majority of races. Using that record as a betting system; that is, consistently betting the favorite to place or show - results in raising the risk level because the bettor would be fortunate to get $3.60 to place or $3.00 to show for this type of bet. Some sophisticated handicappers do manage to make a nominal profit betting *favorite* place and show parlays. I have tried that but found that too often my favorite in the last race of a three race parlay fails to hit the board.

An example of a racing secretary induced false favorite occurred on November 8, 2009, at Aqueduct in the ninth race, a one and one-sixteenth mile $42k maiden special for New York bred fillies and mares three years old and up. The 2, Grace's Valentine, was made the morning line favorite at 2/1; the public bought the line and by the time the gates opened her odds were 6/5.

In examining the previous four consecutive races of the favorite, it seemed clear to me that the horse was short at this distance. The public was no doubt influenced by the fact that her jockey was a 24% winner, her trainer 22%. The public was betting that this time the leading jockey could keep her up to the finish line; notwithstanding that Grace's Valentine had faded in the stretch for four straight races. Today's race was one-sixteenth mile longer than the mile race of August 20 in which Grace led early, was second by two at the head of the stretch before fading to fourth, six lengths back of the winner.

In the horse's last race at a mile and one-eighth, she led to the head of the stretch by two lengths before fading and finishing third, some three and a half lengths back of the winner; she had given up five and a half lengths in the stretch drive. Her best race was the third race back at a mile and one-sixteenth in which she led to the head of the stretch then faded to be second after giving up her half-length lead. In her race of July 5, Grace tried a different tactic, closing some four lengths from the first call to be third by two and a half lengths, again giving up four lengths in the stretch. Clearly, any objective analysis of these four races would lead any experienced handicapper to conclude that she was probably short at today's distance of a mile and one-sixteenth, yet the racing secretary thought she should be the morning line favorite against comparable class horses that included half the field as proven stretch runners.

I marked her as a *false favorite*; that is, my judgment was that her underlay odds were not supported by her past performances. The racing secretary and the betting public were asking Grace's Valentine to do something she had not been able to do: hold her speed in the stretch. And they were betting that she would run to her ridiculous odds of 6/5. Her record did not support those odds; her works were pedestrian, and though the track's leading jockey was up, the betting public - encouraged by the experts - was asking for a miracle.

Instead a hidden horse won at odds of 8.2/1; a mild underlay from its morning line of 12/1. The 12, Split Pot, had the best current work of the field; four furlongs in :48 1/5 just five days before that day's race. Three races back she closed two lengths from the head of the stretch to finish third, just a half length out at the same distance as the current race. She also had the best speed rating of the entire field. The tells were there; you just had to believe what the form was telling you.

Grace's Valentine once again failed. She was a length and a half back of the winner at the head of the stretch, then gave up another length in finishing third, precisely as her previous form indicated; notwithstanding the excellent ride by the track's leading jockey. The crowd was led down the primrose path but did manage to salvage all of $2.60 for the showing of their false favorite.

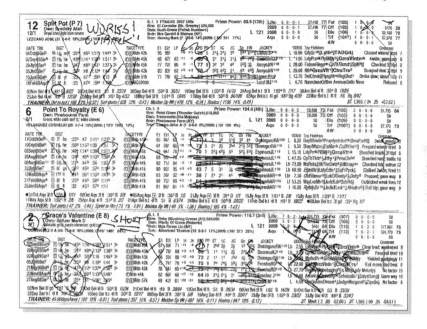

NINTH RACE
Aqueduct
November 8th, 2009

$1\frac{1}{16}$ MILES. (Turf) (1.40^{4}) MAIDEN SPECIAL WEIGHT. Purse $42,000 FOR MAIDENS, FILLIES AND MARES THREE YEARS OLD AND UPWARD FOALED IN NEW YORK STATE AND APPROVED BY THE NEW YORK STATE-BRED REGISTRY. Three Year Olds, 121 lbs.; Older, 122 lbs. (If the Stewards consider it inadvisable to run this race on the turf course, this race will be run at One Mile on the Main Track.). (Clear 64)

Value of Race: $42,000 Winner $25,200; second $8,400; third $4,200; fourth $2,100; fifth $1,260; sixth $120; seventh $120; eighth $120; ninth $120; tenth $120; eleventh $120; twelveth $120. Mutuel Pool $280,626 Pick 3 Pool $80,428 Pick 4 Pool $155,545 Pick 6 Pool $377,236 Daily Double Pool $116,819 Exacta Pool $238,092 Superfecta Pool $100,209 Trifecta Pool $177,328

Last Raced	#	Horse	M/Eqt.	A/S	Wt	PP	St	¼	½	¾	Str	Fin	Jockey	Odds $1
04Oct09 ^{2}Bel^{6}	12	Split Pot	L	3F	121	12	1	$11^{1\frac{1}{2}}$	11^{1}	$11\frac{1}{2}$	4^{1}	$1^{2\frac{1}{2}}$	Lezcano J	8.20
11Oct09 ^{8}Bel^{4}	6	Point to Royalty	L	3F	121	6	4	4^{1}	$4\frac{1}{2}$	5^{1}	$1\frac{1}{2}$	2^{nk}	Velasquez C H	12.60
02Sep09 ^{6}Sar^{3}	2	Grace's Valentine	L b	3F	121	2	3	$5\frac{1}{2}$	6^{1}	$4\frac{1}{2}$	$5^{1\frac{1}{2}}$	$3\frac{1}{2}$	Dominguez R A	1.20
11Oct09 ^{8}Bel^{5}	11	Devilishameye	L	3F	121	11	2	6^{hd}	5^{1}	$3\frac{1}{2}$	$2\frac{1}{2}$	$4^{1\frac{1}{4}}$	Samyn J	28.50
04Oct09 ^{2}Bel^{3}	7	Tom and Dicks Girl	L	4F	122	7	10	$10^{2\frac{1}{2}}$	$9^{1\frac{1}{2}}$	9^{1}	6^{hd}	5^{hd}	Cohen D	7.30
11Oct09 ^{10}Bel^{4}	1	City Vice	L f	4F	122	1	5	$8^{1\frac{1}{2}}$	12	8^{1}	$7\frac{1}{2}$	$6\frac{1}{2}$	Studart M	16.80
11Oct09 ^{8}Bel^{7}	3	Refinery Fire	L bf	3F	121	3	8	9^{hd}	8^{hd}	$7\frac{1}{2}$	$9\frac{1}{2}$	7^{nk}	Maragh R	9.80
03Jan09 ^{9}Aqu^{6}	4	Driven by Energy	L	3F	121	4	6	$2\frac{1}{2}$	2^{hd}	1^{hd}	3^{1}	$8^{3\frac{1}{2}}$	Velazquez J R	4.00
11Oct09 ^{10}Bel^{5}	9	Sweet Baby Blue	L	5M	115	9	9	3^{1}	3^{1}	$6\frac{1}{2}$	$8^{1\frac{1}{2}}$	$9\frac{3}{4}$	Fox K	121.50
24Sep09 ^{4}Bel^{9}	10	Caterina's Term's	L	5M	115	10	12	12	10^{1}	12	10^{4}	$10^{3\frac{1}{2}}$	Davis J A	86.00
11Oct09 ^{8}Bel^{10}	8	Triple Double Kidd	L b	3F	121	8	11	$7\frac{1}{2}$	7^{1}	10^{1}	12	11^{3}	Bisono A	137.00
01Nov09 ^{4}Aqu^{5}	5	Pronto Pronto	L	3F	121	5	7	1^{hd}	$1\frac{1}{2}$	2^{1}	11^{1}	12	Prado E S	27.50

OFF AT 4:16 Start Good. Won driving. Track Firm.
TIME :24^{4}, :51, 1:17^{2}, 1:42, 1:48 (:24.80, :51.00, 1:17.44, 1:42.14, 1:48.15)

$2 Mutuel Prices:

12- SPLIT POT	18.40	9.20	3.90
6- POINT TO ROYALTY		12.20	5.50
2- GRACE'S VALENTINE			2.60

$2 EXACTA 12-6 PAID $239.00 $2 SUPERFECTA 12-6-2-11 PAID $13,984.00
$2 TRIFECTA 12-6-2 PAID $758.00

Bay Filly, (Feb), by El Corredor - Such Grace by Polish Numbers. Trainer Hennig A. Mark. Bred by Mrs. Gerald A. Nielsen(NY).

SPLIT POT reserved near the back of the pack while taking the inside route, came off the rail after entering the far turn, was swung four wide into the lane, took off with a rapid burst of speed after being set down to reach contention with a furlong to go, then sustaining her momentum shot past the leaders and drew clear. POINT TO ROYALTY responded kindly to her rider's rating tactics during the run leading to the opening bend, was kept reserved within striking distance while between rivals, continued to bide her time around the far turn, was taken three wide into the lane, commenced a rally when roused, grabbed the lead approaching the furlong marker, was overhauled by the top one in the vicinity of the sixteenth pole but dug in with determination to preserve the place. GRACE'S VALENTINE within striking distance throughout, came home willingly to grab the show. DEVILISHAMEYE raced three to four wide around both turns, and held well to the end. TOM AND DICKS GIRL saved ground and lacked the needed response after entering the stretch. CITY VICE forwardly placed along the inside, was allowed to drop back leaving the first turn, eased over to the outside approaching the far bend, made a solid three wide move during the run around the second turn to reach contention again, but failed to sustain the bid after turning for home. REFINERY FIRE raced along the outside, was forced to steady when caught in traffic midstretch, losing valuable momentum, angled outward for racing room then displayed some late interest under mild encouragement. DRIVEN BY ENERGY vied inside for the lead, gave way after going three-quarters. SWEET BABY BLUE had a wide journey and weakened during the final furlong. CATERINA'S TERM'S was no menace. TRIPLE DOUBLE KIDD between rivals, folded after completing a half. PRONTO PRONTO disputed the pace from the outside for six furlongs and faltered.

Owners- 12, Brodsky Alan ; 6, Pinebourne Farm ; 2, Spitzer Mark D.; 11, Tri County Stables ; 7, Hoffman, Kathleen, Sullivan, Rosemary and Symansky, Richard ; 1, DeMola Dorothy ; 3, Imperio, Michael and Loftus, Elizabeth ; 4, Repole Stable ; 9, AC Management Racing ; 10, Vangelatos Peter ; 8, Begorragh Stables ; 5, Flying Zee Stable

Trainers- 12, Hennig Mark A.; 6, Campo, Jr. John P.; 2, Albertrani Thomas ; 11, Hertler John O.; 7, Jerkens James A.; 1, DeMola Richard ; 3, Schettino Dominick A.; 4, Pletcher Todd A.; 9, Quick Patrick J.; 10, Sciacca Gary ; 8, Ubillo Rodrigo A.; 5, Kelly Patrick J.

Breeders- 12, Mrs. Gerald A. Nielsen (NY); 6, Pinebourne Farm (NY); 2, MDS Farms, LLC (NY); 11, Tri-County Stables (NY); 7, Kathleen Hoffman (NY); 1, Mr. & Mrs. Rocco Bueti &Patrick Costello (NY); 3, Thomas M. Daly (NY); 4, Mrs. Gerald A. Nielsen (NY); 9, Tea Party Stable Inc. & Stephen J.Dassalis (NY); 10, Peter Vangelatos (NY); 8, Keith Dickstein (NY); 5, Flying Zee Stables (NY)

Scratched- Crystal Galopoff(18Sep09 ^{6}Mth^{9}), Laylaben(04Oct09 ^{2}Bel^{2}), Justify(22Oct09 ^{9}Bel^{4}), All Sew Smooth(22Oct09 ^{9}Bel^{6})

$2 Daily Double (1-12) Paid $69.00; Daily Double Pool $116,819.
$2 Pick Three (2-1-12) Paid $216.00; Pick Three Pool $80,428.
$2 Pick Four (5-2-1-12) Paid $891.00; Pick Four Pool $155,545.
$2 Pick Six (5-7-5-2-1-12) 5 Correct Paid $157.00; Pick Six Pool N/A.
$2 Pick Six (5-7-5-2-1-12) Paid $33,362.00; Pick Six Pool $377,236.

brisnet.com

On the same day at Churchill Downs another false favorite was identified in the fourth race; a one and one-sixteenths mile $15k claimer for fillies and mares three years old and up which had never won two races.

In that race it was understandable that the 4, Sweet Euphoria, was made the mild 3/1 morning line favorite. After analyzing the race, I ended up concluding that she was a false favorite. The betting public observed in the form her four straight second place finishes and bet her down to 1.6/1.

I bet against her for several reasons: she was one of three fillies in the race that were attempting to move up in class from $5k to $10k claimers; she was attempting to win at two classes up, and her four straight seconds had come at Ellis and Turfway Park. Churchill Downs was a considerable step up the class ladder. The speed ratings of her wins were slow, the best being a mediocre 77. Never mind, the public decided: the trainer was a 26% winner; her jockey was 19%.

Once deciding that she was a false favorite, the search began for a hidden horse or two. One that was certainly not hidden was the 6 horse, Nolin Lake. In her previous race at Kentucky Downs she finished second, just one and three-quarter lengths out in a one mile race on the turf after closing from some seven lengths back at the first call, earning a speed rating of 88, by far the best of the current twelve horse field. I thought her morning line should be about 5/2 and as such was my pick as a mild overlay when she went off at 4.9/1.

Searching further I landed on the 10, Miss Amplified, as a hidden horse long shot candidate. In her last race at Turfway Park she finished fifth in a field of twelve after being five wide all the way on an all weather surface. In the current race she was moving to the dirt. In her second race back she stumbled and lost her jockey after being made the odds on .50/1 favorite. Three races back at River Downs she had finished an up close second in a mile race on the dirt after being made the 1.5/1 favorite.

Her morning line odds were set at what I thought to be an unrealistic 20/1; I gave her at least a one in ten chance of winning and a one in five chance of hitting the board. She went off at a whopping 67/1. I had already made a substantial bet to win and place on Nolin Lake or I would have bet more on Miss Amplified on which I placed a small win bet and a sizable bet to show.

The morning line favorite, Sweet Euphoria, was five lengths behind the lead and was fifth at the half mile, then bled badly and was pulled up and vanned off. Nolin Lake, clearly best, broke in the air then recovered to win by six lengths. Miss Amplified was on the lead at three-quarters then was caught by the winner and the 3, Lion Queen.

The winner paid a nice $11.80, 5.80, and 4.80. Miss Amplified paid $23.60 to show. The trifecta paid $10,992 for a $2 ticket while the superfecta paid a life changing $145,856. Some lucky bettor must have had the sole winning ticket.

All overlay betting boats rise when the favorite finishes out of the money.

FOURTH RACE
Churchill
November 8th, 2009

$1\frac{1}{8}$ MILES. (1.41^{1}) CLAIMING. Purse $14,000 FOR FILLIES AND MARES THREE YEARS OLD AND UPWARD WHICH HAVE NEVER WON TWO RACES. Three Year Olds, 121 lbs.; Older, 124 lbs. Non-winners Of A Race At A Mile Or Over Since October 8 Allowed 3 lbs. Claiming Price $15,000, if for $10,000, allowed 2 lbs. (Clear 68)

Value of Race: $14,140 Winner $8,400; second $2,800; third $1,400; fourth $700; fifth $420; sixth $70; seventh $70; eighth $70; ninth $70; tenth $70; eleventh $70. Mutuel Pool $150,224 Pick 3 Pool $18,676 Pick 4 Pool $44,910 Daily Double Pool $14,629 Exacta Pool $142,816 Superfecta Pool $54,225 Trifecta Pool $100,260

Last Raced	#	Horse	M/Eqt.	A/S	Wt	PP	St	¼	½	¾	Str	Fin	Jockey	Cl'g Pr	Odds $1
28Sep09 ^{7}KD^{2}	6	Nolin Lake	L bf	3F	116	6	11	$10^{1\frac{1}{2}}$	$8^{\frac{1}{2}}$	4^{4}	$1^{2\frac{1}{2}}$	$1^{6\frac{3}{4}}$	Court J K	10000	4.90
08Oct09 ^{2}TP^{6}	3	Lion Queen	LA bf	3F	118	3	6	$4^{1\frac{1}{2}}$	4^{2}	$2^{1\frac{1}{2}}$	3^{4}	$2^{\frac{3}{4}}$	Torres F C	15000	13.30
03Oct09 ^{5}TP^{5}	10	Miss Amplified	LA	3F	118	10	4	2^{1}	$2^{\frac{1}{2}}$	1^{hd}	$2^{\frac{1}{2}}$	$3^{1\frac{1}{4}}$	Arroyo E N	10000	67.40
30Sep09 ^{8}TP^{4}	12	Cuddle the Glory	LA b	3F	115	12	2	$1^{4\frac{1}{2}}$	$1^{1\frac{1}{2}}$	3^{hd}	$4^{2\frac{1}{2}}$	4^{2}	Pompell T L	15000	6.50
28Sep09 ^{7}KD^{6}	2	Betty R	L	4F	119	2	5	7^{1}	$7^{\frac{1}{2}}$	7^{2}	7^{3}	5^{hd}	Arguello, Jr. F A	10000	40.10
18Oct09 ^{4}Kee^{8}	5	Shez a Tease	LA b	3F	109	5	12	$9^{1\frac{1}{2}}$	$10^{\frac{1}{2}}$	8^{hd}	6^{hd}	$6^{1\frac{1}{4}}$	Rossi O	10000	4.50
09Oct09 ^{7}Kee^{12}	7	Island Lioness	LA b	3F	118	7	3	3^{1}	$3^{\frac{1}{2}}$	$5^{2\frac{1}{2}}$	5^{2}	$7^{\frac{1}{2}}$	Goncalves L R	15000	8.10
23Oct09 ^{2}Hoo^{4}	9	Marvelous Gaze	LA	3F	118	9	10	11^{1}	$11^{1\frac{1}{2}}$	11^{12}	9^{1}	$8^{2\frac{3}{4}}$	Lopez J	15000	58.20
08Oct09 ^{2}TP^{3}	8	Masai Queen	LA f	3F	118	8	7	12	12	$9^{\frac{1}{2}}$	10^{2}	9^{nk}	Gonzalez, Jr. S	10000	16.10
30Sep09 ^{8}TP^{5}	11	Deputy Sammie	L	5M	118	11	1	$5^{\frac{1}{2}}$	9^{1}	6^{1}	8^{hd}	10^{2}	Canchano A	15000	40.80
03Oct09 ^{5}TP^{3}	1	Last Chance Buddah	L	3F	116	1	8	6^{1}	6^{hd}	10^{1}	11	11	Riquelme J	10000	58.10
08Oct09 ^{2}TP^{2}	4	Sweet Euphoria	LA b	3F	116	4	9	8^{hd}	5^{hd}	12	12	12	Leparoux J R	10000	1.60

OFF AT 2:08 Start Good For All But 5,6. Won driving. Track Fast.
TIME :24, :49^{1}, 1:15, 1:41^{1}, 1:48^{1} (:24.05, :49.26, 1:15.16, 1:41.34, 1:48.24)

$2 Mutuel Prices:

6- NOLIN LAKE	11.80	5.80	4.80
3- LION QUEEN		13.40	8.20
10- MISS AMPLIFIED			23.60

$2 EXACTA 6-3 PAID $164.60 $2 SUPERFECTA 6-3-10-12 PAID $145,856.20
$2 TRIFECTA 6-3-10 PAID $10,992.60

Chestnut Filly, (Feb), by Friends Lake - Delicatessa by Dare and Go. Trainer Newton Troy. Bred by Barr Inman(KY).

NOLIN LAKE broke in the air to get away slowly, settled in hand, ranged up five wide, drew even with a quarter to run, shook clear entering the stretch and widened through the drive. LION QUEEN stalked the pace off of the inside, bid between horses, was no match for the winner but kept on fairly well to earn the place. MISS AMPLIFIED stalked the pace three deep, poked her head in front with five-sixteenths to run, weakened during the drive but had enough left to hold the show. CUDDLE THE GLORY rushed to the fore, angled in and set a clear pace, was collared after five furlongs and flattened out entering the stretch. BETTY R was allowed to settle between horses, came three wide and improved her position through the stretch. SHEZ A TEASE broke a step slow and was rank to place along the inside, settled into stride on the backstretch, angled out to make a mild rally but failed to seriously threaten. ISLAND LIONESS was forwardly placed along the inside for six furlongs and faded. MARVELOUS GAZE was unhurried into stride, angled in to save ground, shifted out and made a belated gain from between rivals. MASAI QUEEN passed only the tiring ones. DEPUTY SAMMIE rushed to contention six wide, but came up empty after five furlongs and dropped out. LAST CHANCE BUDDAH was hustled along the inside for a half and retreated. SWEET EUPHORIA was allowed to settle, closed the gap four wide, but bled badly and stopped after a half, was pulled up entering the stretch and vanned off.

Owners- 6, Porter J. Chester; 3, Family Fun LLC ; 10, Two Jane's Stable, LLC ; 12, Mereworth Farms ; 2, Pierce, Nancy and Danner, Kelsey ; 5, Elbert, James and Bowen, Erica ; 7, Diamant Eli ; 9, Lauer Penny S.; 8, Wittek Karyn ; 11, Dorsey Sam ; 1, Durbin Jerry H.; 4, Ramsey, Kenneth L. and Sarah K.

Trainers- 6, Newton Troy ; 3, Montano, Sr. Angel O.; 10, Rouck Martin L.; 12, Tammaro Michael A.; 2, Danner Mark ; 5, Wilkinson Clifford F.; 7, Bealmear Laura ; 9, Lauer Michael E.; 8, White Brian M.; 11, Dorsey Sam A.; 1, Durbin James R.; 4, Maker Michael J.

Breeders- 6, Barr Inman (KY); 3, Molly Buck Partnership (KY); 10, North Star Equine (FL); 12, Mereworth Farm (KY); 2, Hinkle Farms (KY); 5, Gilbert G. Campbell (FL); 7, SouthShore Stables LLC (KY); 9, William A. Carl (KY); 8, Brian White, Catherine White, DVM &Norris Davidson (KY); 11, Bobby Rankin (KY); 1, Robby Rankin (KY); 4, Kenneth L. Ramsey & Sarah K. Ramsey (KY)

Scratched- Absolutely Smart(21Oct09 ^{3}Haw^{7}), Witty and Wise(28Sep09 ^{7}KD^{3}), Touche(03Oct09 ^{3}TP^{8}), Emerald Gal(30Sep09 ^{8}TP^{3})

$2 Daily Double (3-6) Paid $21.40; Daily Double Pool $14,629.
$2 Pick Three (2-3-6) Paid $92.80; Pick Three Pool $18,676.
PICK 4 6-2-3-6 PAID $140.35

brisnet.com

In the fifth race at Churchill that same day an example of a false favorite was again on display. In a seven furlong $30k claimer on the dirt for fillies and mares three year olds and up which had not won two races, the 6, Elizabeth Park, was made the tepid morning line favorite at 4/1. In fairness to the racing secretary, I thought the odds were about right, yet Elizabeth was bet down to 1.8/1 at post time.

This is a classic example of the crowd going for a substantial class dropper even though she had thrown in two clunkers in a row. Her last race was a $40k allowance race at a mile in which she was fourth, two lengths from the leader, then stopped badly well before the top of the stretch. In her prior race she was entered in a grade 3 stakes at one mile. She was third at the second call, two and a half lengths from the front, then again stopped badly before entering the stretch. Additionally, her three pre-current race works were slow. She was dropping through three classes; in effect, her connections were announcing that they would like to sell her for $30,000.

The astute handicapper must make a decision regarding such a horse: are they trying to steal a purse, hoping they won't get claimed? Or are they looking for a forced buyer of an unsound horse? In this case I thought she was a false favorite, especially at odds of 1.8/1.

Having made that decision, I looked for a hidden horse long shot candidate. While I didn't find a long shot, I found a middle shot at 7/1 hidden in plain sight. The 2 horse, Rajpur Road, had opened the betting with a morning line of 6/1 then went off at

7/1, making her a mild overlay. I thought her morning line should have been at least 3/1, if not the favorite.

Rajpur Road had won her last race at Kentucky Downs, going a mile on the turf in a $20k claimer for non-winners of two races. She pressed the leader to the head of the stretch then closed to win by two lengths as the favorite at 1.4/1, earning a speed rating of 82. In her second race back at Ellis Park she set the pace in a seven furlong race on the dirt and finished third, a length out, earning a speed rating of 83. In her third race back in a $40k maiden claimer at Churchill Downs she wired the field by seven lengths on a muddy track at a mile and one-sixteenth, earning an 86 speed rating. Her pre-current race work was the second best of the field. At today's seven furlong distance, Rajpur Road was cutting back by a full furlong. And finally, her trainer was the redoubtable Bill Mott, a 17% trainer. With all of those kinds of tells - out in the open - I was amazed that the crowd let her go at 7/1.

Rajpur pressed the pace from the start, gained the lead by one and a half lengths at the head of the stretch, then fought off a furious drive from the 10, Differentiate, to prevail by a head. She paid a generous $16.00, 7.40 and 5.40.

Another overlay hidden in plain sight because the crowd was enamored by the class dropping Elizabeth Park, an underlay that broke in the air then led the field to the head of the stretch, before weakening to finish seventh, some seven lengths out.

Class without recent form, either in recent works or a competitive last race or two, will usually *not* tell, but will more often than not produce another false favorite.

FIFTH RACE
Churchill
November 8th, 2009

7 FURLONGS. (1.20^{2}) CLAIMING. Purse $20,000 FOR FILLIES AND MARES THREE YEARS OLD AND UPWARD WHICH HAVE NEVER WON THREE RACES. Three Year Olds, 122 lbs.; Older, 124 lbs. Non-winners Of A Race Since October 8 Allowed 3 lbs. Claiming Price $30,000, if for $25,000, allowed 2 lbs. (Clear 68)

Value of Race: $20,300 Winner $12,000; second $4,000; third $2,000; fourth $1,000; fifth $600; sixth $100; seventh $100; eighth $100; ninth $100; tenth $100; eleventh $100; twelveth $100. Mutuel Pool $189,494 Pick 3 Pool $24,596 Daily Double Pool $11,717 Exacta Pool $173,125 Superfecta Pool $67,971 Trifecta Pool $121,783

Last Raced	#	Horse	M/Eqt.	A/S	Wt	PP	St	¼	½	Str	Fin	Jockey	Cl'g Pr	Odds $1
21Sep09 ^{5}KD^{1}	2	Rajpur Road	LA	3F	119	2	4	2^{hd}	3^{hd}	$1^{1\frac{1}{2}}$	1^{hd}	Melancon L	30000	7.00
11Oct09 ^{5}Kee^{1}	10	Differentiate	LA	3F	122	10	10	12	11^{hd}	$5^{\frac{1}{2}}$	$2^{2\frac{1}{2}}$	Borel C H	30000	3.50
17Oct09 ^{2}Kee^{1}	7	Miss Redoubled	L	3F	122	7	8	7^{hd}	5^{hd}	3^{hd}	3^{1}	Albarado R	30000	13.50
16Oct09 ^{4}Kee^{3}	4	Truck Ride	L bf	3F	119	4	2	3^{hd}	$4^{1\frac{1}{2}}$	$4^{2\frac{1}{2}}$	$4^{\frac{3}{4}}$	Goncalves L R	30000	16.70
13Oct09 ^{6}Mnr^{1}	8	Even Aly	LA b	4F	124	8	11	$10^{2\frac{1}{2}}$	10^{4}	$9^{\frac{1}{2}}$	5^{1}	Mena M	30000	14.50
25Sep09 ^{8}TP^{2}	9	Tellalittlesecret	L	3F	119	9	9	$11^{\frac{1}{2}}$	12	10^{1}	$6^{1\frac{1}{4}}$	Canchano A	30000	31.50
23Sep09 ^{6}Pid^{8}	6	Elizabeth Park	LA	4F	121	6	12	4^{hd}	1^{hd}	2^{1}	$7^{\frac{1}{2}}$	Theriot J	30000	1.80
27Aug09 ^{9}Hoo^{5}	3	Satan's Plume	LA	4F	121	3	7	8^{hd}	9^{1}	$7^{1\frac{1}{2}}$	$8^{\frac{1}{2}}$	Lopez J	30000	39.80
23Oct09 ^{10}Kee^{3}	11	Full of Ideas	LA bf	5M	121	11	6	9^{4}	$7^{1\frac{1}{2}}$	$8^{\frac{1}{2}}$	$9^{1\frac{1}{4}}$	Castanon J L	30000	13.40
16Oct09 ^{4}Kee^{5}	1	Bootprints	LA b	3F	119	1	1	1^{2}	2^{1}	6^{1}	10^{1}	Torres F C	30000	20.20
12Nov08 ^{6}CD^{6}	12	Mud Creek	L f	4F	121	12	5	$6^{\frac{1}{2}}$	$8^{\frac{1}{2}}$	11^{3}	$11^{7\frac{1}{2}}$	Leparoux J R	30000	29.00
16Oct09 ^{4}Kee^{2}	5	Social Charmer	L bf	3F	119	5	3	5^{1}	6^{1}	12	12	Baird E T	30000	8.40

OFF AT 2:36 Start Good For All But ELIZABETH PARK. Won driving. Track Fast.
TIME :22^{4}, :46^{2}, 1:11^{2}, 1:25 (:22.99, :46.46, 1:11.52, 1:25.08)

$2 Mutuel Prices:

2- RAJPUR ROAD	16.00	7.40	5.40
10- DIFFERENTIATE		4.60	3.20
7- MISS REDOUBLED			5.80

$2 EXACTA 2-10 PAID $83.40 $2 SUPERFECTA 2-10-7-4 PAID $5,548.40
$2 TRIFECTA 2-10-7 PAID $744.00

Dark Bay or Brown Filly, (Apr), by Arch - Stormy Blast by Kayrawan. Trainer Mott I. William. Bred by James S. Karp(KY).

RAJPUR ROAD stalked the pace along the inside, shifted out to make his bid three deep, shook clear entering the stretch then was fully extended to just last. DIFFERENTIATE was unhurried into stride, angled in to save ground, swung six wide to launched her bid, finished full of run and was gaining with every stride. MISS REDOUBLED tucked in behind rivals while never far back, split horses entering the stretch to make a mild bid but lacked the needed late response. TRUCK RIDE attended the pace three deep, offered a mild bid entering the stretch but weakened during the drive. EVEN ALY was unhurried early, angled out to make a late rally, but found her best stride too late. TELLALITTLESECRET was unhurried early, circled seven wide to make a belated but failed to threaten. ELIZABETH PARK broke in the air, rushed to the lead from between horses, but was used up after six furlongs and dropped out. SATAN'S PLUME saved ground to no avail. FULL OF IDEAS settled in the second flight and failed to respond. BOOTPRINTS opened clear to set the pace, was collared after a half and gave way readily once headed. MUD CREEK was allowed to settle, came five wide but came up empty entering the stretch and dropped out. SOCIAL CHARMER chased the pace four wide to the stretch and stopped.

Owners- 2, Karp James S.; 10, R. M. Living Trust ; 7, Centaur Farms, Inc. ; 4, Lucky 8 Stables LLC ; 8, Heyer Bob ; 9, Scarpati Joe ; 6, Roof Douglas D.; 3, Stonelea Stable LLC ; 11, Humphrey, Jr. G. Watts; 1, Inforatag Racing Stable X LLC ; 12, England, David P. and Wright, James ; 5, Farmer Tracy

Trainers- 2, Mott William I.; 10, Catalano Wayne M.; 7, Scherer Merrill R.; 4, Sanner Daniel E.; 8, Lucas Ted W.; 9, Cameron Michael C.; 6, Talley Jeff ; 3, Drury, Jr. Thomas ; 11, Oliver Vicki ; 1, Hanna Clark ; 12, England David P.; 5, McKeever Andrew

Breeders- 2, James S. Karp (KY); 10, Alex Lieblong (KY); 7, Centaur Farms, Inc. (KY); 4, Donald Raymond Reuwer (MD); 8, Liam Gallagher, et al. (KY); 9, Patrick Sliney (KY); 6, Eugene Melnyk (FL); 3, Brilliant Stables Inc., Robert Lewis,Beverly Lewis, John Moynihan et al (KY); 11, G. Watts Humphrey Jr. (KY); 1, Richard Kaster & Nathan Fox (KY); 12, Barbara Hunter (KY); 5, Tracy Farmer (KY)

$2 Daily Double (6-2) Paid $130.00; Daily Double Pool $11,717.
$2 Pick Three (3-6-2) Paid $195.80; Pick Three Pool $24,596.

Our final and most extreme example of identifying a false favorite occurred on October 30, 2009, at Aqueduct in the fourth race, a $12.5k claimer for maiden fillies and mares three years old and up going a mile on the dirt. In a field of eight the 2, Crimson Tempest, was made the 1/2 morning line favorite. She had yet to run on the dirt. In her first race on a sloppy track going one mile and one-sixteenth at Belmont, she finished second by a nose in a $35k maiden claiming race. Her next three races were on the turf at a route. On June 26, 2009, the Tempest threw in a clunker in a $65k maiden claimer, finishing sixth, beaten nine lengths in a field of eight. She next ran at Monmouth in a $50k maiden claimer, finishing third, beaten three and a half lengths, giving up a length in the stretch. In her race at the Meadowlands in a $40k maiden claimer she finished third again, giving up a length in the stretch. It was difficult to see what the racing secretary was seeing when he set her line at odds-on.

Then I examined the past performances of the seven other horses. What a pitiful field: all were class droppers; not one horse was at or under class. Ironically, the class (and I use that term loosely) of the race was the 8, Wynot Siyue. Her four races consisted of three maiden specials; two at $45k; one at $42k, the other a maiden claimer for $25k. In those races she finished last, next to last, next to last, and fifth in a field of seven. Her best effort left her seventeen lengths behind the winner. She had lost the four races by a total of 128 lengths. She should have been sent off at odds of at least 50 or 60 to 1; to be exact, she left the gate at 47/1.

Nevertheless, I noticed that her pre-race work on October 26 of :35 2/5 for three furlongs was a wakeup work. In examining all of her works, I noted that in July and August she had worked four furlongs at :48 3/5 and :48 4/5 handily. The favorite's works were slow, slower, and slowest. In addition the field was giving the 8, Wynot Siyue, from seven to nine pounds in the jockey weights for the apprentice allowance. She had not run with less than 118 pounds in the saddle. I then noted that the trainer, though a 3% winner overall, won at a 15% clip with his maiden special to maiden claimer drops.

The public couldn't restrain themselves from betting $109,000 in the show pool on Crimson Tempest: after all, the track expert tabbed her as a "mortal lock." Wasn't she the class of the race? (No, she was the second class of the race.) Look at those four high priced maiden claimers in which she ran, accomplishing two seconds, a third, and a clunker. Now she was dropping to a $12.5 claimer. What a drop! Probably a sure thing; nevertheless, I decided to look elsewhere as I am wary of such a precipitous drop in class that too often presages an attempt to sell an injured horse through the claim box.

When Crimson Tempest: the sure thing - the horse that couldn't lose that race finished a struggling fourth, the show prices ballooned to $58.00, 15.20, and 34.00. A two dollar show bet on each of the other seven horses paid a total of $107.20, netting the bettor $93.30 or nearly 6.5/1 on the wager. Such a finish is the "bridge jumper's" nightmare.

Meanwhile, the class of the race, Wynot Siyue, wired the field on the front, winning by a widening three and a half lengths, returning to the hidden long shot player prices of $96.00, 30.80, and 58.00. All of the exotic payoffs were box car figures.

Beware the cliff-hanging class dropper. Always examine and usually bet the sole maiden special horse when it drops into a cheap maiden claiming race – no matter the past performance record of the maiden special dropper.

FOURTH RACE
Aqueduct
October 30th, 2009

1 MILE. (1.32²) MAIDEN CLAIMING. Purse $15,000 FOR MAIDENS, FILLIES AND MARES THREE YEARS OLD AND UPWARD. Three Year Olds, 120 lbs.; Older, 122 lbs. Claiming Price $12,500. (Cloudy 56)

Value of Race: $15,000 Winner $9,000; second $3,000; third $1,500; fourth $750; fifth $450; sixth $100; seventh $100; eighth $100.
Mutuel Pool $241,757 Pick 3 Pool $25,241 Daily Double Pool $31,584 Exacta Pool $149,203 Quinella Pool $11,767 Superfecta Pool $53,948 Trifecta Pool $120,485

Last Raced	# Horse	M/Eqt. A/S Wt	PP St	¼	½	¾	Str	Fin	Jockey	Cl'g Pr	Odds $1
04Oct09 2Bel⁵	8 Wynot Siyue	L b 3F 113	8 1	1½	1½	1½½	1²½	1³½	Casey A J	12500	47.00
15Oct09 9Bel³	4 Vortices	L 3F 120	4 6	6hd	6½½	2½½	2²½	2³½	Chavez J F	12500	7.50
15Oct09 9Bel⁵	1 Previous Pleasure	L b 4F 122	1 8	8	7²	6²	4³	3²½	Velasquez C H	12500	16.30
02Oct09 4Med⁴	2 Crimson Tempest	L bf 3F 120	2 7	5½½	2hd	3¹	3½	4⁴½	Castro E	12500	0.35
02Oct09 4Bel⁴	5 Bella Karakorum	L b 3F 120	5 3	4hd	4½	5¹	5½	5⁸½	Studart M	12500	22.80
24Sep09 4Bel¹⁰	6 Why Then	L 3F 120	6 4	2¹	3hd	4½	6³	6⁴½	Garcia A	12500	4.80
21Oct09 2Bel⁴	3 Cottage Industry	L 3F 120	3 5	3hd	5hd	7⁴	7⁸	7¹⁸½	Espinoza J L	12500	45.75
21Oct09 2Bel⁶	7 She's Runnin' Wild	L 3F 120	7 2	7hd	8	8	8	8	Rodriguez R R	12500	35.00

OFF AT 1:53 Start Good. Won driving. Track Good.
TIME :23², :46⁴, 1:12¹, 1:39¹ (:23.43, :46.96, 1:12.38, 1:39.35)

$2 Mutuel Prices:
8- WYNOT SIYUE	96.00	30.80	58.00
4- VORTICES		6.10	15.20
1- PREVIOUS PLEASURE			34.00

$2 EXACTA 8-4 PAID $580.00 $2 QUINELLA 4-8 PAID $243.00
$2 SUPERFECTA 8-4-1-2 PAID $11,737.00 $2 TRIFECTA 8-4-1 PAID $5,801.00

Bay Filly, (Apr), by Kalu - Silkworth by Distinctive Pro. Trainer DiSanto B. Glenn. Bred by Advantage Training (NY).

WYNOT SIYUE off to an alert beginning, took command soon after the start, cut the fractions on a loosely contested lead from the two path, emerged from the furlong grounds still unscathed, and held sway under a drive. VORTICES underwent a four wide journey, was put to strong encouragement during the stretch run and was along for the place. PREVIOUS PLEASURE outrun early, displayed a mild rally to take the show. CRIMSON TEMPEST tracked the leader from the pocket, was asked for a response on the far turn, but failed to gain any ground. BELLA KARAKORUM between rivals on the turn, tired. WHY THEN mildly pursued the leader from the three path for six furlongs before backing off. COTTAGE INDUSTRY displayed brief foot. SHE'S RUNNIN' WILD was outrun.

Owners- 8, Markert Karen ; 4, Santucci, John, Tom and Robert and Toscano, Jr., John T. ; 1, Red Oak Stable ; 2, Carliwood Farms ; 5, Karakorum Farm ; 6, Lerman Roy S.; 3, Durst Murray ; 7, Akindale Farm

Trainers- 8, DiSanto, Jr. John T.; 4, Toscano, Jr. John T.; 1, Tesher Howard M.; 2, Weaver George ; 5, Odintz Jeff ; 6, Lerman Roy S.; 3, Martin, Sr. Frank ; 7, Feron Kathleen M.

Breeders- 8, Advantage Training (NY); 4, Paraic Dolan & Stuart Fitzgibbon (KY); 1, Red Oak Farm (FL); 2, Jon A. Marshall (FL); 5, McMahon of Saratoga Thoroughbreds, LLC,Raymond DeStefano & Emma Bell (NY); 6, Roy S. Lerman & Colts Neck Stables (FL); 3, Dr. Patricia S. Purdy (NY); 7, John Hettinger (NY)

Crimson Tempest was claimed by Toscano, Jr. John T.; trainer, Toscano, Jr. John T.

$2 Daily Double (7-8) Paid $383.50; Daily Double Pool $31,584.
$2 Pick Three (3-7-8) Paid $1,444.00; Pick Three Pool $25,241.

As we have seen, one of the most important factors in finding a hidden horse long shot candidate is the ability to recognize a *false favorite* when we see one. Whether or not we are fortunate enough to find that long shot, money saved by passing on the suspect favorite is money better used in backing overlays. Generally, the substantial class dropper is the most likely horse that the racing secretary will usually tab as the morning line favorite. Look carefully at that horse's past performances: examine its works, speed ratings, and last couple of races. So much of eliminating a false favorite involves *pattern recognition*.

Do you really want to bet on a horse whose odds are 4/5 or less; especially if the race is for two year olds? Why not just watch the race, or take a break? My father often cautioned me that I was too impatient. I'm sure he would have been surprised to learn that pari-mutual thoroughbred horse racing taught me something he never could; patience.

The same is true of searching for the hidden horse: be patient, but when you find one supported by the tells we have elucidated, don't hesitate to pull the trigger and make a solid bet. These types of opportunities are few and far between so we must make the most of such a race by betting substantially more than two dollars.

While on the subject of *patience,* the hidden horse hunter will be visited by impatience on those days when it appears that "chalk" is the dominant form. When the favorite or second favorite wins three or four races in a row the temptation is considerable for the long shot player to revert to playing form. Keep in mind that - over time - the favorite will lose two out of three races. In the short run; however, chalk can win often enough to make the hidden horse hunter despair and bring doubt to the methodology of the system. For whatever reason, there appears to be more chalk days on weekdays than there is on weekends. Perhaps that is because the weekends bring out more of the general public and consequently players less sophisticated than the weekday regulars.

Hold your fire on those form winning days and stay alert for the variable or variables that will point you to a long shot play. And when you have found a hidden horse tell in the forest of its past performances, be prepared to make a solid bet.

Depending on your stake, proportion your bets accordingly. I will not bet more than 40 per cent of my stake on any one race. It's a real downer to bet the balance in your account on an apparent excellent prospect, only to have the horse forget to lift its hoofs and finish out of the money. The pros call that: "getting whacked."

With a stake of $100 I will normally bet $10 to win and place on my pick, leaving another $20 for exacta plays which are usually wheels or keys up and back with my pick; that is, with my selected horse to finish first or second with my other keyed horses. When I get my stake up to $200 my standard bet is $20 to win and place and $40 for exacta combinations. I reduce the size of my bets when losing, but never bet more than 40% of the balance. You can see that with an initial stake of $100 I would have to lose four races in a row before getting down to a balance of $10, and if I lose four races in a row it's probably time to call it a day.

Conversely, I increase the size of my bets as I win - still keeping the maximum 40% of my stake bet rule. Through years of trial and error this is the money management system that has worked for me. No known money management system can guarantee a profit at the track if you are not an experienced handicapper, but there are several good ones that can minimize your losses on that inevitable losing day.

As a frequent online horse bettor, I am on many mailing lists of tipsters and system sellers. Over many years I have found few of these to be worth the money, with the exception of the California Handicapper, and even they have their bad days. Too often the system sellers will put you on the favorite, then crow if the horse wins at $4. The years have taught me that you cannot buy consistent winners from the "experts." Consistent handicapping success is hard to come by, but I have found that the most important factor contributing to a winning day is *concentration*. A distracted bettor might as well throw money at the slots. One thing is always with me on winning days: the ability to analyze in depth each past performance of each horse in the field; then to identify the tells that have often predicted a long shot winner.

One of the most important past performances to examine is that of the morning line favorite: does the horse's record support the odds? Never mind that you are probably not going to bet an underlay; identifying false favorites can lead you to the overlay value bet. And overlays hold the key to value bets. Money saved by correctly identifying a false favorite is better invested in a horse that the betting public has overlooked because they did not take the time to enter the *Forest of Hidden Horse Tells*.

Chapter 11

O ne of the problems in identifying hidden horse long shot candidates in Graded Stakes and the Classics is the inability to clearly differentiate relative class, for in these races class droppers - if any are to be found - are few and far between. There are only class climbers in the Kentucky Derby, the Preakness, and the Belmont Stakes. Yet, as we have seen, long shots win their share of those races. One of the more astounding upsets in the history of the race occurred in the 2009 Derby when Make Mine Bird blew away the field at 50/1. In spite of my thorough analysis of the Bird's past performances, I could not honestly land on a tell that could have predicted such a dominating performance as his Derby win. He then proved it was no fluke by his second place finish in the Preakness. Many professional handicappers felt he would have beaten Rachel Alexandra, but for traffic trouble in the stretch.

When the Bird finished a creditable third in the Belmont, he entered the exclusive club of three year old colts to run and finish on the board in all three of the classics. Clearly, the son of Birdstone and the cousin of Summer Bird was no anomaly, nor was his spectacular Derby win a fluke. Why - you may fairly ask - did the public let him leave the gate at monster odds?

It seems to me that it was the modest credentials of his connections; his owners and his trainer were from, of all places, New Mexico. They didn't fly the Bird to Churchill Downs, their laconic improbable trainer simply hooked his horse trailer to his pickup truck and drove him into the history of the Run for the Roses. All credit to the colt's trainer, Bennie Woolley, who changed the Bird's running style from front runner to a deep closing router.

It is a remarkable coincidence that Make Mine Bird's first cousin, Summer Bird, turned out to be the playable long shot in the Belmont. We can't fairly say that he was a hidden long shot, for Nick Zito is known for his ability to get unsuccessful Derby runners into condition for the Belmont when he keeps them out of the Preakness; nevertheless, Summer Bird's troubled Derby try led the public to let him leave the gate at 11.9/1. While Make Mine Bird was the complete router in the Derby and Preakness, it was clear when he led after a mile and a quarter - and then weakened - that he could not get the Belmont distance.

ELEVENTH RACE
Belmont Park
June 6th, 2009

1½ MILES. (2.24) STAKES. Purse $1,000,000 *BELMONT S. (GRADE I)* (UP TO $70,000 NYSBFOA) FOR THREE YEAR OLDS. By subscription of $600 each, to accompany the nomination, if made on or before January 24, 2009, or $6,000, if made on or before March 28, 2009. At any time prior to the closing time of entries, horses may be nominated to The Belmont Stakes upon payment of a supplementary fee of $100,000 to the New York Racing Association, Inc. $10,000 to pass the entry box and $10,000 additional to start. All entrants, supplemental or otherwise, will be required to pay entry and starting fees. The purse to be divided 60% to the winner, 20% to second, 11% to third, 6% to fourth and 3% to fifth. Colts and Geldings, 126 lbs.; Fillies, 121 lbs. The winning owner will be presented with the August Belmont Memorial Cup to be retaine d for one year as well as a trophy for permanent possession and trophies to the winning trainer and jockey. (Clear 75)

Value of Race: $1,000,000 Winner $600,000; second $200,000; third $110,000; fourth $60,000; fifth $30,000. Mutuel Pool $17,632,539 Pick 3 Pool $669,594 Pick 4 Pool $2,243,069 Pick 6 Pool $1,659,251 Daily Double Pool $751,121 Daily Double Pool $483,689 Exacta Pool $10,379,856 Superfecta Pool $5,380,332 Trifecta Pool $12,344,260

Last Raced	#	Horse	M/Eqt.	A/S	Wt	PP	¼	½	1m	1¼	Str	Fin	Jockey	Odds $1
02May09 ^{11}CD^{6}	4	Summer Bird	L b	3C	126	4	5^{1}	6^{1}	9^{2}	4^{1}	4^{5}	$1^{2¾}$	Desormeaux K J	11.90
02May09 ^{11}CD^{11}	2	Dunkirk	L	3C	126	2	$1^{1½}$	1^{1}	1^{1}	$3^{2½}$	2^{1}	2^{nk}	Velazquez J R	4.60
16May09 ^{12}Pim^{2}	7	Mine That Bird	L f	3G	126	7	10	10	$8^{½}$	$1^{½}$	$1^{½}$	$3^{3¾}$	Borel C H	1.25
09May09 ^{9}Bel^{1}	6	Charitable Man	L	3C	126	6	$4^{½}$	$4^{1½}$	3^{1}	$2^{½}$	$3^{1½}$	$4^{3¾}$	Garcia A	4.60
16May09 ^{12}Pim^{6}	5	Luv Gov	L b	3C	126	5	9^{3}	9^{1}	10	$7^{½}$	6^{2}	$5^{4½}$	Mena M	22.40
16May09 ^{12}Pim^{4}	8	Flying Private	L b	3C	126	8	$6^{½}$	$5^{½}$	$6^{½}$	$5^{1½}$	$5^{½}$	6^{2}	Leparoux J R	17.30
09May09 ^{9}Bel^{3}	10	Brave Victory	L	3C	126	10	8^{1}	8^{2}	5^{1}	$9^{½}$	$8^{2½}$	$7^{1¼}$	Maragh R	27.50
02May09 ^{11}CD^{15}	3	Mr. Hot Stuff	L	3C	126	3	$3^{1½}$	$3^{½}$	4^{1}	$6^{½}$	7^{1}	8^{7}	Prado E S	22.60
02May09 ^{11}CD^{5}	1	Chocolate Candy	L	3C	126	1	7^{1}	$7^{½}$	$7^{½}$	8^{2}	9^{14}	$9^{28¾}$	Gomez G K	9.50
02May09 ^{10}Pim^{1}	9	Miner's Escape	L b	3C	126	9	2^{1}	2^{1}	$2^{½}$	10	10	10	Lezcano J	22.00

OFF AT 6:29 Start Good. Won driving. Track Fast.

TIME $:23^{2}$, :47, $1:12^{2}$, $1:37^{4}$, $2:01^{3}$, $2:27^{2}$ (:23.41, :47.13, 1:12.43, 1:37.86, 2:01.66, 2:27.54)

$2 Mutuel Prices:

4- SUMMER BIRD	25.80	9.30	4.70
2- DUNKIRK		5.40	3.60
7- MINE THAT BIRD			2.60

$2 EXACTA 4-2 PAID $121.00 $2 SUPERFECTA 4-2-7-6 PAID $852.00
$2 TRIFECTA 4-2-7 PAID $295.00

Chestnut Colt, (Apr), by Birdstone - Hong Kong Squall by Summer Squall. Trainer Ice A. Tim. Bred by Dr. K. K. Jayaraman &Dr. V. Devi Jayaraman(KY).

SUMMER BIRD steadied between horses on the first turn, angled in entering the backstretch, steadied along the rail while saving ground midway down the backstretch, raced under a hold in traffic along the inside while dropping back losing his position at the half mile pole, swung to the outside for clear sailing at the five-sixteenths pole, circled six wide while rallying at the top of the stretch, made a strong run to challenge inside the furlong marker, surged to the front leaving the sixteenth pole then edged away under strong right handed encouragement in the final seventy yards. DUNKIRK sprinted clear along the rail, set the pace along the inside to the turn, dropped back a bit at the quarter pole, fought back gamely while drifting out a bit in midstretch then outfinished MINE THAT BIRD for the place. MINE THAT BIRD was brushed a bit at the start, angled to the rail after being taken in hand during the early stages, swung to the outside entering the backstretch, trailed for a half while well off the rail, began his move from outside while being carried out a bit by BRAVE VICTORY at the five-eighths pole, made a strong middle move four wide to quickly reach contention on the turn, surged to the front approaching the quarter pole, continued on the lead into midstretch then weakened under pressure through the final sixteenth. CHARITABLE MAN broke outward at the start then moved to the inside, angled out leaving the first turn, raced in good position while three wide for six furlongs, made a run between rivals to challenge on the turn, battled between horses into upper stretch, steadied outside the runner-up in midstretch and gradually tired thereafter. LUV GOV was taken in hand on the first turn, raced far back while saving ground, gradually gained leaving the far turn, swung four wide between horses at the quarter pole then improved his position with a mild late rally. FLYING PRIVATE steadied in traffic on the first turn, raced in the middle of the pack for six furlongs, was in traffic while within striking distance on the turn, lodged a mild move in upper stretch and flattened out. BRAVE VICTORY was outrun for a half, lodged a brief move four wide to get within striking distance on the far turn then faltered at the top of the stretch. MR. HOT STUFF raced just off the pace along the rail, was under a firm hold along the inside, dropped back a bit leaving the far turn and steadily tired thereafter. CHOCOLATE CANDY steadied repeatedly along the inside entering the backstretch and for a good portion of the opening seven furlongs while slightly off the rail, swung five wide on the turn while making a brief move on the turn then flattened out. MINER'S ESCAPE pressed the pace in the two path for seven furlongs and gave way on the turn. Following a stewards inquiry into the stretch run there was no change in the order of finish.

Owners- 4, Jayaraman, Kalarikkal K. and Vilasini D. ; 2, Magnier, Mrs. John, Tabor, Michael and Smith, Derrick ; 7, Double Eagle Ranch and Buena Suerte Equine ; 6, Warren, Jr., Mr. and Mrs. William K. ; 5, Marylou Whitney Stables ; 8, Baker, Robert C. and Mack, William L. ; 10, LaPenta Robert V.; 3, WinStar Farm LLC ; 1, The Craig Family Trust ; 9, LaPenta Robert V.

Trainers- 4, Ice Tim A.; 2, Pletcher Todd A.; 7, Woolley, Jr. Bennie L.; 6, McLaughlin Kiaran P.; 5, Lukas D. Wayne; 8, Lukas D. Wayne; 10, Zito Nicholas P.; 3, Harty Eoin G.; 1, Hollendorfer Jerry ; 9, Zito Nicholas P.

Breeders- 4, Dr. K. K. Jayaraman &Dr. V. Devi Jayaraman (KY); 2, W. S. Farish, James Elkins &W. T. Webber Jr. (KY); 7, Lamantia, Blackburn & Needham/BetzThoroughbreds (KY); 6, Edward P. Evans (VA); 5, Marylou Whitney Stables (KY); 8, John Mulholland & Martha Jane Mulholland (KY); 10, Miller Thoroughbred Farm (KY); 3, WinStar Farm, LLC (KY); 1, Sid Craig & Jenny Craig (KY); 9, Paul Carroll (KY)

$2 Daily Double (5-4) Paid $152.50; Daily Double Pool $751,121.
$2 Daily Double (BROOKLYN-BELMONT 3-4) Paid $337.50; Daily Double Pool $483,689.
$2 Pick Three (2-5-4) Paid $2,577.00; Pick Three Pool $669,594.
$2 Pick Four (4-2-5-4) Paid $17,065.00; Pick Four Pool $2,243,069.
$2 Pick Six (6-7-4-2-5-4) 5 Correct Paid $2,482.00; Pick Six Pool N/A.
$2 Pick Six (6-7-4-2-5-4) Paid $969,345.00; Pick Six Pool $1,659,251.

4 Summer Bird (S 0)
12/1
DESORMEAUX K J
Ch. c. 3
Sire: Birdstone (Grindstone) $10,000
Dam: Hong Kong Squall (Summer Squall)
Brdr: Dr K K Jayaraman &Dr V Devi Jayaraman (KY)
Trnr: Ice Tim A
Prime Power
Blinkr On
L 126

Life:	4	1 - 0 - 1	$123,040	98	Fst (109)	3	1 - 0 - 1	$123,040	98
2009	4	1 - 0 - 1	$123,040	98	Off (112?)	1	0 - 0 - 0	$0	96
2008	0	0 - 0 - 0	$0		Dis (113?)	0	0 - 0 - 0	$0	
Bel	0	0 - 0 - 0	$0		Trf (107?)	0	0 - 0 - 0	$0	
					AW	0	0 - 0 - 0	$0	

DATE TRK	DIST						RACETYPE	E1	E2/	LP	1c	2c	SPD	PP	ST	1C	2C	Str	FIN	JOCKEY		ODDS	Top Finishers	Comment
02May09CD^{11}	1¼	sy	$:47^{1}$	1:12	$1:37^{2}$	$2:02^{8}$	KyDerby-G1	74	82/	92										Rosier CR		L 43.60	MThtBrd Pioneer ofThNile MusktMn	Good 7 wide run 19
11Apr09OP^{11}	1⅛	ft	:46	1:11	$1:36^{3}$	1:49	Arkderby-G2	75	84/	100	+4	-3	98	7	10	10	6	3	3	Rosier CR		L 28.10	PpClnj OldFshnd SumrBrd	Off slow; 5w1/4; gaining 10
19Mar09OP^{9}	1 1/16	ft	$:23^{2}$	$:47^{3}$	$1:13^{1}$	$1:44^{3}$	Mdn 35k	72	81/	101	-1	-4	92	7	7	7	6	1	1	Rosier CR		L (.80)	SumrBrd LvGv CmvlRd	5w bid; drove clear 8
01Mar09OP^{10}	6f	ft	$:22^{1}$	$:46^{4}$	$:59^{2}$	$1:11^{2}$	Mdn 34k	72	67/	103	-2	-3	78	8	11	9	9	5	4	Rosier CR		L 18.60	NLndng CisclChngd Brgn	6w1/4, gaining midtrack 11

30May Bel 5f ft $1:01^{4}$ B 6/9 23May Bel 7f ft $1:26^{2}$ B 1/7 15May LaD 5f ft 1:02 B 8/30 24Apr CD 6f ft $1:15^{4}$ B 3/3 04Apr OP 3f ft 1:30? B 1/15 14Mar OP 5f gd $1:02^{?}$ B 5/35
22Feb OP 5f ft 1:02 B 8/24 15Feb OP 5f ft $1:02^{4}$ Hg 15/30 08Feb OP 4f ft $:49^{3}$ B 6/63 30Dec'08 SA 6f ft $1:13^{4}$ H 6/21 24Dec'08 SA 5f ft $1:01^{1}$ H 25/61 17Dec'08 SA 6f ft $1:15^{2}$ H 9/13

TRAINER: 1stTimeBlinkers (7 14% +13.89) Dirt/Turf (33 18% +1.15) Graded stakes (8 0% -2.00) Routes (49 15% +1.30) Dirt starts (111 14% +0.53)

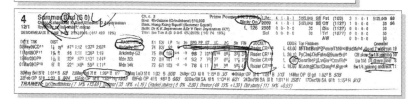

A representative example of clear tells tabbing a hidden horse long shot in a Stakes race occurred at Del Mar in the eighth race on July 25, 2009, with the running of the Eddie Read Handicap, a grade I with a purse of $350k and a field of eight three year olds and up going one and one-eighth mile on the turf.

The racing secretary posted the 1, Monterey Jazz, as the 2/1 favorite. Jazz was a five year old with a lifetime record of eight wins and four shows from 19 starts. He was a consistent front runner that had to have the front to win, never having come from off the pace to contend. While he had never won a Grade I stake, he had won several 2's and 3's. In the current race there was another front runner, the 4, Thorn Song, winner of a million and two and two grade 1's and a record of 8-4-4 out of 28 races. The Thorn also had to have the front to win, never having come from off the pace to contend. His morning line was 8/1.

Since it appeared to me that the Jazz and the Thorn would press each other at the front, I looked for a long shot contender, landing on the 3, Global Hunter. His morning line was 12/1, floating up to 14/1 by post time. The Hunter's last race was just 14 days before; a grade 1 at one mile and one-quarter on the poly, which was not his favorite running surface. Not breaking well in a field of 13, he finished ninth after being hung five wide for the trip and was never in the race, qualifying Global Hunter as a "hidden horse." The tell on him; however, was his work on July 20 - a bullet for three furlongs of :33 1/5 - just five days before the current race. The betting public completely ignored this near world record work, focusing their attention on the poor race of July 11.

My analysis was that the Jazz and the Thorn would hook up on the front and kill each other off, and that's exactly what happened. Global Hunter ran just off the pace and when the Thorn bolted to the outside as he turned into the stretch after taking enough out of the Jazz to make him give it up, the Hunter came on to easily win going away.

His payoff was $30.20, 13.00, and 7.80, anchoring a $234 exacta with an obvious contender. Global Hunter was hidden in the sense that it is extremely difficult for the betting public to invest in a horse with a non-competitive last race unless there is an obvious excuse such as traffic trouble, getting bumped, having to steady, and the like.

Because he was the sole front speed, I had made a successful sizable investment in the Jazz in his last race on July 4 in which he wired the field at odds of 2.7/1, but I wanted no part of him in the current race because of the Thorn's front speed; honoring the trainer's time proven adage that when there is only one front speed in the race, bet the front runner, assuming it is running at class. When there are two or more who usually contest the front early, look elsewhere for the winner of that race.

EIGHTH RACE
Del Mar
July 25th, 2009

1⅛ MILES. (Turf) (1.44⁵) STAKES. Purse $350,000 *EDDIE READ S. (GRADE I)* FOR THREE-YEAR-OLDS AND UPWARD. By subscription of $350 each, which shall accompany the nomination, and $3,500 additional to start, with $350,000 Guaranteed, of which $210,000 to first, $70,000 to second, $42,000 to third, $21,000 to fourth and $7,000 to fifth. Three-year-olds 118 lbs.; Older 123 lbs. Non-winners of a Grade I at one mile or over in 2009 allowed 2 lbs.; of a Grade II at one mile or over in 2009 or a Grade I at one mile or over in 2008, 4 lbs. A trophy will be presented to the owner of th e winner. Nominations Closed Thursday, July 16, 2009, with 15. (Cloudy 78)

Value of Race: $350,000 Winner $210,000; second $70,000; third $42,000; fourth $21,000; fifth $7,000. Mutuel Pool $723,128 Pick 3 Pool $137,942 Daily Double Pool $40,756 Exacta Pool $344,050 Quinella Pool $19,417 Superfecta Pool $173,724 Trifecta Pool $304,925

Last Raced	#	Horse	M/Eqt.	A/S	Wt	PP	St	¼	½	¾	Str	Fin	Jockey	Odds $1
11 Jly 09 ⁸Hol⁸	3	Global Hunter (ARG)	BL	6H	119	3	2	3¹	2²½	2⁴½	1½	1¹	Nakatani C S	14.10
27 Jun09 ⁹Hol¹	5	Awesome Gem	BL b	6G	119	5	8	7¹	5hd	6hd	6²½	2½	Solis A O	8.70
04 Jly 09 ⁸Hol³	8	Whatsthescript (IRE)	BL	5H	119	8	3	4½	4²	4½	3½	3hd	Rosario J	2.90
04 Jly 09 ⁸Hol²	6	Artiste Royel (IRE)	BL b	8R	121	6	5	6½	6¹½	5¹	5hd	4¹¾	Talamo J	7.00
04 Jly 09 ⁸Hol¹	1	Monterey Jazz	BL	5H	121	1	4	2¹½	1⁴½	1⁵	2³	5½	Baze T	1.10
11 Jly 09 ⁸Hol⁹	2	Dakota Phone	BL b	4G	119	2	7	5¹½	3¹	3¹	4¹	6hd	Gomez G K	16.20
16May09 ⁴Pim⁴	7	Richard's Kid	BL b	4C	119	7	6	8	7	7	7	7	Espinoza V	21.80
04 Jly 09 ¹⁰CD⁴	4	Thorn Song	BL b	6H	123	4	1	1²	8	8ᶜᵐ	8ᶜᵐ	8	Smith M E	11.60

OFF AT 5:44 Start Good. Won driving. Track Firm.

TIME :24, :47, 1:10, 1:34, 1:46¹ (:24.02, :47.18, 1:10.11, 1:34.12, 1:46.24)

$2 Mutuel Prices:

3- GLOBAL HUNTER (ARG)	30.20	13.00	7.80
5- AWESOME GEM		9.80	5.60
8- WHATSTHESCRIPT (IRE)			3.80

$1 EXACTA 3-5 PAID $117.20 $2 QUINELLA 3-5 PAID $105.60
$1 SUPERFECTA 3-5-8-6 PAID $2,119.00 $1 TRIFECTA 3-5-8 PAID $487.70

Bay Horse, (Oc), by Jade Hunter - Griffe de Paris (BRZ) by Telescopico (ARG). Trainer Avila C. A.. Bred by La Providencia(ARG).

GLOBAL HUNTER (ARG) chased inside, moved up then came out leaving the second turn and into the stretch, gained the lead outside a rival in midstretch, kicked clear while drifting out a bit under left handed urging and held gamely. AWESOME GEM saved ground off the pace, came out into the stretch and rallied between foes in deep stretch for the place. WHATSTHESCRIPT (IRE) angled in and settled outside a rival chasing the pace, came out some in the stretch, also split rivals in deep stretch and edged a foe for the show. ARTISTE ROYAL (IRE) allowed to settle between horses early then came out outside a rival, came out into the stretch and just missed third. MONTEREY JAZZ pulled his way along inside then stalked a bit off the rail, steadied off heels into the first turn then inherited the lead, tugged his way clear to set the pace inside, came a bit off the rail into the stretch, drifted in some in midstretch and weakened in the final furlong. DAKOTA PHONE a bit slow to begin, chased inside to the stretch and lacked the necessary response. RICHARD'S KID allowed to settle outside then off the rail, came out into the stretch and did not rally. THORN SONG sent to the early lead, angled in and set the pace inside, bolted to the outside fence on the first turn and was pulled up. The stewards conducted an inquiry into the incident on the first turn before ruling THORN SONG was responsible for his own trouble.

Owners- 3, L-Bo Racing and Pyle, Monte ; 5, West Point Thoroughbreds ; 8, Tommy Town Thoroughbreds LLC ; 6, Heerensperger, David and Jill ; 1, A and R Stables LLC and Class Racing Stable ; 2, Carver, John, Halo Farms, Todaro, George and Hollendorfer, Jerry ; 7, Arnold Zetcher LLC ; 4, Zayat Stables, LLC

Trainers- 3, Avila A. C.; 5, Dollase Craig ; 8, Sadler John W.; 6, Drysdale Neil D.; 1, Dollase Craig ; 2, Hollendorfer Jerry ; 7, Baffert Bob ; 4, Mitchell Mike R.

Breeders- 3, La Providencia (ARG); 5, Runnymede Farm Inc., Catesby Clay &Peter Callahan (KY); 8, C. Mac Hale and J. Hyland (IRE); 6, Dayton Investments Ltd (IRE); 1, Danzel Brendamuehl (KY); 2, Cashmark Farms, Inc. & Dakota Stables (KY); 7, Fitzhugh, LLC (MD); 4, Pinnacle Racing LLC &Taylor Made Farm Inc. (KY)

$2 Daily Double (10-3) Paid $74.40; Daily Double Pool $40,766.
$1 Pick Three (11-10-3) Paid $379.60; Pick Three Pool $137,942.

The tells on Global Hunter were:

1) His work five days before the race at three furlongs in :33 1/5.

2) He was cutting back from one mile and one-quarter to one mile and one-eighth.

3) He was moving from poly track to the turf, his favorite distance.

Another good example of finding a hidden long shot candidate in a handicap or graded stakes race occurred on August 8, 2009, in the Whitney Handicap for three year olds and up, going one mile and one-eighth on the dirt at Saratoga for a purse of $750k. The racing secretary tabbed the 4, Macho Again, with a morning line of 7/2. A proven router, the horse had won nearly one and a half million dollars and was coming off a seven week layoff after winning a grade one stakes on June 13 at Churchill Downs. He was not, however, the morning line favorite, for the 7 horse, Commentator, was given that role with a morning line of 8/5. He was a confirmed front runner, never having come from off the pace to contend. Since there was another front runner in the race, the 5 horse, Tizway, who also had to have the front or else, I tabbed Commentator as a false favorite. I thought Macho Again's record and recent form deserved the favorite's mantle.

In my search for a long shot candidate I landed on the 3, Bullsbay. The horse last ran on July 9 at Hollywood in a Grade I at one mile and one-quarter, turning in a clunker on the all weather track after contending to the head of the stretch. Bullsbay's favorite distance appeared to be at one mile and one-eighth and his style of running was to attend the pace and close. His jockey, Jeremy Rose, was a 24% winner; his trainer 33% when moving horses from all weather surfaces to the dirt.

A few minutes before post time his odds floated up to 19/1. My analysis of the race was that Tizway and Commentator would duel on the front for the lead, with Bullsbay stalking them and that Macho Again would put in his deep close. That is what happened, with Bullsbay just holding off the fast closing Macho Again for the win.

Another cutback horse winner at a great price! I had bet Bullsbay to win and place which paid $39.60 and 12.00 with the exacta paying $179.50, proving again that you can find hidden tells even in a three-quarter of a million dollar Grade I Handicap Stake.

TENTH RACE
Saratoga
August 8th, 2009

1⅛ MILES. (1.46³) STAKES. Purse $750,000 *WHITNEY H. (GRADE I)* A HANDICAP FOR THREE YEAR OLDS AND UPWARD. No nomination fee. $7,500 to pass the entry box. All starters will receive a $4,000 rebate. The purse to be divided 60% to the winner, 20% to second, 10% to third, 5% to fourth, 3% to fifth and 2% divided equally among the remaining finishers. Any horse that competed in the Suburban Handicap will have their entry fee waived for the Whitney Handicap and any horse that competes in both the Whitney Handicap and the Woodward will have their entry fee waived for the W oodward. Trophies will be presented to the winning owner, trainer and jockey.
Closed Saturday, July 25, 2009 with 24 Nominations. (Clear 73)

Value of Race: $750,000 Winner $450,000; second $150,000; third $75,000; fourth $37,500; fifth $22,500; sixth $15,000. Mutuel Pool $824,941 Pick 3 Pool $110,822 Daily Double Pool $155,367 Exacta Pool $477,858 Trifecta Pool $313,987 Grand Slam Pool $35,952

Last Raced	# Horse	M/Eqt.	A/S Wt	PP St	¼	½	¾	Str	Fin	Jockey	Odds $1
11 Jly09 ⁸Hol¹⁰	3 Bullsbay	L	5H 116	2 3	4²	4¹	4⁴	1¹	1¹½	Rose J	18.80
13Jun09 ¹⁰CD¹	4 Macho Again	L b	4C 119	3 4	6	6	5³½	3²	2¹½	Albarado R	3.65
12Jun09 ³Bel¹	7 Commentator	L	8G 12⅟	6 2	1¹	1¹	1²	2¹½	3²¾	Velazquez J R	2.20
12Jly 09 ⁹Bel¹	5 Tizway	L b	4C 113	4 5	2¹	2½	3²	4²	4²¾	Maragh R	10.70
04 Jly 09 ¹⁰Bel²	6 Dry Martini	L b	6G 117	5 6	5½	5¹	6	6	5ʰᵈ	Prado E S	3.55
04 Jly 09 ⁹Mth²	1 Smooth Air	L f	4C 118	1 1	3⁹	3¹⁰	2¹½	5¹	6	Lezcano J	2.15

OFF AT 5:50 Start Good. Won driving. Track Fast.
TIME :23², :46¹, 1:10, 1:35, 1:48   (:23.49, :46.38, 1:10.11, 1:35.14, 1:48.12)

$2 Mutuel Prices:

3-BULLSBAY	39.60	12.00	5.90
4-MACHO AGAIN		4.90	3.40
7-COMMENTATOR			3.20

$2 EXACTA 3-4 PAID $179.50 $2 TRIFECTA 3-4-7 PAID $554.00
$2 GRAND SLAM 3/6/7-1/5/8-1/2/6-3 PAID $166.50 4 Correct

Bay Horse, (Mr), by Tiznow - The Hess Express by Lord Carson. Trainer Motion Graham H. Bred by Brad Anderson(KY).
BULLSBAY saved ground on the first turn, moved out on the backstretch, raced three wide for five furlongs, made a strong moved along the rail at the three-eighths pole, split horses on the turn, angled out entering the stretch, charge to the front in midstretch and edged clear under strong right hand urging. MACHO AGAIN raced far back for five furlongs, launched a bid from outside on the turn, swung five wide at the quarter pole and closed late in the middle of the track to gain the place. COMMENTATOR angled in on the first turn after sprinting clear, set a quick pace along the rail to the top of the stretch, relinquished the lead to the winner nearing the furlong marker and weakened late to lose the place. TIZWAY raced up close in the two path to the turn and steadily tired thereafter. DRY MARTINI never reached contention. SMOOTH AIR raced up close along the inside, lodged a brief move on the turn and gave way.

Owners- 3, Mitchell Ranch, LLC, Lewkowitz, Frank and Rice, Joe ; 4, West Point Thoroughbreds ; 7, Farmer Tracy ; 5, Clifton, Jr. William L; 6, Nyren Carol ; 1, Mount Joy Stables, inc.

Trainers- 3, Motion H. Graham; 4, Stewart Dallas ; 7, Zito Nicholas P.; 5, Bond H. James; 6, Tagg Barclay ; 1, Brown Chad C.

Breeders- 3, Brad Anderson (KY); 4, Milan Kosanovich (FL); 7, Michael Martinez (NY); 5, Whisper Hill Farm (KY); 6, Carol Hershe & Marty Hershe (FL); 1, Mount Joy Stables (FL)

Scratched- Asiatic Boy (ARG){04 Jly 09 ¹⁰Bel²}

$2 Daily Double (6-3) Paid $314.50; Daily Double Pool $155,367.
$2 Pick Three (8-6-3) Paid $705.00; Pick Three Pool $110,822.

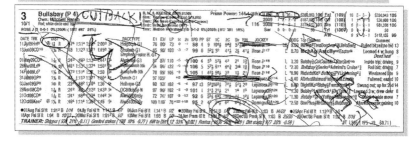

The tells for Bullsbay were:

1) He was cutting back by one-eighth mile.
2) His trainer and his jockey had 16% and 24% winning records.
3) His trainer was 33% when moving his horses from all weather to dirt.

Another example of finding a hidden horse long shot in a handicap or stakes race occurred on August 15, 2009, in the Sword Dancer Invitational Stake at Saratoga, when a field of ten three year olds and up went a mile and a half on the turf for a purse of $500k.

It is puzzling that the racing secretary made the 1, Grand Couterier, the morning line favorite at 3/1. The horse had just completed a dull race on July 11 at Belmont in a Grade I mile and three-eighths turf try. His recent works were poor. In the ten races listed in his past performances, Grand Couterier had left the gate at odds of 3/1 or better only twice. His odds in his last three races were 5.1/1, 5.7/1, and 6.9/1. Through August of 2009 the horse had won just $21k for the year, though his lifetime earnings exceeded a million two. I thought this was a case of an older horse on his way down the class ladder. Nevertheless, the public bought the morning line odds and sent the Couterier off at 2.9/1.

Another older class horse in the race was the ten year old, Better Talk Now, winner of over four million dollars. He would be ridden by the leading Belmont jockey, Ramon Dominguez. The betting public let the old warrior get away at overlay odds of 11.9/1.

In searching for a hidden horse long shot candidate, I landed on the 7, Telling. In all fairness his tells were well hidden; you had to look deep for them, but several were there. Obviously the racing secretary missed them for Telling's morning line was 20/1, which was understandable because the horse had only finished second and third in three of his last ten races. Telling had not won a race in fifteen months. Nevertheless, his lifetime record was 4-4-4, out of 16 races he had hit the board at a 75% rate.

Close examination of his last three races indicated he was a determined router. In his race of July 11 at Arlington Park at a mile and one-quarter in a Grade 3 handicap on the turf, Telling closed nine lengths from the first call to the finish - though he finished sixth, just one and a half lengths from the winner. In his race of June 6 at Arlington he again closed nine lengths from the first call to the finish and again finished off the board, but was only one and a half lengths from the winner. In his race of May 9 at Arlington, a non-graded stakes race at a mile and one-sixteenth, he closed ten lengths from the first call to the finish, this time finishing second, just one and three-quarter lengths from the winner. Telling was clearly a deep closing router.

Once again he closed nine lengths from the first call, but this time he closed to win by two lengths, paying $68.00, 28.00, and 13.00. When Better Talk Now finished second, the exacta paid $645; the trifecta and superfecta paid four and five figures. The false favorite, Grand Courterier, limped in at fifth. Not only can the discerning hidden horse hunter find an overlooked long shot in non-graded stakes, but in this class when a long shot wins the odds are extra long as the public is usually over betting the underlay morning line favorite.

One other angle that is often overlooked in stakes races, and not infrequently produces a long shot price, is when a promising three year old enters a stakes for the first time; having success- fully – and perhaps *consecutively* - climbed the beginning classes of maiden special; the allowance conditions of non-winner of a race other than maiden, claiming, or starter allowance; and an allowance race for non-winners of two other than the preceding conditions.

The public generally will shy away from a horse that has not yet run in a stakes race when entered against proven stakes class competitors. Such a horse is, in that sense, hidden, but often wins at double digit odds. In that example the tells are usually an excep- tional pre-race workout after successfully climbing his conditions with quality performances.

TENTH RACE
Saratoga
August 15th, 2009

1½ MILES. (Inner Turf) (2.23¾) STAKES. Purse $500,000 *SWORD DANCER INVITATIONAL S. (GRADE I)* INNER TURF FOR THREE YEAR OLDS AND UPWARD. By invitation only with no subscription fees. The purse to be divided 60% to the owner of the winner, 20% to second, 10% to third, 5% to fourth, 3% to fifth and 2% divided equally among the remaining finishers. Selection of fourteen (14) invitees, Saturday, August 1. Alternate list Monday, August 10. Three Year Olds, 115 lbs.; Older, 123 lbs. TURF: Non-winners of a Grade 1 on the turf in 2009 allowed 3 lbs.; a Grade 1 on the turf in 2008 or a Grade 2 twice onthe turf in 2008-09, 5 lbs.; a Grade 2 on the turf in 2008-09, 7 lbs. DIRT: Non-winners of a Graded Sweepstake over a mile on the dirt in 2008-09 allowed 3 lbs.; A sweepstake over a mile on the dirt in 2008-09, 5 lbs. Trophies will be presented to the winning owner, trainer and jockey. The New York Racing Association reserves the right to transfer this race to the Main Track. In the event that this race is taken off the turf, it may be subject to downgrading upon review by the Graded Stakes Committee. (Clear 86)

Value of Race: $500,000 Winner $300,000; second $100,000; third $50,000; fourth $25,000; fifth $15,000; sixth $2,000; seventh $2,000; eighth $2,000; ninth $2,000; tenth $2,000. Mutuel Pool $1,010,570 * Pool $108,598 Daily Double Pool $129,918 Exacta Pool $710,282 Superfecta Pool $215,337 Trifecta Pool $523,754 Grand Slam Pool $38,567

Last Raced	#	Horse	M/Eqt.	A/S	Wt	PP	¼	½	1m	1¼	Str	Fin	Jockey	Odds $1
11 Jly09 12AP5	7	Telling	L f	5H	116	7	5⁴	4½	6⁶	6²	1¹½	1²	Castellano J	33.00
06Jun09 10Bel3	4	Better Talk Now	L f	10G	116	4	8¹	8½	8²½	7½	2½	2¹	Dominguez R A	11.90
04Jly09 10Mth3	9	Brass Hat	L bf	8G	117	9	7³	7½	10	9½	8¹	3½	Borel C H	14.60
11 Jly09 12AP2	2	Gentleman Chester	L	5H	116	2	9½	9½	9½	10	7¹	4nk	Leparoux J R	26.25
11 Jly09 7Bel5	1	Grand Couturier (GB)	L f	6H	120	1	10	10	7½	8²	3½	5⅜	Garcia A	2.90
11 Jly09 7Bel3	8	Quijano (GER)		7G	123	8	4hd	5⁸	4¹	2hd	4²	6⁶½	Starke A	4.20
17May09 LCH1	6	Americain	L	4C	116	6	2½	3¹½	3hd	5hd	5½	7¹	Velazquez J R	4.00
04Jly09 10Bel3	5	Rising Moon	L b	6H	116	5	6²½	6⁷	5¹	4½	9¹½	8²	Desormeaux K J	11.00
11 Jly09 7Bel2	10	Musketier (GER)	L	7H	117	10	3¹½	2½	2¹½	1½	6¹	9²½	Jones J C	6.20
04Jly09 10Mth2	3	Lauro (GER)	L	6H	118	3	1½	1¹	1½	3½	10	10	Chavez J F	7.20

OFF AT 5:51 Start Good. Won driving. Track Firm (Rail at 9 ft).
TIME :23², :46⁴, 1:11, 1:36, 2:01, 2:25² (:23.48, :46.80, 1:11.13, 1:36.02, 2:01.05, 2:25.43)

$2 Mutuel Prices:

7- TELLING	68.00	28.00	13.40
4- BETTER TALK NOW		11.00	6.90
9- BRASS HAT			7.80

$2 EXACTA 7-4 PAID $645.00 $2 SUPERFECTA 7-4-9-2 PAID $79,644.00
$2 TRIFECTA 7-4-9 PAID $9,045.00 $2 GRAND SLAM 3/6/8/10/12/13–1/2/4/10/11–3/7 PAID $574.00 4 Correct

Bay Horse, (Apr), by A.P. Indy - Well Chosen by Deputy Minister. Trainer Hobby Steve. Bred by Darley(KY).

TELLING tucked in along the rail, raced in good position for a mile, split horses while angling four wide at the quarter pole, charged to the front in midstretch and drew clear under steady urging through the final sixteenth. BETTER TALK NOW was unhurried while racing well back through the opening mile, launched a rally leaving the far turn, swung five wide at the quarter pole, made a run from outside to threaten in midstretch but couldn't gain on the winner through the final eighth while clearly best of the others. BRASS HAT was outrun to the turn, circled five wide into the stretch and rallied belatedly in the middle of the track. GENTLEMAN CHESTER was outrun to the turn, saved ground nearing the quarter pole, swung out in upper stretch and finished full of run from outside in the late stages. GRAND COUTURIER (GB) trailed for most of the way, closed the gap inside on the turn, raced in traffic while gaining in upper stretch, made a run to threaten while splitting horses nearing the eighth pole then flattened out late. QUIJANO (GER) was rated just off the pace, lodged a move four wide to challenge nearing the quarter pole, then tired in upper stretch. AMERICAIN raced up close along the inside to the top of the stretch and

The tells for Telling were:

1) The Grade 3 race of July 11 at Arlington at one and one-quarter mile in which he closed eight lengths from the first call, finishing just one and a half lengths from the winner.

2) He had run three races at the one and a half mile distance, two on the turf. In the October 18, 2008, Grade 3 race at Keeneland Telling finished third, a length from the winner after closing four and a half lengths from the first call to the finish. In his Grade 3 race at Arlington on July 3, 2008, he closed thirteen lengths from the first call to finish second, just two lengths behind the winner.

3) His trainer was a 16% winner for the year overall, 15% with shippers and route starts.

The exception to the assertion that you don't find class droppers in handicap or stakes races occurs in the non-graded stakes, usually with purses of $100k and below. Sometimes a former Grade 1, 2, or 3 contender that has lost a step or two will drop into one of these races; this qualifies the horse as a class dropper, and it is usually over bet as an underlay.

Such was the case in the ninth race at Belmont on July 3, 2009, when a field of eight entered the non-graded Caress Stakes for three year olds and up competing on the inner turf at six furlongs for a purse of $65k.

Four of the entries had run in graded stakes: two in grade 1's and two in grade 3's; they were therefore legitimate class droppers. I judged the 6, Smart and Fancy, as the false favorite. Her morning line of 5/2 was shaved to 6/5 by the time the gate opened. The filly had not run since May 9 at Pimlico in a $50k stake on the turf at five furlongs, indicating that she may have suffered some kind of minor injury. Her works since the layoff were undistinguished.

The 6, J Z Warrior, was made the 7/2 morning line second favorite on the basis of her win on June fifth at Belmont on a sloppy track at six furlongs in a $65k stakes. At post time she was an overlay at 6.5/1.

In searching for a hidden horse long shot play, I landed on the 5, Jazzy. On April 9 at Keeneland, Jazzy threw in a clunker in a five and a half furlong $100k stakes. She then reverted to the hands of her original trainer, Mark Henning, a 13% winner with layoff horses. In examining Jazzy's works, a note was made of her June 8 work at Belmont at 5 furlongs in 1:00 breezing, the eighth best time of the 58 horses that worked that distance that day at that track. It was the best five furlong work of the field for the current race. In her second race back at Gulfstream Park she finished sixth, just three and a half lengths out for the win. My guess was that she suffered some kind of minor injury in that race.

Her morning line was 10/1; by post time she was a huge overlay at 24.5/1. Jazzy rallied from seven and a half lengths at the first call to win by a half length. This was an example of a horse that obviously suffered a serious injury in her race at Tampa Bay

Downs on December 13. Her work of June 8 at Belmont was the tell that this horse was ready to put in a good effort in her return from a two and a half month layoff.

Jazzy paid the hidden horse hunters $51.00, 19.00, and 6.70. Coupled with the second place finisher, J Z Warrior, the exacta paid $305.50. The odds-on underlay favorite, Smart and Fancy, finished third.

The tells are in the form: not on the odds board. Keep searching the forest of detail in the form. Only there will you find a hidden horse long shot candidate.

NINTH RACE
Belmont Park
July 3rd, 2009

6 FURLONGS. (Inner Turf) (1.07) STAKES. Purse $65,000 *CARESS S.* INNER TURF FOR FILLIES AND MARES THREE YEAR OLDS AND UPWARD. No nomination fee. $1,000 to enter, starters to receive a $750 rebate. A supplemental nomination fee of $200 may be made at time of entry. The added money and all fees to be divided 60% to the o wner of the winner, 20% to second, 10% to third, 5% to fourth, 3% to fifth and 2% divided equally among the remaining finishers. Three year olds 119 Older 123 lbs. Non-winners of a sweepstakes on the turf since November 1, 2008 allowed 2 lbs. Three races, 4 lbs. (Maiden, claiming, starter and restricted allowance races not considered in allowances). A presentation will be made to the winning owner. Nominations Closed Friday, June 26, 2009 with 26 original nominations and 1 supplement. (Showery 75)

Value of Race: $65,200 Winner $40,920; second $13,640; third $6,820; fourth $3,410; fifth $2,046; sixth $455; seventh $455; eighth $454. Mutuel Pool $403,816 Pick 3 Pool $50,313 Daily Double Pool $80,355 Exacta Pool $294,511 Superfecta Pool $93,555 Trifecta Pool $210,400 Grand Slam Pool $26,879

Last Raced	# Horse	M/Eql	A/S	Wt	PP	St	¼	½	¾	Str	Fin	Jockey	Odds $1
18Apr09 8Kee11	5 Jazzy (ARG)	L	7M	121	4	7	7²½	5½	4½	1½	1½	Garcia A	24.50
05Jun09 8Bel1	6 J Z Warrior	L b	4F	121	5	2	2hd	2½	2½	2½	2½	Desormeaux K J	6.50
15May09 5Pim1	7 Smart and Fancy	L b	6M	123	6	1	3¹	3½	1½	1½	3½	Dominguez R A	0.90
25May09 4Bel7	3 Mohegan Sky	L b	6M	121	2	8	5hd	7¹½	7¹½	4nk		Velasquez C H	10.60
30May09 8Bel6	8 Stormy Relations	L	4F	119	7	6	8	8	8	5¹		Prado E S	29.75
06Jun09 7Bel7	9 Modern Look (GB)	L	4F	121	8	5	4¹	4²½	5¹	6½		Coa E	5.30
06Sep08 9AP2	2 Lucky Copy	L	4F	121	3	3	1¹½	1½	3¹½	7¹½		Castellano J	4.90
17Oct08 NEW8	4 Masada (IRE)	L	4F	119	3	4	6¹½	6¹	6¹	8		Maragh R	16.60

OFF AT 5:20 Start Good. Won driving. Track Yielding (Rail at 9 ft).
TIME :22⁴, :46⁴, :59², 1:12² (:22.94, :46.84, :59.57, 1:12.58)

$2 Mutuel Prices:

5- JAZZY (ARG)	51.00	19.00	6.70
6- J Z WARRIOR		7.30	3.40
7- SMART AND FANCY			2.20

$2 EXACTA 5-6 PAID $305.50 $2 SUPERFECTA 5-6-7-3 PAID $6,336.00
$2 TRIFECTA 5-6-7 PAID $798.00 $2 GRAND SLAM 2/4/5-2/4/6-6/7/9-5 PAID $141.00 4 Correct

Bay Mare, (Sep), by Mutakddim - Jollie Fille (ARG) by Southern Halo. Trainer Hennig A. Mark. Bred by La Quebrada(ARG).
JAZZY (ARG) was reserved along the backstretch, lodged a rally three wide at the quarter pole, closed the gap to reach contention in midstretch and wore down J Z WARRIOR in the final fifty yards. J Z WARRIOR pressed along the inside, rallied along the rail to gain a brief lead a sixteenth out then yielded grudgingly. SMART AND FANCY raced in close contention while three wide between horses for a half, surged to the front a furlong out then yielded late. MOHEGAN SKY raced in the middle of the pack while saving ground for a half and rallied mildly between horses. STORMY RELATIONS dropped back early, trailed for a half, angled out in upper stretch and rallied belatedly. MODERN LOOK (GB) stalked the leaders from outside, lodged a brief three wide bid at the quarter pole and flattened out. LUCKY COPY set the pace along the rail into upper stretch and gave way. MASADA (IRE) was under a firm hold along the rail for a half and lacked a late response.

Owners- 5, Team Valor International ; 6, Scheumann Ty ; 7, Park Avenue Racing Stable ; 3, Enterline Larry ; 8, Bloom, William, Behrendt, John T. and Marquis, Charles K. ; 9, Juddmonte Farms, Inc. ; 2, Wertheimer and Frere ; 4, Ballymacoll Farm

Trainers- 5, Hennig Mark A.; 6, Mott William L; 7, Dutrow Anthony W.; 3, Rice Linda ; 8, Donk David G.; 9, Frankel Robert J.; 2, Pletcher Todd A.; 4, Clement Christophe

Breeders- 5, La Quebrada (ARG); 6, Gulf Coast Farms LLC (KY); 7, Dr. & Mrs. Thomas Bowman (MD); 3, Adam Staple, Michaelyn Scott & JamesScott (NY); 8, John T. Behrendt & William Bloom (NY); 9, Juddmonte Farms Ltd. (GB); 2, Wertheimer & Frere (KY); 4, Ballymacoll Stud Farm Ltd (IRE)

Scratched- Are We Dreamin(14Jun09 3Bel3), Matchless Orinda(14Jun09 3Bel1)

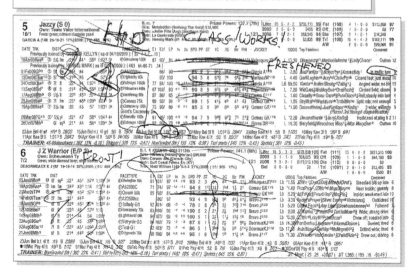

While on the subject of the Triple Crown, I have found that these races can be a fertile field for betting a three race parlay. Each year I follow the Derby trial races avidly. By the time it is Derby Day I have seen each of the entries run several times over and then again in several replays. I am looking for a horse that can not only win the Derby, but hit the board in all three classics. If I can land on one I pull out my $500 "classics" stakes and begin working on a three race parlay. It doesn't work for me every year but I cashed some nice parlay bets in 2004 and 5, and again in 2007. My 2009 parlay turned out to be for two races as I (like nearly all of the Derby punters) did not give Mine That Bird a beggar's chance to hit the board, much less to win it all.

In the spring of 2004 I followed Smarty Jones to the Derby after watching him at Oaklawn Park, which has seen its share of Derby winners after graduating from the Arkansas Derby. He had this turn of foot that I favor for a Derby contender, not a deep closing router, but the ability to get out close to the pace then unleash that powerful mid-stretch kick for which he would become noted. After spending hours watching the replays of all the Derby contenders, Smarty was my parlay horse.

When he drew the 15 post I was tempted to just put my $500 on him to show but on Derby day his odds never fell below 4/1. I knew that if he won the Derby I would be lucky to get $4 on him to win the Preakness, so I bet $360 to win and $140 to place on him. When he attended the pace early then made that strong kick of his in mid-stretch and won going away, I thought we might have a Triple Crown winner.

When Smarty paid $10.20 to win and $6.20 to place, my $500 had turned into $2,274. I couldn't wait for the Preakness. The only question was whether to bet him to win and place or win only or place only. I knew that he would probably be odds-on. And so he was. When Smarty's odds with five minutes to post were 4/5 I was torn between betting $2,274 to place only, or to split win and place with bets of $1,137 each. I reasoned that I would be lucky to get $3.00 for place and such a result would still leave me about $1,600 up on my parlay so I made the win and place bet. When Smarty won by eleven and a half lengths, he paid $3.40 and $3.00 bringing my average return to $3.20 and my parlay total to $3,368. I couldn't wait for the Belmont!

When at last Belmont day arrived - discretion being the better part of valor - I decided to hold back my original $500 stake and parlay the remaining $2,868. The worst that could happen was that Smarty would not hit the board, in which case my parlay was a break even proposition.

Could my pick get the one and half mile distance of the Belmont? That was the question. When I examined his breeding, I could not honestly assure myself that he could. I reasoned that a place bet was the right strategy, and entered my bet of $2,868 just two minutes before post time. In the middle of the stretch it was clear that it was a two horse race. When the long shot Birdstone caught Smarty with under a furlong to the finish, I breathed a heavy sigh of relief. I thought $3.30 was generous pay when my original parlay stake of $500 had turned into net winnings of $4,732.20.

Smarty Jones showed me the money, though he failed in his heroic effort to win the Triple Crown.

My horse in 2005 was Afleet Alex, who had a similar style of running as Smarty Jones. When Alex placed third in the Derby at $4.60; first in the Preakness at $8.60, 5.00, and 3.20, then first in the Belmont at $4.30, 3.60, and 3.00 - my $500 stake returned better than 10/1. I had bet Alex to show in the Derby, to win and place in the Preakness and to place in the Belmont, remembering that the object of handicapping is not *how* but *how much money* our horse will bring home for us.

The first time I saw Curlin race in 2007, I thought I was looking at a monster horse - perhaps another Secretariat. Though his connections were less than stellar, I was excited about his potential. After the Arkansas Derby victory, he was my Triple Crown play pick.

I decided to raise my beginning stake to $600. To make a long story short, Curlin finished third in the Derby, won the Preakness, and placed in the Belmont. My bet on the Derby was $600 to show; the price was $5.60, returning $1,680. He then won the Preakness, paying $8.80, 3.80, and 2.80. My split win and place bet of $840 each brought back $5,272. After pulling back my original $600 stake I was prepared for the Belmont with a stake of $4,672.

My strategy left no question as to the nature of my bet in the Belmont - all to place on Curlin. When the distance bred filly Rags to Riches won by a head and my horse paid $3.00 to place, the parlay paid $7,008 in net winnings. I had only bet my horse to win in one of the three races.

Parlays are difficult to successfully execute, especially in the cheaper races. My early attempts at this system were frustrating because I usually ended up looking for the "sure thing" in the third and final race of the parlay. Experience has taught me that the best class of race in which to place such a bet is the *highest* class; the Triple Crown of American racing.

Following that reasoning, it would appear at first glance that the Breeder's Cup races would be a fertile field in which to find promising candidates for three race parlays but because all the runners are experienced horses with considerable earnings it is extremely difficult to separate their form and class. It is frustrating to the American handicapper who is used to the detailed form and transparency of both the Bloodstock Research Information Systems past performance charts as well as the Daily Racing Form with its inclusion of the Beyer's Figures, to be confronted in the Cup's races with the Chinese Hieroglyphics recaps of the past performance's of the foreign horses. The European chart writers appear to take pains to provide as little information as possible to the bettor. They will not reveal how a horse broke from the gate and there are no intermittent calls at the quarter, half, or into the stretch. You get what kind of race it was and in what position the horse finished the race, that's about it. In their old world way, the chart writers give us a few nearly unintelligible abbreviated comments about how a specific horse ran the race.

For example: from our friends in Great Britain we learn how Masada, an Irish bred racing in the UK and entered in a turf race at Belmont, progressed in her previous race in England: *Chsd ldr; led ov 1f out; hdd; edgd lft; no ext insd fnl f.* Is the translation: *chased leader; led over 1 furlong out; headed; edged left* ("bore in?" No, they run from left to right overseas so he must have meant "bore out"); *no extension inside final furlong?* On this side of the pond the chartist's comment would have been: *weakened.*

At least the American punter could discern the final time of the winner and the information that Masada finished eighth, some five lengths back of the winner. If we do a little inverse deduction analysis we can even discern that her final time was one second slower than the winner's.

Here is another of Masada's race calls which defies interpretation: *Hmped s;* (we honestly hope he meant "Hampered start") *bhd;* (behind?) *hdwy ov 2f out;* ("headway over 2 furlongs out?") *nvr trbld dlrs* ("never troubled dealers? Or was it "dollars?" Surely he didn't mean "*dawdlers?*"). Compounding the confusion, I believe it was a transposition and that he actually meant "leaders."

Because of the paucity of information in the American past performance forms for races outside the United States, I have generally shied away from wagering on foreign horses, having a strong bias against them for the reason that you can't bet on them, but you had better not bet against them. That is why in the Breeder's Cup races I will generally pass any race in which there are two or more foreign horses.

While I believe that the Triple Crown presents a good opportunity for a three race parlay, I do not recommend that any sane handicapper try it in the Breeder's Cup races. Nevertheless, the Handicap and Stakes races produce their share of hidden long shot winners. Even in the tallest forest of tells, there are hidden horse contenders to be found.

Chapter 12

O ver the career of any serious handicapper he or she will encounter many frustrating *beats:* a head bob loss at the wire; a disqualification of your chosen steed, but the worst downer of all is being shut out at the window or seeing on your computer screen the red paged message: "No further betting on this race." Two emotions then ensue; the hope that you were wrong and saved some money, or that sinking feeling when your shutout bet is successful and you miss a sizeable payoff.

Such an occurrence happened on December 26, 2009, in the seventh race at Aqueduct, when a field of eleven three year olds and up went six furlongs over a muddy track in a $10k claimer for non-winners of two races.

I thought the race was ripe for a long shot winner. The racing secretary assisted in this perception when the 7, Great Debater, was tabbed the morning line favorite at 7/2. Trained by Richard Dutrow who had won in 2009 at a 28% clip, red flags were immediately raised on examination of that horse's past performances. His works were poor; he had raced but five times in a year, and had been steadily dropped in class since his poor effort on October 16 in a Grade 2 stakes at The Meadowlands in which he ran on the lead to the second call then stopped badly. He was dropped to a $40k open claiming race in his last start at six furlongs at the same track and was a half length from the leader at the half, only to abruptly stop again. In two races the trainer had dropped the Debater from a Grade 2 stakes to nearly the bottom of the barrel at Aqueduct in a race in which the winner's purse was a grand $9,000. The public bit, betting him down to the 2.1/1 favorite. I thought *false favorite* was written all over the sum of his past performances, and that probably his connections would be only too happy to sell him through the claim box.

After examining the rest of the field I landed on the 2, Brendan's Warrior. In his last race at the same conditions of the current race he was tenth at the half then closed three and a half lengths to finish sixth, some four lengths from the winner in a twelve horse field. It was a marked improvement from his four previous races in which he had descended the class ladder from a $61k allowance race at Saratoga. He fit my definition of a "wake-up" horse.

I thought the 3, Gimmee Getme, had a long shot chance from his last two races in which he closed some six lengths from the first call to the finish. In examining the 4, Sinister Storm, I noted the sudden marked improvement in his last race over the poor performances in his previous three tries. I tabbed Sinister Storm as another "wake up" horse.

The 8, Triple Glory, appeared to me to be a horse in good form and on class. The 9, Khan of Khans, appeared to be a notorious front running quitter and I eliminated him. The 11, Enduro, had changed trainers four times in four months and was trying to move up one class. His form in his last two races was good and I thought he was a contender.

This left the 12, Smarty Karakorum, for me to consider. The racing secretary assisted in my search for a hidden long shot when he made the line on Smarty 20/1. The current race would be over a muddy track. Three races back in a $15k claimer for non-winners of two races, he led from the gate on a muddy track and was barely caught at the wire; finishing second, a half-length behind the winner. The trainer's record when dropping his horse one class down was 16%. Smarty left the gate at odds of 39/1.

In constructing my bets I started with six candidates after leaving the favorite out. The proposed structure of my bets was a $2 exacta box 8-12 over the 2-3-4-8-11-12; a trifecta key with the 8-12 over the 2-3-4-8-11-12 over the 2-3-4-8-11-12. I intended to bet a dime super including the six horses in a box. I got my first bet down which was $10 to win and place on the 12. I barely got my exacta key in; when I attempted to enter my trifecta and super bets I was shut out by the red screen. They were off!

You can probably guess what happened. The racing secretary and the betting public's pick, Great Debater, finished dead last. Smarty Karakorum was third, a length and a half from the lead at the half, then closed steadily to win by a widening length. The 2 "woke up," finishing a closing second, and another "wake-up" horse, the 4, Sinister Storm, closed to finish third. When I saw the 8, Triple Glory, finish a clear fourth my stomach turned over for reasons that will shortly become clear.

The 12 paid $81.50, 28.60, and 19.40. The 2 paid $14.80 and 9.80 and the 4 paid $10.60 to show. The exacta paid $1,633 and the straight bets paid $505.50; the $40 investment returned $2,138.50 in less than two minutes. What a nice hit!

When they flashed the trifecta and dime super prices; however, I was astounded. The $1 trifecta paid $12,508.50; the dime super paid $10,573. No one had a $1 or $2 superfecta so the pool was split between all holders of a dime super. I was sick when I realized that being shut out cost me winnings of over $23,000, but the fault was mine alone. When you find a hidden horse make sure you get paid for being right! It is one thing to have a good idea, but without timely execution that idea is worthless. Be decisive; once you have made up your mind – get the bet down!

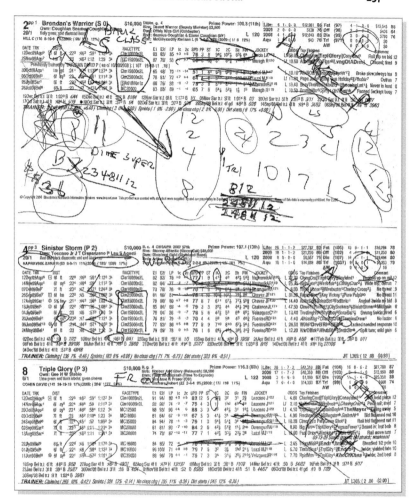

SEVENTH RACE
Aqueduct
December 26th, 2009

6 FURLONGS. (1.074) CLAIMING. Purse $15,000 INNER DIRT FOR THREE YEAR OLDS AND UPWARD WHICH HAVE NEVER WON TWO RACES. Three Year Olds, 122 lbs.; Older, 123 lbs. Non-winners of a race since October 26 Allowed 3 lbs. Claiming Price $10,000 (Races where entered for $7,500 or less not considered). (Rainy 40)

Value of Race: $15,000 Winner $9,000; second $3,000; third $1,500; fourth $750; fifth $450; sixth $50; seventh $50; eighth $50; ninth $50; tenth $50; eleventh $50. Mutuel Pool $361,029 Pick 3 Pool $40,373 Daily Double Pool $58,318 Exacta Pool $309,232 Superfecta Pool $86,613 Trifecta Pool $186,055

Last Raced	#	Horse	M/Eqt.	A/S	Wt	PP	St	¼	½	Str	Fin	Jockey	Cl'g Pr	Odds $1
29Nov09 ¹Aqu⁵	12	Smarty Karakorum	L b	3G	119	10	2	5¹	3¹½	3¹½	1¹	Studart M	10000	39.75
12Dec09 ⁹Aqu⁵	2	Brendan's Warrior	L fg	4G	120	1	9	9³	9¹½	7²	2ⁿᵏ	Hill C	10000	16.90
12Dec09 ⁹Aqu⁵	4	Sinister Storm	L	4C	120	3	5	8⁴	7¹	5¹½	3½	Napravnik A R	10000	19.00
12Dec09 ⁹Aqu²	8	Triple Glory	L f	3G	122	6	4	4½	5½	2½	4¾	Cohen D	10000	3.65
06Dec09 ⁵Aqu⁵	1A	The Mayor	L bf	3C	122	11	1	7²	6¹	6½	5¹	Bocachica O	10000	4.60
27Nov09 ¹Med²	11	Enduro	L bf	4G	120	9	6	2½	2½	4ʰᵈ	6²½	Chavez J F	10000	5.20
12Dec09 ⁹Aqu⁷	9	Khan of Khans	L b	3C	119	7	3	1¹½	1²	1²	7²½	Lopez C C	10000	7.20
30Nov09 ²FL⁸	5	Fotografia	L bf	3G	119	4	11	11	10²	9²	8²¾	Bermudez J E	10000	74.25
12Dec09 ⁹Aqu⁴	3	Gimmee Getme	L g	6H	115	2	10	10¹½	11	10½	9²½	Davis J A	10000	26.50
29Nov09 ¹Aqu⁷	10	Forty Third Recon	L	3G	119	8	7	6½	8²	11	10ⁿᵏ	Bisono A	10000	55.50
17Nov09 ²Med⁷	7	Great Debater	L	3C	119	5	8	3¹½	4½	8¹½	11	Rodriguez R R	10000	2.10

OFF AT 3:24   Start Good. Won driving. Track Good (sealed).
TIME :23, :47², 1:00³, 1:14¹   (:23.16, :47.41, 1:00.76, 1:14.20)

$2 Mutuel Prices:

12- SMARTY KARAKORUM	81.50	28.60	19.40
2- BRENDAN'S WARRIOR		14.80	9.80
4- SINISTER STORM			10.60

$2 EXACTA 12-2 PAID $1,633.00 $2 SUPERFECTA 12-2-4-8 PAID $213,475.00
$2 TRIFECTA 12-2-4 PAID $25,017.00

Bay Gelding, (Apr), by Wiseman's Ferry - Sr. Ferra by Jeblar. Trainer Odintz Jeff. Bred by Jo A. Halleck-Finley & James Lamonica(NY).

SMARTY KARAKORUM moved up from outside on the turn, circled five wide at the quarter pole and edged clear while drifting out at the wide. BRENDAN'S WARRIOR rail move, angled wide in upper stretch and rallied belatedly. A claim of foul against the winner was disallowed. SINISTER STORM raced well back for a half then closed late between horses to gain a share. TRIPLE GLORY raced evenly and lacked a late response. THE MAYOR failed to mount a serious rally. ENDURO pressed outside for a half and tired. KHAN OF KHANS raced uncontested on the lead into midstretch and gave way. FOTOGRAFIA steadied in the start and was never close thereafter. GIMMEE GETME never reached contention. FORTY THIRD RECON steadied between horses at the half mile pole and was never close thereafter. GREAT DEBATER rushed up along the inside, steadied while lacking room on the turn and gave way.

Owners- 12, Karakorum Farm ; 2, Coughlan, Seamus and Eileen ; 4, Toscano, Jr., J. T., Crapanzano, P., Lau, S., Agostinello, G. and Mondello, B. ; 8, Gee H. W. Stable ; 1A, Western Resources Racing, LLC and Jacobson, David ; 11, Bulger Joseph ; 9, Me You and Magoo Stable ; 5, Flying Zee Stable ; 3, Durst Murray ; 10, GPC Racing Stables ; 7, Four Roses Thoroughbreds

Trainers- 12, Odintz Jeff ; 2, Mcgillycuddy Keriann L. ; 4, Toscano, Jr. John T. ; 8, Barbara Robert ; 1A, Jacobson David ; 11, Saliusto Justin ; 9, Imperio Joseph ; 5, Barrera, Jr. Oscar S. ; 3, Martin, Sr. Frank ; 10, Duggan David P. ; 7, Dutrow, Jr. Richard E.

Breeders- 12, Jo A. Halleck-Finley & James Lamonica (NY); 2, Seamus Coughlan & Eileen Coughlan (NY); 4, Arthur I. Appleton (FL); 8, Mrs. Jane N. Fraser (OH); 1A, Hindman Limited Partnership, L.L.L.P. (KY); 11, Arthur I. Appleton (FL); 9, Carlos Perez (KY); 5, Flying Zee Stables (NY); 3, Lillian Durst & Murray Durst (NY); 10, Robert L. Losey (NY); 7, Oliver B. Brooks Jr. (FL)

Scratched- Living Out a Dream(06Dec09 ⁵Aqu⁵), Turaath(21Nov09 ¹Aqu³), Carter's Store(13Dec09 ⁴Aqu⁷), Driven by Royal(03Dec09 ⁵Aqu⁶), Bold Vindication(13Dec09 ⁴Aqu⁴)

$2 Daily Double (1-12) Paid $459.50; Daily Double Pool $58,318.
$2 Pick Three (11-1-12) Paid $5,430.00; Pick Three Pool $40,373.

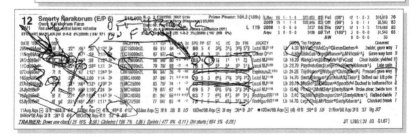

The final examples of races in which "hidden" horses hit the board includes the 2010 *Run for the Roses* – the 136th running of the Kentucky Derby. The results unequivocally validate the systematic methodology set out in the 58 examples described in the previous chapters. The basic premise in identifying potential long shot winner candidates is that there are certain "tells" in their past performances and recent workouts that – though not apparent to the average bettor – are strongly predictive of a top effort from the horse or horses that have one or more of the variables that tell the bettor that a particular horse is in top current condition and ready for an exceptional effort. The premise is that current pre-race workouts coupled with a detailed analysis of that horse's past performances will tell the handicapper whether or not the runner is a potential long shot.

I have heard a number of owners and trainers say "workouts don't mean anything." They and Andy Beyer notwithstanding, the exhaustive examples in this work tell us that *works are nearly everything,* and especially in identifying long shot winner candidates.

In many professional public handicappers' opinion the 2010 Derby was one of the weakest fields in the recent history of the race. The winner was the highest priced favorite in several years at 8/1, as the race came up sloppy for the second year in a row; nevertheless, the hidden horse formula produced the second, third, and fourth place finishers at delicious odds. Boxed underneath the winner, Supersaver – who certainly wasn't hidden – a one dollar superfecta bet would have cost six dollars and would have brought home what daughter Elaine calls a "life-changing win" of $101,284.46.

The "tells" on the second, third, and fourth place finishers were simple: the 2, Icebox, had the second best work of the field with a four furlong workout on April 26 of :46 2/5 – a bullet work, the best of 28; the 10, Paddy O'Prado, had the best five furlong work of the field at :58 2/5 on April 23; the 9, Make Music for Me, had the best four furlong work of the field when he ran "a hole in the wind" with a :46 1/5 work on April 19. These works were clear indications that these three horses were in top condition and should have been considered top contenders. Instead, the public let them leave the gate at odds of 11.7/1, 12.3/1, and 30/1 respectively.

This method of searching for and identifying the "tells" in a horse's past performances and its workouts will work whether the race is a $2,500 claimer or the Kentucky Derby. It requires a certain amount of analytical ability, an eagle's eye for detail, and a considerable amount of patience. While the variables involved in thoroughbred horse race handicapping are nearly infinite, the most important of the"tells" required to locate a hidden horse winner can be counted on the fingers of one hand. Learn them well. You will be rewarded for your hard work. If it were easy there wouldn't be such a thing as a long shot winner.

ELEVENTH RACE
Churchill
May 1st, 2010

$1\frac{1}{4}$ MILES. (1.59^2) STAKES. Purse $2,000,000 *KENTUCKY DERBY PRESENTED BY YUM! BRANDS (GRADE I)* FOR THREE-YEAR-OLDS WITH AN ENTRY FEE OF $25,000 EACH AND A STARTING FEE OF $25,000 EACH. (Cloudy 68)

Value of Race: $2,185,200 Winner $1,425,200; second $400,000; third $200,000; fourth $100,000; fifth $60,000. Mutuel Pool $47,944,683 Pick 3 Pool $1,139,397 Pick 3 Pool $563,000 Pick 4 Pool $1,999,504 Pick 6 Pool $1,306,381 Daily Double Pool $837,115 Daily Double Pool $2,046,573 Exacta Pool $21,608,785 Future Wager Pool $80,053 Future Wager Pool $60,053 Future Wager Pool $86,547 Future Wager Pool $86,547 Future Wager Pool $85,796 Future Wager Pool $385,995 Future Wager Pool $269,309 Future Wager Pool $224,358 Superfecta Pool $8,516,113 Super High Five Pool $182,546 Trifecta Pool $25,451,417

Last Raced	#	Horse	M/Eqt.	A/S	Wt	PP	$\frac{1}{4}$	$\frac{1}{2}$	$\frac{3}{4}$	1m	Str	Fin	Jockey	Odds $1
10Apr10 ^{9}OP^{2}	4	Super Saver	LA	3C	126	4	5^{hd}	6^{hd}	4^{hd}	2^{1}	1^{2}	$1^{2\frac{1}{2}}$	Borel C H	8.00
20Mar10 ^{11}GP^{1}	2	Ice Box	LA	3C	126	2	19^{3}	19^{4}	19^{2}	15^{3}	11^{hd}	2^{nk}	Lezcano J	11.70
10Apr10 ^{9}Kee^{2}	10	Paddy O'Prado	LA	3C	126	10	13^{2}	$11^{2\frac{1}{2}}$	$10^{1\frac{1}{2}}$	5^{hd}	3^{2}	3^{2}	Desormeaux K J	12.30
10Apr10 ^{9}Kee^{6}	9	Make Music for Me	LA b	3C	126	9	20	20	20	13^{hd}	$7^{\frac{1}{2}}$	$4^{1\frac{1}{4}}$	Rosario J	30.00
10Apr10 ^{9}OP^{5}	3	Noble's Promise	LA	3C	126	3	$8^{1\frac{1}{2}}$	4^{1}	3^{3}	$1^{\frac{1}{2}}$	$2^{1\frac{1}{2}}$	5^{1}	Martinez W	24.90
03Apr10 ^{6}SA^{3}	1	Lookin At Lucky	L	3C	126	1	18^{3}	18^{2}	$18^{1\frac{1}{2}}$	$14^{\frac{1}{2}}$	6^{hd}	$6^{\frac{1}{2}}$	Gomez G K	6.30
10Apr10 ^{9}OP^{3}	17	Dublin	LA b	3C	126	17	$14^{\frac{1}{2}}$	$15^{\frac{1}{2}}$	12^{1}	7^{hd}	5^{hd}	$7^{1\frac{1}{4}}$	Thompson T J	20.00
10Apr10 ^{9}Kee^{1}	6	Stately Victor	LA	3C	126	6	$17^{2\frac{1}{2}}$	17^{4}	14^{hd}	$10^{\frac{1}{2}}$	$8^{\frac{1}{2}}$	8^{2}	Garcia A	20.20
27Mar10 ^{10}FG^{1}	14	Mission Impazible	LA	3C	126	14	5^{2}	7^{1}	7^{1}	$11^{1\frac{1}{2}}$	$9^{1\frac{1}{2}}$	$9^{1\frac{1}{4}}$	Maragh R	16.70
20Mar10 ^{7}GP^{1}	11	Devil May Care	LA b	3F	121	11	10^{1}	9^{1}	8^{hd}	$3^{\frac{1}{2}}$	$4^{\frac{1}{2}}$	$10^{6\frac{3}{4}}$	Velazquez J R	10.90
03Apr10 ^{7}Haw^{1}	7	American Lion	LA	3C	126	7	7^{hd}	8^{1}	$9^{1\frac{1}{2}}$	$9^{\frac{1}{2}}$	$12^{1\frac{1}{2}}$	11^{nk}	Flores D R	23.20
03Apr10 ^{9}Aqu^{2}	13	Jackson Bend	LA	3C	126	13	$9^{1\frac{1}{2}}$	10^{1}	$11^{1\frac{1}{2}}$	8^{hd}	$10^{\frac{1}{2}}$	$12^{6\frac{1}{2}}$	Smith M E	23.00
27Mar10 ^{10}FG^{4}	15	Discreetly Mine	LA	3C	126	15	4^{hd}	$5^{1\frac{1}{2}}$	5^{hd}	$6^{\frac{1}{2}}$	13^{2}	$13^{3\frac{1}{4}}$	Castellano J	31.60
27Mar10 ^{9}TP^{1}	8	Dean's Kitten	LA b	3C	126	8	15^{2}	$12^{\frac{1}{2}}$	13^{2}	$16^{2\frac{1}{2}}$	15^{3}	$14^{14\frac{1}{2}}$	Albarado R	25.70
28Mar10 ^{12}Sun^{2}	12	Conveyance	L	3C	126	12	1^{1}	$1^{1\frac{1}{2}}$	1^{1}	4^{hd}	14^{2}	$15^{10\frac{1}{2}}$	Garcia M	27.00
27Feb10 ^{3}GP^{2}	19	Homeboykris	L b	3G	126	19	11^{hd}	14^{2}	$17^{3\frac{1}{2}}$	20	$18^{\frac{1}{4}}$	$16^{\frac{1}{2}}$	Dominguez R A	27.00
03Apr10 ^{6}SA^{1}	20	Sidney's Candy	LA	3C	126	20	2^{2}	2^{4}	$2^{2\frac{1}{2}}$	$12^{\frac{1}{2}}$	$16^{1\frac{1}{2}}$	$17^{6\frac{1}{4}}$	Talamo J	9.50
10Apr10 ^{9}OP^{1}	5	Line of David	LA b	3C	126	5	$3^{\frac{1}{2}}$	3^{hd}	6^{1}	$18^{2\frac{1}{2}}$	19^{2}	18^{nk}	Bejarano R	19.90
03Apr10 ^{9}Aqu^{3}	16	Awesome Act	LA	3C	126	16	$16^{1\frac{1}{2}}$	$16^{\frac{1}{2}}$	$16^{\frac{1}{2}}$	17^{4}	17^{4}	$19^{9\frac{1}{2}}$	Leparoux J R	11.60
03Apr10 ^{7}Haw^{3}	18	Backtalk	L	3C	126	18	$12^{\frac{1}{2}}$	13^{hd}	15^{hd}	$19^{1\frac{1}{2}}$	20	20	Mena M	23.10

OFF AT 6:32 Start Good. Won driving. Track Sloppy (sealed).
TIME :22^{3}, :46, 1:10^{2}, 1:37^{3}, 2:04^{2} (:22.63, :46.16, 1:10.58, 1:37.65, 2:04.45)

$2 Mutuel Prices:

4- SUPER SAVER	18.00	8.80	6.00
2- ICE BOX		11.20	8.00
10- PADDY O'PRADO			7.40

$2 EXACTA 4-2 PAID $152.40 $2 FUTURE WAGER EAXCTA POOL 1 19-24 PAID $176.40
FUTURE WAGER EXACTA POOL 1 19-24 PAID $176.40 $2 FUTURE WAGER EXACTA POOL 2 21-24 PAID $259.20
FUTURE WAGER EXACTA POOL 2 24-24 PAID $259.20 $2 FUTURE WAGER EXACTA POOL 3 22-11 PAID $1,077.40
$2 FUTURE WAGER POOL 1 - 19 PAID $43.20 $2 FUTURE WAGER POOL 2 - 21 PAID $51.20
$2 FUTURE WAGER POOL 3 - 22 PAID $73.00 $2 SUPERFECTA 4-2-10-9 PAID $202,569.20
$2 SUPER HIGH FIVE 4-2-10-9-3 PAID $0.00 Carryover Pool $147,055 $2 TRIFECTA 4-2-10 PAID $2,337.40

The 135th running of the Preakness was another notable example of finding hidden horse contenders when the hidden horse hunter methodology produced the place and show finishers at odds of 23.8/1 and 11.6/1, respectively. The winner, Lookin at Lucky, was certainly not hidden. Though badly roughed up in the slop of the Derby, he closed 15 lengths from the quarter call to the finish. Additionally, in his three previous races he earned late pace ratings of 106 and 108; by far the best of the field. On the other hand, Derby winner Supersaver had poor late pace ratings. He was a proven "mudder," but his stamina in the stretch on a fast track was open to question

First Dude was well hidden but his tells were clear to the hidden horse hunters. He had been roughed up in his last two races which were therefore *throw-outs*. The hidden key for this long shot was his :46 3/5 and :46 4/5 first quarter times in his second and third races back, making him a good bet to be on the front at the quarter pole in the Preakness. And so he was.

Jackson Bend had been roughed up in the Derby but his pre-race workout for the Preakness was the best of the field at :46 3/5 handily for four furlongs. He was clearly the "work" horse for discerning hidden horse hunting punters.

Yawanna Twist had the third best late pace rating and was a lightly raced horse, therefore rested and fresh for the Preakness.

Handwritten notes:

7 — BEST LATE PACE

11 — BEST FRONT — TROUBLE RACE THROW OUTS

6 — BEST WORKOUT @ :46³

5 — 3RD BEST LATE PACE

TWELVETH RACE
Pimlico
May 15th, 2010

1⅛ MILES. (1.52²) STAKES. Purse $1,000,000 *PREAKNESS S. (GRADE I)* FOR THREE-YEAR-OLDS. $10,000 to pass the entry box, starters to pay $10,000 additional. 60% of the purse to the winner, 20% to second, 11% to third, 6% to fourth and 3% to fifth. Weight 126 pounds for Colts and Geldings, 121 pounds for Fillies. A replicao f the Woodlawn Vase will be presented to the winning owner to remain his or her personal property. First closing January 16, 2010. Second closing March 27, 2010. (Clear 72)

Value of Race: $1,000,000 Winner $600,000; second $200,000; third $110,000; fourth $60,000; fifth $30,000. Mutuel Pool $20,101,004 Pick 3 Pool $538,846 Pick 4 Pool $1,663,081 Pick 6 Pool $285,790 Daily Double Pool $592,784 Daily Double Pool $837,210 Exacta Pool $11,739,228 Superfecta Pool $5,667,984 Super High Five Pool $244,889 Trifecta Pool $13,944,671

Last Raced	#	Horse	M/Eqt.	A/S	Wt	PP	St	¼	½	¾	Str	Fin	Jockey	Odds $1	
01May10 ^{11}CD^{6}	7	Lookin At Lucky	LA	3C	126	7	4	$6^{2\frac{1}{2}}$	5^{hd}	5^{1}	$1\frac{1}{2}$	$1\frac{3}{4}$	Garcia M	2.40	LATE PACE!
10Apr10 ^{9}Kee^{3}	11	First Dude	LA	3C	126	11	6	$1^{1\frac{1}{2}}$	$1^{1\frac{1}{2}}$	1^{1}	2^{2}	2^{hd}	Dominguez R A	23.80	2 THROW OUTS!
01May10 ^{11}CD^{12}	6	Jackson Bend	LA	3C	126	6	1	3^{1}	$3^{1\frac{1}{2}}$	3^{1}	4^{hd}	3^{1}	Smith M E	11.60	BEST WORK!
03Apr10 ^{7}Haw^{2}	5	Yawanna Twist	L	3C	126	5	7	5^{hd}	6^{1}	$6\frac{1}{2}$	3^{hd}	4^{4}	Prado E S	16.60	3 BEST LATE PACE
01May10 ^{11}CD^{7}	12	Dublin	LA b	3C	126	12	12	12	12	12	7^{hd}	$5^{4\frac{3}{4}}$	Gomez G K	9.80	
01May10 ^{11}CD^{3}	10	Paddy O'Prado	LA	3C	126	10	8	7^{1}	8^{1}	8^{1}	$9^{1\frac{1}{2}}$	6no	Desormeaux K J	7.50	
03Apr10 ^{6}SA^{4}	9	Caracortado	LA	3G	126	9	5	4^{hd}	$4^{1\frac{1}{2}}$	4^{hd}	$5^{4\frac{1}{2}}$	7^{1}	Atkinson P	18.80	
01May10 ^{11}CD^{1}	8	Super Saver	LA	3C	126	8	3	$2\frac{1}{2}$	$2\frac{1}{2}$	$2\frac{1}{2}$	8^{2}	$8\frac{3}{4}$	Borel C H	1.90	
03Apr10 ^{9}Aqu^{4}	2	Schoolyard Dreams	LA bf	3C	126	2	2	8^{2}	7^{1}	7^{1}	6^{hd}	$9^{2\frac{1}{2}}$	Coa E	15.40	
24Apr10 ^{10}CD^{2}	1	Aikenite	LA	3C	126	1	10	11^{5}	$11^{5\frac{1}{2}}$	11^{3}	10^{1}	$10^{3\frac{1}{2}}$	Castellano J	30.00	
24Apr10 ^{10}CD^{3}	3	Pleasant Prince	LA	3C	126	3	11	10^{2}	10^{1}	$10\frac{1}{2}$	11^{4}	$11^{3\frac{1}{2}}$	Leparoux J R	23.50	
10Apr10 ^{9}OP^{9}	4	Northern Giant	LA b	3C	126	4	9	$9^{2\frac{1}{2}}$	9^{2}	9^{1}	12	12	Thompson T J	31.20	

OFF AT 6:19 Start Good For All But DUBLIN. Won driving. Track Fast.
TIME :22^{4}, :46^{2}, 1:11^{1}, 1:36^{1}, 1:55^{2} (:22.91, :46.47, 1:11.22, 1:36.26, 1:55.47)

$2 Mutuel Prices:

7- LOOKIN AT LUCKY	6.80	4.60	3.80
11- FIRST DUDE		16.60	9.20
6- JACKSON BEND			6.60

$2 EXACTA 7-11 PAID $188.60 $1 SUPERFECTA 7-11-6-5 PAID $17,126.00
$2 SUPER HIGH FIVE 7-11-6-5-12 PAID $61,014.40 $2 TRIFECTA 7-11-6 PAID $2,771.00

Bay Colt, (May), by Smart Strike - Private Feeling by Belong to Me. Trainer Baffert Bob. Bred by Gulf Coast Farms LLC(KY).

LOOKIN AT LUCKY, between rivals entering the first turn, angled out four wide for the backstretch run, rallied four deep leaving the three furlong marker, moved to a short lead in upper stretch, dueled outside FIRST DUDE through the final three sixteenths and proved best under strong right handed urging. FIRST DUDE cleared under the wire the first time, set the pace under a light hold inside, was joined by rivals leaving the far turn, dueled under a vigorous ride into the lane, was overtaken soon after then continued gamely inside the winner while drifting out late. JACKSON BEND came in at the break putting YAWANNA TWIST in tight, gained a forward position along the rail entering the clubhouse turn, chased the dueling leaders into the stretch, angled out for room with three sixteenths to go then finished with good energy between rivals. YAWANNA TWIST, in tight at the break, angled in nearing the first turn, was lightly steadied near the seven furlong marker, advanced inside into the far turn, eased out and moved between foes mid way on the final turn, shifted out five wide for the stretch run, made a menacing move approaching the furlong marker but could not sustain his bid. DUBLIN bore out at the break then steadied to avoid the outrider, recovered and moved to the inside nearing the wire the first time, lagged well back for six furlongs, angled out five wide for the drive and finished with interest. PADDY O'PRADO lost ground four wide while in mid pack, was put to a strong ride three furlongs out, steadied briefly leaving the three sixteenths marker when appearing to get out then lacked any further response. CARACORTADO, within range early while three wide, moved in tandem inside the winner leaving the far turn, dueled on near even terms a quarter mile out, held well to the eighth pole then surrendered. SUPER SAVER was angled outside FIRST DUDE before the wire the first time, prompted that rival two wide, moved to challenge leaving the far turn, dueled between rivals to the quarter pole, gave way and steadied when in tight leaving the three sixteenths marker. SCHOOLYARD DREAMS, bumped at the break, was taken in hand to rate early while off the rail, moved up between rivals nearing the half mile marker, made a threatening four wide run approaching the quarter pole then lacked a further response. AIKENITE lacked speed, came five wide for the drive and failed to reach contention. PLEASANT PRINCE, pinched back at the break, settled back towards the inside, raced between rivals leaving the five sixteenths pole but failed to make an impact. NORTHERN GIANT broke outward then steadied when put in tight when JACKSON BEND came over, angled to the inside in early backstretch, made a mild run nearing the far turn then tired after seven furlongs.

Owners- 7, Watson, Karl, Pegram, Michael E. and Weitman, Paul ; 11, Dizney Donald R.; 6, LaPenta, Robert, V. and Brei, Fred, J. ; 5, Steel Your Face Stables ; 12, Baker, Robert C. and Mack, William L. ; 10, Donegal Racing ; 9, Blahut Racing LLC and Lo Hi Racing ; 8, WinStar Farm LLC ; 2, Fein, Eric and Milola, Anthony ; 1, Dogwood Stable ; 3, Ramsey, Kenneth L. and Sarah K. ; 4, Westrock Stables, LLC

Trainers- 7, Baffert Bob ; 11, Romans Dale L.; 6, Zito Nicholas P.; 5, Dutrow, Jr. Richard E.; 12, Lukas D. Wayne; 10, Romans Dale L.; 9, Machowsky Michael ; 8, Pletcher Todd A.; 2, Ryan Derek S.; 1, Pletcher Todd A.; 3, Ward Wesley A.; 4, Lukas D. Wayne

Breeders- 7, Gulf Coast Farms LLC (KY); 11, Donald R Dizney (FL); 6, Jacks or Better Farm Inc. (FL); 5, Steel Your Face Stable, LLC (NY); 12, Peter E. Blum & Gerry Dilger (KY); 10, Winchell Thoroughbreds, LLC (KY); 9, Mike Machowsky (CA); 8, WinStar Farm, LLC (KY); 2, John E. Little (KY); 1, Brylynn Farm, Inc. (FL); 3, Adena Springs (FL); 4, Dell Ridge Farm, LLC & Ashford Stud (KY)

$2 Daily Double (8-7) Paid $117.20; Daily Double Pool $592,784.
$2 Daily Double (SUSAN-PREAKNESS 4-7) Paid $89.60; Daily Double Pool $837,210.
$2 Pick Three (8-8-7) Paid $1,643.60; Pick Three Pool $538,846.
$2 Pick Four (4/6-8-8-7) Paid $3,594.80; Pick Four Pool $1,663,081.
$1 Pick Six (2/6/8/9/12-4/7/8-4/6-8-8-7) 5 Correct Paid $110.00; Pick Six Pool N/A.
$1 Pick Six (2/6/8/9/12-4/7/8-4/6-8-8-7) Paid $14,466.00; Pick Six Pool $285,790.

The final example of finding a hidden horse long shot winner occurred in the third leg of the Triple Crown – the 142nd running of the Belmont Stakes on June 5, 2010. The field of 12 did not include the winner of the Derby or the Preakness; for another year there would not be a Triple Crown threat in the mile and a half Belmont. The runner up in the Derby, Ice Box, was certified as the morning line favorite by the racing secretary and the huge crowd promptly bet the "sure thing" down to 8/5; after all, hadn't he closed some 24 lengths from the first call to be second, only two and a half lengths behind the winner? And that was at a mile and a quarter: the Belmont was for an additional quarter mile.

At first glance, Icebox's work of :46 3/5 on May 27 at the Saratoga training track appeared to be, and was in fact, the best pre-race work of the field; nevertheless, I and my punting partner discounted the value of that work. First, we did not know the nature of the Saratoga training track surface; second, we were unsure of the value of such a break-neck speed from the gate work-out for a horse whose proven running preference was to saunter out of the gate some 10 to 20 lengths back of the field and then to start pealing off horses in his closing drive, as in the Florida and Kentucky Derby contests. I thought that Icebox was a "false favorite" and that perhaps he could close for third or fourth, at best.

In searching for the hidden horse my attention was drawn to the 7, Drosselmeyer, trained by the redoubtable Bill Mott. I considered his works pattern of four furlongs at :47 3/5 breezing on May 17 at Belmont and his five furlong work of :59 3/5 breezing at Belmont on May 31 to be the best works pattern of the field.

In his eight races he was on the board seven times. His last race was the Dwyer – at Belmont – in which he encountered trouble at the 3/8 pole ("blocked" was the chart writer's comment) yet stayed on, finishing second to the second favorite in the Belmont – Fly Down.

I was amazed to see that Drosselmeyer's odds were set at 12/1; and at post time he was a mild overlay at 13/1. Here was a long shot candidate *hidden in plain sight.* When you come across this kind of situation believe what you see! Do not be influenced by the racing secretary's unrealistic setting of an overly generous morning line on the horse you are considering or the amount of money the unsophisticated public bettors are pouring into the false favorite.

The next best work pattern belonged to the 5, Fly Down, who had beaten Drosselmeyer in the aforementioned Dwyer. His work on May 30 at the Saratoga training track of four furlongs at :47 2/5 was exceptional and comparable to Drosselmeyer's five furlong work at :59 3/5 on May 31. I thought that Fly Down was the better horse of Nick Zito's duo.

It appeared that the 11, First Dude, was the sole front speed for his performance in the Preakness indicated that he could probably carry that speed past the mile and a quarter distance of the Derby.

My only reservation about backing Drosselmeyer was his rider. I don't know how many bettors have "nemesis" jockeys; that is, riders that nearly always lose when you back them and nearly always win when you bet against them. Such a generally inconsistent jock can drive a seasoned punter up the wall. So it is that Mike Smith was my "nemesis" rider. The fault, of course, is not with Mike but with the author. My reservations were raised when I considered the fact that Mike had not ridden my *hidden in plain sight* long shot pick. Needless to say, Mr. Smith is no longer my "nemesis" rider.

The construction of my final bets began with a substantial win and place on Drosselmeyer. I then boxed my top pick with Fly Down and First Dude in a substantial exacta and trifecta.

Mike gave the winner a perfect ride. Dominguez got every thing he could out of First Dude and did a hell of a job in holding his horse up for third. But for traffic trouble, John Velazquez would have guided his horse to the winner's circle. *Ah, if only: woulda, shoulda, coulda…*

Drosselmeyer's tells were in the form; hidden in plain sight. His works and his troubled previous race were there in the form for all to see, yet those predictive variables were ignored by the crowd intent on getting in on the "sure thing" that was Icebox who finished a struggling ninth in the third leg of racing's Triple Crown.

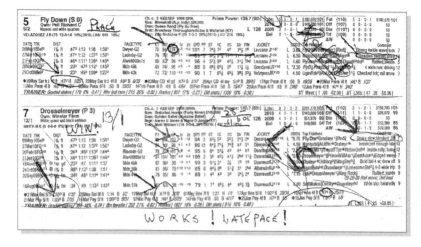

ELEVENTH RACE
Belmont Park
June 5th, 2010

1½ MILES. (2.24) STAKES. Purse $1,000,000 *BELMONT S. (GRADE I)* FOR THREE YEAR OLDS. By subscription of $600 each, to accompany the nomination, if made on or before January 16, 2010, or $6,000, if made on or before March 27, 2010. At any time prior to the closing time of entries, horses may be nominated to The Belmont Stakes upon payment of a supplementary fee of $100,000 to the New York Racing Association, Inc. $10,000 to pass the entry box and $10,000 additional to start. All entrants will be required to pay entry and starting fees; but no fees, supplemental or othe rwise shall be added to the purse. The purse to be divided 60% to the winner, 20% to second, 11% to third, 6% to fourth and 3% to fifth. Colts and Geldings, 126 lbs.; Fillies, 121 lbs. The winning owner will be presented with the August Belmont Memorial C up to be retained for one year as well as a trophy for permanent possession and trophies to the winning trainer and jockey. (Clear 85)

Value of Race: $1,000,000 Winner $600,000; second $200,000; third $110,000; fourth $60,000; fifth $30,000. Mutuel Pool $14,061,140 Pick 3 Pool $634,407 Pick 4 Pool $2,026,444 Pick 6 Pool $1,442,500 Daily Double Pool $652,639 Daily Double Pool $503,733 Exacta Pool $8,946,327 Superfecta Pool $4,835,244 Trifecta Pool $9,884,213

Last Raced	#	Horse	M/Eqt.	A/S	Wt	PP	¼	½	1m	1¼	Str	Fin	Jockey	Odds $1
08May10 ^{9}Bel^{2}	7	Drosselmeyer	L	3C	126	7	6^{1}	$5^{\frac{1}{2}}$	$5^{\frac{1}{2}}$	$4^{1\frac{1}{2}}$	$3^{1\frac{1}{2}}$	$1^{\frac{3}{4}}$	Smith M E	13.00
08May10 ^{9}Bel^{1}	5	Fly Down	L	3C	126	5	5^{1}	6^{3}	6^{2}	6^{2}	$5^{1\frac{1}{2}}$	2^{nk}	Velazquez J R	5.20
15May10 ^{12}Pim^{2}	11	First Dude	L	3C	126	11	$1^{1\frac{1}{2}}$	1^{1}	1^{1}	1^{1}	1^{1}	$3^{1\frac{1}{2}}$	Dominguez R A	5.90
08May10 ^{9}LS^{1}	8	Game On Dude	L b	3G	126	8	$4^{1\frac{1}{2}}$	$3^{\frac{1}{2}}$	3^{hd}	$3^{\frac{1}{2}}$	2^{hd}	$4^{\frac{1}{2}}$	Garcia M	17.00
17Apr10 ^{9}Kee^{3}	3	[D]Uptowncharlybrown	L	3C	126	3	3^{1}	$4^{1\frac{1}{2}}$	$4^{\frac{1}{2}}$	$5^{\frac{1}{2}}$	4^{1}	$5^{3\frac{3}{4}}$	Maragh R	10.90
01May10 ^{1}CD^{1}	10	Stay Put	L b	3C	126	10	$10^{\frac{1}{2}}$	10^{1}	$9^{\frac{1}{2}}$	7^{1}	7^{2}	$6^{1\frac{1}{4}}$	Theriot J	26.25
10Apr10 ^{9}Kee^{4}	12	Interactif	L	3C	126	12	2^{hd}	2^{1}	2^{1}	2^{hd}	6^{1}	$7^{2\frac{1}{2}}$	Castellano J	19.80
01May10 ^{11}CD^{6}	9	Stately Victor	L	3C	126	9	$8^{\frac{1}{2}}$	$9^{1\frac{1}{2}}$	$10^{2\frac{1}{2}}$	$10^{2\frac{1}{2}}$	$9^{3\frac{1}{2}}$	$8^{\frac{3}{4}}$	Garcia A	14.30
01May10 ^{11}CD^{2}	6	Ice Box	L	3C	126	6	9^{2}	$8^{\frac{1}{2}}$	7^{1}	$8^{4\frac{1}{2}}$	8^{1}	$9^{4\frac{1}{2}}$	Lezcano J	1.85
01May10 ^{11}CD^{4}	4	Make Music for Me	L b	3C	126	4	12	12	$11^{3\frac{1}{2}}$	$9^{1\frac{1}{2}}$	10^{8}	$10^{11\frac{1}{4}}$	Rosario J	12.30
03Apr10 ^{7}Haw^{5}	1	Dave in Dixie	L	3C	126	1	11^{2}	$11^{1\frac{1}{2}}$	12	12	11^{10}	$11^{19\frac{1}{2}}$	Borel C H	14.70
24Apr10 ^{9}Aqu^{3}	2	Spangled Star	L b	3C	126	2	$7^{1\frac{1}{2}}$	$7^{1\frac{1}{2}}$	8^{1}	$11^{\frac{1}{2}}$	12	12	Gomez G K	23.30

[D] - Uptowncharlybrown disqualified and placed 12th

OFF AT 6:35 Start Good. Won driving. Track Fast.
TIME :24, :49, 1:14^{4}, 1:40^{1}, 2:04^{4}, 2:31^{2} (:24.15, :49.19, 1:14.94, 1:40.25, 2:04.97, 2:31.57)

$2 Mutuel Prices:

7- DROSSELMEYER	28.00	11.60	7.70
5- FLY DOWN		6.80	5.10
11- FIRST DUDE			4.90

$2 EXACTA 7-5 PAID $144.50 $2 SUPERFECTA 7-5-11-8 PAID $10,658.00
$2 TRIFECTA 7-5-11 PAID $766.00

Chestnut Colt, (Ap), by Distorted Humor - Golden Ballet by Moscow Ballet. Trainer Mott I. William. Bred by Aaron U. Jones & Marie D. Jones(KY).

DROSSELMEYER was unhurried in the early stages, was strung out five wide leaving the first turn, raced under a snug hold while in good position continuing well off the rail along the backstretch, rapidly closed the gap circling five wide approaching the quarter pole, gained on the leaders when roused sharply under left hand whipping in upper stretch, made a run to challenge in midstretch, surged to the front inside the sixteenth pole then edged away with the rider switching to the right hand whip in the final seventy yards. FLY DOWN steadied in a bit of traffic briefly nearing the first turn, raced in good position on the backstretch, saved ground approaching the far turn, launched a rally just behind the winner in the three path on the turn, angled to the outside leaving the three-sixteenths pole then closed late from outside to narrowly gain the place. FIRST DUDE sprinted clear soon after the start, angled to the inside, set the pace along the rail while being pressured mildly to the turn, maintained a clear advantage into midstretch then weakened under pressure in the final sixteenth. GAME ON DUDE raced just off the pace from outside for six furlongs, made a run four wide to threaten at the quarter pole then flattened out in upper stretch.
UPTOWNCHARLYBROWN was well placed along the rail in the early stages, saved ground into the backstretch, lost the eight pound weight pad at the seven-eighths pole, saved ground in good position to the turn, lodged a mild bid in upper stretch and lacked a strong closing response. Following a stewards inquiry UPTOWNCHARLYBROWN was disqualified from fifth and was placed last for losing the eight pound lead pad on the backstretch. STAY PUT broke in the air at the start, raced well back for seven furlongs, gained along the rail on the turn, swung six wide at the quarter pole and lacked a late response. INTERACTIF pressed the pace from outside to the quarter pole and gave way. STATELY VICTOR failed to mount a serious rally while three wide throughout. ICE BOX raced in hand while unhurried for six furlongs, gained inside on the turn, swung five wide at the quarter pole and lacked a further response. MAKE MUSIC FOR ME steadied after being pinched back while bobbling at the start and was never close thereafter. DAVE IN DIXIE was outrun while saving ground throughout. SPANGLED STAR saved ground, angled out and gave way on the turn.

Owners- 7, WinStar Farm LLC ; 5, Pell Richard C.; 11, Dizney Donald R.; 8, Lanni Family Trust, Mercedes Stable, Diamond Pride LLC and Schiappa, Bernie ; 3, Fantasy Lane Stable ; 10, Bertram, Richard and Klein, Elaine ; 12, Wertheimer and Frere ; 9, Conway, F. Thomas and Jack ; 6, LaPenta Robert V.; 4, Johnson, Ellen and Peter O. ; 1, Thrash, Ike and Dawn ; 2, Roman, Lawrence P. and Levine, Jeff

Trainers- 7, Mott William I.; 5, Zito Nicholas P.; 11, Romans Dale L.; 8, Baffert Bob ; 3, McLaughlin Kiaran P.; 10, Margolis Steve ; 12, Pletcher Todd A.; 9, Maker Michael J.; 6, Zito Nicholas P.; 4, Barba Alexis ; 1, Sadler John W.; 2, Dutrow, Jr. Richard E.

Breeders- 7, Aaron U. Jones & Marie D. Jones (KY); 5, Broadway Thoroughbreds Inc. & W.S.Farish (KY); 11, Donald R Dizney (FL); 8, Adena Springs (KY); 3, Juan Bruno & Rose Hill Farm (KY); 10, Reklein Stables (KY); 12, Wertheimer & Frere (KY); 9, Adena Springs (KY); 6, Denlea Park, LTD. (KY); 4, Richard Shultz (KY); 1, Glencrest Farm LLC (KY); 2, Grapestock LLC (KY)

$2 Daily Double (4-7) Paid $596.00; Daily Double Pool $652,639.
$2 Daily Double (8-7 (BROOKLYN-BELMONT)) Paid $283.00; Daily Double Pool $503,733.
$2 Pick Three (12-4-7) Paid $36,107.00; Pick Three Pool $634,407.
$2 Pick Four (3-12-4-7) Paid $167,056.00; Pick Four Pool $2,026,444.
$2 Pick Six (5-5-3-12-4-7) 5 Correct Paid $3,180.00; Pick Six Pool $1,442,500; Carryover Pool $930,495.

Data provided or compiled by Equibase Company, which includes data from The Jockey Club, generally is accurate but occasionally errors and omissions occur as a result of incorrect data received by others, mistakes in processing and other causes. Equibase Company and Bloodstock Research Information Services, Inc. and Thoroughbred Sports Network disclaim responsibility for the consequences, if any, of such errors, but would appreciate being called to their attention. Copyright 2010.

Having tackled the technical aspects of successful thoroughbred horse race handicapping for hidden long shots, we must now move on to the more challenging side of this game which never seems to lose its edge; the structuring and the execution of our bets.

How often the phrases heard at the betting windows consist of: *would have, should have, could have.* And the saddest words heard at the track are surely: *if only!* These words should be put to music and sang as "The Punter's Lament" with a blues beat. Oh, in all these years, I have sung that tune too often to count.

Experience; however, has taught me that every bad beat I have taken later evened out when my horse won by a nose at the wire in a head-bob finish or when I received a much better payoff than I had any right to expect. Equanimity is a trait sorely earned at the track or in life: it is a treasure which can only be earned by trial and error and a thousand gut wrenching shouts at your horse to: "Get up! Get up!" in the final hundred yards to the wire. Whenever you take a bad beat, step back and remind yourself that there will be other races on other days.

The psychologists tell us that money is a "charged" word. If that is the case, then it is supercharged at the race track where fast money changes hands at a rate nearing the speed of light. *A fool and his money are soon parted,* should be the motto of the bettor as he enters the track. Better yet, the law should require that every racing program print on its cover in large block letters: *Caveat Emptor!* Let the buyer beware.

Gambling is one of man's oldest instincts. Carried to an extreme it can destroy lives, just as alcohol and a number of other addictions can bring an otherwise good person down. As members of the human race none of us can escape risk in our lives. We take a risk when we choose a mate, or make an investment, or decide on a specific career. Some risks we can calculate and control: with others we are at the mercy of coincidence, chance and circumstance.

One risk you can control is that of handicapping and betting on thoroughbred horse racing unless you are a compulsive-obsessive personality. In that case you should never go near the track. But for the normal horse racing fan and bettor, it is great entertainment. And for those of you who take the time to learn the lessons that only a thousand races teach; the rewards can be life changing, or at the worst just a hell of a lot of fun.

The first lesson to be learned at the track is a simple, common sense one; that is, a money management plan. You can become an excellent handicapper, able to compete with many of the best professional handicappers in the racing industry – but without the ability to systematically manage your wagering capital you cannot over a long period of time profit from your hard earned expertise in selecting winners; hidden horse long shots, or odds-on favorites, or anything in between.

Over the years I have studied numerous money management systems; some mundane, many complicated. In the end I have come to the conclusion that the best money management system you can bring to the track is the one called *common sense*. That system tells us that when we are winning we need to increase the size of our bets, and when we are losing to decrease them – and to never *bet the farm*.

When you go to the track (either in person or online) your first goal, of course, is to win money. Failing that, you need to control your loss for the day to a reasonable amount that you can chalk up to entertainment. In either event make sure you have some fun!

While the subject of this work is how to find and bet long shot candidates, I am not suggesting that the handicapper exclusively bet long shots. There are many moderate overlay horses that are well worth backing when you can't find a hidden horse long shot candidate for any particular race. I am saying that if you consistently play favorites you will lose two of three tries, for the sweet spot is somewhere in between. Long shots are few and far between, but you must be eternally vigilant in seeking them, and when you find a hidden horse candidate you must have the courage of your convictions and make a decent bet.

The size of your bet on a long shot is determined by your bankroll and your comfort level of wagering. My comfort level in betting long shots is a minimum of $10 to win and place and a $5 exacta box of my selection with the first and second favorites. My normal bet is twice that amount, and when I am up substantially for the day, I increase the size of my bets.

The first thing I do when looking over a race card is to go to the last race for I have found that it is a fertile field in which to go hunting for long shots. I will frequently work that race before going back to the first race. In reviewing each race I begin from the bottom up in each horse's past performances: the second line up is always the workout line; there is the pattern of that horse's works. From left to right, the most current first, I mark the exceptional works of that horse, if any. Normally, works of :48 4/5 and below for four furlongs will attract my attention as will works for five furlongs of 1:00 4/5 or below. These are the common workout distances. If I find such an exceptional work, I will examine the horse's entire works pattern. (For first time starters I will examine each work of each horse in the entire field.) Of course, the good work must have been prior to the current race. If the horse has run a race since the good work, but finished out of the money, I disregard the workout unless that race was a troubled one in which the horse was bumped, steadied, checked, in between, or encountered other serious traffic trouble.

Regarding the value of workouts generally; no less an authority than the legendary Andy Beyer comments in his *The Winning Horseplayer*: "...It is best not to base many serious handicapping decisions on published workout information." The 60 examples we have listed of hidden horse long shot winners contradicts that conclusion, as well as my experience as an owner. One can be a genius in some areas of their chosen field, and not necessarily a genius in *all* the facets of their field of expertise.

Next, I look for a cutback horse. I have found that many long shot winners are horses that are cutting back in distance from their last race in which they would have finished close up had that race been run at the current distance. You do not; however, want to back a cutback horse that is a habitual slow breaker in a distance race and is cutting back to a sprint.

I next determine the class of the horse, and whether it is moving up or down or is right at the current race class. And of course I ask: Is this horse a front runner, a pace horse, or a router? I then examine the records of the trainer and the jockey. If the horse has been away from the track for more than 30 days, what is the trainer's record with layoff horses? The variables are many and they must all be checked.

In reviewing the long shot winners we have listed, it is notable that only a few were ridden by a top ranked jockey. Many bettors will not bet a horse unless the jockey is a big hitter; therefore, hidden horse hunters should not be dissuaded from backing a long shot because of an inexperienced or lower ranked jockey. And over half of the long shots winners we have listed were guided by trainers in the lower half of the standings.

When a horse is ready to run a big race - it is ready, and it will generally signal that readiness by a sudden hot work or sudden improvement in its last race. Has it just come off an "excuse" race that the hidden horse hunter can reasonably disregard?

After an analysis of these some 60 examples of hidden horse long shot winners, I was surprised to learn that in fully 82.8 per cent of these races, the common denominator was either the best pre-race workout of the field, or an otherwise superior work that predicted the winner or place horse. In 34.5 per cent of the sampling, the determinant factor was that of a cutback horse. Many of the hidden long shot winners were both works *and* cutback horses. The next most important variable for identifying long shot candidates is that their last race was a "throw-out race" in which the horse encountered serious trouble, though its race or races immediately prior to that were good efforts. The fourth in importance tell consists of finding a "wakeup" horse; one that has run three, four, or five straight clunker races before suddenly showing improvement in its last race, whether or not it finished on the board.

After all is said and done, a successful hidden horse hunter must bring to the track that rarest of qualities possessed by the betting public...patience. You will not find a long shot candidate in every race; you may not find one in a complete race card. On those days when it seems that only chalk wins, you may be tempted to "chase the chalk;" but be patient, for over time the favorites will not win in two of every three starts. Hold your fire; keep your betting powder dry until you find the tells of a hidden horse candidate, for *pattern recognition* is the key to finding long shots. And when you recognize the patterns that tell you the horse is ready for a big try, pull the trigger; make a substantial bet.

Hopefully, this work has given you the ammunition you need to bring home the bigger game; perhaps even that fifty to one long-shot, and the delicious reward for finding a hidden horse winner! Though in thoroughbred horse race handicapping *there's many a slip 'tween the cup and the lip*, it is a game in which you *can* have your cake and eat it too when you find a hidden horse winner deep within the forest of its tells.

Happy hunting!

BIBLIOGRAPHY

Finding the Hidden Horse

Heller, Bill: *Overlay, Overlay.* Chicago: Bonus Books, Inc., 1990.

Beyer, Andrew: *The Winning Horseplayer.* Boston-New York: Houghton Mifflin Company, 1994.

_____*Beyer on Speed.* Boston-New York: Houghton Mifflin Company, 1993.

Davidowitz, David and Beyer, Andrew: *Betting Thoroughbreds: a Professional's Guide for the Horseplayer.* New York: Penguin Books, 1995.

Dostoyevsky, Fyodor: *Notes From Underground.* London: Penguin Books, 1972.

_____*The Gambler.* London: Penguin Books, 1972.

Le Bon, Gustave: *The Crowd: A Study of the Popular Mind.* (1895) London: Dover Publications, 2008.

Mackay, Charles: *Extraordinary Popular Delusions and the Madness of Crowds.* Radford, VA: Wilder Publications, 2008.

Malmuth, Mason and Sklansky, David: *Gambling for a Living.* Las Vegas: Crest Printing Co., 1998.

Mamis, Justin: *The Nature of Risk.* New York: Addison-Wesley Publishing Company, 1991.

Meadow, Barry: *Money Secrets at the Racetrack.* Anaheim, CA: TR Publishing, 1990.

Pizzola, Michael: *Handicapping Magic*. Las Vegas: I.T.S. Press, 2000.

Wong, Stanford and Spector, Susan: *Gambling Like a Pro*. Indianapolis: Alpha Books, 2003.

15386997R00156

Made in the USA
Lexington, KY
24 May 2012